JOSSEY-BASS TEACHER

Jossey-Bass Teacher provides educators with practical knowledge and tools to create a positive and lifelong impact on student learning. We offer classroom-tested and research-based teaching resources for a variety of grade levels and subject areas. Whether you are an aspiring, new, or veteran teacher, we want to help you make every teaching day your best.

From ready-to-use classroom activities to the latest teaching framework, our value-packed books provide insightful, practical, and comprehensive materials on the topics that matter most to K–12 teachers. We hope to become your trusted source for the best ideas from the most experienced and respected experts in the field.

Teach
— LIKE A —
CHAMPION
FIELD GUIDE

DOUG LEMOV

Teach
— LIKE A —
CHAMPION
FIELD GUIDE

A Practical Resource to Make
the 49 Techniques Your Own

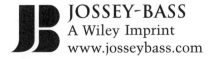

JOSSEY-BASS
A Wiley Imprint
www.josseybass.com

Published by Jossey-Bass
A Wiley Imprint

One Montgomery Street, Suite 1200, San Francisco, CA 94104-4594—www.josseybass.com

Jossey-Bass books and products are available through most bookstores. To contact Jossey-Bass directly call our Customer Care Department within the U.S. at 800-956-7739, outside the U.S. at 317-572-3986, or fax 317-572-4002.

Library of Congress Cataloging-in-Publication Data

Lemov, Doug, 1967-Teach like a champion field guide : A practical resource to make the 49 techniques your own / Doug Lemov. —1st ed.
    p. cm. —(Jossey-Bass teacher)
  Includes index.
    ISBN 978-1-118-11682-1 (pbk.)
    ISBN 978-1-118-21858-7 (ebk.)
    ISBN 978-1-118-21859-4 (ebk.)
    ISBN 978-1-118-21860-0 (ebk.)
1. Effective teaching. 2. Academic achievement. 3. College preparation programs. I. Title.
  LB1025.3.L485 2012
  371.102—dc23

Printed in the United States of America

FIRST EDITION

PB Printing 10 9 8 7 6 5 4 3 2 1

CONTENTS

> Use the checkboxes to track your progress through this *Field Guide.*
>
> | Making Progress | A Strength |
> |---|---|

Section 1   Setting High Academic Expectations

Technique 1   NO OPT OUT | 11

Turn "I don't know" into a success by helping students who won't try or can't succeed practice getting it right (and being accountable for trying).

○   ○

Technique 2   RIGHT IS RIGHT | 22

When you respond to answers in class, hold out for answers that are "all-the-way right" or all the way to your standards of rigor.

○   ○

Technique 3   STRETCH IT | 37

Reward "right" answers with follow-up questions that test for reliability, challenge students, and extend knowledge.

○   ○

Technique 4   FORMAT MATTERS | 52

Help your students to "format" responses to your questions grammatically, in complete sentences, audibly, and according to other worthy criteria.

○   ○

Technique 5   WITHOUT APOLOGY | 65

Get beyond labeling what students need to learn as "boring," out of your control, or too remote or hard for them. Keep it rigorous, not watered down.

○   ○

Section 2   Planning That Ensures High Academic Achievement

Technique 6   BEGIN WITH THE END | 73

Progress from unit planning to lesson planning. Define the objective, decide how you'll assess it, and then choose appropriate lesson activities.

○   ○

	Making Progress	A Strength

Section 3   Structuring and Delivering Your Lessons

	Making Progress	A Strength

Section 4   Engaging Students in Your Lessons

	Making Progress	A Strength

	Making Progress	A Strength

DVD CONTENTS

Here is an overview of the video clips for your quick reference. The teachers in these clips often demonstrate more than one technique in the few minutes captured. We've named the main technique that the clip demonstrates first, followed by other techniques it also reflects. The technique called Control the Game is not mentioned in the *Guide* but is discussed in *Teach Like a Champion*. All these clips are worth watching on more than one occasion.

Clip 1   NO OPT OUT

Shadell Noel calls on a second student to help a first one correct an answer.

Clip 2   NO OPT OUT

Patrick Pastore makes sure a student does not opt out of answering.
Clip also includes *Format Matters*.

Clip 3   CIRCULATE

Unpredictable teacher Lauren Catlett calls on her students for expressive reading.
Clip also includes *Control the Game*.

Clip 4   FORMAT MATTERS

Stacey Shells positively insists on standard English in her literature lesson.
Clip also includes *Take a Stand, Explain Everything, SLANT, Do It Again*.

Clip 5   RIGHT IS RIGHT

Alexandra Bronson persists in helping members of her fifth-grade class grasp a basic relationship between variables.
Clip also includes *Check for Understanding, No Opt Out, Warm/Strict*.

Clip 6   RIGHT IS RIGHT

Colleen Driggs supportively pushes her students to get the answer "really right."

Clip 7   RIGHT IS RIGHT

Khushali Gala involves many members of the class in answering a question about an important mathematical concept.

Clip 8   RIGHT IS RIGHT

As students discuss what they are reading aloud, Patrick Pastore presses them to get answers "really right."
Clip also includes *SLANT*.

Clip 9   NO OPT OUT

Lauren Catlett draws lots of students into a question sequence about predicates needing subjects.
Clip also includes *Circulate*.

Clip 10   WITHOUT APOLOGY

Dinah Shepherd and her class work hard to understand paradoxical language in a novel.
Clip also includes *Circulate*.

Clip 11   CONTROL THE GAME

Nikki Frame quietly tends to other students while also correcting the performance of students who read aloud.
Clip also includes *Circulate, No Warnings, Warm/Strict, Normalize Error, Precise Praise*.

Clip 12   CHECK FOR UNDERSTANDING

Bob Zimmerli checks his students' understanding and follows up to correct misunderstanding.
Clip also includes *Circulate*.

Clip 13   EXIT TICKET

Isaac Pollack issues and collects math exit tickets that he checks at the door as students leave.
Clip also includes *Check for Understanding*.

Clip 14   EXIT TICKET

Leanna Picard uses *Exit Ticket* results to follow up on student misunderstandings.
Clip also includes *Check for Understanding*.

Clip 15   DO IT AGAIN

Lauren Whitehead shows a *Do It Again* moment in this clip.
Clip also includes *Tight Transitions*.

Clip 16   COLD CALL

Hannah Lofthus makes effective cold calls.
Clip also includes *Check for Understanding*.

Clip 17   COLD CALL

Summer Payne excites a student group with fast-paced cold calls.

Clip 18   CALL AND RESPONSE

Lauren Whitehead builds academic purpose into *Call and Response*.
Clip also includes *Vegas, Tight Transitions*.

Clip 19   WAIT TIME

As Yasmin Vargas waits to pick a scholar to answer, she "notices" more and more students "thinking."

Clip 20   WAIT TIME

Katie Bellucci provides a *Wait Time* narrative.
Clip also includes *Check for Understanding*.

Clip 21   WAIT TIME

More hands go up as Christine Ranney narrates *Wait Time*.
Clip also includes *Stretch It, Circulate*.

Clip 22   VEGAS

Laura Palma has a lively routine to prepare her young class for attending to a story.
Clip also includes *Tight Transitions*.

Clip 23 TIGHT TRANSITIONS

Lauren Whitehead uses a silent, smooth transition routine to shift her students to the reading area.
Clip also includes *Call and Response*.

Clip 24 TIGHT TRANSITIONS

Marisa Segel's students pass up their seat work papers in no time.

Clip 25 DO IT AGAIN

Katie Bellucci asks the class to *Do It Again* and gets a stronger show of hands.

Clip 26 DO IT AGAIN

Alexandra Bronson and her class practice to tighten a transition.
Clip also includes *SLANT, Tight Transitions*.

Clip 27 THRESHOLD

Shadell Noel greets each student at the threshold of her classroom.

Clip 28 JOY FACTOR

Kelli Ragin's class celebrates with its "Angle Shuffle."

Clip 29 JOY FACTOR

Tamika Boykin rivets her class with an academic competition—them versus her.

Clip 30 RATIO

Amelia Herbert's students debate contrasting views of the American Revolution.

*With thanks and gratitude to the teachers and leaders at Uncommon
Schools, from whose work I have tried to learn*

ACKNOWLEDGMENTS

Teach Like a Champion was written for teachers and, for all intents and purposes, is by teachers. As its author, I had the job of observing and explaining what the most talented teachers I could find did that made them successful. Its underlying belief is that in the end it is teachers who hold the solutions to teaching problems and that observing them and tapping their wisdom is more than just an effective way for individuals to get better. It's the most promising way to rethink the profession, how it trains people, and the degree to which it affords teachers the full measure of respect they deserve as thinkers and entrepreneurs.

This book, in a way, applies the same lens to teacher training. It contains not only further observations about how the masters do it but also ideas developed by a smaller group of peers, both within and beyond Uncommon Schools, about how to help great people practice, reflect, and improve. Those peers include school leaders, lead teachers, coaches, and others who support educators at work.

Among those, the greatest debts of gratitude go to my colleagues Erica Woolway, Colleen Driggs, Rob Richard, and Katie Yezzi, whose insight was invaluable to practically every idea in the book. Even more than their work developing the activities we use in our workshops (many of which are adapted here), their understanding of people—a profoundly optimistic belief in their desire to be the best they can be—has been deeply inspirational to me. Our colleagues John Costello, Tracy Koren, and Alex Salinsky also worked tirelessly and contributed ideas and expertise.

The ideas we developed in workshops and trainings were often improved, bettered, or overshadowed by the insightful work of so many of Uncommon Schools' brilliant school leaders: Stacey Shells, David McBride, Paul Powell, Julie Jackson, Julie Kennedy, Lauren Harris, Hannah Solomon, JT Leiard, Jesse Rector, Sultana Noormuhammad, and Serena Savarirayan among others, all under the guidance of my fellow managing directors, Dana Lehman, Paul Bambrick-Santoyo, and Brett Peiser. At Uncommon I've also benefited from the tireless support of Laura Maestas, Evan Rudall, Josh Phillips, and Carolyn Hack. I also learned from principals and administrators of top schools and networks around the country: Ben Marcovitz, Caleb Dolan, Heather Kirkpatrick, Dan Cotton, and Chi Tschang, to name a few.

Finally, there was the messy work of turning all of this into a book that someone might actually read. For that I offer my gratitude to the tireless and unflappable Alan Venable, who put the pieces together from the other side of the country; to the always can-do Kate Gagnon, my editor at Jossey-Bass, who willed this into being; and to the rest of the team there and at John Wiley and Sons. And of course to Rafe Sagalyn, my agent, whose partnership has helped me survive life as a sometime (usually between 5 and 7 AM) writer.

And of course the last thank you is always closest to home—to my wife, Lisa, and our three amazing children. I don't know whether to thank you first for inspiring me to take on projects like this or for putting up with the result.

THE AUTHOR

Doug Lemov is a managing director of Uncommon, which runs twenty-eight high-performing urban charter schools in the Northeast. Doug is also the author of the best-selling book *Teach Like a Champion* and has shared the results of his study of high-performing teachers with school leaders and teachers through workshops as well as his writing. He has taught English and history at the university, high school, and middle school levels. He lives in upstate New York with his wife, Lisa, and three children. Visit him at www.douglemov.com.

Uncommon Schools | Change History.

Uncommon Schools (Uncommon, www.uncommonschools.org) starts and manages great schools in urban areas across the Northeast. We currently have twenty-eight schools in Boston, New York City, Newark, Rochester, and Troy. Although each school is unique, we are similar in the ways that matter most:

- We believe that *all* students should have access to the best teachers and resources.
- We go the distance to make sure that all our students are ready to go to college.
- We hold ourselves—both students and the adults who serve them—to high standards of excellence.
- We're unapologetic about our focus on rigor and structure.
- We believe in the power of data and pride ourselves on focusing our instructional energy accordingly.

These themes shine through when Uncommon staff members talk about what makes us "Uncommon":

"Uncommon believes that the educational inequity in America is a crisis. Our response is to focus deeply on student achievement by finding ways to free our educators of distractions. Uncommon teachers are able to focus solely on executing instruction that is both rigorous and engaging. Our principals are instructional leaders who spend at least 70 percent of their day observing teachers and giving actionable feedback. This supports all teachers to continue to grow their practice—essential because our shared goal is that every student will attend college. It is 'Uncommon' for urban teachers and principals to be able to focus on instruction for the majority of the day, enabling every student who sits in every chair to make dramatic learning gains."

—Julie Jackson, Associate Managing Director, North Star Academy Schools, Newark, New Jersey

"Although you can learn a lot about us from our name alone, you'd be remiss not to step foot inside one of our schools to observe what truly makes us 'Uncommon.' What would you find? You'd see data-driven instruction that has been painstakingly prepared to help students master their daily objectives. You'd see teachers striking the elusive yet critical balance of creating a warm learning environment while setting high behavioral standards. You'd witness teachers who receive hundreds of hours of professional development every year to ensure that they are masters in their field. You'd hear a collective sigh (of sadness!) among students when they are told that there will be no Saturday School this weekend. You'd see students whose parents chose to send them to a school where they can receive a superior education with absolutely no out-of-pocket costs. Are we Uncommon? Yes."

—Bob Zimmerli, Dean of Curriculum and Instruction, Rochester Preparatory Middle School, Rochester, New York

"The top 10 things that make us 'Uncommon:'

10. We have some of the smartest people in the field of education on staff.

9. In the words of Carolyn DiProspero, Leadership Prep Bedford Stuyvesant kindergarten teacher, 'I love that I work at a school where we take a whole day to talk about assessments!'

8. Chanting and singing with our scholars is like living in *High School Musical.*

7. Our scholars say the darndest things.

6. We don't reinvent the wheel but instead share best practices across teachers, classrooms, and schools.

5. Watching our students working diligently at their desks inspires us to improve our posture and diligence.

4. Our schools are filled with people who support each other through thick and thin.

3. The mantra 'Work hard, get smart' is true for our scholars and for all of us.

2. We challenge previously held assumptions about what is possible in education.

1. We change the trajectory of children's lives every day."

—Sultana Noormuhammad, Principal, Leadership Preparatory Bedford Stuyvesant Collegiate Charter School, New York, New York

INTRODUCTION

HOW TO USE THIS FIELD GUIDE AND DVD

Whether you are a teacher-in-training, a master teacher whose goal is constant improvement, or an educator who simply loves the art of getting better, this field guide can help you get the most out of the techniques profiled in *Teach Like a Champion: A Practical Resource to Make the 49 Techniques Your Own*. Drawing on the experience of top trainers, teachers, and school leaders, the *Field Guide* provides hands-on activities and guidance that you can use to reflect on your own practice and then work to explore, experiment with, and master any or all of the forty-nine techniques.

Under the best circumstances, you're collaborating in this challenge with a small group of colleagues who can stimulate, share, and support one another's discoveries and deepening skills. But even if you're using the *Field Guide* alone, we think the tools included here can help you achieve the results you and your students deserve.

START WITH THE BIG PICTURE

Most of the techniques in this book work best when you apply them alongside other, complementary techniques; so a good place to begin is to become familiar with the overall pattern of the forty-nine techniques, as summarized in the table of contents. Or use the map following the Introduction to get the general lay of the land.

As you use the book, you'll notice that frequent icons in the margins signal points at which one technique supports another. But of course the connections we point out are an incomplete list. As you use and practice the techniques, look for synergies between and among them to emerge.

An important step in self-improvement is self-assessment. This book is designed to help you reflect on where you stand and what techniques will be most valuable for you—at the outset or as you hone your skills. The "Where Am I Now?" charts that begin each technique are designed to help you in this area, as are a variety of reflection questions interspersed throughout. The charts will help you think about your own comfort, confidence, and proficiency. But if you find yourself saying "I already do that," you've uncovered an even greater reason to study a technique. The fact that an idea comes naturally to you and jibes with your overall approach is a starting point, not an end point.

In fact, it's been fascinating to all of us who use this material at Uncommon Schools to observe that almost no champion teacher we know is without weaknesses, even those who humble us and take our collective breath away when we observe them at work. What champions have in common, both within our organization and in other great schools of every stripe and variety where we've observed, is a portfolio of five or six skills at which they truly excel. The skills aren't the same ones for every teacher—the combinations are as unique as the applications. But it is these skills, the things they are best at, that drive much of their success. The lesson from this is clear: strengthen your strengths, make them exceptional, and use them as a foundation from which to improve what you perceive to be your weaker areas.

As a general principle, then, we urge you to *begin by improving upon your strengths as much as upon your weaknesses*. Consolidate major skills with which you feel more confident, then use those techniques to build your confidence and ability to learn new challenging ones. Consider these questions:

- Are you strong at planning, but not so strong yet as a classroom performer? Consider starting with one of the planning techniques, and look for ways that further improvements in planning can strengthen your classroom preparedness and confidence.
- Are you strong in classroom interaction skills, but not so strong in planning the lesson? Consider beginning by muscling up your classroom skills, and fold in improvements in planning as well.

One other thing we've discovered is that studying classroom technique is best done as a team sport. When possible, try to work with a partner or group, so that you can discuss what you learn and learn from each other as you explore a given concept.

CHOOSING WHICH TECHNIQUES TO START WITH

If you still don't know where to begin, here are several possible starting points.

Starting with *Cold Call* (and Some *No Opt Out*)

Of all the forty-nine techniques, *Cold Call* backed up by *No Opt Out* is likely to revolutionize the culture of academic expectations in your classroom more quickly than any other combination. Together, they help you normalize the expectation that everybody gives his or her best every day and is always "in the game." Therefore, starting with techniques 1 and 22 can be especially effective.

Starting from Routines

Some champion teachers argue that great classrooms rest on an everyday culture of strong, apparently (but not really) mundane routines that empower you to teach efficiently and empower students to excel at academics. Making routine tasks automatic frees more time—often astounding amounts of it—for teaching. You can make almost any routine automatic, efficient, and a source of useful habit, from entering the classroom to shifting from one task to another.

The Section Five techniques, 28 through 35, all focus on building strong routines. They are preceded by an overview that includes advice about creating strong routines generally and also activities for identifying and improving the routines you need.

If you want to start from routines, begin with the Section Five overview. After that, three good specific routines to start with are techniques 28, *Entry Routine;* 30, *Tight Transitions;* and 41, *Threshold.*

Starting from Planning

A third place to begin is at planning. In that case, you might choose to start with techniques 6 and 10, *Begin with the End* and *Double Plan.* What does your class look like—and what are its goals—from your perspective and that of your students?

CHART AND NAVIGATE

Beyond the starting point you choose, chart your continuing course as a journey you need not map entirely in advance. The table of contents includes a checklist with which you can neatly log techniques you've visited and ones to which you'll want to return. Likewise, the map following the Introduction shows what are likely the most important techniques to cover and subsidiary ones you will probably want to visit from there.

As you work, remember what you probably already know from your experience with students: that deep mastery trumps partial skill, even of a larger number of things. Rather than starting by touching briefly on all forty-nine techniques, set out with a goal of mastering a handful or so that seem most important for you at this time. With those secured, expand. Every essential teaching skill develops with repeated practice and time, and the material for each technique in this book is designed to benefit you every time you visit it again, aware of your continuing progress.

RECORD SOME OPTIONS NOW

No matter how you are using the *Field Guide,* take a minute now to reflect on your strengths and weaknesses. Identify one or two broad preliminary goals that address what you want to learn and improve—for example, using questioning to be more rigorous, or remaining calm and poised in the face of nonproductive behavior.

1. _____

2. _____

Now flip through the book and, at closer range, note some specific techniques that could help you address the general topics you've listed. Your goal is ultimately to master these and a variety of related content, including that related to your strengths.

1. _____

2. _____

3. _____

Considering your strengths and weaknesses, your interests and style, the needs of your students, and perhaps your partners in applying this book, consider which techniques in this guide look like the best places for you to start. Choose three or four. Then glance through those techniques, noting one single, focused idea from within each that you're excited to master. Record the technique names and smaller ideas here:

_____

_____

_____

_____

From among the ones you've listed here, choose your starting point. If you're new to this, starting with one technique (or even part of one!) may be sufficient. As you work on it, it may lead you to start work on one or two other related techniques. But avoid spreading yourself thin; keep the number small. Make progress on these techniques that will show up dramatically on "Where Am I Now?" before you tackle additional techniques.

ACTIVITIES WITHIN EACH TECHNIQUE

For each technique, your hands-on learning is supported by numerous activities. For example, technique 1, *No Opt Out,* includes the following order of coverage, with various resources under each heading. The materials for the other forty-eight techniques are similarly organized (although not every technique includes all of these headings):

Overview	A thumbnail sketch of *No Opt Out*
Where Am I Now?	A simple self-assessment to update as you go
Analyze the Champions	Prompts for analyzing video clips on the accompanying DVD (with some sample answers provided)
Expand Your Skills and Repertoire	Explanations and individual practice exercises (often adaptable for partner or group work)
Practice with Study Group or Partners	Group role plays, discussions, and exercises (often adaptable for individual work)
Try *No Opt Out* in the Classroom	Step-by-step suggestions
Trouble-Shoot	Common temptations and other challenges in applying *No Opt Out*
Be Creative	Creative suggestions
Sustain Your Progress	A place to update notes on issues and progress toward mastery

As you will see, the activities constitute a process for assessing outcomes and sharpening your efforts. Nearly all of them are useful to do more than once.

GET FULL VALUE FROM THE VIDEO CLIPS

This book often refers to one or more of the brand-new video clips that accompany it on DVD. Every clip shows a highly accomplished teacher at work, and all of them will be new (and, we hope, exciting) to you even if you've repeatedly watched the clips included in *Teach Like a Champion.* Most demonstrate numerous techniques, some more subtly than others. Independent of your work on techniques, dip into them periodically to absorb more from these champion teachers. Although "Analyze the Champions" is presented for individual work, the clips can be used very effectively by groups working on a specific technique. If you are facilitating the group work, consider having participants also watch clips together to answer the questions in a group setting. You'll also notice that we often provide several videos for one technique, so that you can compare different ways of applying the technique and model a version that best matches your own classroom goals, demeanor, and methods.

AUDIO- OR VIDEO-RECORD YOUR TEACHING

We strongly recommend that you videotape yourself in the classroom. For some of the techniques, we will ask you to view and reflect on your recordings. You won't necessarily need to rerecord each time. One audio or video recording may suffice to visit and revisit to study your words and behaviors and those of your students. Begin the recording with some private thoughts about the objective for the session, as well as thoughts about any champion technique(s) on which you intend to focus.

After you make the initial recording, listen to it and note down at which points various activities begin; among others, the following points will be especially useful to mark so that you can find them quickly in the future:

- Your private thoughts about the *objective* for the session
- Your private thoughts about the champion *technique*(s) on which you wanted to focus
- *Greeting* students at the door
- Students entering and *preparing* for class
- *Beginning* the lesson
- *Transitions* from one activity to another
- Direct *instruction*
- *Question-and-answer*

- *Checking students understanding*
- *Desk work*
- Moments at which you are dealing with some issue of classroom *control*
- Moments of *shared satisfaction*
- Bringing the lesson to a *close*
- *Dismissal*
- Private *debriefing*
- Conversation with an *observer*

You can also profit greatly by rerecording and studying more sessions or by being observed by a supportive partner at several points, as the school year and your skills advance.

WORK WITH A GROUP OR PARTNER

If you are starting work on the *Field Guide* alone, begin to look right away for *at least one other teacher with whom you can partner.* You may find someone in your school or district, but you can also work via phone, e-mail, or social media with someone you know and trust, perhaps posting videos and reflections on Facebook. Both of you can benefit by this in terms of motivation, support, resources, and the power and enjoyment of these activities.

If you can't find a partner, still *begin to talk with at least one other teacher colleague* about matters related to the techniques. What does he or she do to deal with something related to the technique you're on? Share your own ideas as well.

Partners or groups will likely want to arrive at some consensus about where to start among the techniques and periodically where to go next. Often, you may wish to go to a technique that is related to one you've worked on already and that feels within reach.

In a large group, someone may need to be an ongoing facilitator and manager. But ideally group members will take turns as *Facilitator* for each technique or meeting. In most instances, the *Facilitator* also can participate in the activity as everyone else is doing. The following are basic *Facilitator* tasks:

- Read the technique materials ahead of the rest of the group to notice and call general attention to things that members should do to prepare.
- Lead decision making and communication about what activities the group wants to do.
- Prepare shared materials.
- Lay meeting ground rules.
- Moderate.
- Decide when to switch from one activity to the next.
- Keep track of time or deputize someone else to do it.
- Lead new decision making about what technique(s) the group will do next time.
- Summarize at the end of a meeting.

BRAINSTORMING IN GROUPS

The group activities often involve brainstorming. If your group does not already have its own effective method, you may want to follow this one, presented here from the perspective of the member of the group who is acting as *Facilitator* for a given technique.

1. Set the context by refreshing the group on whatever topic or materials the brainstorming will be about.
2. Appoint a *Timekeeper* and a *Recorder* who will use board, overhead, large paper, or other means to capture all ideas.
3. Go in order around the circle, giving each person a limited number of seconds (thirty to sixty) to contribute one idea. If needed, the *Timekeeper* can call "Time."
4. Allow anyone who has no idea at that moment to say "Pass."
5. As you go around, no one disrupts by expressing any judgment of or modification to another person's idea.
6. Keep going for an agreed-on time, or call a stop when you've gone around several times and four or five people pass in a row. Invite hands for any last ideas.
7. When the brainstorm is over, keep the recorded results in view of the group. Also, as a group, examine the recorded results to order, cluster, or refine them as needed.

USING A JOURNAL

This guide does not involve keeping an outside journal, but it is compatible with doing so in handwritten or digital form. If you want to make journaling part of your work, be sure to develop a system by which you can easily revisit what you wrote in connection with a given prompt in the book. Design it to help you monitor your progress and benefit more deeply each time you return to a technique. Also index the journal in a way that will let you cull it quickly as you go through the planning, preparation, and follow-up for "Try [Technique X] in the Classroom."

USING THIS BOOK AS A COACH OR ADMINISTRATOR

We also recognize that some administrators may wish to use this book to assist their teachers in developing the craft, either in groups or on their own. If this is your situation, we provide the following reflections to help support your work.

1. *Success begins with practice.* Especially adults are often reluctant to practice or rehearse, to get in front of a group of four or five peers and, for example, practice cold-calling them in order to get better at *Cold Call.* But practice before the game is the single most reliable driver of success. So strive to build a setting for safe practice where it's okay to experiment, and participants are supported if they fail. And where teachers can practice over and over again to get ready.

2. *Peer-to-peer accountability drives success.* People are at least as motivated by accountability to their peers as they are by their accountability to authority. Although it's important for teachers to be accountable to their organizations, consider letting your teachers form groups (by subject area or grade level or some other common interest) and commit as a group to working on techniques they want to master together—and for which they will hold each other accountable. Giving them vested autonomy is both a gesture of respect and a tool to ensure their success.

3. *Make it safe to fail.* Champions seek to expose their weaknesses. Exposing them is the only way to fix them. Thus good-faith struggle and difficulty are good things, and we urge you not to punish or chastise teachers who try but struggle or even fail. Encourage them and help them improve. If you don't, you risk fostering a culture where people try to hide their weaknesses, and this only causes those weaknesses to fester. Further, if people struggle and know they can safely come to you with challenges and problems, and if you are able to help them find solutions, you will earn their trust and faith.

WHERE THESE IDEAS AND ACTIVITIES CAME FROM

Much of the material here has been developed as part of the workshops and training we've helped run (or observed being run) with and by the incredible and inspiring teachers and leaders at Uncommon Schools. Most of the techniques have gone through a variety of iterations to improve and refine them, often based on feedback from the folks who've attended our workshops. The more trainings we do, the more we realize that, as inspiring as the videos are, the work that comes after one watches them is more important. Practice and reflection are what drive results, and that means studying a technique multiple times over the course of a year.

Please also know that we believe that these tools truly work. We have seen them change teachers' and students' lives—making the former love the work and achieve their goals and helping the latter to do something fairly similar. We know this from watching talented peers within and outside our organization put them to the test—in charter schools and district schools; private and public schools; urban, rural, and suburban schools. So we are excited to share this material with you and wish you the best of success at the most important and most rewarding work in the world.

A MAP OF THE 49 TECHNIQUES

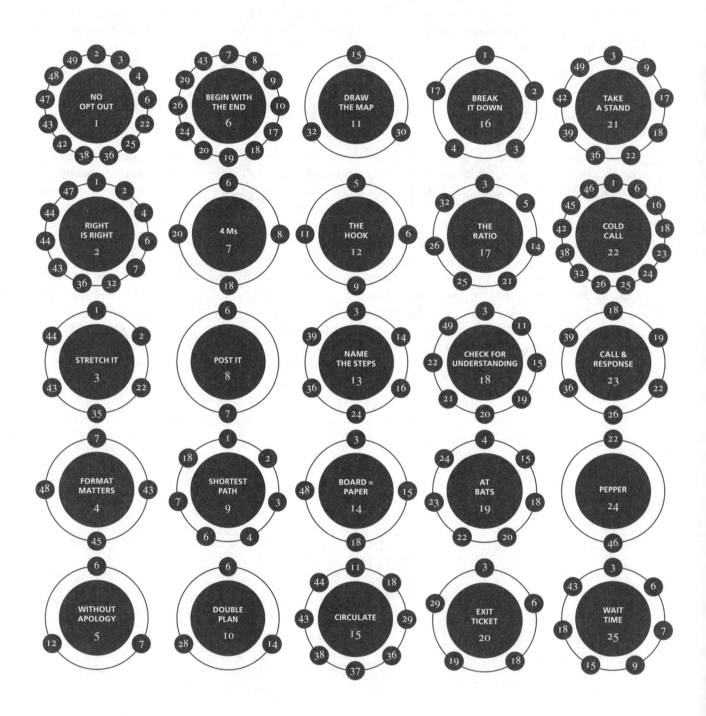

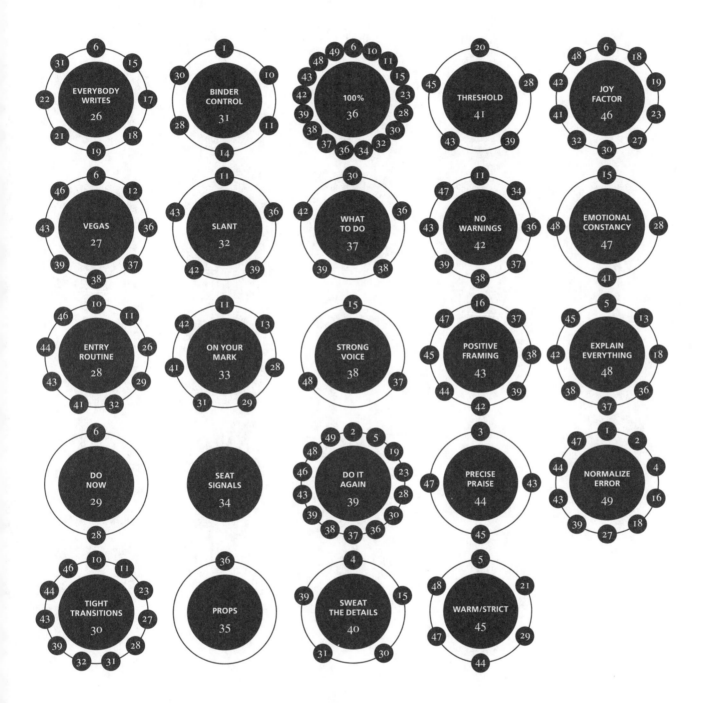

NO OPT OUT

OVERVIEW

In a high-performing classroom, a verbalized or unspoken "I don't know" is cause for action. When a student begins by being unable or unwilling to answer, you should strive to make the sequence end as often as possible with the student giving a right or valid answer. Choose among four basic formats to respond:

Format 1. You provide the answer; your student repeats the answer.

Format 2. Another student provides the answer; the initial student repeats the answer.

Format 3. You provide a cue; your student uses it to find the answer.

Format 4. Another student provides a cue; the initial student uses it to find the answer.

This is surely among the most helpful and efficient techniques for raising classroom expectations, especially if

- Students tend to duck away from questions rather than answer them.
- Students don't hear themselves getting answers right.
- The class lacks a culture of accountability and incentive for each individual.

Take the rigor of your interaction up a notch by wrapping up the sequence with a request for another correct answer or an explanation of the "why."

WHERE AM I NOW?

	Proficiency			
Comfort & Confidence	**I'm brand new to *No Opt Out* . . .**	**I'm in the planning and practice stage, though I haven't tried it yet in class . . .**	**I'm beginning to try *No Opt Out* in my classroom . . .**	**I use *No Opt Out* regularly . . .**
	❏ . . . and excited to try it.	❏ . . . but know that with more practice I'll make it work.	❏ . . . and love how it basically works.	❏ . . . and am adding my own distinctive touch.
	❏ . . . and undecided about my ability to pull it off.	❏ . . . because I still have questions about how to do it right.	❏ . . . with mixed results I need to evaluate.	❏ . . . but I may be overusing it.
	❏ . . . and not at all sure it's for me.	❏ . . . because, frankly, I still have serious doubts.	❏ . . . but it doesn't seem to work or suit me.	❏ . . . but when class isn't going well, I do it poorly and it doesn't help.

Work from your strengths! If you find yourself in the bottom left portion, leaf through this technique to locate related ones that could help you build the classroom culture that will make you more confident and able to execute *No Opt Out*—perhaps *100%*, *Positive Framing*, or *Cold Call*. Or look for a setting in which to try it out first with greater safety and less risk, perhaps in a smaller group in which you interact with students or with a group of especially positive students. But take on *No Opt Out* as soon as you can. It's a game changer in building a culture of accountability and high expectations.

NO OPT OUT

ANALYZE THE CHAMPIONS

| 22 **COLD CALL** |
| 36 **100%** |
| 38 **STRONG VOICE** |
| 43 **POSITIVE FRAMING** |

View each video clip, ideally more than once, and answer the following questions. See the end of the technique for some possible answers.

 Clip 1. Teacher Shadell Noel, Grade K

1. Which format(s) of *No Opt Out* is Ms. Noel using? Do you already use the same format(s) often and with ease?
2. What seems to be Kayla's attitude when she says, "I don't know"? What is it when she repeats the answer?
3. How do the other students seem to feel about the sequence and Kayla's answer?

 Clip 2. Teacher Patrick Pastore, Grade 6

1. Which format(s) of *No Opt Out* is Mr. Pastore using? Do you already use the same format(s) often and with ease?

 Clip 9. Teacher Lauren Catlett, Grade 5

1. Which format(s) is Ms. Catlett using? Do you already do the same?
2. What is Ms. Catlett's initial question? Where does the *No Opt Out* technique begin?
3. How many students does she go back to at the end for correct answers? Who and why?

EXPAND YOUR SKILLS AND REPERTOIRE

An incorrect answer is not opting out. But saying "I don't know" in good faith or with impassivity *is* opting out. The goal of *No Opt Out* is that *the student will eventually state the answer,* even if that amounts to repeating an answer that you or another student supplied. Your goal should be to establish *No Opt Out* as the norm in your classroom, so that students will try to answer, knowing they will succeed with dignity even if they're not right the first time.

No Opt Out and *Cold Call*

No Opt Out is especially useful in supporting *Cold Call*—selecting a student to answer without asking

| 22 **COLD CALL** |

for hands. Teachers who use *No Opt Out* well often *Cold Call* effectively also. What do you think the connection might be? How might the techniques support each other?

The Moment of "I Don't Know"

Have you already noticed moments when you've received silence or some form of "I don't know" and accepted that response? What keeps you from addressing the problem?

_____

_____

What simple language could you rehearse and use to indicate that you don't accept it and plan to come back to the student for an actual answer? Consider these examples and add some of your own:

"Take a little more time to speak your thoughts. I'll wait."

"Give it some more thought. I'll be back."

"Let's see how you might begin to answer. I'll come back to you shortly."

"We can work on this problem together. I'll bring it back to you in a moment."

_____

_____

_____

_____

_____

_____

What Is an Answer?

In order to take on opt-out responses, you need to have a clear idea of what kind of response is *not* opting out. In other words, what would be an acceptable attempt at responding? One solution is the "However/Best" approach. In it, a student can say, "I don't know" if it's followed by the word "however" and his best try, as in "I don't know; however, I think I need to multiply here."

Try scripting a few "However/Best" phrases that you could model for your students:

1. _____

_____

2. _____

_____

You can always repeat the question in case it wasn't heard or understood. *Format Matters* suggests several criteria you can request the student to follow before you conclude he is opting out, including audibility and complete sentence format. When a student is opting out by mumbling, you can comment,

> **4 FORMAT MATTERS**

"John, please speak up so everyone can hear. I'll repeat the question . . ."

"I didn't catch that. Can you say it again more loudly and at a little more length? Say it as a complete sentence. The question I'm asking is . . ."

"I'll accept that you don't know all of it if you follow that statement by summarizing what you *do* know. Try it again."

Try writing two similar responses that would fit your style and grade level of students:

1. _____

   _____

2. _____

   _____

Rehearse them by speaking them aloud, preferably to a peer or colleague. What did you learn from speaking them aloud? Did you make any changes or adaptations?

_____

_____

_____

_____

_____

Rather than remaining silent or saying they don't know, students may also try to opt out using strategies mentioned in *Right Is Right*: they may "answer" some question other than the one you asked. In that case, stick with them with a response like this:

| 2 **RIGHT IS RIGHT** |

"Delia, I'd like you to focus on the question I've asked. My question right now is . . . "

Try writing and speaking two similar responses that would fit your style and grade level of students:

1. _____

   _____

2. _____

   _____

Rehearse these as well. Or go back and rehearse several prompts that would request that the student answer the question you asked and do so in the correct format. Did you make any changes after speaking them aloud?

Start Simple

When students aren't used to the discipline of *No Opt Out*, start out with questions that have one clear, correct answer and can be answered in a *single sentence*:

"What did you get for problem 24? Paula?"

"What phrase shows that Hemingway's old man is tired? Anna?"

What are two other ways to get students used to *No Opt Out* by starting simple?

1. _____

_____

2. _____

_____

Supplying Answers or Cues

The goal of No Opt Out *is to get the student to answer.* One way to get him to do so is to get the answer from another student (or supply it yourself) and have the first student repeat the answer. This does train him to know that he can't opt out, and it helps him keep his mind on the lesson and listen to what other students are saying. So you can turn to another student and ask,

"How would *you* answer that, Yolanda?"

But often better is to arrange some cue (a precise and intentional clue that helps students recall critical information), especially by asking a question of another student. By *Cold Calling* on that student as well, you signal all students to regard themselves as potential call-ons for assistance.

Perhaps the best kind of cue is one that calls attention to a resource that a student has overlooked, such as

- *The place where the answer can be found.* "Who can tell James where he could find the answer?" This is especially useful in reading classes.
- *The step in a process that's required.* "Who can tell James what the first thing he should do is?"

A cue can also directly simplify the question in some helpful way, such as by supplying another name for a term that the student may not know:

"Who can tell us what *synchronous* means in this question?"

As a fallback, you can also provide a cue yourself:

"By synchronous, I mean two things occurring simultaneously—at the same time."

"Let's all look at the top of page 25. James, what do you see there?"

"There's some useful information on the board. James, what looks useful there?"

"Let's all look at our notes from yesterday."

Adding Rigor

Think how you might add rigor after a successful sequence of *No Opt Out*. One way is to ask a follow-up question (see *Stretch It*) that lets the student show himself and others what he can do. Phrases such as "Good, let's try a harder one," "Good, now give me another example," or "Good, can you tell me why?" are important for older students who will want to show that they can do more than repeat an answer. Add several more questions that add rigor in language appropriate to your students and subject.

3 STRETCH IT

_____

_____

_____

Negative Reactions

In some classrooms, a student may be inclined to react negatively to being called on, or mock or laugh at another student who can't answer the question. Prevent this by teaching students how to react before it happens for real. See the "rollout" ideas in the "Try *No Opt Out* in the Classroom" section. As part of rollout, you can ask students how they should react. Give them a clear model of what it should look like, role-play it, and practice it with simulated examples.

| 42 **NO WARNINGS** |

Once a student does react with clear disobedience, however, tackle the behavior with a consequence as described in *No Warnings*.

PRACTICE WITH STUDY GROUP OR PARTNERS

Revisit the individual work you did in the previous section to share and compare your responses and see other options.

Why Students May Try to Opt Out

1. Brainstorm as many possible reasons as you can for why students might be unable to answer a given question in your classes. You might think about reasons students may not know the answer, reasons they may know the answer but not want to say it, or reasons they don't want to hazard a guess.

_____

_____

_____

| 47 **EMOTIONAL CONSTANCY** |
| 49 **NORMALIZE ERROR** |

2. In most cases, you won't know what is causing a student to opt out, but when you do, discuss how that cause should affect your tone and manner in responding.

3. Pairing off, ask a simple question (for example, What's 3 plus 5?) and have the partner opt out in a way that reflects the various motivations the group identified. Practice responding to each.

No Opt Out Role Play

Practice the *No Opt Out* techniques with two other people. Start simply. Rotate roles before moving on to the two variations here. Listen for how your tone and body language change so that you can find versions of each format that are natural to you.

The roles are *Teacher, Student A,* and *Student Z.* Here is the basic sequence:

1. *Teacher* asks *Student A* a simple question. ("What's 3 plus 5?")
2. Unable to answer, *Student A* responds in a way that suggests genuine effort.
3. *Teacher* asks *Student Z* to provide a correct answer.
4. *Student Z* answers directly and correctly.
5. *Teacher* returns to *Student A* for repetition of correct answer.
6. *Student A* answers correctly.
7. *Teacher* acknowledges correct answer.

Practice this way to *Normalize Error* so that it makes *Student A* feel as though getting it wrong and then getting it right are a normal part of school. Record your observations.

_____

_____

Variation 1

1. *Teacher:* Follow the basic sequence several times, but notice differences in your own tone and manner of response when *Student A* responds as follows.
2. *Student A* says "I don't know" negatively, challengingly, indifferently.
3. *Student Z* answers directly and correctly.

   Teacher: What was more or less effective about your choices of tone and manner?

   Reflection: How did your response change when *Student A* was negative, challenging, sarcastic? What were the two most effective things that members of the group did?

_____

_____

Variation 2

Teacher: Follow a similar pattern, but now also try formats 3 and 4.

   Format 3: You provide a cue; your *Student* uses it to find the answer.

   Format 4: Another *Student* provides a cue; the initial *Student* uses it to find the answer.

Students: Start out with relatively cooperative responses. As the *Teacher* gets more comfortable, become a little more challenging.

   Reflection: What actions or phrases were effective in this situation?

_____

_____

   What useful feedback did you get from this group work? What else did you learn? What parts of this were particularly challenging that you'd like to plan for or practice more?

_____

_____

_____

_____

TRY *NO OPT OUT* IN THE CLASSROOM

Basketball coach Bobby Knight would say, "Everyone has the will to win; only some people have the will to prepare to win." Remember, you won't get it right the first time. You will master this on the tenth or fifteenth try!

1. A "rollout speech" tells your students in advance that you're going to use a technique and explain why and how they should respond. By rolling out the technique, you head off any potentially awkward misunderstandings and publicly commit yourself to trying it. Then you have to follow through! Draft your rollout speech for *No Opt Out*. (You may recall the video of Colleen Driggs's *Cold Call* rollout speech in *Teach Like A Champion*; rewatching it now may help you draft a similar one for *No Opt Out*.) Try to frame things as positively as you can. You might address

| 43 **POSITIVE FRAMING** |
| 48 **EXPLAIN EVERYTHING** |
| 49 **NORMALIZE ERROR** |

- What will happen when you use *No Opt Out*
- How students should respond
- What will be tricky about it
- What it will be like over time as they get used to it
- Why you are doing this

2. While you are learning the basics, anticipate *No Opt Out* moments in your lesson plan. Working with a partner if you can, script three questions into your lesson plan that you think students might

| 6 **BEGIN WITH THE END** |

struggle with and require *No Opt Out* help on. Write out the responses you anticipate and how you'd respond. Your answers can include what students say or what they do (if their actions speak as much as their words).

| 22 **COLD CALL** |

3. Revisit your thoughts in "Why Students May Try to Opt Out." Draft a *No Opt Out* response for each reason you identified. Practice saying it aloud five times.

4. After class, go back to the lesson plan and write what you want to pay attention to next time you teach.

5. In future sessions, continue to focus *No Opt Out* on questions with relatively clear-cut answers. As you improve, script and try more open-ended questions. Practice until the format is a comfortable part of your style.

| 25 **WAIT TIME** |

6. One of the reasons students might opt out is that they haven't had enough thinking or processing time. How could you remind yourself to leave sufficient *Wait Time*?

TROUBLE-SHOOT

Steady On

You may need to fight the temptation to let students opt out—or to slide to the simplest format (providing the answer yourself). Think about what you can learn from Mr. Harris in this example. How does he avoid these temptations? What's the message he sends to Jalon and the rest of the class?

Mr. Harris *Cold Calls* Jalon with a question about something the class covered yesterday. Jalon says truthfully, "I don't know. I wasn't here."

In response, Mr. Harris

- Acknowledges that Jalon was absent
- Says he will ask someone else
- Forewarns Jalon to expect to be called on to answer again in a moment because Jalon needs to be able to move forward today
- Asks another student
- Returns to Jalon for the correct answer
- Provides cueing to Jalon as needed

Other Challenges

Ultimately, you'll learn *No Opt Out* by practice supported by planning and frequent referral back to the basics, rather than by trying to memorize situations and how to respond. But these suggestions might be useful. Discover and add your own.

Possible Challenge	Possible Solutions
No Opt Out slows me down, and we don't get everything done.	True. Balance using *No Opt Out* against the need to keep momentum going. Focus *No Opt Out* most on questions closest to the session's main learning objective. The earlier in the year that *No Opt Out* becomes the norm, the less students will slow things down by trying to opt out. In the long run, you will have more time to teach. **6 BEGIN WITH THE END**
I call on another student for the answer, but she doesn't know it.	Give *that* student a clue to find the answer. Give the answer and have *both* students repeat it together for the class. Or have the whole class repeat it using *Call and Response.* Remember, you are building culture.
I call on a student to give a cue, but he does not know how to give it and wants to give the answer instead.	Say, "When I ask you for a cue, I am not asking you to answer. The difference is important, and I expect you to pay attention to it." Then (1) ask him to provide the cue he could have provided after the fact, or (2) for the very next question, call on the helper student to provide a cue before you ask for someone to answer the next problem.
I ask a question that no one can answer.	Did they hear it? Were you sure there was a right answer? Were you sure of exactly what it was? Have you used *Wait Time* well? **25 WAIT TIME** Was there a more effective cue you could have used? (Ask a peer to suggest some!) Was the question appropriate to the moment? Was it clear? If not, say, "Let me ask a better question for now."
The initial student resists repeating the answer out of embarrassment, shame, and so on.	Build culture. Say, "Thank you, Jeremy. It's great you struggled the first time around. It helped us all see this is challenging. Say the answer now to solidify." Or "Thank you, Jeremy. I'm proud of you for persevering."
The other students grow impatient waiting for someone to get to the right answer.	Stop the lesson. Teach your class how to respond. "Just a second. Kareemah is doing what we'll all be doing at some point in this class, working hard towards getting it right. I'll expect you to show your support just as she'll show it to you. That means silence, tracking, and a supportive expression on your face."

BE CREATIVE

Grade 1 teacher Sultana Noormuhammad devised a routine that allows students to call on other students for either a cue or an answer (within a limiting countdown of time). Usually she frames a question for the "helper student" in a way that elicits a cue, thus putting cognitive work back on the initial student.

SUSTAIN YOUR PROGRESS

1. Using feedback from your study group or other peers, and reviewing your own lesson notes and observations, monitor your progress on *No Opt Out*.

Date	Attempt to Opt Out	What I Did or Could Have Done

2. Revisit "Where Am I Now?" Are you ready to build out to some other new technique?

ANALYZE THE CHAMPIONS: SOME OBSERVATIONS

 Clip 1. Teacher Shadell Noel, Grade K

You may have noticed that at the start of Ms. Noel's phrase "Do you know . . . ," all students enthusiastically raise their hands, but when the teacher mentions the word "clever," Kayla puts her hand down. Seeing this, Ms. Noel asks her if she knows what it means, and Kayla honestly answers that she doesn't. Ms. Noel then uses format 1 with a slight variation—she has another student provide the definition of clever, which she then repeats before going back to Kayla to provide (by repeating) the definition. The entire exchange takes no longer than fifteen seconds and ends with Kayla confidently providing a right answer.

 Clip 2. Teacher Patrick Pastore, Grade 6

Mr. Pastore first tries format 3, providing a cue himself. Then he uses format 2, getting the answer from another student. He is sterner than Ms. Noel and persists in requiring the initial student to repeat the answer as a complete sentence, per *Format Matters*. He's sure to praise the second student's answer as a model—"flawless"—and after it's over, they move on quickly. No lecture necessary (or worthwhile).

| 4 **FORMAT MATTERS** |

 Clip 9. Teacher Lauren Catlett, Grade 5

Ms. Catlett first uses format 3, attempting to prompt the student herself. Then she uses format 2: another student provides the answer; the initial student repeats the answer. But she also uses a *No Opt Out* within a *No Opt Out* to address multiple students. This normalizes the process and underscores that it applies to everyone. Her positive tone is critical to achieving this.

| 49 **NORMALIZE ERROR** |

NO OPT OUT

RIGHT IS RIGHT

OVERVIEW

This technique helps you set and defend a high standard of correctness in your classroom. There's an important difference between partially right and all-the-way right answers. *Right Is Right* means that when you respond to students' answers in class, you set a high standard by holding out for all-the-way right or, if there is no one "right" answer, holding out for thorough, rigorous answers. There are four main criteria for *Right Is Right*:

1. Is the answer all-the-way correct? (When there is no precise correct answer, is the answer up to my standard of thoroughness and rigor?)

2. Has the student answered my question?

3. Is this the right answer at the right time?

4. Are my students using technical vocabulary?

WHERE AM I NOW?

	Proficiency			
Comfort & Confidence	**I am brand new to *Right Is Right* ...**	**I'm in the planning and practice stage, though I haven't tried *Right Is Right* yet in class ...**	**I'm beginning to try *Right Is Right* in my classroom ...**	**I stick with *Right Is Right* ...**
	❏ ... and excited to try it.	❏ ... but know with more practice I'll make it work.	❏ ... and love how it basically works.	❏ ... and my students understand its value.
	❏ ... and undecided about my ability to pull it off.	❏ ... because I still have questions about how to do it right.	❏ ... with mixed results I need to evaluate.	❏ ... but I may need to frame it more positively.
	❏ ... and not at all sure it's for me.	❏ ... because, frankly, I still have serious doubts.	❏ ... but it doesn't seem to work or suit me.	❏ ... but when class isn't going well, I do it poorly and it doesn't help.

Work from your strengths. If you find yourself in the bottom left portion, leaf through this technique to locate related ones you might prefer to work on right now or first steps to help you get started!

ANALYZE THE CHAMPIONS

View each video clip, ideally more than once, and answer the following questions. See the end of the technique for some possible answers.

Clip 5. Teacher Alexandra Bronson, Grade 5

1. What criterion of *Right Is Right* is Ms. Bronson addressing in this clip?
2. Why not just tell the student that the word "increase" wasn't necessary to the answer and go on from there?
3. What does Ms. Bronson do to reinforce the nature of the correction with the entire class, rather than just the first responder?
4. What about the class's behavior suggests that Ms. Bronson has established a strong norm of *Right Is Right* and *No Opt Out*?

> 1 **NO OPT OUT**

 Clip 6. Teacher Colleen Driggs, Grade 5

1. When the student responds, "Madeleine L'Engle was born in 1918 and died in 2007," what *Right Is Right* criterion is at stake?
2. How does Ms. Driggs respond to that student, and how does she move the class closer to right?
3. In the second part of the clip, when the student responds with "Less," what criterion of *Right Is Right* is at stake?
4. How does Ms. Driggs respond to that student, and how does she move the class closer to right?

 Clip 7. Teacher Khushali Gala, Grade 9

1. What *Right Is Right* criterion does this clip demonstrate?
2. Why is Ms. Gala's pursuit of the phrase "rate of change" important even though it initially may seem trivial?
3. About how many students does Ms. Gala involve as respondents in the class's effort to reach the precise answer? How many times does Ms. Gala praise a student's response? Where does that happen?
4. How would you describe Ms. Gala's general tone as she applies *Right Is Right*? How do the students react to that tone?

 Clip 8. Teacher Patrick Pastore, Grade 8

1. How many criteria of *Right Is Right* does Mr. Pastore call into play? What are they?
2. Is there any difference in how he pursues them?
3. What is Mr. Pastore's general demeanor with his students while he pursues *Right Is Right*? How do they react to it?

EXPAND YOUR SKILLS AND REPERTOIRE

How can *Right Is Right* apply to questions where there is no "right answer"? Substitute "thorough" or "rigorous" (or both) for "right," and you've got something worth defending. In other words, you can still apply and defend a standard of quality even when answers are subjective or based on opinion. In fact, Colleen Driggs, one of the champions we studied in *Teach Like a Champion* reflected on *Right Is Right* as follows:

RIGHT IS RIGHT

Possibly the biggest separator between good and great teachers, I think, is how they handle it when there isn't one clear right answer. The great teachers I know set incredibly high standards even when answers are subjective! It's much easier to apply *Right Is Right* when there is a clear right answer, but applying it when the question is more open ended is the real test! Great teachers, to me, always think through the components of their target responses and push to get students there.

In light of this, what are your standards of quality for questions for which there are no right answers? (For example, how well formed should an argument be, how should it martial evidence, and how should it reflect the ideas from readings?)

_____

_____

_____

Holding Out for All-the-Way Right

Try to avoid settling for an answer that you must add to yourself, as in, "Right, except you need to move the decimal." When you ask for the definition of a noun and get "a person, place, or thing," don't do students the disservice of overlooking the fact that the answer is incomplete (a noun is a person, place, thing, *or idea*). Here are some productive ways of holding out.

Keep a Positive Tone

Praise students for their effort, but try not to confuse effort with mastery. When answers are nearly correct, tell students that they're almost there, that you like what they've done so far, that they're closing in on the right answer, that they've done some good work or made a great start. Use simple, positive language that expresses your appreciation *and* your expectation that the student or the class as a whole will now march the last few yards. Here are some phrases that convey that:

> 43 **POSITIVE FRAMING**
> 44 **PRECISE PRAISE**

"I like what you've done. Can you get us the rest of the way?"

"We're almost there. Can you find the last piece?"

"I like most of that . . ."

"Keep going with that . . ."

"You're using the rules we talked about . . ."

"Well, there's a bit more to it than that . . ."

"James just knocked a base hit. Who can bring him home?"

What other phrases have you used or would be useful in your classroom . . .
To acknowledge effort and stay focused on the student?

_____

_____

_____

_____

RIGHT IS RIGHT

To acknowledge effort and open the task to responses from others in the class?

_____

_____

_____

_____

Repeat the Student's Words

Repeat the student's words back to him or her, with cueing if necessary—for example, by emphasizing problematic parts:

"A peninsula is *water* indenting into *land*?"

"You just said that a noun is a person, place, or thing . . ."

"You just said that a noun is a person, place, or thing, but *freedom* is a noun, and it's not exactly any of those three."

"You just said that first you would solve the exponent and then you'd go to what's in parentheses."

First, try reading these examples out loud as if you were using them in the classroom. Strive to achieve the combination of *Emotional Constancy,* supportive encouragement, and high expectations that matches your style. Make some notes on what worked:

> 47 **EMOTIONAL CONSTANCY**

_____

_____

Now that you've got the tone, try writing a few of your own repeat-back responses to these less-than-correct statements:

"A spider is an insect with eight legs." (A spider has eight legs but isn't an insect.)

Your response: _____

_____

"Lewis and Clark traveled across Louisiana to the Pacific Ocean." (Louis and Clark explored the Louisiana *Purchase* [and then some] before reaching the Pacific.)

Your response: _____

_____

"A preposition is a little bitty word."

Your response: _____

_____

Answer My Question

Insist that the student answer the question you asked. Students learn quickly that when they can't answer a question, they may get by by answering a different one or by saying something true and heartfelt. But the "right" answer to any question other than the one you asked is *wrong*.

Make your students aware of the differences between their answers and the kind of answer a particular question implies. Students may conflate two pieces of information about a topic. You ask for a definition, and they give you an example. You ask them to describe a concept, and they provide the formula to solve it. If you ask your students for a definition and get an example, say, "James, that's an example. I want the definition."

How could you respond to each of these?

Example:

You ask: Define a square, James.   Student answers: The floor of this room is square.

You respond: *James, the floor might be an example of a square. We can find out later. Right now we want a definition—what every square must have.*

1. Q: How many different digits are   A: 1, 2, 3, 4, 5, 6, 7, 8, 9.
    there in base 10, Ella?

You respond: _____

_____

2. Q: Read the first word, Cheyenne.   A: "Once upon a time . . . "

You respond: _____

_____

3. Q: I'd like an example of something   A: Well, he was probably the greatest inventor ever.
    Thomas Edison invented, Derrek.

You respond: _____

_____

4. Q: What other animals have fur?   A: Rabbits feel soft.

You respond: _____

_____

5. Q: What can you tell from the pic-   A: Where's that taken? Not anywhere near here!
    ture about where groundhogs live?

You respond: _____

_____

Everyday excellence: two teachers whom we know practice this together every day. They meet at lunch, and each one brings five questions they intend to ask in their lesson the next day. One teacher reads those questions to the other, who gives her best guess at the *wrong* answers students are likely to give. The first teacher then practices reacting. They report incredible progress. Could you pull this off? With whom? When? With what adaptations?

_____

_____

RIGHT IS RIGHT

Right Answer, Right Time

The entire class deserves a full understanding of a process, so don't accept answers that are out of step with your teaching. If you're asking about step two of a problem and someone gives the overall solution, stop and refocus on step two.

"My question wasn't about the solution to the problem. It was about what we do next. What *do* we do next?"

Write a response for these next examples.

1. Q: "What's our next step, William?"   A: "You divide and you get an answer of 23!"

You respond: _____

_____

2. Q: "What's step four, Cecilia?"   A: "That one's easy. It's step five I don't understand."

You respond: _____

_____

3. Q: "What does Shakespeare imply
    is on Romeo's mind as he enters
    the masquerade party where he's
    about to meet Juliet?"   A: "He's about to meet Juliet and they fall in love."

You respond: _____

_____

4. Q: "What might the author be sug-
    gesting by titling this novel *Conti-
    nental Divide*?"   A: "Oh, I have a question."

You respond: _____

_____

5. Q: "Then what's the last stage of
    mitosis?"   A: "Can we go back to how it started?"

You respond: _____

_____

Using Technical Vocabulary

Good teachers get students to develop effective right answers using terms they are already comfortable with ("volume is the amount of space something takes up"); *great* teachers get them to use *precise* technical vocabulary ("volume is the amount of space an object occupies"). This expands students' comfort and command in using vocabularies they will need in college.

Write down at least four "technical" terms that your students need to master. For each, also write down at least one word or phrase with which your students are likely to approximate the precise term. Also write some wording that would launch a *Right Is Right* response to the student's words.

Example:

Precise term: *"Species"*   Likely student usage: *"kind of animal"*

Right Is Right response: *Well, you might speak of "four-legged" as a kind of animal, so a lizard and a dog would be the same "kind." We need the precise biological term here that refers to deeper similarities that make two specific creatures extremely alike . . .*

Precise Term   **Likely Student Usage**

1. _____   _____

Right Is Right response: _____

_____

_____

2. _____   _____

Right Is Right response: _____

_____

_____

3. _____   _____

Right Is Right response: _____

_____

_____

4. _____   _____

Right Is Right response: _____

_____

_____

PRACTICE WITH STUDY GROUP OR PARTNERS

Revisit the individual work you did in the previous section to share and compare your responses and see other options.

Peer Observation

If you are training with a group of teachers, do this after you've completed the group and other activities in this chapter.

Have a peer observe your use of *Right Is Right* in the classroom. (In the absence of a peer, consider making an audiotape of a lesson to review yourself.)

Also sit in on another teacher's class and listen for *Right Is Right* moments. On an observation sheet like this one, make notes about what happened:

Right Is Right Peer Observation Sheet

Teacher Question	Student Response	Teacher Follow-Up	What's Effective? How Could It Be More Effective?

Positive Language for "Almost Right"

This activity will help you develop short, positive phrases you can say to encourage students to add to and develop their "almost right" answers to get them to "right."

Before the group convenes, spend some time reflecting individually on these questions:

Why are we, as teachers, sometimes inconsistent about holding out for right answers? What incentives or factors make us vulnerable to letting "almost right" slip past us?

_____

_____

_____

_____

How can we address and overcome these challenges? How do the teachers in the video clips do that?

_____

_____

_____

_____

Think back on and describe some situations in which you didn't hold out for the completely right answer. What were (or could have been) the consequences of not holding out for the right answer?

_____

_____

_____

_____

_____

_____

When the group convenes, share your responses. Then use a flipchart or other device to collectively brainstorm phrases you can use to respond to "almost right" answers quickly, positively, and comfortably.

After you brainstorm many phrases, look at them for these qualities:

- Positive and upbeat about what's been accomplished
- Clear and honest about the fact that more work is needed
- Useful when an answer is 80% right, not when it's just wrong

Ideally, by the end you will have a dozen phrases you can all draw on easily and effectively. Make copies of the list for everyone to take away and try in class.

Choose three phrases that you'll definitely try to use in your next teaching session.

_____

_____

_____

Bounce (Game)

This game requires at least three participants; the more the merrier. Before you convene, designate one participant as *Facilitator*. In the game, you will take turns being *Teacher* and *Students*.

Sit in a circle and let the role of *Teacher* travel around the circle with each round. The goal is for the *Teacher* to practice effective *Right Is Right* responses on the fly, when the *Students* avoid, deflect, evade, or partially answer their question. All participants are free to think creatively but realistically.

1.   The *Facilitator* asks participants to think of examples of times when students did or might answer a different question than the one their teacher asked. Share your examples aloud. Examples can be general (for example, "When they don't know the answer") or specific (for example, "Once I asked for the definition of a compound word, and four kids in a row gave me an example").

2.   The *Facilitator* asks that each participant select one question that she asked of her students during a recent lesson, or would ask in an upcoming one. In the participant's round as *Teacher,* she will pose that question to the *Student* on her left.

3.   The *Student* then deflects the question in some way, such as by answering a different question, answering part of the question, jumping ahead, bringing up another point, and so on.

Example: *Teacher* asks, "What is the setting of the story?" *Student* replies, "I really liked this story."

4. Now the *Teacher* must respond by using a *Right Is Right* technique to redirect the *Student* back to the original question.

Example: "I liked the story too. But I want to know the setting."

The *Student* does not need to respond again.

5. The *Teacher* puts the same original question to each of the next two *Students* to the left, and those *Students* also deflect, each in a different way. After each deflection, the *Teacher* responds with a different *Right Is Right* technique that redirects that *Student* back to the original question.

6. When you've all had enough, the *Facilitator* leads a group discussion using these questions:

- Describe the different ways you found to get off track or to evade the questions.

- As a *Student,* what was your internal reaction when the teacher offered a *Right Is Right* response?

- What are the advantages of using this approach?

- Can you anticipate any difficulties in adding this to your repertoire in your classroom? How would you address or prevent these?

- What is your main takeaway from this exercise?

Small Group Discussion: Related Techniques

Before the group convenes, the *Facilitator* asks each participant to prepare some thoughts and examples (preferably from his or her own experience) of how the *Right Is Right* technique might work together with another technique. As much as possible, arrange for each different participant to prepare to describe how a related technique would work well with *Right Is Right*. (Especially good choices include *No Opt Out, Format Matters, 100%,* and *SLANT.*)

> 1 **NO OPT OUT**
> 4 **FORMAT MATTERS**
> 32 **SLANT**
> 36 **100%**

As a group, share and extend your thoughts. Discuss whatever challenges and questions come to mind. Write down your key takeaways:

_____

_____

_____

_____

TRY *RIGHT IS RIGHT* IN THE CLASSROOM

Work on this with a peer partner if you can (not necessarily of your own grade level or subject).

1. On your own, think about an upcoming lesson or larger unit you are planning to teach. Identify ten technical vocabulary words that your students will need to know in order to be successful. For example, your students might need these terms for a writing unit on poetry: stanza, verse, rhythm, rhyme, alliteration, metaphor, simile, onomatopoeia, italics, and haiku.

> 6 **BEGIN WITH THE END**

Unit/Lesson: _____

1. _____   6. _____

2. _____   7. _____

3. _____   8. _____

4. _____   9. _____

5. _____   10. _____

2.   With a partner if possible, brainstorm three ways that could systematically help students in your classroom use the technical vocabulary. For example:

- For homework, students create their own dictionaries for the unit, looking up the definitions. In class, the teacher has students refer to their dictionaries to make sure that they are using the appropriate vocabulary in writing and discussion.
- Create a word wall that shows how the terms are related.
- Organize quick silent cheers whenever a student uses one of the terms.

Record your three best ideas here:

_____

_____

_____

_____

_____

_____

3.   Integrate at least one way to reinforce technical vocabulary and other *Right Is Right* thinking into your plan for an upcoming lesson. If possible, have a peer review it.

- Note where in the lesson students are most likely to give partially or mostly correct answers that leave out key details. Find the three most risky places and mark them. Then write out and insert for each an "anticipated partially correct answer" and your "anticipated response."
- Make a list of technical vocabulary terms that your students know (or should know and can be taught!) and could be asked to substitute for common terms of discussion during the lesson. For example, you might list

  "Predicate," which could be used in place of "verb" in some grammar lessons

  "Occupies," which could be used in place of "takes up" in a volume lesson

  "Integer," which could be used in place of "number"

  "Antagonist," which could be used in place of "bad guy"

  "Author," which could be used in place of "writer"

4.   Look back on your work for the section "Positive Language for 'Almost Right.'" Note any problems or questions that have multiple steps a student could potentially jump ahead on. Insert language to remind them that they should focus on one step at a time.

5.   Consider what you may already know about which of your students are likely to respond in ways that require you to address particular criteria for *Right Is Right*.

6.   While you deliver the lesson, don't worry if all four *Right Is Right* criteria aren't constantly in your mind. Teach according to your plan and what you notice regarding

- All-the-way correct answers
- Students answering your questions
- Right answers at the right time
- Technical vocabulary

7.   After you deliver the lesson, talk with a peer or reflect about how it went, including these questions:

Were some moments particularly effective? Why?

_____

_____

_____

Were there one or two missed opportunities to apply *Right Is Right* to specific students or situations? How can you do that in your next lesson plan and actual lesson?

Opportunity: _____

Strategy: _____

Opportunity: _____

Strategy: _____

TROUBLE-SHOOT

Right Is Right or *No Opt Out*?

Compare your use of *Right Is Right* to *No Opt Out*. Which is more often needed in your class? Which is easier for you to use? Why in both cases do you think so? How might the techniques work in synergy?

| 1 **NO OPT OUT** |

_____

_____

_____

Steady On

1.   Are you worried about being perceived as negative when you respond? Create and try more *positive and encouraging* phrases.

| 43 **POSITIVE FRAMING** |
| 44 **PRECISE PRAISE** |
| 45 **WARM/STRICT** |

2.   Every teacher has a vested interest in student success—if they are successful, it means you are successful, so there's a strong temptation to believe that student answers were better than they were and perhaps to say things like "I knew what she was trying to say." What can you tell yourself to combat this vested interest in order to become more objective in your evaluation of student responses?

_____

_____

_____

3.   It's easy to respond to almost-correct answers by "rounding up"—that is, affirming the student's answer and adding some detail of your own to make it fully correct even though the student didn't provide it and may not recognize the difference.

Imagine a student who's asked, at the beginning of *Romeo and Juliet,* how the Capulets and Montagues get along. The student answers, "They don't like each other." Rounding up, the teacher might say, "Right, they've been feuding for generations." Rather than round up, get the student or the class to articulate a better response: "Don't like each other? Is there more to it than that?"

You may find yourself under pressure to round up because your lesson planning is (as mine was on a recent lesson) too jam-packed and doesn't leave enough time to master content with students.

| 7 **4 MS** |

Consider cutting the amount of content you're trying to cover—especially on days when you want to be extra rigorous. You also might consider whether your objectives are truly Manageable (see *4 Ms*).

Other Challenges

Possible Challenge	Possible Solutions

SUSTAIN YOUR PROGRESS

1. Using feedback from your study group or other peers, and reviewing your own lesson notes and observations, monitor your progress on *Right Is Right*.

Date	Things I'm Doing Well	A Type of Right I Want Students to Get "Righter"

2. Revisit "Where Am I Now?" Are you ready to build out to some other new technique?

ANALYZE THE CHAMPIONS: SOME OBSERVATIONS

Clip 5. Teacher Alexandra Bronson, Grade 5

You may have noticed that Ms. Bronson does not reveal the problem with the student's answer, only that a word was incorrect. From there on, she holds out for all-the-way right. Students will be more likely to learn to be careful about language if they themselves correct it (in this case by omitting "increase") than if teachers do it for them. Also, it's not just that "increase" isn't necessary to the answer. It makes the answer *wrong* because it refers to an entirely different positive variable, and the sharper students are likely to see that. Ms. Bronson reinforces the nature of the correction with the entire class by calling on another student to identify the word that needed to be left out.

Clip 6. Teacher Colleen Driggs, Grade 5

Ms. Driggs begins by asking a question that requires students to make a general statement supported by evidence: "This is a biography because . . . ," and she notices that *the student hasn't answered her actual question.* She praises the effort ("a really good detail") and at the same time describes how it doesn't answer her actual question. Then she reformulates the task as "to show what a biography is" and turns to another student who may have a stronger grasp.

When Ms. Driggs asks for a word similar to "scarce," she knows she's venturing into new and possibly challenging territory, but she still holds out for all-the-way right. She is careful not to dismiss the student's not all-the-way correct response of "less." But she shows respect by saying she wants to "push back" and by praising the student's moving the class "in the right direction."

 Clip 7. Teacher Khushali Gala, Grade 9

Ms. Gala is pursuing the need for careful technical vocabulary in math, and "rate of change" is both a subtle and indispensable concept as the students enter the subject of functions. She involves five students directly in the process, creating a strong sense of total class involvement in this genuinely difficult challenge. She keeps interest high by withholding praise until the end, when the goal has been reached.

 Clip 8. Teacher Patrick Pastore, Grade 8

Mr. Pastore notices and addresses a response that doesn't answer his question. Later, he holds out for all-the-way right when the student says "don't" instead of "can't." If he had simply corrected the student on that, many students in the class might have gone away less certain about an important and not obvious denotation of "illiterate." These behaviors are in line with Mr. Pastore's goal of getting students to read *alertly* even when a story seems to breeze along.

STRETCH IT

OVERVIEW

Learning shouldn't end at the first "right" answer. *Stretch It* rewards "right" answers with more knowledge and further challenge: follow-up questions that test for reliability, extend knowledge, and ask students to apply skills in new ways. It checks whether the student can *replicate* success by getting the right answer again and again and allows students to think on their feet and tackle harder questions. This keeps them engaged and sends the message that the reward for achievement is more knowledge!

Stretch It can help you differentiate instruction for students of different skill levels and meet the ever-expanding horizons of students who might otherwise be coasting. Here are six effective ways to *Stretch It* (there are more). Ask students to

1. Explain how or why.
2. Answer in a different way.
3. Answer with a better word.
4. Provide evidence.
5. Integrate a related skill.
6. Apply the same skill in a new setting.

WHERE AM I NOW?

	Proficiency			
	I am brand new to *Stretch It* . . .	I'm getting familiar with *Stretch It,* though I haven't tried it yet in class . . .	I'm beginning to *Stretch It* in my classroom . . .	I *Stretch It* regularly . . .
Comfort & Confidence	❏ . . . and excited to try it.	❏ . . . but know with more practice I'll make it work.	❏ . . . and love how it basically works.	❏ . . . and my students see it in a positive light.
	❏ . . . and undecided about my ability to pull it off.	❏ . . . because I still have questions about how to do it right.	❏ . . . with mixed results I need to evaluate.	❏ . . . but the class is still adjusting to it.
	❏ . . . and not at all sure it's for me.	❏ . . . because, frankly, I still have serious doubts.	❏ . . . but it doesn't seem to work or suit me.	❏ . . . but when class isn't going well, I do it poorly and it doesn't help.

Work from your strengths. If you find yourself in the bottom left portion, leaf through this technique to locate related ones you might prefer to work on right now.

STRETCH IT

▼ EXPAND YOUR SKILLS AND REPERTOIRE

| 1 **NO OPT OUT** |
| 22 **COLD CALL** |
| 44 **PRECISE PRAISE** |

Stretch It pushes your students to demonstrate and apply knowledge in new ways. It makes your teaching dynamic and responsive, and it's a great way to differentiate.

     Precise Praise will help make *Stretch It* work. *Stretch It* is an ideal follow-up to a successful *No Opt Out* or *Cold Call*. It's often used in combination with *Right Is Right*.

Compare with *Right Is Right*

| 2 **RIGHT IS RIGHT** |

Right Is Right and *Stretch It* are both similar and different. List three ways they are alike:

1. _____

2. _____

3. _____

What are three ways that they differ?

1. _____

2. _____

3. _____

Six Ways of Asking

How or Why

The best test of whether students can get answers right consistently is whether they can explain how they arrived at the answer they did. (Increasingly, state assessments also ask them to do so.)

1	*Teacher:*	How far is it from Durango to Pueblo?
2	*Student:*	600 miles.
3	*Teacher:*	How'd you get that?
4	*Student:*	By measuring three inches on the map and adding 200 plus 200 plus 200.
5	*Teacher:*	How'd you know to use 200 miles for each inch?
6	*Student:*	I looked at the scale in the map key.

     Look over some of your recent lesson plans. Write down a sample of questions you planned to ask in class where it would be appropriate for students to be able also to narrate how they arrived at their answers. For each question, note how you could follow up to ask for an explanation, and jot down what a good answer would look like. (Sometimes the why isn't so easy to explain, and it's always easier to evaluate the quality of the answers if you know what you're looking for.)

1. Question: _____

   _____

   Follow-up: _____

   _____

   _____

   Model student answer: _____

   _____

2. Question: _____

   _____

   Follow-up: _____

   _____

   _____

   Model student answer: _____

   _____

3. Question: _____

   _____

   Follow-up: _____

   _____

   _____

   Model student answer: _____

   _____

STRETCH IT

Another Way to Solve

Often there are multiple ways to answer a question. When a student solves it one way, it's a great opportunity to make sure she can use all available methods. Ask the student to solve the same problem using a different set of skills.

1	*Teacher:*	How far is it from Durango to Pueblo?
2	*Student:*	600 miles.
3	*Teacher:*	How'd you get that?
4	*Student:*	By measuring three inches on the map and adding 200 plus 200 plus 200.

5	*Teacher:*	Is there a simpler way than adding three times?
6	*Student:*	I could have multiplied 200 by 3.
7	*Teacher:*	And when you do that, you'd get what?
8	*Student:*	600.
9	*Teacher:*	Very nice. That's a better way.

Or, in some classes, you might focus on alternative sources of evidence or alternative interpretations. That approach might look like this:

1	*Teacher:*	Who can tell me what kind of person Jonas is?
2	*Student:*	He's curious and independent minded.
3	*Teacher:*	Okay, why do you say so?
4	*Student:*	Well, there's that moment where the apple looks different to him, and he keeps thinking about it and wondering why. And the other people in the community don't seem to do that much.
5	*Teacher:*	Interesting. But if they're really strong traits, we should see other examples for curiosity and independence of mind. Can you find another?

Or (with the same initial sequence):

	Teacher:	Interesting. But I wonder if we think that because we know so much about how Jonas develops over the course of the novel. Is there another way to interpret the scene with the apple in terms of how it characterizes our protagonist?

Look over some of your recent lesson plans. Write down a sample of questions you planned to ask where there might be another way for students to find the answer. For each question, note how you could follow up to ask for another way and jot down what a good answer would look like. (Again, it always helps to know what you're looking for when you are evaluating the quality of student answers.)

1. Question: _____

    _____

    Follow-up: _____

    _____

    _____

    Model student answer: _____

    _____

2. Question: _____

    _____

    Follow-up: _____

    _____

    _____

Model student answer: _____

_____

3. Question: _____

_____

Follow-up: _____

_____

_____

Model student answer: _____

_____

A Better Word

Students often begin framing concepts in the simplest possible language. Give them opportunities to use better, more specific words, as well as new words.

1	*Teacher:*	Why did Sophie gasp, Janice?
2	*Student:*	She gasped because the water was cold when she jumped in.
3	*Teacher:*	Can you answer with a better word than "cold," one that shows how cold it was?
4	*Student:*	Sophie gasped because the water was freezing.
5	*Teacher:*	Okay, how about using one of our vocabulary words?
6	*Student:*	Sophie gasped because the water was frigid.
7	*Teacher:*	Very nice.

Write down at least five ways you could ask a student to use a new, more specific, or otherwise better word or phrase in his answer to a question you asked.

1. _____

_____

2. _____

_____

3. _____

_____

4. _____

_____

5. _____

_____

STRETCH IT

Evidence

As students advance, they must increasingly build and defend their conclusions. Both tasks depend on using evidence. Who's to say what the theme of the novel is or what the author intended to show in a given scene, except by evidence in the author's words?

You don't have to say you don't agree with the student. Instead, just ask for evidence or proof. This encourages students to analyze their responses and helps them avoid subjective interpretations of material.

1   *Teacher:*   How would you describe Dr. Jones's personality? What traits is he showing?

2   *Student:*   He's spiteful.

3   *Teacher:*   And *spiteful* means?

4   *Student:*   Spiteful means that he's bitter and wants to make other people unhappy.

5   *Teacher:*   Okay, so read me two sentences from the story that show us that Dr. Jones is spiteful.

Review a recent lesson or lesson plan. List five times you could have asked for evidence to support a viable answer.

1. _____

   _____

2. _____

   _____

3. _____

   _____

4. _____

   _____

5. _____

   _____

Evidence comes in a variety of types. Look through your examples to see how many ask students to use evidence in the ways shown in the following list. If none of your examples met some of the formats listed, try drafting some more so that you are asking students to use evidence a wide variety of ways.

- Evidence is cited in the moment and as you read. (For example, "What evidence do we have that shows that the deep sea is not an easy place to live?")

- Evidence is cited from recollection. ("When else have we seen critical moments of unusual curiosity from Jonas?")

- Students are asked to directly cite evidence. ("Who can read me a sentence that shows Carlos can be selfish?")

- Students are asked to paraphrase evidence. ("Who can describe some other times we've seen that selfishness?")

STRETCH IT

- Students are asked to use evidence to support their own conclusion. ("Okay, perhaps Carlos is brave. Can you prove it?")
- Students are asked to use evidence to support someone else's conclusion. ("Petra says Carlos is brave. Who can give us some evidence that would show she's right?")

List your additional examples of evidence requests here and note which of the listed formats each one demonstrates.

_____

_____

_____

_____

_____

A Related Skill

In the real world, skills must overlap. To prepare students for that, try responding to mastery of one skill by asking students to integrate the skill with others recently mastered.

1	_Teacher:_	Who can use the word "stride" in a sentence?
2	_Student:_	I stride down the street.
3	_Teacher:_	Can you add some detail to show more about what stride means?
4	_Student:_	I stride down the street to buy some candy at the store.
5	_Teacher:_	Can you add an adjective to modify street?
6	_Student:_	I stride down the wide street to buy some candy at the store.
7	_Teacher:_	Good. Now can you add a compound subject to your sentence?
8	_Student:_	My brother and I stride down the wide street to buy some candy at the store.
9	_Teacher:_	And can you put that in the past tense?
10	_Student:_	My brother and I strode down the wide street to buy some candy at the store.
11	_Teacher:_	Those were very challenging questions, Charles, and look how well you handled them!

Review a few of your recent lessons. Select several of the questions you asked in class and, for each, identify the skill (or content area) you're asking students about. Then identify two overlapping skills or content areas your students would already be familiar with (either they're working on them at the same time or have already mastered them). Frame one (or several) related-skill _Stretch It_ questions for each.

Question A: _____

_____

Skill addressed: _____

STRETCH IT

Overlapping skill 1: _____

Question: _____

_____

Overlapping skill 2: _____

Question: _____

_____

Question B: _____

_____

Skill addressed: _____

Overlapping skill 1: _____

Question: _____

_____

Overlapping skill 2: _____

Question: _____

_____

Question C: _____

_____

Skill addressed: _____

Overlapping skill 1: _____

Question: _____

_____

Overlapping skill 2: _____

Question: _____

_____

_____

STRETCH IT

Same Skill, New Setting

Ask students to apply a newly mastered skill in a more challenging situation.

1	*Teacher:*	So what's the setting of our story?
2	*Student:*	The setting is in a town called Sangerville, in the recent past.
3	*Teacher:*	Good. I notice that you remembered both parts of setting. Can you remember the setting of *Fantastic Mr. Fox,* then?
4	*Student:*	It was on a farm in the recent past.
5	*Teacher:*	How do you know it was the recent past?
6	*Student:*	They had tractors.
7	*Teacher:*	Good. But what about fairy tales? Do fairy tales have a setting?
8	*Student:*	Usually, yes. Though sometimes they don't tell you much about it.
9	*Teacher:*	Good. Then these will be really fun and challenging! I'll tell you a fairy tale, and you tell me the setting. Or I'll give you a setting, and you see if you can find a fairy tale that fits.

Look back over a recent lesson plan. Identify a few questions you asked where applying the skill in a new setting could have been a useful and productive challenge for students. Draft some *Stretch It* questions for each.

_____

_____

_____

_____

Stretch It Vocabulary Case Study

You can also do this with a partner or group. The goal is to focus on ways to improve asking for a better word. Read the case and answer the questions that follow it.

Case: Mr. Jones is standing at the head of an attentive grade 3 class, having just finished reviewing sentences that his students wrote about a reading selection they completed earlier in the day. Recognizing that he has completed the task three minutes early, Mr. Jones begins to ask students to describe one thing that they learned from reading the selection.

1	*Erik:*	I learned that whales are bigger than sharks.
2	*Mr. Jones:*	Yes, they are. But are whales just big? Who can use a better word than "big" to describe a whale? John?
3	*John:*	Large?
4	*Mr. Jones:*	Large? Who can use a different word?
5	*Jamal:*	Enormous.
6	*Mr. Jones:*	Enormous. Who can use a different word?

7	*Jayquon:*	Huge.
8	*Mr. Jones:*	Huge. One more. Malik?
9	*Malik:*	Gigantic.
10	*Mr. Jones:*	Gigantic. Excellent.

1. What method(s) of *Stretch It* is this teacher using? What's his goal?

_____

_____

_____

_____

2. How is the effectiveness of *Stretch It* limited by the way in which he uses the technique?

_____

_____

_____

_____

3. What specific things could the teacher have done or said to make better use of the *Ask for a better word* technique? That is, how could he improve his use of the technique? How could he make it more rigorous? More effective in reinforcing vocabulary knowledge? More responsive to his students' specific skills and needs?

_____

_____

_____

_____

4. What are some positive responses he could have used to validate a student's initial answer and still push the student to reach for a more rigorous response? For example: "Large. You've got the right idea; now fit it into this sentence."

_____

_____

_____

_____

STRETCH IT

Here's a revised version of Mr. Jones's interaction with his third graders. Underline at least two effective changes that Mr. Jones made and note in the margin why you think they help. Circle one place where you could revise further to add even more rigor. Make that change directly into the text.

1	*Erik:*	I learned that whales are bigger than sharks.
2	*Mr. Jones:*	Yes, they are. But are whales just big? Who can use a better word than "big" to describe a whale? John?
3	*John:*	Large?
4	*Mr. Jones:*	Large? I still think we can do better than that!
5	*Jamal:*	Enormous.
6	*Mr. Jones:*	Good, Jamal, enormous. Now we're getting somewhere. But remember that "enormous" isn't the same part of speech as "bigger." So can you use enormous but in a complete sentence?
7	*Jamal:*	Whales are enormous … enormouser …
8	*Mr. Jones:*	Good. You're getting there. Try this phrase: "even more enormous."
9	*Jamal:*	Whales are even more enormous than sharks.
10	*Mr. Jones:*	Okay, Jamal really showed us something there. Who can do the same with a different word? Malik?
11	*Malik:*	Gigantic.
12	*Mr. Jones:*	Okay, now in a sentence like Jamal, BUT …
13	*Malik:*	Whales are even more gigantic than sharks.
14	*Mr. Jones:*	Okay, but I wonder, are sharks really gigantic? Our words are getting so big that the sharks can't keep up. So see if you can make your sentence focus not so much on whales being "more gigantic" but on the fact that only one of the two is truly gigantic.
15	*Malik:*	Whales are gigantic, but sharks really aren't.
16	*Mr. Jones:*	Nice work, third grade.

5.   What do you notice in your responses that you could apply to using *Ask for a better word* in your lesson planning process?

_____

_____

_____

PRACTICE WITH STUDY GROUP OR PARTNERS

Revisit the individual work you did in the previous section to share and compare your responses and see other options.

STRETCH IT

Roundtable Brainstorm

You can do this with as few as two participants. With more, the *Facilitator* can appoint a *Timekeeper* and a *Recorder* to capture the group's ideas on a flipchart or another means of display. When you convene, the *Facilitator* can also post a list of the six kinds of *Stretch It* questions.

1.   With a partner, review the six kinds of *Stretch It* questions and write an example of each in response to the following question, context, and answer. The *Recorder* will record each example generated by each pair.

    Question 1: What is evaporation?

        Context: Identifying the water cycle components and how they are related: evaporation, condensation, and precipitation.

        Student answer: Evaporation is when liquid turns into vapor.

2.   The *Facilitator* announces a time limit that the *Timekeeper* will impose, based on the size of the group but allowing enough time for everyone in the circle to have about four fifteen-second shots (plus time for the *Recorder* to record each suggestion).

3.   In each next round, the *Facilitator* poses one of the following questions aloud (begin with Question 2), along with the context and student's answer. (Or as a group, come up with other questions tailored to your shared grade level or subject.)

    Question 2: 6 plus 5 equals . . . ?

        Context: Simple computations: addition, subtraction, multiplication, division.

        Student answer: 6 and 5 equals 11.

    Question 3: Who can use the word "reassure" in a sentence?

        Context: Increasing vocabulary through drills that explore the use of synonyms, antonyms, and different parts of speech.

        Student answer: My mom reassured me that I would be okay.

    Question 4: What is the lesson of the story "The Boy Who Cried Wolf"?

        Context: Exploring the moral of the story and the genre of fables in general.

        Student answer: The lesson in the story is that you shouldn't cry for help unless you really need it.

    Question 5: What is one branch of the U.S. government?

        Context: Understanding the three branches of the U.S. government and how they relate to each other and current events.

        Student answer: One branch of the U.S. government is the judicial branch.

4.   Going around the circle, each person has fifteen seconds to share a question he would ask in response to the correct answer to this question, in order to get the student to stretch her answer. If no idea comes, say "Pass." The *Recorder* writes down the questions. Meanwhile, no one attempts to answer the questions, and no one passes judgment on them, good or bad.

5.   Continue through the full time limit, even if several people pass in a row.

6.   When time has expired, allow a minute of independent silent reflection for each participant to select his favorite three.

7.   As a group, discuss what types of *Stretch It* methods the questions reflect. Also discuss favorite questions and what made them favorite.

8.   Go around the circle again, asking everyone to come up with another *Stretch It* for the original question.

9.   As time allows, continue rounds through Question 5.

10.   Discuss and record your thoughts overall: What questions were asked that you would not have thought of? What are your takeaways?

_____

_____

_____

_____

11.   After the meeting, the *Recorder* should distribute the list of proposed *Stretch It* questions to all participants.

TRY *STRETCH IT* IN THE CLASSROOM

1.   What insights from the case study and other activities in the previous section will help you apply *Stretch It* in your classroom?

_____

_____

_____

_____

2.   Select a lesson plan you are creating for an upcoming class. Identify the following points:
- Two or more times when *Stretch It* questions would be applicable in this lesson.
- Specific questions you want to ask. Make sure they are scaffolded. Draft the specific language you'd use.
- Try to anticipate what you will do if students do not get the answer.
- Look back over the six (and more) ways that *Stretch It* can be applied. Add to the plan for how you will integrate forms of *Stretch It*.
- If possible, exchange lesson plans with a partner and give mutual feedback on how you will use *Stretch It*.

| 1 **NO OPT OUT** |

3.   After the class session, note the following on your plan:
- Where and how you used *Stretch It* in the lesson and when it was effective
- Missed opportunities or moments that were less effective

4.   What other forms of *Stretch It* could you have tried as well?

_____

_____

5.   Apply these insights to future lesson plans.

TROUBLE-SHOOT

Possible Challenge	Possible Solutions
My students just don't want to "stretch." 35 **PROPS** 43 **POSITIVE FRAMING**	Consider giving a rollout speech to introduce *Stretch It* concepts to your class. Celebrate successful *Stretch Its* with a *Prop*: "Two snaps and two stomps for Daequan for taking it up a level!" Frame it positively: "Of course it's hard. But challenges are fun, and everything I know about this class is that they love a challenge." Is it possible that it's not the right moment for *Stretch It*? Are kids just trying to keep track of a great deal of new information? Are kids loving the story and just want to keep reading without distraction? Are kids (or you) suffering from *Stretch It* fatigue?
Stretch Its might make the lesson drag on too long or can be hard to think of on the spot.	Plan them into your lesson. *In advance,* choose four or five questions where you will be likely to get the chance to have students stretch. Script three or four *Stretch Its* for each and write them into your lesson plan.

BE CREATIVE

There are lots of ways to "stretch" in addition to the initial six. Can you think of another type of question you could ask to stretch kids in class? Describe it here. If you're working with a group or partner, this is a great time to share ideas and examples!

_____

_____

_____

SUSTAIN YOUR PROGRESS

1. Using feedback from your study group or other peers, and reviewing your own lesson notes and observations, monitor your progress on *Stretch It*.

Date	Great *Stretch It* Moment	A Type of Stretch to Work on More

2. Revisit "Where Am I Now?" Are you ready to build out to some other new technique?

FORMAT MATTERS

OVERVIEW

What students *say* matters, but so does *how* they say it. For example, it matters to colleges, and most employers expect "standard" English. At some Uncommon Schools, we call this the language of opportunity or the language of college. That makes it easy to ask for.

Format Matters includes ways to get students to learn to "format" responses to your questions and the questions students will face later on. The main areas are

- *Grammatical* format
- *Complete sentence* format
- *Audible* format (so others can hear the response)

- *Unit* format (accompanying numerical answers with unit information)

WHERE AM I NOW?

	Proficiency			
Comfort & Confidence	**I am brand new to *Format Matters* . . .**	**I'm in the planning and practice stage, though I haven't tried this yet in class . . .**	**I'm beginning to try *Format Matters* in class . . .**	**I use *Format Matters* regularly . . .**
	❑ . . . and excited to try it.	❑ . . . but know with more practice I'll make it work.	❑ . . . and love how it basically works.	❑ . . . and it's part of our classroom culture.
	❑ . . . and undecided about my ability to pull it off.	❑ . . . because I still have questions about how to do it right.	❑ . . . with mixed results for one or more aspect.	❑ . . . and still bringing some students up to speed on it.

Work from your strengths. If you find yourself in the bottom left portion, leaf through this technique to locate related ones you might prefer to work on right now.

ANALYZE THE CHAMPIONS

View the video clip, ideally more than once, and answer the following questions. See the end of the technique for some possible answers.

Clip 4. Teacher Stacey Shells, Grade 7

1. What aspect(s) of format is Ms. Shells requiring in this clip?

2. Where are her eyes as the first student reads? Why?

3. How does Ms. Shells deflect any sense of passing moral judgment on the word choice of the student who apparently says "they mom"?

EXPAND YOUR SKILLS AND REPERTOIRE

Without denying that dialect has its place in many students' families and communities, champion teachers expect and reinforce—every chance they get—the patterns of English that will be required in college and the workplace. They don't debate the values this implies, but teach it as a "language of opportunity" for scholarship, business, and general work. They may introduce it with an explanation of why they expect it and occasionally reinforce, but for the most part they make little fuss.

The Four Aspects of Format

Grammatical Format
Great teachers correct slang and nonstandard syntax, usage, and grammar in the classroom through simple and efficient (that is, low transaction cost) techniques to identify and correct errors with minimum distraction. That way they correct consistently and seamlessly. Here are two simple methods that involve no discussion and no judgment beyond identification of the error itself:

1. *Identify the error, then allow the student to correct.* When a student makes a grammatical error, merely repeat the error in an interrogative tone:

"We *was* walking down the street?"

"There *gots to be* eight of them?"

2. Then allow the student to self-correct. If the student fails to self-correct, use the *Begin the correction* technique described here or quickly provide the correct verb forms (or whatever correction is called for) and ask him or her to repeat. This builds familiarity with the language of opportunity and removes any incentive to pretend not to know the answer, in that the student will still have to repeat it anyway.

3. *Begin the correction.* When a student makes a grammatical error, you *begin* to rephrase the answer as it would sound if grammatically correct, and allow the student to complete it. In the previous examples that would mean saying, "We *were* . . ." or "There *must be* . . ." and expecting the student to provide the full correct answer.

Complete Sentence Format
Insist that students answer in complete sentences, and give them plenty of practice at this critical skill. To scaffold and support their learning, you can, for example,

1. *Provide the first words of a complete sentence.* This shows students how to begin sentences. This is especially important when students are not yet ready to answer every question on their own in a complete sentence, as in this exchange:

Teacher: James, how many tickets are there?

James: Six.

Teacher: There are . . .

James: There are six tickets in the basket.

2. *Remind students before they start to answer.* Top teachers at Boston Preparatory Charter School end their questions to students by "punctuating" them with the letters "RTQ," short for "repeat the question." They do this after every question as students are learning this skill. For example,

Teacher: Jamal, what's the setting of the story? RTQ.

Student: The setting is the city of Los Angeles in the year 2013.

3. *Remind students afterwards with a quick and simple reminder with the lowest possible transaction cost:*

Teacher: What was the year of Caesar's birth?

Student: 100 BC.

Teacher: Complete sentence, please.

Student: Julies Caesar was born in 100 BC.

Or say, "Like a scholar" to remind students to use complete sentences.

Audible Format

Insist that answers be delivered in a loud, clear voice. What's the point of discussing answers if the rest of the class can't hear? Asking for a loud, clear voice tells students that their ideas matter. Underscore that students should be listening to their peers, so the speaker needs to make himself heard.

Reinforce these expectations with a clear, quick, crisp reminder that creates the minimum distraction from the business of class. Rather than saying, "Maria, we can't hear you in the back of the room; would you speak up, please?" train the class to understand an efficient, one-word instruction, such as "Voice."

The instruction itself can signify that you don't need to explain why they should speak up and that speaking up is an *expectation,* not a favor. The word "Voice" is better than "Louder" because it can refer to more important aspects of audibility than just raising one's voice.

Once you've trained students to know what you expect when you say "Voice," you can also weave it into your wording of a question, as in these examples:

"Jayshon, can you use your *voice* to tell me how I'd find the least common multiple?"

"I need someone with *voice* to tell me what I need to do next!"

Unit Format

In math, science, *and* other subjects, don't accept "naked numbers" (numbers without units). If you ask for the area of a rectangle and a student tells you, "It's twelve," ask for the units, or merely note that her numbers "need some dressing up" or are "hanging out a bit underdressed."

Shorthand Corrections for Written Work

You can do this activity on your own, but working with a partner or group in your subject area is better.

1. Look over some typical uncorrected drafts of writing that students in your class have done. Create a list of evidence of incorrect format, according to the standards of your class.

2. For each type of error, or for the ten most common ones, devise a shorthand correction that can be written onto a student's paper that will indicate the needed correction. Examples: CS = "Need complete sentence"; SVA = "Subject verb agreement"; in math or science, SYW = "Show your work."

3. With a partner or group, compare your shorthand inventions and notice improvements you might make.

4. If you're working with other teachers at your school, find out what shorthand they use and explore standardizing and systematizing these corrections among you.

Format Matters **Case Study**

This activity will help you apply the audibility criterion to your classroom work. When using a code command like "Voice" for audibility, you will always need to strike a balance between saying the command by itself and selectively reminding students what it means. As the year progresses, of course, fewer and fewer reminders should be needed.

1. This sixth-grade English teacher is asking questions of his students in succession. Read the interchange, then proceed with the instructions following the dialogue.

1	*Teacher:*	What was the vocabulary word you just learned in Ms. Smith's class? Rashonna?	
2	*Rashonna:*	Ancient.	
3	*Teacher:*	Complete sentence. Voice. I need to hear you.	
4	*Rashonna:*	*(somewhat louder)* We learned the word "ancient."	
5	*Teacher:*	And what does "ancient" mean again? Jaiquon? They need to hear you in the back, so nice and loud.	
6	*Jaiquon:*	Very old.	
7	*Teacher:*	Ancient means . . . loud and proud.	
8	*Jaiquon:*	Ancient means very old.	
9	*Teacher:*	Yes, it does, and can you then tell me what this word "ancestor" means? It's related . . .	
10	*Jaiquon:*	Somebody who is related to another person from long ago.	
11	*Teacher:*	Whoops, start again . . . An ancestor is someone who . . .	
12	*Jaiquon:*	An ancestor is someone who is related to another person from long ago.	

13	*Teacher:*	Okay, and so can someone read this sentence for me containing the word "ancestor"? I need somebody to read this sentence for me, loud and proud. I need voice. Who can give me voice today? Let's see ... Deandre.	
14	*Deandre:*	*(reading quietly)* "My grandfather told me a lot of interesting things about my ancestors."	
15	*Teacher:*	That was good, but do you think that Mahogany can hear you at the back of the class? Try again, with voice.	
16	*Deandre:*	*(reading)* "My grandfather told me a lot of interesting things about my ancestors."	

2. Underline the *Format Matters* corrections (grammatical, complete sentence, audible, units) and write their names in the boxes, as appropriate. (Not all the teacher's comments and questions concern *Format Matters*.)

3. Judging from the opening lines, how far into the year would you guess the class has come?

_____

4. Considering your answer to point 3, how efficiently and effectively do you think the teacher is setting his *Format Matters* expectations throughout the dialogue? Mark at least one area where you think he could make improvements.

_____

5. What are the *Format Matters* expectations in *your* classroom? For each *Format Matters* expectation, write down some brief prompts you do use or could use with your students for the four different format criteria.

Grammatical prompt phrases: _____

_____

Complete sentence prompt phrases: _____

_____

Audible prompt phrases: _____

_____

Units prompt phrases: _____

_____

6. Write some notes about how you think the case study teacher's *Format Matters* response would or should change, according to the time of the year.

Example (at line 15)

September: *That was good, but do you think that Mahogany can hear you at the back of the class? Try again, with voice.*

Or better:

September: *That was so good; we need to make sure Mahogany can hear it in the back. Try again, with voice.*

December: *Good sentence. Try again with voice.*

April: *Voice.*

At line 3

September: _____

_____

_____

December: _____

April: _____

At line 5

September: _____

_____

_____

December: _____

April: _____

At line 7

September: _____

_____

_____

December: _____

April: _____

At line 9

September: _____

_____

_____

43 **POSITIVE FRAMING**

FORMAT MATTERS

December: _____

April: _____

At line 11

September: _____

_____

_____

December: _____

April: _____

At line 13

September: _____

_____

_____

December: _____

April: _____

7. Consider the formats you expect in your classroom. For each one, word an ideal interaction with your students at each given point in the school year.

Grammatical

September: _____

_____

_____

December: _____

April: _____

Complete sentence

September: _____

_____

_____

December: _____

April: _____

Audible

September: _____

_____

_____

December: _____

April: _____

Units

September: _____

_____

_____

December: _____

April: _____

PRACTICE WITH STUDY GROUP OR PARTNERS

Revisit the individual work you did in the previous section to share and compare your responses and see other options.

Speed Role Play

This role play simulates the *Teacher*'s experience of correcting various incorrectly formatted answers. You can play it with one partner as *Student,* but the more *Students* the better.

To prepare, the *Facilitator* should photocopy and cut out (or adapt) the "flash card" questions.

1. As a group, brainstorm different ways to address *Format Matters* moments in the classroom. Consider applicable verbal and nonverbal cues for each. For example, for *audible* format you could say "Voice" or cup your hand to your ear.

2. In each round, half the participants are *Teachers* and stand opposite the *Students.* The *Facilitator* distributes a card to each *Teacher.* The *Facilitator* reminds the group that there are four criteria for format: *grammar, complete sentence, audible,* and in appropriate *units.*

3. Taking turns, briskly, each *Teacher* asks the question on the card of the *Student* standing (or sitting) opposite.

4. The *Student* answers the question correctly in terms of content, but incorrectly in terms of at least one format criterion.

5. The *Teacher* leads the *Student* to correct the format using an appropriate *Format Matters* technique.

6. Switch sides and continue until the *Facilitator* thinks the group has done enough.

SPEED ROLE PLAY FLASH CARD QUESTIONS

Speed Role Play	Speed Role Play	Speed Role Play	Speed Role Play
What is the capital of [your state]?	Name one part of the water cycle.	How many sides does a pentagon have?	What is the product of 4 times 8?
What was the most significant event of the 20th century?	True or false? The light bulb was invented by Albert Einstein.	What are the three branches of the U.S. government?	Name the author of [War and Peace or other famous novel].
How many criteria of Format Matters are there?	What is the area of a rectangle that has a length of 4 inches and a width of 3 inches?	Who is buried in the Tomb of the Unknown Soldier?	Why do you think students must answer in the proper format?
Who was the first president of the United States of America?	Which U.S. states are not adjoined by any other state?	What is the greatest novel of the 20th century?	How many original colonies became part of the United States?
What was Beethoven's greatest symphony?	What is the most important quality of a leader [or of an artist, scientist, etc.]?	Identify the subject of this sentence: "To encourage students to comply with Format Matters criteria, a master teacher finds quick and unobtrusive methods of reminding students to answer in complete sentences."	Why did President Thomas Jefferson send Lewis and Clark on their expedition west?
If you have one piece of rope that is 8 feet long and one that is 10 feet long, how much rope do you have altogether?	What is the capital of [some other state or country]?	What do we call money that is invested in an industry?	How many sides does a Stop sign on the road have?

7. Use these questions to guide a discussion:
   - What were the various methods of eliciting *Format Matters* responses?
   - Were any more successful than others?
   - What are the most common *Format Matters* errors you experience in your classroom? How will you attend to these?

Roll Out *Format Matters*

Before the group convenes, each participant writes two introductions to his or her *Format Matters* expectations, to deliver to students who are learning about *Format Matters* for the first time. One introduction is intended for the beginning of the year, the other for beginning *Format Matters* in the middle of the year. The introduction should cover some or all of the following points (you may think of others to include):

- What are the expectations?
- Why is it important always to answer in the proper format?
- How should students respond if they are corrected regarding format?

Each participant delivers at least one of the introductions to the group. After all have done so, the group then discusses further thoughts on these questions:

- Is there anything else you might want to tell students about your *Format Matters* expectations and why?
- What do you expect will be challenging about introducing *Format Matters* expectations to your students?
- What do you expect will be different about introducing *Format Matters* expectations in the middle of the year?
- Are there any objections from students that you anticipate having to overcome?
- Are there particular ways that you think would be effective in introducing *Format Matters* to make it easier? Hand signals? Trigger words? Explain.

What useful feedback or key takeaways do you want to remember from this group work?

_____

_____

_____

_____

TRY *FORMAT MATTERS* IN THE CLASSROOM

If you hesitate to jump in, spend a class session listening to the format issues that your students present, or listen to students in a similar class conducted by another teacher. Make notes about what needs to be done. Then, in your own next teaching session, begin with whatever aspect of format you feel most confident about.

If you're working with a group of teachers at your school, find out what spoken and written format shorthand other teachers use and explore coordinating your usage with theirs.

Introduce Your Shorthand for Written Work

Look back at your earlier work in "Shorthand Corrections for Written Work." By yourself or with a peer, as part of a lesson plan, devise a plan for rolling out your expectations about your students' writing. Do this when you are returning student written work for the first time.

7 **4 MS**

Include a process or activity for conveying the meanings of your shorthand marks. Consider letting the students try applying those marks to a sample of writing you have created that is in clear need of corrections they should be able to notice.

Introduce Your Broader Format Expectations

1. To maintain format expectations among your students, you first need to tell them what those expectations are. Write and practice a brief, positive introduction to each of your main format expectations. Introduce as many in a given session as you think the class can digest. Consider putting up a succinct poster that reminds the class of your main expectations.

2. Explain the language you will be using for your expectations (for example, what you mean by "Voice" or "Complete sentence"). Model the behavior for the class and solicit questions that will clarify understanding of your expectations. In lower grades, you may also want to create a simple game in which the students can demonstrate and practice correct format with each other.

3. If you have past experience with these students, think about who among them is likely to need some particular format guidance. But prepare to discover similar format needs in other students in the class.

Integrate *Format Matters* into Normal Class Procedure

1. On the same day in which you introduce an expectation, also begin to apply it, and continue to do so on subsequent days.

2. Look back at your work at step 7 of the "*Format Matters* Case Study" on page 58. Note where in the lesson plan specific format issues are likely to arise. For these places, note down and practice some wording that will remind students about format *before* they start to answer.

3. For grammar and complete sentences, also practice

    • Identifying the error and cueing the student to correct it

    • Beginning the correction by providing a stem that the student can use to provide the full correct answer

4. After a lesson, note on the lesson plan where and how you might improve your work on *Format Matters*.

TROUBLE-SHOOT

Steady On

When audibility is at stake, notice any tendency you may have to nag at length. Nagging can be a sign that you need to train the class to follow a simple, easily understandable instruction, like "Voice."

FORMAT MATTERS

Other Challenges

Possible Challenge	Possible Solutions
I find it awkward to point out instances when students use nonstandard language. It feels uncomfortable and even judgmental to me.	Focus on your rollout. Make a crisp, clear statement that explains the "why" to *you* as well as to them. Rewrite it until you've captured the nuance. You might say: **48 EXPLAIN EVERYTHING** "We all speak differently outside of school and work. This might be surprising to you, but that includes teachers! I don't speak like a teenager, of course, but I am more casual with my language outside of work. And I **45 WARM/STRICT** know that sometimes the way you speak with your friends, say, is part of your true voice. So there's no judgment when I correct you. But I will correct you. Because here in this room we need to practice a form of speaking that's expected in certain settings. And so I'm going to ask that of you every time." Ask students to remind each other. If they are old enough, ask them how you can best remind them in a way that is supportive and respectful but clear and direct.

FORMAT MATTERS

SUSTAIN YOUR PROGRESS

1. Using feedback from your study group or other peers, and reviewing your own lesson notes and observations, monitor your progress on *Format Matters*:

Date	Things I'm Doing Well	Format to Emphasize

2. Revisit "Where Am I Now?" Are you ready to build out to some other new technique?

ANALYZE THE CHAMPIONS: SOME OBSERVATIONS

 Clip 4. Teacher Stacey Shells, Grade 7

In the first part of this clip, Ms. Shells understands audibility as a compact between reader and listeners. The reader reads aloud with voice, so she wants to verify that the rest of the class is giving him their full attention. Later, she prompts another student to speak more audibly. She also tackles his nonstandard way of saying "their mom." She avoids moral judgment in part by avoiding calling his usage an error but insisting he use the "standard," and by addressing her justification to the class as a whole.

WITHOUT APOLOGY

OVERVIEW

Champion teachers find a way to make the material students need to know meaningful and engaging. They keep it rigorous by disciplining themselves to avoid labeling what students need to study as "boring," out of their control, or too remote or hard for their scholars. They are careful to avoid such "apologies"—that is, excuses for watering down the content and rigor of what they teach.

Teachers sometimes "apologize"—at times unconsciously—by

- Telling students that something will be boring

- Blaming some outside entity for the fact that they are teaching certain material

- Diluting material under the rationale of making it "accessible" to minds they've already assumed will be unreceptive

- Classifying students as unable to learn challenging material

We are all at risk of these apologies. In fact, let's assume that we've all allowed them to change our teaching at least once. But becoming aware of these risks enables you to stay vigilant and find alternatives, such as a dynamic *Hook* or allowing a bit more time to read a challenging text deeply.

7 **4 MS**

12 **THE HOOK**

WHERE AM I NOW?

	Proficiency			
Comfort & Confidence	I am brand new to *Without Apology* . . .	I'm in the planning and practice stage, though I haven't tried it yet in class . . .	I'm beginning to apply *Without Apology* in my classroom . . .	I use this technique as often as needed . . .
	❑ . . . and want to try it.	❑ . . . but know with more practice I'll make it work.	❑ . . . and see how it improves the learning.	❑ . . . and am adding my own distinctive touch.
	❑ . . . and have some immediate hesitation.	❑ . . . because I still have questions about how to carry it off.	❑ . . . with mixed results I need to evaluate.	❑ . . . and find it reliable.
	❑ . . . and not at all sure it's workable.	❑ . . . because, frankly, I still have serious doubts.	❑ . . . but have trouble letting go of some negative feelings.	❑ . . . but still backslide on occasion in some respect.

Work from your strengths. If you find yourself in the bottom left portion, leaf through this technique to locate related ones you might prefer to work on right now.

ANALYZE THE CHAMPIONS

View the video clip, ideally more than once, and answer the following questions.

 Clip 10. Teacher Dinah Shepherd, Grade 8

1. What, if anything, does Ms. Shepherd say or do that convinces you that she thinks the question she has posed is really worth answering?
2. At several points, Ms. Shepherd persists in going back in order to go deeper. What does she say at these points? What does she ask the students to do?
3. How do Ms. Shepherd's students benefit from her persistence? Give evidence.

EXPAND YOUR SKILLS AND REPERTOIRE

Apologies

"Guys, I know this is dull. Let's just do our best to get through it."

"You need to know this for the test."

"This isn't my favorite story, but it's not I who decides what we read."

"This probably seems irrelevant to some of you, but . . ."

"Spelling time. Oh, well, let's do it."

"This may be a little beyond some of you, but . . ."

"I know your iPhone can tell you this, but . . ."

Is there anything *you've* said in class that apologized for the material that your students needed to learn? (*All* of us, or at least every teacher we've met, have done this. The goal here is to recognize, not judge.) Jot down your best recollection of what you've said (or might be inclined to say). Why do you think you said it? Can you think of any alternatives or solutions right away?

1. What you said: _____

Why you think you said it: _____

Alternatives? _____

_____

| 6 **BEGIN WITH THE END** |

2. What you said: _____

Why you think you said it: _____

Alternatives? _____

_____

WITHOUT APOLOGY

Nothing That Matters Is Boring

1. Think through the material you are teaching this year. Identify two or three parts of that material that you or someone else might be inclined to regard as boring for students.

_____

_____

2. Why is that material important on the path to college? (Sometimes framing this for students can be a way in.)

_____

_____

3. Cite any evidence you have that students are bored by it.

_____

_____

4. How reliable is your evidence? Does it apply to all students? What, other than the topic itself, could account for the evidence you perceive?

_____

_____

5. What signs of interest do you also notice?

_____

_____

6. How might you stoke those flickers of interest?

_____

_____

7. For people who are fascinated by this material—people who spend their lives studying it or who use it every day or who find it gratifying—and there are such people for every topic—why do you think it's interesting? Put yourself in their shoes. How would they introduce it?

_____

_____

_____

_____

Expanded Horizons

1. What do you think are the main interests of your students?

_____

_____

_____

2. Do those interests apply to all of your students? For your most engaged students, the ones you wish they could all be like, what experiences or interactions, with whom, made them that way?

_____

_____

_____

3. What do you think your students aren't interested in?

_____

_____

_____

4. How might you probe further for possible evidence to the contrary?

_____

_____

_____

5. All of us have things we once had no interest in but for which we later developed a love. For some of us, this is a description of our college major or even our decision to teach! Think of something that you developed an interest in over time—something that you once had no time for but ultimately found fascinating. What changed you? Something you read or heard? Someone you met? How can you bring that kind of experience to your students?

_____

_____

_____

_____

_____

Blaming Outside Forces

1. Name something large or small that you include in a lesson mainly out of responsibility to some outside authority or standardized test.

_____

_____

2. What about the material feels unworthy to you? Push yourself to be specific and demanding here. Try to put your concerns into writing.

_____

_____

3. What's the academic reason for its being there? Why might an authority decide that it was critical for students to learn this material? How can you communicate that to students?

_____

_____

4. Is there a different place for it, serving some other learning objectives than the one where it is now?

_____

_____

Dilutions and Substitutions

1. Write down one, if any, way you may have diluted material in order to make the lesson more "accessible."

_____

_____

2. What more might you yourself be able to learn about the *original* material that might lead you to an effective *Hook* into it?

12 THE HOOK

_____

_____

3. The fact that material is challenging is a good thing. Can you use the challenge as part of a *Hook*? Take a shot at drafting a *Hook* here—one that draws on the fact that achieving what's hard will set your students apart and that the ability to rise to a challenge is both rewarding and another word for excellence.

_____

_____

WITHOUT APOLOGY

Not Apologizing for Students

1. What, in the material you teach, do you worry your students may not be able to "handle"?

_____

_____

2. What skills or background knowledge do you think they lack that prevents them from successfully working through the material?

_____

_____

3. Do you have hard evidence that they can't successfully work through the material? If so, what activities could help them overcome that? If not, what could you ask them to do to show you they had the wherewithal to do it?

_____

_____

Alternatives to Apology

"You can take real pride in knowing . . ."

"Don't be rattled by a few fancy words here. Once you know them, you'll see her meaning."

"This is tricky, but you guys can do it. I haven't seen much you couldn't do if you put your minds to it."

"I know you can do this, DaJuan. So I'm going to stick with you on this question."

"It's okay to be confused at this point. We're going to get it. Let's take another try."

"This challenge is terrific!"

"Lots of people don't understand this until they study it in college. You're going to be a step ahead."

"This gets more and more exciting as you come to understand it better."

"A lot of [second graders, high school students, adults] don't know this, but you'll know it before we're done!"

"There's a great story behind this problem . . ."

What other alternative language can you add to your repertoire when . . .

You anticipate boredom?

_____

_____

You sense low confidence among the students?

_____

_____

You want to blame?

_____

_____

You're deliberately not diluting?

_____

_____

Your students might not be up to the challenge?

_____

_____

PRACTICE WITH STUDY GROUP OR PARTNERS

Revisit the individual work you did in the previous section to share and compare your responses and see other options.

Sorry!

1. Go around in a circle for each of the following topics. The first person makes an apology for the topic. After that, each person apologizes for a different reason or in a different way from the previous speakers. Have a *Recorder* post each group member's response.

Topic: Conversion of a fraction to its decimal equivalent (no calculators, of course).

Topic: Spelling unit on *-ight* words.

Topic: The origins of the Vietnam War.

Reflection: How do you react to hearing so many apologies? How does it make you reflect on your work as a teacher and/or on the lives of students? What if you heard such apologies over and over in your life? Share some of your reactions with the group.

2. Go around the circle again, and for each apology, one at a time brainstorm alternative, non-apologetic things to say instead.

Reflection: How did it feel different to be sitting in the circle the second time around? How might those differences, if multiplied by dozens of interactions over the year, affect students? Share some of your reactions with the group.

Mandated Tests

Discuss how statewide or other mandated tests affect your teaching, especially how they may affect your creation of lesson plans based on objectives. What are the tensions? Where do your students' best long-term academic interests lie? How can you best support those interests?

> 6 **BEGIN WITH THE END**
> 7 **4 MS**

TRY *WITHOUT APOLOGY* IN THE CLASSROOM

1. Where in your next lesson plan might you be at risk of apologizing for or diluting content? Why might you be tempted? Script a phrase or two to use in that moment to keep your expectations at their highest.

2. Deliberately remove anything from the plan that you worry might be diluted or that might distract students from reaching the objective. Replace it with full-strength material. Consider any scaffolding you may need to add to reach that material.

| 12 **THE HOOK** |

3. Script a great *Hook*. Even if you end up not using it, it can help by exciting *you* about the lesson!

BE CREATIVE

Do your students ever make apologies for themselves—for example, assuming they will not be able to do something yet or excusing themselves from trying? Come up with three good responses, verbal or otherwise.

1. _____

2. _____

3. _____

SUSTAIN YOUR PROGRESS

1. Using feedback from your study group or other peers, and reviewing your own lesson notes and observations, monitor your progress on *Without Apology*.

Date	How I Was Tempted to Apologize	What I Did Instead

2. Revisit "Where Am I Now?" Are you ready to build out to some other new technique?

BEGIN WITH THE END

OVERVIEW

Planning is essential for daily success in the classroom. *Begin with the End* is a process whereby you begin with larger objectives, those that would be achieved over the course of a unit, and then break those objectives down into smaller objectives, and finally create lessons and activities designed to achieve them. Specifically, you would go through the following sequence:

1. Start with unit planning, then lesson planning.

2. Clearly frame an objective for each lesson.

3. Determine how you'll assess your effectiveness in meeting your objective, ideally every day (see *Exit Ticket*).

4. Choose lesson activities that work toward the goal and align to your assessment.

20 **EXIT TICKET**

Begin with the End establishes a framework for all other lesson planning techniques, including whatever use you make of homework. (The latter is discussed in *Ratio*.) The following discussion contains many references to the other planning techniques in this section of the Guide.

17 **RATIO**

WHERE AM I NOW?

<table>
<tr><td rowspan="2">Comfort & Confidence</td><td colspan="4" align="center">Proficiency</td></tr>
<tr><td>I am brand new to some part of Begin with the End ...</td><td>I haven't tried it yet ...</td><td>I'm beginning to try this in my planning ...</td><td>I always Begin with the End ...</td></tr>
<tr><td></td><td>❏ ... and excited to try it.</td><td>❏ ... but know with more practice I'll make it work.</td><td>❏ ... and love how it basically works.</td><td>❏ ... and my lessons stay on track.</td></tr>
<tr><td></td><td>❏ ... and undecided about my ability to pull it off.</td><td>❏ ... because I still have questions about how to do it right.</td><td>❏ ... with mixed results I need to evaluate.</td><td>❏ ... but am still working on efficiency or effectiveness.</td></tr>
</table>

If you are not already using *Begin with the End,* start working on it now.

EXPAND YOUR SKILLS AND REPERTOIRE

If possible, do these activities together with a partner who is also planning or learning to plan classroom lessons. If you can't meet face-to-face, consider exchanging your thoughts and samples of your work by phone, e-mail, or social media. Follow the steps suggested in the "Overview" section.

The Planning Sequence

Progress from Unit Planning to Lesson Planning

Unit planning means planning lessons in groups. The goal of the unit is achieved in the course of progress through daily lessons, each with its own, smaller objective.

1.   Begin by planning a "unit" on a major topic in your curriculum. Review all information about the unit and the number of sessions you have to complete it. What is the overarching goal of the unit as you see it, and how will it be assessed?

_____

_____

2.   In plain language and as concretely as possible, what are the three to five most important things students will have to master to be successful in this unit? Even if you see more than five, it's powerful to distill them down to this small of a number to ensure that, when in doubt, you know what to spend your time on.

_____

_____

_____

_____

_____

_____

_____

3.   If you have not already done so, consider roughly the number of sessions or classroom weeks you have and organize them in a syllabus in which you indicate which goals will be covered each week or each session.

Try to draft a sequence of objectives, one for each day in the unit. Each objective should cover a slightly different aspect of the larger skill or content you are building toward. Even if objectives vary only slightly (for example, one day's goal is to introduce common denominators, the second day's goal is for students to be able to find them independently, the third day's goal is to find them with automaticity), each day should be different.

4.   Reserve a few lessons (10 to 20 percent is a decent rule of thumb) for going back and reteaching anything your students struggle with.

5.   As teachers we are quick to overlook the need for students to keep practicing skills they have mastered to keep those skills alive and, we hope, extend students' ability to use them. Use a template

like the one provided to plan for places in your lesson to reinforce and extend content students have mastered, including during the *Do Now* and a five- to ten-minute block of spiraled practice (a great time for *Pepper*).

Template for Weekly Reinforcing and Extending

	Monday	Tuesday	Wednesday	Thursday	Friday
Do Now Periodically use your 3- to 5-minute class intro to review mastered skills.					29 **DO NOW**
Core Lesson Objective Key daily objective goes here.					
Pepper Embed skills students have mastered or are close to mastering in a 5- to 10-minute session of fast, high-energy practice to reinforce content from previous lessons.					24 **PEPPER**
Homework Use it to review mastered skills from your most recent lessons and occasionally add a few questions on important lessons students previously mastered. (See *At Bats*.)					19 **AT BATS**

6. At this point you will need to be willing to circle back occasionally as you move forward through your lessons, because you need to make sure that one day's lesson builds off the previous day's real outcome and prepares for the next day's, and that these three fit into a larger sequence of objectives that lead to mastery.

Be prepared to change your plan for the next session based on what happened in the one before. If you know you've failed to achieve full mastery of one day's objective on which the next day's objective depends, go back and reteach the content to ensure full mastery before moving on. In general, it's a good idea to plan to begin lessons by circling back to anything that may still need attention from the day before.

Apply the following steps as you design an actual lesson plan. To begin your lesson plan, note any goals you have that carry over from the previous session.

Identify and Test Your Goal or Objective for the Lesson

1. Identify the main goal of the lesson you are planning. Write it down in your plan.

2. Use *4 Ms* to evaluate and possibly improve the precision of the goal: ask whether the goal is "Made first" (determined before any activity is chosen), Most important, Measurable, and Manageable.

7 **4 MS**

Decide How You'll Assess Your Effectiveness in Reaching Your Goal

> 18 **CFU**
>
> 20 **EXIT TICKET**
>
> 24 **PEPPER**

Exit Tickets are such a good means of assessment that some champion teachers believe that every lesson plan should include one. As often as is possible, try to include them. Also consider how you can use techniques like *Check for Understanding* and *Pepper* to understand how well you're doing in reaching student mastery *throughout the lesson.*

Choose Lesson Activities That Work Toward the Goal

1. Think in terms of what the activity will cause students to *do* in pursuit of the goal. How will the activities build on what students can already do, so that by the end of the session they've shown that they can do whatever the lesson goal required?

> 9 **SHORTEST PATH**

2. Before you settle on an activity, come up with at least two other activities you could consider using in its place. Are there strong aspects of alternative activities that could be combined in one new, more effective one? Will this activity be the best and fastest way to help you reach the goal?

3. Consider whether the activity could be tightened in some way to use the time more efficiently and maintain pacing. There are no throwaway two minutes at the end of class. A year full of throwaways like that adds up to more than six hours of instruction—a whole school day.

> 10 **DOUBLE PLAN**

4. Now *Double Plan*. Go through your lesson and write out what students should be doing during each section. Challenge yourself to make sure their task is always something active.

Saving Time During Planning

Planning does take time, and it's important to be realistic about how much time good planning needs for you at your own stage in the mastery of teaching. You'll spend less time planning if you always plan from objectives and continually *Check for Understanding.*

> 18 **CFU**

You can also reduce planning time by developing standard "events"—recurring activities that you frequently use. This allows you to insert your content into a trustworthy framework rather than having to design a framework from scratch. Here are four examples of recurring lesson features.

> 26 **EVERYBODY WRITES**

1. *Everybody Writes*

Humanities, ELA, history:

"Stop and jot." Read a key passage from a novel or primary text and respond to it in writing. Then discuss.

Later, students can suggest or nominate passages, and you can choose the best suggestions.

Math and science:

Take a formula or problem and describe what it does in clear, direct, narrative prose.

> 24 **PEPPER**

2. *Pepper/Oral drill*

Script ten to twelve questions of increasing rigor reviewing key content. Ask students to stand, and rapidly move around the room cold-calling students. Entertain no discussion between questions—*keep it fast.*

Humanities, the novel The Giver:

"The first time Jonas sees colors, this is the object he observes."

"The relationship of the Giver to the young person appointed before Jonas to be receiver of memory."

"The form of government we said *The Giver* was raising questions about?"

"The speaker of the statement: 'The veins in your arms are still teeny-weeny.'"

"Who the speaker is talking to."

"Who else overhears him (later)."

"Let's go back to the statement 'The veins in your arms are still teeny-weeny.'"

"Why is this statement ironic?"

"Who can remind us of the definition of dramatic irony?"

"Who can tell me why the scene in which the statement is made demonstrates dramatic irony?"

Geometry:

"I am a parallelogram with opposite angles of 100 degrees each. What's the measure of my other two angles?"

"What type of angle will the two remaining angles be? Why?"

"Now I am a square. My angles are $2x$ plus 10 degrees. What's the value of x?"

"I am a rhombus with a side of $7x$ plus 2 inches. What's my perimeter?"

"If the measure of one angle is 90 degrees, what's my area if x equals 3?"

"What's the formula for my area if you don't know the value of x?"

3. **Timed practice**

Humanities:

Adapt the old saw of math teachers (see the next activity) with, for example, a series of quotations from the text to identify the speaker of, paraphrase, explain the importance of, and so on.

Math:

Many math teachers are familiar with "Mad Minute," which can be adapted to more rigorous and far-ranging content, such as a page of one- or two-variable equations solved for a given x or y or a series of triangles with angle measures partially complete.

4. **Passage or text analysis**

Students, working individually or in pairs, get a section of text and ten minutes in which to identify and analyze it in writing. Who wrote it? What text is it from? If it's fiction, who are the characters in it, and what are they doing? What themes or ideas from class does it reflect or discuss? How is it like or unlike another passage from something else we've read?

Lesson Plans for Teaching Reading

Great lesson plans whose objectives relate to developing students' reading skills tend to look very different from great lesson plans in other content areas. But although it may not be apparent right away, they, too, contain all the elements we've described as crucial to a successful lesson. Here briefly is how objectives, assessment, and activity might look in a reading lesson plan.

A Well-Framed Objective

All good reading lessons have one! It should align to your state or school standards and should be capable of being taught and practiced using whatever passage the class is reading on a given day. For example, if the class is reading a novel together, the lesson objective needs to be applicable to the passage of the novel they are reading on that day.

8 **POST IT**

In front of the class, champion teacher Patrick Pastore calls his daily objective an "Active Reading Job," and students in his class know that they'll be responsible for demonstrating mastery by the end of the day's reading. Actually, his plan often includes three Active Reading Jobs. One is the primary objective, which is also posted on the board. The other two are review skills.

Reading objectives may differ from those in other content areas because effective reading objectives can, in some cases, be more explicit about an activity. For example, "Define satire and its characteristics and show how *Harrison Bergeron* is an example" or "Find elements of absurdity in Dave Eggers's *Zeitoun.*" This is particularly true of students in older grades who often use a combination of tools and skills to comprehend and analyze a given text.

Assessment

20 **EXIT TICKET**

Assessment takes three primary forms that are similar to forms used in other content areas: written responses, verbal responses, and *Exit Tickets*.

Activity

Most of a reading lesson is spent in reading. Although most champion reading teachers include other activities as part of their lesson (vocabulary building, written responses to the reading, and so forth), for them the most important part of planning a reading lesson is thinking about what students will be doing *during* reading. They ask themselves,

- How much reading will be done altogether in the session, using independent reading and reading aloud?

- Are my students ready to do some portions of the reading on their own?

- What questions can I ask or tasks can I give to make sure that students understand the reading they've done on their own?

They think about and plan the questions they will ask of the students during reading in order to

20 **AT BATS**

- Provide students with *At Bats* for the lesson objective

- Check for basic understanding of the small passages within the story (sentence level, paragraph level)

- Support understanding of the overall story and its themes

They plan ahead also about what the proper response format will be for answering their questions, in either verbal or written form.

Reading teachers often find it useful to write their questions and stopping points directly into the text the class is reading and use this marked-up text during their in-class reading with students. It's more efficient than typing their questions into a separate lesson plan because the questions (and answers) are directly based on the content of the text, and they don't have to flip back and forth between the text the class is reading and their lesson plan as they ask a question.

PRACTICE WITH STUDY GROUP OR PARTNERS

Revisit the individual work you did in the previous section to share and compare your responses and see other options.

If your group totals more than eight, the *Facilitator* should make some decision about dividing into smaller working groups for some of this work and let the other members know in advance of the meeting how many copies they need to bring.

Before the meeting, make enough copies (for your working group) of two lesson plans you've used in the past: one that went relatively well and another that you'd like to improve before you use it again in the future.

Also bring at least one copy of the unit overview materials from which you derived your syllabus or basic breakdown of lessons.

Units to Lessons

Go around the circle describing how each of you goes about breaking down your unit materials into teachable lesson units. What problems do you and others encounter? How do you deal with them? What new thoughts emerge from this for you?

_____

_____

_____

_____

If you broke into smaller groups, reunite to share insights.

Evaluate Past Lesson Plans

1. In the working group, exchange copies of the plan that went well. Allow a few minutes for everyone to look over these plans.

2. Go around the circle talking first about how the plan reflects any or all of the four main ideas covered in "Expand Your Skills and Repertoire": (1) starting with unit planning, (2) framing each lesson's objective, (3) knowing how you will assess effectiveness, and (4) choosing activities.

3. Go around again sharing comments about what else you liked and possibly found useful about someone else's plan.

4. Go around the circle again discussing any ways in which you feel you might further improve your plan. Invite input from the rest of the group about it.

5. Do steps 1 to 3 again with the second plan that did not work as well.

6. Write down and share observations of what you learned in this group work.

_____

_____

_____

_____

7. If you broke into subgroups, reconvene as a whole to share insights.

8. Revise one or both of your plans for possible future reference.

BEGIN WITH THE END

Share and Evaluate Upcoming Plans

1. Using a lesson plan you haven't tried yet, follow the same general process you followed in steps 1 through 4 for past lesson plans.

2. After step 4, go around addressing each member of the group with comments and questions that might help that teacher improve some aspect of the plan. The member whose plan is under discussion can (but does not need to) respond directly to any of the comments or questions.

3. Write down and share observations of what you learned in this group work.

_____

_____

_____

_____

4. After the session, improve your plan in any way you see fit.

5. After you have taught the lesson, report back to the group (in meeting or by message) about how it went and what you learned.

TRY YOUR PLAN IN THE CLASSROOM

Depending on your experience and other factors, you may need to have your lesson plan in front of you more or less frequently during the lesson and in more or less detail. Prepare it in a format or medium that will work for you in class. Consider having two versions—a detailed one that you can refer to if necessary, and a more skeletal one that you can glance at quickly from a card.

TROUBLE-SHOOT

Sometimes the complexity of lesson planning can cause the best of us to procrastinate. It's tiring and challenging to work out all the details of a series of lessons. Start simple. *Plan just your objectives first.* Knowing the objective of the unit, breaking it down into parts, and knowing your weekly objectives will help you focus easily and rapidly on objectives and goals for each lesson in the coming week.

The earlier you start planning for sets of lessons, the more time you have to let each lesson percolate in your mind to be sure you have the right objective and your own (and others') best thoughts about the right activity.

You might need less time consolidating your next lesson plan if you start shortly after the one you just taught.

Devise a standard lesson plan outline or form that will make planning easier to start and faster to do each time. Here are some categories the form would have. Add others that will serve your needs.

- Unit
- Date
- Mastered skills or content from last lesson
- Objective for this lesson
- Means of assessment

- *Hook*
- Activities and their steps
- *Exit Ticket*
- Evaluation of the plan
- Teaching technique I'm working on

BE CREATIVE

Variety adds spice. If the activity you settle on is one you've already used recently, vary it a little. Select a future lesson objective that you think might be served best by a basic activity that is similar to one you've used before.

Objective: _____

Basic activity: _____

Previous objective when you used it: _____

How do the objectives differ? Therefore, how should the activity differ?

_____

_____

How might you announce or otherwise introduce the difference to your students in a way that underscores the change in *challenge*?

| 43 **POSITIVE FRAMING** |

_____

_____

SUSTAIN YOUR PROGRESS

1.   Using feedback from your study group or other peers, and reviewing your own lesson notes and observations, monitor your progress on *Begin with the End.*

Date	Things I'm Doing Well	Ways to Improve

2.   Revisit "Where Am I Now?" Are you ready to build out to some other new technique?

BEGIN WITH THE END

4 MS

OVERVIEW

| 6 BEGIN WITH THE END |

Begin with the End is based on the idea that starting with *objectives* gives lesson planning meaning, discipline, and direction. The *4 Ms* technique focuses on how to ensure that the objectives are crafted with care and for maximum impact. As I noted in *Teach Like a Champion,* I am indebted to my colleague Todd McKee for coming up with this technique. Here are his four "M" criteria for an effective objective.

Made first. The objective was chosen first and determines what activities the lesson plan includes. It wasn't thought up to justify doing an appealing activity that may or may not advance class learning toward the overall unit goal.

Most important. The objective focuses on what's most important for the class right now on its path to higher education. It describes the next step straight up the mountain.

Measurable. It's possible to measure how fully the objective has been realized. Ideally you have measured that by the time the class period is over.

Manageable. The objective can be reached within the time of the lesson.

WHERE AM I NOW?

	Proficiency			
Comfort & Confidence	**I am brand new to *4 Ms* . . .**	**I'm familiar with *4 Ms* now, but haven't tried it yet in planning . . .**	**I'm beginning to try *4 Ms* in my planning . . .**	**I use all *4 Ms* . . .**
	❏ . . . and excited to try it.	❏ . . . but know with more practice I'll make it work.	❏ . . . and love how it basically works.	❏ . . . because they sharpen my teaching.
	❏ . . . and undecided about my ability to pull it off.	❏ . . . because I still have questions about how to do it right.	❏ . . . with mixed results I need to evaluate.	❏ . . . but still have occasional trouble addressing them all.

If you are not already using some technique closely akin to the *4 Ms,* start working on it now.

EXPAND YOUR SKILLS AND REPERTOIRE

MMMM

Made First

The objective comes first. It requires and shapes a certain activity rather than justifying an activity that came up in the absence of an objective.

> 6 **BEGIN WITH THE END**

On the lines that follow, if you can, name an activity you used recently in class whose purpose was not particularly aligned with the overall learning objective of that day's lesson. (Perhaps it was an activity you do simply because it is enjoyable or puts the class in a good frame of mind.) What was the learning objective for that day? What may have led you to use the activity? Is there some element of the activity that would actually have been useful as part of some other activity that would have truly served the objective?

Activity: _____

Lesson objective: _____

Why you did the activity: _____

A useful element: _____

Most Important

An effective objective should focus on what's most important on the path to higher levels of education, including college.

Measurable

An objective should be *written down* so that your success in achieving it can be *measured,* ideally by the end of the class period. This lets you better understand in your own mind what worked in your implementation. It makes every lesson a learning opportunity for *you,* rather than a vague experiment.

"Measured" doesn't necessarily mean a "test" or a result you can quantify in a rigorous way, but it does mean that you are systematic. For example, it could mean the use of any careful form of *Check for Understanding.* You want to have some idea beforehand about what you will define as success. Not all students in the class will reach the same high level of success during a given session.

We urge you to include an *Exit Ticket* to assess whether students have reached the objective for the day. If you have been using them, look back at the *Exit Ticket* forms you used in ten recent lessons. Put the *Exit Ticket* forms in one stack and the lesson plans in another; then shuffle each stack. Can you match them? Can a partner teacher match them? How well do you (or your partner) think the *Exit Tickets* match the objectives you've written?

> 18 **CFU**
> 20 **EXIT TICKET**

_____

_____

_____

4 MS

If you sometimes tend to hold off some large "assessment" until tomorrow or the end of the week, in what ways can you be sure to measure progress today on today's objective?

_____

_____

_____

Manageable

Can the objective be taught in a single lesson? Is there a good activity that will fit within the time frame, including time for enough practice and repetition?

Is there a means of assessment that will also fit within the time? It's best for you to know by the time class has ended whether or not your students have met the goal of the session—and they should want to know that, too.

If a proposed objective says that students should reach a deep understanding that actually takes numerous sessions, days, or weeks to gain, it's too grand for a lesson plan. Instead, determine what you can accomplish *today* that will advance them toward eventual mastery.

Of course, you should let your students know the larger goal and how what they do today will help them get there. A well-expressed, manageable lesson objective is brief enough that you can *Post It* for the class.

| 8 **POST IT** | Think of when you ran out of time in a recent lesson. What got cut? Why do you suspect you ran short? |

_____

_____

_____

| 8 **POST IT** | Have your students shown signs recently of confusion about their objectives or frustration in trying to meet them? What may have caused those reactions? |

_____

_____

_____

Critique Some Statements of Objectives

Each of these objectives fails to meet at least one *4 Ms* criterion. For each, say which criterion it misses and how. How would you improve on these? Try rewriting each so that it meets all the criteria. Some possible answers are shown at the end of this technique.

1. *Students will see why Shakespeare is the greatest author in the English language, and possibly in all languages.*

_____

_____

_____

Rewrite: _____

_____

2.   *Students will develop a four-point list of criteria for whether a group of words is a complete sentence.*

_____

_____

_____

Rewrite: _____

_____

3.   *The class will learn a short song about climate change.*

_____

_____

_____

Rewrite: _____

_____

4.   *Students will be able to name the parts of a cell and describe their functions.*

_____

_____

_____

Rewrite: _____

_____

5.   *Students will discuss chapter 2 of* To Kill a Mockingbird.

_____

_____

_____

Rewrite: _____

_____

4 MS

Work on Objectives for a Week

1. Less than success in meeting Monday's objective would likely require you to revise your objective for Tuesday, and so on; but for the purposes of this exercise, working with a unit you are teaching or are likely to teach, create the objectives for each of five related lessons that you will teach in sequence. Apply the *4 Ms* to each. Write your finished forms here:

Objective 1: _____

_____

Objective 2: _____

_____

Objective 3: _____

_____

Objective 4: _____

_____

Objective 5: _____

_____

2. If you aren't meeting with a group, exchange your work on this and the other activities in this section with a partner for mutual feedback.

PRACTICE WITH STUDY GROUP OR PARTNERS

Revisit the individual work you did in the previous section to share and compare your responses and see other options. Bring enough copies of your answers to "Critique Some Statements of Objectives" and "Work on Objectives for a Week" to share and discuss with the group.

Also bring the written objective for a lesson you will be teaching soon, along with notes about how you will measure progress or success.

1. As a group, compare your rewrites for "Critique Some Statements of Objectives." Apply the *4 Ms* criteria to all of them. What gray areas might there be with respect to any of the Ms? Make and share any useful changes.

2. Also compare your sets of five objectives from "Work on Objectives for a Week." Describe how they relate to the larger unit and to each other. Again apply the *4 Ms* criteria. What improvements can be made?

3. Go around the circle reading the objective of the lesson you will be teaching soon. Field questions from the group about how each of the Ms apply or about other issues or opportunities they see in the objective.

TROUBLE-SHOOT

Steady On

As a teacher you will help students learn and master knowledge and skills, including powers of reason and, to some extent, taste. And chances are that the more knowledgeable and skilled students become at something, the more they will enjoy it. People often enjoy what they're good at. But in the end, some well-educated people never come to *like* poetry, literary criticism, math, Shakespeare, and so on. And even if you plan to make them love it, your objective should always be skill or content based. Loving something is not a daily objective but an effect of mastering objectives with verve and insight under the tutelage of a great and inspiring teacher. As an English teacher I very intentionally set out to make my students love a certain story or book (and certainly reading and writing generally), but that larger effect wasn't reflected in my daily lesson objective. It was—I hope—reflected in whatever passion and insight I was able to bring to the classroom.

Other Challenges

Possible Challenge	Possible Solutions
Often my lesson objectives turn out to have been too big, not really Manageable within the time we had in class.	Can you be stricter with yourself about how much you can realistically expect to achieve? You might try inserting more intentional internal timings in the lesson plan—for example, that you should be at point one at 20 minutes and point two at 35 minutes. In case you miss these timings, plan a "first drop" activity that you'll shorten or exclude if you're running behind. (Plan a back-pocket activity, too, that you can include in case you come up short.)
I don't believe that the outcomes of some of my lessons can be described well in terms of the *4 Ms.* Not all we do as educators can be boiled down.	Ask a colleague to listen to you describe the lesson for 5 minutes and then write a *4 Ms* analysis of it for you.

BE CREATIVE

Try to write some objectives for other important moments in your life. For example, here is an objective for changing a flat tire:

"Drivers will safely remove a flat tire and replace it with a spare within 30 minutes and following two keys to safety: tight bolts and safe jack placement."

How about these (or others)?

- Cooking dinner
- A conversation with your spouse about the most important challenge you face
- A social event you plan to attend

4 MS

SUSTAIN YOUR PROGRESS

1. Using feedback from your study group or other peers, and reviewing your own lesson notes and observations, monitor your progress on the *4 Ms*.

Date	Ms I Nailed	Ms That Got Away

2. Revisit "Where Am I Now?" Are you ready to build out to some other new technique?

The following are possible responses to "Critique Some Statements of Objectives."

1. *Students will see why Shakespeare is the greatest author in the English language, and possibly in all languages.* This objective aims at belief, which cannot be measured. A *Measurable* objective would be a set of reasons that other people have argued in support of or against Shakespeare's preeminence.

2. *Students will develop a four-point list of criteria for whether a group of words is a complete sentence.* This statement is a mix of objective and activity (writing a list). Perhaps the objective is, more briefly, "Identify the difference between complete and incomplete sentences." A more rigorous version might be "Identify the difference between complete and incomplete sentences and successfully correct incomplete sentences to make them complete." Notice how *Measurable* the second part of the objective is.

3. *The class will learn a short song about climate change.* This objective isn't *Most important* unless perhaps as part of a music unit on choral singing. In that case, the objective probably doesn't need to include the particular choice of song (activity). What basic understandings of the arguments about climate change is the teacher trying to get at? In a unit about weather, those might become the lesson's objective. A song might be a way to reinforce that understanding. But an effective objective would sound more like this: "Students will describe three important causes of climate change and provide examples of human activities that accelerate each."

4. *Students will be able to name the parts of a cell and describe their functions.* This objective isn't *Manageable*. Realistically, this objective may be large enough to occupy an entire unit.

5. *Students will discuss chapter 2 of* To Kill a Mockingbird. This is an activity, not an objective. Therefore it's not *Made first*. The objective might ask students to characterize the relationship between Jem and Dill or to identify a key theme that is developed in the chapter and compare it with a similar theme in another novel.

POST IT

OVERVIEW

Post It means displaying your lesson plan objective where others can see it, in the same location every day, so that everyone who walks into the room—students, peers, administrators—can identify your purpose. This will help students pursue the objective more intentionally and will help peers give you useful feedback on whether you are doing what you set out to do.

If your students are learning basic reading skills, you can use the posting as material for them to read aloud each day at the start of class or at some moment of transition.

Before you actually try *Post It,* make sure you've read and are close to mastering *Begin with the End.*

6 **BEGIN WITH THE END**

WHERE AM I NOW?

	Proficiency			
Comfort & Confidence	I am brand new to *Post It* . . .	I understand it well enough to try it . . .	I'm beginning to try this in my classroom . . .	I use *Post It* regularly . . .
	❑ . . . and excited to try it.	❑ . . . and will try it soon.	❑ . . . and love how it basically works.	❑ . . . and have added a distinctive touch.
	❑ . . . and not sure it's for me.	❑ . . . but I still have doubts.	❑ . . . but it doesn't seem to work or suit me.	❑ . . . and refer to the posting during class.

EXPAND YOUR SKILLS AND REPERTOIRE

1. Look around at various ways to *Post It* in your school and classroom. Writing on "the board" may be simplest and best, but a poster can be more attractive, especially if your board handwriting needs improvement. You can also *Post It* by putting the objective on student handouts and on your lesson plans—leaving a copy of the latter by the door for observers.

2. Get the right equipment—*colored* markers, for example, perhaps some tape to mark the spot on the whiteboard where you post your objective every day. Practice using these tools in a consistent way.

POST IT

PRACTICE WITH STUDY GROUP OR PARTNERS

Complete the "Try *Post It* in the Classroom" section before you meet in a group to discuss it. At the meeting, share examples of objectives you have already posted. Discuss the opportunities and challenges of

- Alternative ways to *Post It* (for example, different practical "low-" or "high-tech" technologies)
- Getting all members of the class to read the post
- Wording the post briefly but unmistakably
- Ensuring that all students understand it

TRY *POST IT* IN THE CLASSROOM

1. Base your *Post It* on the daily objective you have planned as part of *Begin with the End*.

| 6 BEGIN WITH THE END |

2. Decide on your wording before you get to class. Ensure that you choose a location that you can use every day and in a way that makes it visible throughout the session (not, for example, where it will get erased to clear more space on the board).

3. Call attention to your first *Post It* and let the class know your expectations about what they will do with it. Check that students understand this.

4. During class, refer to it verbally and by gesture. At the end you might refer back to it as well: "We set out to do X and Y. How'd we do?"

5. After class, reflect on your posted objective. Was any substantial part of the session taken up by something else? Could and should that have been avoided? How?

TROUBLE-SHOOT

| 6 BEGIN WITH THE END |
| 7 4 MS |

Some teachers write state learning standards on the board as objectives—for example, "3.7.6 Students will read for understanding." Be sure that what you write is the daily objective as *you* defined it in your lesson plan.

BE CREATIVE

1. Do a "pre-mortem." Imagine that a skeptical student saw your lesson plan before class and said, "Aw, Teach, why does that even matter?" Plan your answer to the student beforehand.

2. In what ways do you communicate the "why" when you post the lesson?

3. You can *Post It* both visually and audibly—by referring to the visual posting and reflecting on it to your class. Working by yourself or with a group of peers, brainstorm three visual and three auditory ways you could *Post It* for your next five objectives. (Remember, your purpose is to brainstorm—don't stop just because your ideas aren't "realistic"; unrealistic ideas often give rise to realistic ones.)

4. When you have visitors to class, be sure to encourage them to give you feedback that addresses how well you helped your students master the posted objective.

SUSTAIN YOUR PROGRESS

1. Monitor your progress on *Post It*.

Date	How I *Post It* Now	What Needs Improving?

2. Revisit "Where Am I Now?" Are you ready to build out to some other new technique?

POST IT

SHORTEST PATH

OVERVIEW

All other things being equal, the simplest solution is the best. In your lessons, taking the *Shortest Path* means finding the most direct route to student mastery. Getting there faster leaves more time for practice or application or questions from students—or to move on to a new and equally important topic.

| 6 **BEGIN WITH THE END** |

Watch out for sexy "state-of-the-art" ideas and practices that may not actually help you achieve your lesson objective. Use any instructional approach because it is the best way to get you to your goal, not because your goal affords (or can be adapted to provide) the opportunity to use the approach.

| 18 **CFU** |

Less clever, less complex, less cutting-edge methods may sometimes yield a better result. Consider new approaches that are likely to support your lesson objective, but regularly use what the *data* on student understanding tells you works best to advance their mastery.

WHERE AM I NOW?

	Proficiency			
Comfort & Confidence	I am brand new to *Shortest Path* . . .	I understand the idea and some methods of applying *Shortest Path* to my lesson planning . . .	I'm beginning to try *Shortest Path* in my planning . . .	I regularly evaluate my plans in terms of *Shortest Path* . . .
	❏ . . . and look forward to learning more.	❏ . . . and plan to try it soon.	❏ . . . and find it useful.	❏ . . . and find it.
	❏ . . . but am not sure it's something I need to do.	❏ . . . but don't plan to try it at this point.	❏ . . . with mixed results I need to evaluate.	❏ . . . but suspect I miss it fairly often.

Work from your strengths. If you find yourself in the bottom left corner, leaf through this technique to locate related ones you might prefer to work on right now.

EXPAND YOUR SKILLS AND REPERTOIRE

Can It Be Simpler?

1.   Think of some activity from a lesson you recently taught that turned out to be more complicated than you expected, or more difficult to keep focused on the lesson plan objective. What was the activity, and why do you think it ended up being so complex?

_____

_____

_____

How might you have simplified it or kept better focus on the objective?

_____

_____

_____

2.   Even though the lesson plan might look more elaborate, a well-planned and connected series of short activities might be a shorter path than one long activity. The switch from one short activity to another can often help sustain student attention, energy, and participation. Champion teachers often make lessons more motivating by moving through a series of reliable activities with a variety of tones and paces.

Could the aim of the activity you're analyzing have been broken down into smaller parts? Could a series of simpler, varied activities have worked better?

_____

_____

_____

3.   Look at an activity you're currently planning to use in line with a lesson plan objective. Is it more complex than it needs to be? Is any part of it not really squarely addressing the objective?

_____

_____

_____

4.   How might you simplify it or break it into a sequence of shorter, simpler activities?

_____

_____

_____

SHORTEST PATH

Cutting Edges

No classroom approach or method is good or bad except in terms of how well it provides the *Shortest Path* to your lesson and unit objectives.

Think about some teaching approach you're considering in light of a specific lesson objective you are planning. What is the objective?

_____

What in the approach keeps the class focused on the objective you have planned?

_____

_____

_____

How does the approach fulfill the objective?

_____

_____

| 1 **NO OPT OUT** |
| 2 **RIGHT IS RIGHT** |
| 3 **STRETCH IT** |
| 4 **FORMAT MATTERS** |
| 6 **BEGIN WITH THE END** |
| 7 **4 MS** |

Our experience tells us that the techniques in Section One in this guide are essential to maintaining high academic expectations. How well does the approach you're examining mesh with those techniques? If the mesh is less than perfect for your particular class and students, what challenges might this raise for reaching the lesson objective?

_____

_____

_____

For the objective you have chosen, brainstorm what might be an effective *Shortest Path*.

_____

_____

The Other Dr. J

Samuel Johnson—a.k.a. Dr. Johnson, the eighteenth-century polymath who created what is regarded as the first modern dictionary—once wrote, "Read over your compositions, and wherever you meet with a passage you think is particularly fine, strike it out." In writing, and in lesson planning, loving something can blind us to the fact that it is more clever than useful. Choose three lesson activities you love and apply the Dr. Johnson test to them: find the part you think "particularly fine." Is it truly useful or merely clever? (There is nothing wrong with strategically using engaging activities in order to keep students motivated, but it is important that you can justify their use.)

Activity 1: _____

_____

What's useful about it? _____

_____

Activity 2: _____

_____

What's useful about it? _____

_____

_____

Activity 3: _____

_____

What's useful about it? _____

_____

_____

PRACTICE WITH STUDY GROUP OR PARTNERS

Simpler?

As a group, share and compare what you found and learned from "Can It Be Simpler?" and "The Other Dr. J" in the previous section.

More Cutting Edges

As a group, revisit and retry "Cutting Edges" in the previous section.

The *Facilitator* can prepare by polling members about what novel approach or approaches they want most to examine. The *Facilitator* can also poll them about what sort of lesson plan objectives they'd like to test against the approach and draft a common objective accordingly. Members can prepare by bringing any brief descriptive materials they have about an approach.

Conclude by discussing, overall, for what types of lesson plan objectives and unit objectives the approach might be the *Shortest Path*.

TRY *SHORTEST PATH* IN YOUR PLANNING

1.   Apply *Shortest Path* to your next lesson plan. It may or may not lead to some change in the plan.

2.   After the lesson, look back at the plan and your experience in the class. What might have been a useful *Shorter Path*?

3.   Consider *Shortest Path* as part of your next several lesson plans. If it's valuable to you as a separate step, build it in. If it's not, shorten your own planning path. Come back to it when you think you need it.

SHORTEST PATH

SUSTAIN YOUR PROGRESS

1. Using feedback from your study group or other peers, and reviewing your own lesson notes and observations, monitor your progress on *Shortest Path*.

Date	How I Tried *Shortest Path*	Results?

2. Revisit "Where Am I Now?" Are you ready to build out to some other new technique?

SHORTEST PATH

DOUBLE PLAN

OVERVIEW

To *Double Plan* means that you plan what your students will be doing at each point in the class. For example, what will *they* be doing while you're introducing or reviewing certain ideas, details, or skills? When you say, "Discuss key aspects of oxygenation," are you discussing it or are they? If so, how? And how are those who aren't talking tracking the discussion?

A tool for this could be a lesson plan with two columns—one noting what you are doing and the other noting what students are doing at the same moment. This literal doubling can get you into the habit of thinking about lessons from both sides—yours and the students'. Once you absorb the concept of *Double Plan,* you probably won't need to do it quite so literally all the time. But it's good discipline to return to it now and then to make sure you are keeping your students engaged.

WHERE AM I NOW?

	Proficiency			
Comfort & Confidence	I am brand new to *Double Plan* . . .	I'm familiar with it, though I haven't tried it in my planning . . .	I'm beginning to *Double Plan* . . .	I *Double Plan* all the time . . .
	❏ . . . and excited to try it.	❏ . . . but know with more practice I'll make it work.	❏ . . . and love how it basically works.	❏ . . . efficiently, in terms of my planning time.
	❏ . . . and not at all sure it's for me.	❏ . . . because, frankly, I doubt its value.	❏ . . . but it doesn't seem to work or suit me.	❏ . . . but sometimes it seems unnecessary.

EXPAND YOUR SKILLS AND REPERTOIRE

Options

1. Which of the following behaviors do you ask of your students when you find it necessary to speak for an extended moment about something they need to be learning? How effectively do they follow through?

Repeating what you say

_____

_____

_____

Listening attentively, eyes on you, pencils down

_____

_____

_____

Listening for the answer(s) to a question you have posed in advance

_____

_____

_____

Mentally forming some response

_____

_____

_____

Mentally predicting what question or conclusion you are leading up to

_____

_____

_____

Making some specific response on a worksheet or blank sheet of paper

_____

_____

_____

Looking at something you're using to demonstrate

_____

_____

_____

Searching the page of a book for some specific information

_____

_____

_____

Studying other evidence

_____

_____

_____

Taking notes

_____

_____

_____

Writing occasional reflections

_____

_____

_____

Marking up a text with margin notes and underlines

_____

_____

_____

Working at the board

_____

_____

_____

Reflecting with a partner

_____

_____

_____

DOUBLE PLAN

Drafting questions of their own raised by your presentation

_____

_____

_____

2.   What other things do you or might you want students to be doing while you speak? What would be the learning benefit of each?

_____

_____

_____

3.   In the "What I and They Do" grid, write some things you often do in class. What should students be doing at the same time? What are some of them actually doing that's different from what you desire? What better things can you *plan* for them to be doing?

What I and They Do

What I'm Doing	What They Should Be Doing (Desired Response)	What Else They Are Doing (Undesired)	Better or Additional Things for Them to Do

Taking Notes

1. Starting with the basic concept described in *Board = Paper,* the advice in Overview to Section 5: The Importance of Routines, and the bulleted points that follow here, what routine or activity ideas can you use to sharpen your students' behavior when they should be "taking notes"?

14 **BOARD = PAPER**

- Where will they be taking notes? On a blank sheet of paper? On an organizer you've designed?
- Will they then review those notes and write a quick one-sentence summary?

2. Under what circumstances might you want students to be marking or writing on a schematic drawing, map, graph, or similar image that deserves their attention? (If you need to provide a preprinted sheet, is there a way that the same sheet can serve some related objective-driven activity in the next class session, too?)

Whole Class Questions

What preparations do you need to make or instructions do you need to plan to give to make sure students will be playing their expected role?

If you can, describe a recent moment when students shifted away from what you thought they should be doing in pursuit of the lesson objective. Include what you were doing at the time.

1. _____

_____

_____

Describe two similar recent moments.

2. _____

_____

3. _____

_____

At each of these moments, what did you intend the students to be doing, or what would have been their best use of the moment? Write your ideas in brief language that you could insert into a lesson plan.

6 **BEGIN WITH THE END**

1. _____

_____

2. _____

_____

3. _____

_____

DOUBLE PLAN

PRACTICE WITH STUDY GROUP OR PARTNERS

Bring several of your lesson plans to the meeting.

1. Compare thoughts with the group about how *Double Plan* works for you. If you incorporate it into your written lesson plan, show or explain where and how.

2. What benefits, if any, does *Double Plan* produce in terms of meeting the lesson's objective?

3. Look over your lesson plans for places (or more places) you might want to *Double Plan*. Mark up the plan. Share your rationale and actual wording with the group.

Your takeaways:

_____

_____

_____

TRY *DOUBLE PLAN*

1. Add some *Double Plan* thinking to the next lesson plan you create. Also plan to ensure that students know what you expect them to be doing.

2. After class, look back at the plan. Were the *Double Plan* parts of it helpful? Add notes about what you might want to change in future lesson plans.

SUSTAIN YOUR PROGRESS

1. Using feedback from your study group or other peers, and reviewing your own lesson notes and observations, monitor your progress with *Double Plan*.

Date	How I *Double Plan* Now	Ways to Improve

2. Revisit "Where Am I Now?" Are you ready to build out to some other new technique?

DRAW THE MAP

OVERVIEW

Draw the Map refers to consciously designing and shaping the physical environment in which you teach. Take an ongoing interest in evaluating seating arrangements, posted materials, and so forth to ensure that they support each day's lesson plan and objectives, rather than some general philosophical or personal preference.

You can start to *Draw the Map* by considering what questions you ask yourself (or not) about the physical setting you control.

WHERE AM I NOW?

Proficiency			
❏ I am brand new to *Draw the Map*.	❏ I'm currently making notes about things I may want to change and how.	❏ I'm actively improving the physical layout.	❏ I'm maintaining a system of layout that serves ongoing and changing needs.

ANALYZE THE CHAMPIONS

Every video clip that comes with this guide shows ways a classroom can be arranged to good advantage. Browse the clips for insights now or as you work on the activities for this technique. Especially watch to whom the students are oriented, paths for the teacher to *Circulate,* and what is and isn't on the walls. Often, you'll see the *SLANT* expectation prominently displayed.

15 **CIRCULATE**
32 **SLANT**

EXPAND YOUR SKILLS AND REPERTOIRE

Seating

Your Current Thoughts

1. When should your students interact in school?

_____

_____

2. When should your students interact mainly with each other in your classroom? What physical arrangements best support this?

_____

_____

3. When should they interact mainly with you rather than one another? What physical arrangements best support this?

_____

_____

4. How much time do they spend working independently? What physical arrangements best support this?

_____

_____

5. What signs have you seen that your current classroom layout either promotes or detracts from what you want (as stated for questions 2 through 4)?

_____

_____

Your Current Map

Draw the Map includes making space planning part of your unit and lesson planning. With pencil on graph paper or some other equally convenient and revisable surface, diagram the existing desk and seating pattern and the locations of doors, windows, blackboards, and any other significant objects.

How would you generally describe your current seating: rows, pods, in the round, or some other form? Did you lay it out or inherit it? Do you share it with other teachers? What seems good about it? What activities does it support well, and from what activities does it detract?

_____

_____

_____

_____

Pods Versus Rows

Kindergarten and early elementary rooms often have places where students can gather on a matted floor for activities like listening to reading. They may also do activities that require table space rather than small desk surfaces. Generally, however, most teachers of large classes need to choose a default seating arrangement based on pods or rows. Which is your best default?

Pods

Pods generally arrange students to face each other, with the rationale that students should be socialized to interact in school. But it's worth asking what advantages or disadvantages pods present.

Advantages

- When an activity requires students to be interacting mainly with each other in a small group, the pod places them face-to-face and facilitates exchange of speech and visual contact.

- Pods make it easy for students to generally support each other in their work.

- Pods make it easy for small groups to share or exchange materials.

- Clustering students in a pod around one large table at the center can offer more space than having separate desks all facing a center point.

- What other advantages do you see in pods for your classroom?

_____

_____

Disadvantages

- When students need to watch the teacher or study something on a board or wall, they may need to twist around or swivel back and forth between the teacher and their work materials. Or their view (and the teacher's of them) may be blocked by other students.

- Students are more likely to pay attention to another student directly across from them than to a teacher who is outside their normal view.

- Territorial squabbles can arise, especially involving feet and leg room. Property squabbles can also arise.

- It may be difficult for students to interact with students in another pod when the teacher wants them to do so.

- What other disadvantages do you see in pods for your classroom?

_____

_____

Rows

Rows orient all students toward the "front" of the room—the board or other main display and the usual spot of the teacher.

Advantages

- Row layout is tidy and orderly, and it socializes students to attend to the board and the teacher as their primary focus.

- Rows allow the teacher to stand directly beside any student as he or she teaches, checks work, or ensures that students are on task. Rows allow teachers to track students' eyes more directly and make it easier to scan the room for attentiveness.

- Row seating gives every student a place to write that is directly in line with what he or she is supposed to be writing about in most cases.

- The orientation of seats eliminates the distraction of always looking directly into other students' faces.

- Rows make it easy for students to distribute or pass materials quickly and efficiently.
- What other advantages do you see in rows for your classroom?

_____

_____

Disadvantages
- Rows put some students at the backs of others, where they may hide or distract the student in front of them.
- Rows place some students at the "head" of the class and others at the "back."
- What other disadvantages do you see in rows for your classroom?

_____

_____

A third option is "seminar seating." It's harder to arrange if you have thirty students (or close to that), but involves students sitting in a squared semicircle around the room. This makes it easy to attend both to teacher instruction and to discussion from and among the whole class. Thus it might be ideal for discussion of a novel.

There is no one right answer to your classroom layout. But the value of some traditional structures can often be underestimated. Columns of paired rows like those shown in Figure 11.1 allow students to work independently, in pairs, or as a whole group, or to attend to teacher-led content. Could this work for you?

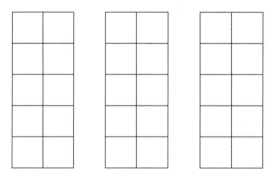

FIGURE 11.1. Three Paired Columns of Rows

Aisles and Alleys

| 15 **CIRCULATE** |
| 30 **TIGHT TRANSITIONS** |

Circulate and *Tight Transitions* both depend on the teachers' and students' being able to move about individually and as groups.

As you *Draw the Map,* pay as much attention to aisles and alleys as you do to seating. As teacher, you should be able to get anywhere in the room (preferably to within a foot of any student, so that you can whisper in his or her ear to encourage, correct, observe, or instruct without leaning across anyone)—without a word to anyone else. Once you have to say "Excuse me" to ask students to push in a chair or move backpacks, you are essentially asking permission and interrupting your lesson. Lay out paths so that you don't cede your full natural access to every part of the room.

Walls

Items on walls can help or hinder the focus and work of the class. Use the points here as the basis for a checklist as you plan and change the objects on the walls:

- Do they stimulate students as you intend and from the directions you want students to face?

  _____

  _____

- Do they distract or overstimulate or divert attention from what matters to the course objectives?

  _____

  _____

- Are potential distractions too close to the primary instructional space you are using?

  _____

  _____

- Is there clutter?

  _____

  _____

- Is there order that supports your objectives?

  _____

  _____

- Are *most* posted items useful tools (key steps, concepts, typologies, rules for interaction or for bathroom use) rather than student work? Teachers are frequently told to post student work, but posting tools like these is actually more important.

  _____

  _____

- Have you given prime location to the tools?

  _____

  _____

- Is there attractive student work that reinforces pride, participation, and mastery? Have you annotated the work not just with "Great job!" but with notes that show how other students can replicate success? (Example: "Your care in aligning these numbers makes adding them easy!")

  _____

  _____

DRAW THE MAP

- Is the overall look appropriately cheerful for the grade level of your class?

_____

_____

- Are objects current? Once you've taught a key skill, posting a related tool quickly thereafter helps students review it and use it frequently.

_____

_____

PRACTICE WITH STUDY GROUP OR PARTNERS

To the group, bring photos of the walls and the current map of your classroom. Come prepared also to describe how well the arrangement serves your needs.

1. Going around the group, show and tell how your arrangement helps you
    - Maintain focus on each day's learning objective.
    - *Circulate* and allow students to move about as needed.
    - See which students are paying attention at any given moment.
    - Avoid unnecessary distractions from inside or outside the room.
    - Make important tools available.
    - Stay abreast and keep students abreast of where the class is in its overall unit progress.
    - Make your classroom a pleasant place throughout the day.

2. After everyone has shown and told, go around again to say what you may want to change and why. Invite suggestions from the group. What help did you get?

_____

_____

_____

_____

BE CREATIVE

Notice how things are arranged in the school outside your classroom, such as in the immediate hall. Whether or not you personally control that space, is there anything you'd like to change because, for example, you might be able to reduce hallway noise that distracts students from the lesson?

DRAW THE MAP

SUSTAIN YOUR PROGRESS

1. Using feedback from your study group or other peers, and reviewing your own lesson notes and observations, monitor your progress on *Draw the Map*.

Date	Latest Way to Improve	How and When to Start

2. Revisit "Where Am I Now?" Are you ready to build out to some other new technique?

THE HOOK

OVERVIEW

You don't need a *Hook* every day, but an exciting opening can inspire students and introduce *any* material to *any* class in a captivating, inspiring, and stimulating way. This ensures that there is no boring content, just the challenge of finding a compelling way in. A *Hook* should strive to be

- Short—a few minutes at most
- Energetic and optimistic
- A smooth transition to more substantive things

WHERE AM I NOW?

	Proficiency			
	I am brand new to *The Hook* . . .	I'm familiar with *The Hook,* though I haven't planned it very often . . .	I'm beginning to plan and use *The Hook* . . .	I *Hook* 'em good! . . .
Comfort & Confidence	❑ . . . and excited to try it.	❑ . . . but know with more practice I'll make it work.	❑ . . . and love how it basically works.	❑ . . . in my own distinctive, varied ways.
	❑ . . . and undecided about my ability to pull it off.	❑ . . . because I still have questions about how to do it right.	❑ . . . with mixed results I need to evaluate.	❑ . . . but may need to vary it more.
	❑ . . . and not at all sure it's for me.	❑ . . . because, frankly, I still would rather wing it.	❑ . . . but it doesn't seem to work or suit me.	❑ . . . but when class isn't going well, I do it poorly and it doesn't help.

Work from your strengths. If you find yourself in the bottom left portion, leaf through this technique to locate related ones you might prefer to work on right now.

EXPAND YOUR SKILLS AND REPERTOIRE

The Hook is a compelling transition into the main objective of the lesson. It can be an anecdote or an intriguing fact, and the more you ponder it, the more likely you can make it stimulate and surprise students and grab their attention.

Objects, photos, and other visuals can add fascination to *The Hook,* and you can mount them in view throughout the session to strengthen interest and focus. Actual objects, photos, and such will probably be more exciting than things shown on a computerized screen. Brief audio recordings can also draw students to many topics.

The Hook dwells on what's great about numbers or about Shakespeare, not what's hard or daunting or difficult about them—unless that's what's great. Try this:

| 11 **DRAW THE MAP** |

| 5 **WITHOUT APOLOGY** |

1. Choose a topic that you teach: _____

2. List all the things that make that topic interesting or important:

_____

_____

_____

_____

3. After selecting one or two items from your list, briefly describe the interesting and important aspects of the topic aloud and with full animation. If you can, tell a story about it.

4. Describe it again two more times in other terms of greatness.

5. For the same topic, briefly describe "to the class" the excitement of what you and the class are about to do and learn.

"You're going to be amazed at . . ."

6. Now describe "to the class" how they will be "masters" of this great topic by the end of the session (in other words, what will they know or be able to do).

PRACTICE WITH STUDY GROUP OR PARTNERS

1. Bring (or at the meeting, write down) *Hooks* that you have used in your classroom. Each member of the group should share at least one example of how he or she has effectively hooked the class on a challenging lesson objective. How did he or she get the idea and material that were needed to make *The Hook* work?

2. Think of a *Hook* that "went wrong." What happened? Which of the criteria listed in the "Overview" did *The Hook* not meet? Discuss your experience with the group and jot down notes about how you might adapt it in the future to make it more effective:

_____

_____

_____

_____

3. Share instances of lessons that may have lacked a *Hook*. What was the objective? What sort of *Hook* might have worked? Share examples of effective *Hooks* for a similar objective and how the successful angler came up with it.

THE HOOK

Your takeaways:

_____

_____

_____

_____

TRY *THE HOOK* IN THE CLASSROOM

1. You may not need a *Hook* for every lesson, but when you need one, do not leave it to chance. Develop it and include it in the lesson plan.

| 6 **BEGIN WITH THE END** |

2. Consider adding some visual element to the verbal that can be on display throughout the session.

3. Plan to combine *The Hook* with short questions whose answers lead into the more substantive next phase of the session.

4. What value may there be in revisiting *The Hook* near the end of the class session?

5. When one lesson plan is closely linked to the next, one basic *Hook* idea might be extended in some way to serve (and unite the themes of) several sessions. For example, in session one, give one intriguing fact about the strange *anatomy* of a snail; in session two, give another related intriguing fact about snail *behavior*.

6. Reflect back on your last five *Hooks*. Is there one type of *Hook* you tend to use more frequently than others? (Overuse of one type can sometimes limit its effectiveness.) Are there other types you never use? Plan to use one type of *Hook* you rarely or never use.

7. The biggest risk of a *Hook* is that it goes on too long. Too short is better than too long, as it intrigues students and leaves them wanting more. Protect yourself by starting with the minimum and timing how long it takes.

TROUBLE-SHOOT

| 9 **SHORTEST PATH** | Be brief. Know how you'll transition soon to the substance of the lesson.

BE CREATIVE

A fishing hook has more than a sharp point. It has a barb that keeps the point in place, a curve that secures the lip of the fish, a size and shaft to match the size of fish you are after, a way to fasten the fisherman's line to the hook, and tempting bait! What further, analogous thoughts does this spark in you about *The Hook*?

Is there a way you can involve one or more students in the actual delivery of *The Hook,* with or without prior arrangement with them?

SUSTAIN YOUR PROGRESS

1.   Using feedback from your study group or other peers, and reviewing your own lesson notes and observations, monitor your progress at employing *The Hook*.

Date	Good *Hook* I Used	New Type of *Hook*

2.   Revisit "Where Am I Now?" Are you ready to build out to some other new technique?

THE HOOK

Technique 13

NAME THE STEPS

OVERVIEW

Champion teachers notice that skills might seem easy to them but still often need to be broken apart for new learners. *Name the Steps* is the technique of breaking down complex tasks into discrete steps. Doing so allows students to follow the individual steps when a task is not intuitive or when they are confused. But the technique is not just a scaffold; it includes a surprising amount of metacognition: What am I doing now? Why? What am I doing next? This metacognitive work can allow students to develop intuition around whys and hows. *Name the Steps* can be divided into four activities:

1. Identify the steps.
2. Make steps "sticky" (memorable) by naming them and other means.
3. Help students see how the steps are related and how to build from step to step.
4. Switch back and forth between how students are solving this immediate problem and what basic process they are using or deriving. We call this "using two stairways." The goal is for students to be able to narrate separately the ongoing work on both the immediate problem and the underlying process.

| 16 **BREAK IT DOWN** |

Name the Steps is part of the broader technique called *Break It Down*.

WHERE AM I NOW?

<table>
<tr><th colspan="5">Proficiency</th></tr>
<tr><th rowspan="7">Comfort & Confidence</th><th>I am brand new to Name the Steps . . .</th><th>I'm in the planning and practice stage, but haven't tried it yet in class . . .</th><th>I'm beginning to try Name the Steps in my classroom . . .</th><th>I use Name the Steps whenever it's needed in class . . .</th></tr>
<tr><td>❑ . . . and excited to try it.</td><td>❑ . . . but know I'll make it work.</td><td>❑ . . . and am pleased by how it works.</td><td>❑ . . . and am adding my own distinctive touches.</td></tr>
<tr><td>❑ . . . and undecided about my ability to pull it off.</td><td>❑ . . . because I still have questions about how to do it right.</td><td>❑ . . . with mixed results I need to evaluate.</td><td>❑ . . . but may need to consider how much time it sometimes takes.</td></tr>
<tr><td>❑ . . . and not sure it's for me.</td><td>❑ . . . because I still doubt I can use all four aspects of the technique.</td><td>❑ . . . but it doesn't seem to work or suit my setting.</td><td>❑ . . . but don't often climb on that second "stairway."</td></tr>
</table>

Work from your strengths. If you find yourself in the bottom left portion, leaf through this technique to locate related ones you might prefer to work on right now.

EXPAND YOUR SKILLS AND REPERTOIRE

1. Identify Steps

The first order of business is for you to identify steps. One objective of a great science teacher might be for students to learn how to study a specimen of an animal in order to determine what species it belongs to. This might involve posing an initial question or step and then, depending on the answer, posing a certain second question or step, and so forth. The exercise might lead to learning a broader *process* of steps for assessing other animal specimens.

The Steps of a Library Skill

Suppose you're about to send four eighth-grade students to the library. They've been there before, but this is the first time that their task is to *check out one book that they can start with* in writing a paper about a species of animal they've chosen to research. You want them to accomplish this in about fifteen minutes. The library has an easy-to-use computer catalogue for its books, which are on open shelves.

Write a list of up to seven steps that the students will take with them to the library in order to choose the book. Express each step as an instruction the students can follow. Take several minutes now to do it.

1. _____

2. _____

3. _____

4. _____

5. _____

6. _____

7. _____

Now go back to your list and make sure that you haven't included too many steps. Limit the number by making sure that you've included only steps that are absolutely essential to checking out one book, and eliminating those that are not.

2. Make Steps "Sticky"

Once you've got your steps, try to give each one a brief, memorable name that is likely to stick in your students' minds. Also try making the set of steps and their names even "stickier" by creating a story or a mnemonic device around the names for your steps.

A Stickier Library List

Realistically, once they're on the loose in the library, your eighth graders may not read every item on the list with great care. Try revising the list into shorter language that's easier to follow. Then create a name (a word or two) for each step and add it in the brackets. Then name the list as a whole.

List name: _____

1. [   ] _____

_____

2. [   ] _____

_____

3. [   ] _____

_____

4. [   ] _____

_____

5. [   ] _____

_____

6. [   ] _____

_____

7. [   ] _____

_____

8. [   ] _____

_____

A Stickier *Field Guide*

The *Field Guide* contains various lists of steps for you, the reader, or for students to follow. Browse through them (and other lists of component ideas, such as "What's *Pepper* Made Of?" in *Pepper* and "Calm Finesse" in *100%*) for any you could make stickier by naming the steps, rephrasing the wording of the steps or their names to create a useful acronym, creating a mnemonic device, or by any other means. Apply those methods to at least one of the lists. Write down your results:

| 24 **PEPPER** |
| 36 **100%** |

_____

_____

_____

_____

_____

3. Build the Steps

As the teacher, you want to know ahead of time the list of steps that will serve your students best. But a valuable activity might be getting the class to plan the steps themselves, perhaps starting from a short list of questions that you supply, such as, in the library example,

"How might you discover what books or group of books might be about your subject?"

"Beyond the title, how can you quickly figure out what is actually in the book?"

"If the entire book isn't about your subject, how can you figure out whether it contains a fair amount about your subject?"

From these three questions, students or the class at large might come up with a workable list that makes use of the computerized catalogue, the arranging of books in terms of subjects, and items inside the book itself, like the table of contents or index.

This kind of challenge also involves students in figuring out the steps to follow if something stumps their basic list (for example, if the library computer is "down").

3 **STRETCH IT**

4. Use Two Stairways

Once students know the steps, classrooms can have two parallel conversations going at once: how to find a solution to the current problem and how to solve any similar problem. In other words, students can narrate the *process* or the *problem,* and a great teacher switches back and forth. For example:

1	*Teacher:*	What's the next step, Paul? [process]
2	*Paul:*	Multiply the numerators.
3	*Teacher:*	Okay, what are the numerators? [problem]
4	*Paul:*	The numerators are 4 and 1.
5	*Teacher:*	So the numerator in our solution is going to be? [problem]
6	*Paul:*	It's going to be 4.
7	*Teacher:*	Okay, good. So, Sasha, what do we need to do next? [process]
8	*Sasha:*	We need to multiply the denominators.
9	*Teacher:*	And the answer is? [problem]
10	*Sasha:*	The denominator should be 2.
11	*Teacher:*	So I'm done; right, Conrad? [process]
12	*Conrad:*	No, you have to reduce.
13	*Teacher:*	Perfect. So what's our final answer? [problem]
14	*Conrad:*	The answer is 2.

Remember that you can ask a student to

- Explain the *process* while you perform the concrete steps in this case.
- Perform the steps while *you* explain the process.
- Both do the steps and explain the process.

You can also

- Ask one student to concentrate on the problem while another student concentrates on the process.
- Make mistakes and ask students where you went wrong or might have used a better step.

PRACTICE WITH STUDY GROUP OR PARTNERS

Back to the Library

To the group, bring your library activity work from "Expand Your Skills and Repertoire."

1. Compare your experiences as you worked on the problem.

2. Compare your actual lists of steps. Do any lists stand out for

- Steps other lists missed?
- A good level of ease and precision in each step?
- A good sequence of steps?
- Stickiness of steps?
- Other reasons?

3. Overall, which lists seem likely to work best for the students? Why?

4. What's another search activity you might want your students to learn in another setting, such as a museum, gallery, or zoo?

- What similarities in process might that bear to the library task?
- What actual process steps might apply well to both?

Back to the Guide

As a group, compare what you did individually in "Make Steps 'Sticky'" to make a stickier *Field Guide*. Possibly select and work together on a different list in the *Field Guide*.

Challenges for Different Grade Levels

In the group, discuss the challenges that you and your particular students have in the following areas. Explain what you do to work on them. Ask other group members to share possible strategies or solutions. Challenges can include

- Understanding and following lists
- Moving to the level of process
- Applying the level of process back to specific instances
- Switching between the two stairways

Your takeaways:

_____

_____

_____

_____

TRY *NAME THE STEPS* IN THE CLASSROOM

1. Consult your next few lesson plans and find one whose objective can be served in part by an activity that involves breaking down some task into steps.

2. Identify the steps as they would apply to a single instance or problem, and plan how you will present them or how you will help the class build them.

3. Possibly identify each step with an underlying process that generalizes to similar problems.

4. Script some pairs of questions to ask that will move students back and forth between steps to solve the immediate problem and the steps as a general process.

5. If appropriate, ahead of time or as part of class activity, create a poster of process steps as a tool that students can consult in future sessions.

6.   Consider an activity that involves the students *taking notes* on steps. Consider the notes as a resource they can look back to when they get stuck in another problem for which they might need to retrace their steps to see where they strayed. Students can also use the notes as a tool for working out the underlying, more generalized pattern of steps in a process, possibly to consult during homework.

14 **BOARD = PAPER**

TROUBLE-SHOOT

Steady On

Test your list of steps on a variety of examples before you teach it to students. Are there cases to which the steps won't apply? Adapt the steps or plan how you'll explain limitations to students.

Other Challenges

Possible Challenge	Possible Solutions

BE CREATIVE

Have your students reached a point at which they've learned a certain set of steps so well that they might try the whole task without deliberate "stepping-stones"? Could such a whole-task activity help them see which, if any, steps they might need to shore up?

39 **DO IT AGAIN**

NAME THE STEPS

NAME THE STEPS

SUSTAIN YOUR PROGRESS

1. Using feedback from your study group or other peers, and reviewing your own lesson notes and observations, monitor your progress on *Name the Steps*.

Date	Good Stairway I Just Taught	Steps That Might Need Repair

2. Revisit "Where Am I Now?" Are you ready to build out to some other new technique?

BOARD = PAPER

OVERVIEW

Board = Paper is a technique for modeling the habit of taking classroom notes—the kind that capture information you present (or the class itself discovers). Ultimately the notes may also record the student's own perspective on that knowledge.

In their written notes, younger students generally should start by replicating exactly what their teacher writes on the board (or shows on an overhead), and the teacher makes that expectation explicit at first by using an overhead projector (or other device) that displays a copy of the sheet on which students take their own notes.

Over time, students learn to take notes on their own, gradually earning more autonomy as they learn structured note-taking skills through modeling.

WHERE AM I NOW?

	Proficiency			
	I am brand new to *Board = Paper* . . .	**I'm in the planning and learning stage, though I haven't tried it yet in class . . .**	**I'm beginning to try *Board = Paper* in my classroom . . .**	**I use this *Board = Paper* as needed . . .**
Comfort & Confidence	❑ . . . and excited to try it.	❑ . . . but feel confident it will work in developing note-taking skills.	❑ . . . and love how it basically works.	❑ . . . and gradually shifting more responsibility onto the students.
	❑ . . . and undecided about my ability to pull it off.	❑ . . . because I still have questions about how to do it right.	❑ . . . with mixed results I need to evaluate.	❑ . . . adapting it to my students' current level of writing and note-taking skills.
	❑ . . . and not at all sure it's for me.	❑ . . . because I still have serious doubts.	❑ . . . but I'm not sure how it moves students toward fuller note-taking skills.	

EXPAND YOUR SKILLS AND REPERTOIRE

Students need to learn how to take effective notes. Even late into high school (and after), many have not acquired the skills to make sense of an instruction like "Take careful notes" or know what to do when there's no instruction given.

Board = Paper involves modeling and scaffolding. It starts with your modeling exactly what the notes should be and allows you to gradually shift more and more actual note-taking thought and work onto the students themselves.

At the start, students fill out blank sections in a graphic organizer. Over time the blanks get larger.

***Board = Paper* Overhead Example**

SETTING

The Basics

The basic definition of the setting of a story is its (*time*) and (*place*).

Taking Setting to the Collegiate Level

This year, we are going to consider the (*five*) facets of setting.

1. (*Place*): (*geographic*) location. (*Where*) is the action of the story (*taking*) place?
2. (*Time*): (*When*) is the story taking place?
   - (*historical*) period, time of (*year*)
3. (*Weather*) conditions: Is it (*rainy, stormy*), sunny, etc.?
4. (*Social*) conditions: What is the (*daily*) life of the (*characters*)?
5. Mood or (*atmosphere*): What (*feeling*) is created in the story?
   - Is it bright and (*cheerful*) or (*dark*) and frightening?

Marking Up the Text

When you see any of these facets in the text, mark it up as follows in the margin . . .

- P = (*place*)
- T = (*time*)
- WC = (*weather*) conditions
- SC = (*social*) conditions
- MOA = mood or (*atmosphere*)

Gradually, students should progress in the amount of the note taking over which they exercise discretion, filling out longer and longer passages of their graphic organizers on their own and finally taking notes on a separate sheet of paper as you write terms and definitions on the board exactly as you wish students to copy them down. In the long run, the exercise can shift to students' helping determine what the stems should be and eventually taking notes from the board or other sources on their own.

In the course of scaffolding, tell students what to title their notes, when to skip a line, and how to make subheadings and headings. When they can reliably do this, you can also begin to divest yourself gradually of responsibility for exact phrasing and let students own that, too. Remember that it takes years before most students are ready to own full responsibility for such a critical process as taking notes.

PRACTICE WITH STUDY GROUP OR PARTNERS

The *Facilitator* may need to arrange equipment in advance. If possible, work with other teachers who teach at grade levels close to your own, but not all at exactly your level.

Before the meeting, create a *Board = Paper* organizer that you might use in a future lesson. If you don't yet have such a plan, create the organizer based on notes you wrote on the board in a previous lesson. Make copies for everyone in the group.

1. Depending on the size of your group, availability of an overhead, and so on, each group member might take a turn as *Teacher* and actually do *Board = Paper* with the other members as *Students*. Then discuss the experience from both perspectives.

2. Share copies and discuss them.

- What challenges arose as you created your organizer?
- Did creating the page cause you to alter your plans for what notes to present to the class? How so?
- What previous *Board = Paper* work prepared your class for this current level of note-taking challenge?
- What might be the next small step?
- What might be the next fairly large step?

3. Take advantage of what you learned from the group to improve your short- and longer-term plans for teaching note-taking skills.

TRY BOARD = PAPER IN THE CLASSROOM

1. In an upcoming lesson plan, identify an objective that can best be advanced in part by an activity involving *Board = Paper*.

> 6 **BEGIN WITH THE END**

2. In the lesson plan, consider how you can *Circulate* to *Check for Understanding* several times before you and the class have completed the page. Decide whether you will have your copy of the notes filled in ahead of time or will fill in the notes during class, or some combination of the two. Also plan how students will save their notes over the course of the year.

> 15 **CIRCULATE**
> 18 **CFU**

3. When you pass out the organizers, tell the class how they are part of a process of learning to take great notes. Explain what role note taking plays in important learning. Be explicit about what you expect them to do while taking notes and when you expect them to take notes during class (for example, while you're writing? when you've finished writing?).

4. Check the students' work often enough to be sure that no one is falling behind or having some persisting problem. The first

> 48 **EXPLAIN EVERYTHING**

few times, you may want to collect the sheets so that you can evaluate how well students are handling the level of challenge. Hand back the sheets at the next session, and, depending on what you found, give necessary feedback and possibly slightly increase the level of student responsibility. Let students know how and why you are shifting more responsibility to them.

TROUBLE-SHOOT

Steady On

Don't let yourself or your students slip into thinking of *Board = Paper* as filling out "worksheets." Keep *Board = Paper* consciously tied to the broader goal of learning to take one's own effective *notes*.

Other Challenges

Challenge	Possible Solutions
Students work at vastly different paces when filling in notes. Some students are finished and simply waiting for their classmates to finish note taking.	Provide a copy of the filled-in notes for "slower" note-taking students to fill in after class. Have challenge problems prepared for "faster" note-taking students to work on while they wait for classmates to complete notes.

BE CREATIVE

3 STRETCH IT

How might you extend the basic idea of *Board = Paper* to situations where students are taking notes on reading or on other things they can observe? How will you frame these activities in terms of building note-taking skills? And how will you gradually *Stretch It*?

SUSTAIN YOUR PROGRESS

1. Using feedback from your study group or other peers, and reviewing on your own lesson notes and observations, monitor your progress on *Board = Paper*.

Date	What the Class Can Handle Now	Likely Next Step

2. Revisit "Where Am I Now?" Are you ready to build out to some other new technique?

CIRCULATE

OVERVIEW

OVERVIEW

Circulate involves moving strategically around your room during a lesson, getting nearer to students when that's necessary for learning or for managing behavioral expectations.

Circulate doesn't assume that proximity itself is necessarily all that's required. *Circulate* means building your consciousness of how closer proximity can *abet* what else you do to address a need.

The classroom belongs to you. Move through it constantly and intentionally, and ally your movement with these aims and practices:

- Break the plane—the imaginary line separating the front of the room from students' desks.
- Maintain full access.
- Engage when you *Circulate*.
- Move systematically.
- Position for control and your rightful authority.

Consult *Check for Understanding* for many other suggestions related to engaging as you *Circulate*.

18 **CFU**

WHERE AM I NOW?

	Proficiency			
	I rarely *Circulate* . . .	I'm thinking about access and other issues, but I haven't tried yet to *Circulate* more effectively in class . . .	I'm beginning to *Circulate* more in my classroom . . .	I *Circulate* regularly, beginning early in every session, and use the benefits it bestows . . .
Comfort & Confidence	❏ . . . and am excited to do more of it.	❏ . . . but know with more preparation I'll start.	❏ . . . and love how it basically works.	❏ . . . and have my own style when I do.
	❏ . . . and am undecided about my ability to do it more.	❏ . . . because I still have questions about how to do it right.	❏ . . . with mixed results I need to evaluate.	❏ . . . but am still firming up certain uses of it.
	❏ . . . and am not at all sure these uses are for me.	❏ . . . because, frankly, I still have doubts or hesitations.	❏ . . . but am often not sure why I'm moving around.	❏ . . . but sometimes need to remind myself not to stay put.

Work from your strengths. If you find yourself in the bottom left portion, leaf through this technique to locate related ones you might prefer to work on right now.

CIRCULATE

ANALYZE THE CHAMPIONS

View each video clip, ideally more than once, and answer the following questions. See possible answers for clip 11 at the end of this technique.

 Clips 3 and 9. Teacher Lauren Catlett, Grade 5

How does Ms. Catlett's circulation make her teaching stronger?

 Clip 10. Teacher Dinah Shepherd, Grade 8

1. Why does Ms. Shepherd *not Circulate* during much of this clip?
2. What does she gain when she does *Circulate*? What's effective about how she *Circulates*?
3. What does she gain from moving to the back of the class?

 Clip 11. Teacher Nikki Frame, Grade 6

1. How does Ms. Frame engage with individual students in the course of her circulation?
2. How does she do so without impeding the progress of the class as a whole?
3. What purposes does she have when she engages?
4. Is Ms. Frame's circulation predictable?

EXPAND YOUR SKILLS AND REPERTOIRE

The "plane" of your classroom is the imaginary line that runs the length of the room, parallel to and about five feet in front of the board, usually about where the first student desks start. Don't hesitate to cross that line. It's *your* space. Range constantly and intentionally.

Break the Plane

Why?

*   To show that the classroom is yours
*   So that you can check and assist with the work of any individual student
*   To allow you to conduct behavioral interactions less visibly and less disruptively to other students in the class

Break It Early and Often

"Early" means—at the latest—within the first five minutes of every class session. This makes it clear to students that you "own the room" and that it is normal for you to go anywhere you want in it, at any time, without giving a reason.

| 36 **100%** |

Break it before a student behavior requires you to break it. This shows that you move where you want as a product of *your* decisions about *teaching*. Your movement is not controlled by negative behavior. Also, you want to be able to make most corrections as subtly as possible, rather than drawing everyone's attention to off-task students. If you *Circulate* early and often, your movement among the students will be less obvious and won't suggest that something is wrong.

Maintain Full Access

You must be able to

- Get anywhere at any time simply and easily without interrupting your teaching. For this you need wide, clear causeways (length *and* width) unencumbered by chairs or anything else.

11 **DRAW THE MAP**

- Get there *with no verbal interaction,* no matter how polite the "Excuse me" or other forms of asking for permission. Find a better place for backpacks than on the back of chairs.

- Simply and naturally stand next to any student in your room at any time and be able to keep talking about your lesson content. Seat your students in pairs so that you can stand directly next to anyone at any time.

- Do simple things simply, such as closing a door or adjusting the blinds, without diverting students to such nonlearning tasks.

Engage When You Circulate

Frequently interact verbally and nonverbally as you *Circulate*. As you *Circulate, Check for Understanding*.

18 **CFU**

Add to this list of things you could do or say as you *Circulate*. Notice that positive reinforcement can be a major part of the mix:

Put your hands subtly on a student's shoulders to remind him to sit up.

Say to a student, "You're close. Try that again."

Say "Just right; I like it" as you glance at a student's graph.

Say "Check your last step" as you gaze at a student's notes.

36 **100%**
37 **WHAT TO DO**
38 **STRONG VOICE**

Ask a question about what a student has written, such as, "But what about the mother? Does she question society?"

Show "thumbs up" to a student.

Notice that a student is on track without needing to point that out.

_____

_____

_____

_____

_____

With other techniques, prepare for the fact that proximity alone may not cause a student to correct an inappropriate behavior. Among other preparations, decide on some additional simple, obvious gestures that you can use to supplement proximity. (See clip 11.)

Move Systematically

Don't only address "trouble spots." Get to everyone. But vary your movement patterns and vary how much or how long you interact in different instances.

When there is a "trouble spot," keep relaxed and don't show anxiety. (Moving by "strolling" can help with this.) If you announce to your class, "I need everyone's eyes on me" and march directly toward Alphonse, you are telling him that you are worried that he will not comply. Alphonse may think you can be rattled.

To address Alphonse without creating any perception of anxiety, go somewhere else first and approach Alphonse just after, perhaps while students are jotting down notes. Or systematically move down each row. This signals that you regard and treat Alphonse as just another member of the class.

Be systematic yet not predictable. Avoid following the same pattern (left to right; clockwise around the room) all the time. Predictable patterns leave students freer to do as they wish until the moment they *know* you'll arrive at them. Routinely skip students here and there and take longer with some than with others so that your movements are less predictable.

Position for Control and Your Rightful Authority

Face the Room

As you *Circulate,* generally remain facing as much of the class as possible. This allows you to see what's going on around you at a glance and with the most minimal transaction cost. You can lift your eyes quickly from a student's paper and then return to reading in a fraction of a second. Turning your back, by contrast, invites opportunistic behavior.

Leverage Students' Blind Spots

The most authoritative position to be in with another person is one where you can see him, he knows you can see him, and where he can't see you. Standing just over a student's shoulder as you peruse his work and standing at the back of the classroom as a class discusses a topic are great ways to build subtle but pervasive control of your domain and keep it focused on learning.

PRACTICE WITH STUDY GROUP OR PARTNERS

Revisit the individual work you did in the previous section to share and compare your responses and see other options.

Circulate Role Play

This role play requires a *Facilitator.* There need to be at least five participants, but a larger number is better. If the size of the group allows, let everyone take a turn as *Teacher.* In each *Teacher*'s round, everyone else is a *Student.*

1. Before you meet, the *Facilitator*
   - Photocopies and cuts out the activity cards (make enough for all the *Students*). You can also devise and add other Distractive Activity Cards similar to the ones shown here.
   - Reproduce this Mock *Do Now* onto enough separate sheets of paper that there will be enough for each *Student* to use a fresh one in each round. (Participants don't need to fill in their names and the date; we include them here because in the classroom *Do Now* forms do generally require that information.)

2. In each round, the *Facilitator* selects one participant to play *Teacher.* If possible, arrange student seating to match the arrangement that the participant normally uses in the classroom.

3. The *Facilitator* also passes out two items to each *Student.* (When it's the *Facilitator*'s turn to be *Teacher,* someone else can pass them out.):
   - *Role play card.* Be sure to pass out a proportionate number of positive and distractive cards to simulate as close to a real classroom as possible, which tends to be more positive than distractive. If there are just four *Students,* make it two and two.
   - *Mock* Do Now *sheet.*

29 **DO NOW**

MOCK *DO NOW*

Name _____

Date _____

What have you done in the past few months that makes you feel proud?

_____

_____

_____

Write about the last time you were late for something.

_____

_____

_____

Write about how the Internet affects your life and your work.

_____

_____

_____

If you could have any superpower, what would it be and why?

_____

_____

_____

CIRCULATE ROLE PLAY CARDS

Positive Activity Cards

Circulate Role Play Work silently	**Circulate Role Play** Work silently
Circulate Role Play Work silently	**Circulate Role Play** Work silently
Circulate Role Play Work silently	**Circulate Role Play** Work silently

Distractive Activity Cards

Circulate Role Play Distraction Raise hand to say, "I don't understand this question."	**Circulate Role Play Distraction** Stare out the window, not working.
Circulate Role Play Distraction Move desk or chair slightly out of position. (Create a reason for doing so and tell the teacher if he or she asks you about it.)	**Circulate Role Play Distraction** Drop your pen or pencil in front of you where you can't reach, then spend time obviously trying to get it.
Circulate Role Play Distraction Slouch down in your chair.	**Circulate Role Play Distraction** Yawn and stretch repeatedly, every 5–10 seconds.

Taken from *Teach Like a Champion Field Guide: A Practical Resource to Make the 49 Techniques Your Own.* Copyright © 2012 by Doug Lemov.

4. The *Facilitator* explains to the group that the cards describe what *Students* should do while they are writing their answers. Mention that the instructions on the cards are not meant to be acted out in any markedly disruptive manner; they are merely small details that the *Teacher* should be able to notice and deal with as he or she *Circulates*.

5. While the *Students* are working on the Mock *Do Now,* the *Teacher* moves about, applying *Circulate* and other relevant techniques as called for.

6. The *Facilitator* stops the round after no more than three minutes. Between rounds and at the end, discuss ways the *Teacher* effectively used techniques, and what opportunities he or she might have overlooked. Also discuss the seating arrangement and how it affected *Circulate*.

What insights did you gain from this role play?

_____

_____

_____

_____

TRY *CIRCULATE* IN THE CLASSROOM

Know Your Lesson Plan

Liberate yourself from your desk by knowing your lesson plan inside out. If you need to glance at your plan or some other resource, put it on a clipboard and bring it with you.

Get to It

If you don't have time right now to "map" and "plan" (as described in the next two sections), start breaking the plane early and *Circulating* frequently anyway. This will get the precedent going and may also show you opportunities that will motivate you to map and plan.

Map It

Draw the Map of your classroom if you haven't already done it. Or consult your current map and make deliberate choices about how to maximize student engagement through your use of *Circulate*. Make changes that address these questions:

| 11 **DRAW THE MAP** |

- Are you able to break the plane of your classroom?
- Do you have access to *all* parts of the room?
- Are there any areas that are inaccessible or uncomfortable?
- Can you stand at the side and "over the shoulder" of each student?
- Are backpacks or paraphernalia a problem in your current layout?
- Currently, do students maintain any "no fly zones" by obvious or subtle means?
- Is outside light or any other factor hindering your ability to see or hear any student?
- As needed, can you easily—without interrupting your teaching or any student—close doors, open windows, adjust blinds, and so on?

Plan It

1. In your lesson plan, mark what you think will be the five-minute point. *Before* that point, mark where you intend to first break the plane and move out among the students if things are going along as expected.

2. When are the best moments of the lesson to remain in the front of the room? When are the best parts to use *Circulate*? Does the plan allow you to do so?

3. Are there specific locations you want to be in at certain moments of the lesson? Where are they?

4. How will you *Circulate* systematically but not too predictably? Can you plan for this?

| 18 **CFU** |
| 43 **POSITIVE FRAMING** |
| 44 **PRECISE PRAISE** |

| 36 **100%** |
| 37 **WHAT TO DO** |
| 38 **STRONG VOICE** |
| 42 **NO WARNINGS** |

5. How will you maximize your engagement with students while you *Circulate*? What will you be looking for and possibly saying?

6. Are there any new gestures you want to add as part of *Circulate*?

7. Try to anticipate the first moment that any "trouble spot" is likely to become troublesome. Plan to be *Circulating* before and at that moment.

8. Have you already noticed a moment in which, by itself, proximity to a student did not correct a misbehavior? If it arises again, what could you add to mere proximity?

9. After class, think back on the session and make notes for future sessions about

- Any tendency on your part not to "face the room," or other things you might improve
- Anything you noticed about positions of control and authority, blind spots, or other features of the room you could use more fully next time

TROUBLE-SHOOT

Steady On

By sprawl of body or belongings or by other means, students may try to cordon off "their" part of the classroom. Don't let this slide. Have expectations already in place about what space students occupy and how. When a student crosses those expectations, let him or her know *What to Do*. If one student often challenges you, start with a general direction and direct eye contact with her: "We're about to start. Backpacks fully under chairs in five, four, three . . ."

| 37 **WHAT TO DO** |

Other Challenges

Possible Challenge	Possible Solutions

SUSTAIN YOUR PROGRESS

1. Using feedback from your study group or other peers, and reviewing your own lesson notes and observations, monitor your progress on *Circulate*.

Date	Things I'm Doing Well	Ways to Improve

2. Revisit "Where Am I Now?" Are you ready to build out to some other new technique?

ANALYZE THE CHAMPIONS: SOME OBSERVATIONS

 Clip 11. Teacher Nikki Frame, Grade 6

As she *Circulates,* you see Ms. Frame keeping every student accountable with fast pacing and unpredictable *Cold Calls*. It's hard to catch the details in this clip, but when a student isn't ready to read, as she *Circulates* Ms. Frame quickly assigns a consequence (a $2 deduction from the student's paycheck) and moves on to the next student. Afterwards, Ms. Frame uses proximity to ensure that the student is in the right place and calls on him again, allowing him to feel success.

BREAK IT DOWN

OVERVIEW

When a student makes an error, *Break It Down* means turning the original material into a series of smaller, simpler parts (not necessarily "steps") and asking the students to work back to the right answer. The following are six especially effective ways to *Break It Down*:

1. *Provide an example:* "Salt is a compound. But sodium, of which it is partially made, is not. Can you define compound now?"

2. *Provide context:* "Remember that the world's population has been growing steadily."

3. *Provide a rule:* "A complete sentence has to have a subject. Can you find a subject in this one?"

4. *Provide the missing (or first) step:* "What do we always do when one number is a fraction and the other is a decimal?"

5. *Roll back:* Repeat a student's answer back to him or her.

| 1 **NO OPT OUT** |
| 2 **RIGHT IS RIGHT** |
| 3 **STRETCH IT** |
| 4 **FORMAT MATTERS** |

6. *Narrow or eliminate false choices:* "Let's consider the possibilities. A word can be a noun, a verb, a preposition, an article. What's a common preposition? . . . What does it do? . . . Does this word seem to be doing that?

Depending on the subject and what the student is struggling with, *Break It Down* can be a complex and challenging technique. You may want to work on developing and perfecting it after you feel at ease with *No Opt Out* and other techniques in Section One.

WHERE AM I NOW?

	Proficiency			
Comfort & Confidence	I am brand new to *Break It Down* as a broad technique . . .	I'm in the planning and practice stage, though I haven't tried it yet in class . . .	I'm beginning to try each kind of *Break It Down* in my classroom . . .	I use *Break It Down* regularly . . .
	❑ . . . and excited to master it.	❑ . . . but know with more practice I can make these ways work.	❑ . . . and love how they work so far.	❑ . . . and am adding my own touches.
	❑ . . . and undecided about my ability to pull off most of the ways described in the "Overview."	❑ . . . because I still have questions about how to do some part of it right.	❑ . . . with mixed results I need to evaluate.	❑ . . . but I may be spending too much time this way.
	❑ . . . and not at all sure it's for me.	❑ . . . but I still have doubts about some of these methods of *Breaking It Down*.	❑ . . . but most don't seem to work or suit me.	❑ . . . but when a student is really having trouble, I do it poorly and it doesn't help.

Work from your strengths. If you find yourself in the bottom left portion, leaf through this technique to locate related ones you might prefer to work on right now.

EXPAND YOUR SKILLS AND REPERTOIRE

Break It Down is an important, powerful teaching tool, but it can be challenging to use because it is primarily a *reactive* strategy. At the moment a student responds with an error, you help him *Break It Down* to correct it. Most times, simply re-asking the question isn't going to help. But what to do instead?

Ask another question or present new information that simplifies the part of the material that you think may have caused the error. From there, you help the student build back to a *Right Is Right* answer.

> **2 RIGHT IS RIGHT**

How *Break It Down* Works

A teacher never knows exactly how big the gap is between the student's knowledge and the knowledge necessary for mastery, but ideally he seeks to bridge just enough of the gap to allow the student to cross the rest of the way on her own. In other words, he wants to *break the original question down only a small amount*. Here's how any *Break It Down* tries to work:

1. The student answers incorrectly due to some lack of knowledge.
2. The teacher makes an educated guess about what the lack or gap might be—how close the student is to being able to answer correctly.
3. The teacher provides a cue (a strategic hint) or asks a question that focuses on some portion of the gap. How big a portion? It's a judgment call:
   - Breaking down some smaller portion (giving a smaller cue) demands more rigor from the student, which is good.
   - Breaking down in a larger sense (giving a larger cue) is faster, which may be necessary.
   - Ideally, the teacher's cue is just enough to close the actual gap in the student's knowledge. In some way the cue should help build the student's base of knowledge.

But even if you plan in this way, inevitably you must still often think on your feet. You can learn to think faster and better on your feet by being aware of general options like those in the "Overview."

Provide an Example

Examples work well and will come to mind most easily when a question has asked for a *definition*. You can ask other students to provide the example.

> **1 NO OPT OUT**

If the question involved an example, especially an abstract one, give an additional, possibly more concrete example.

"Cal, we're trying to determine what part of speech *owner* might be. Suppose the owner was Nancy over there . . . ?"

What could you say to provide an (or another) example that might help in each of the following situations? Try to fill a gap by building a student's base of knowledge.

"How did West Virginia come into being?"

(Additional knowledge you might want to employ: When Virginia joined the Confederacy in the Civil War, the western part of Virginia seceded from Virginia.)

"In grammar, what does *object* mean?"

   (*Additional knowledge you might employ:* Object *means the recipient of an action. Some are direct objects:* Mary *in "John kissed* Mary." *Others are indirect objects: "John sent* Mary *flowers"—sent* flowers *to Mary.)*

_____

_____

"Is a whale an example of a mammal?"

   (*Additional knowledge: Yes, and it lactates, has hair, gives live birth with an umbilical cord, has similar bone structure . . .)*

_____

_____

"For example, suppose I wanted to turn ice into water. What would I need to add?"

   (*Additional knowledge: One would need to add heat or calories or energy.)*

_____

_____

Provide Context

Context can serve to help students recall information they've encountered before:

Teacher: Is 23 prime?

Jethro: No.

Teacher: How so? Remember on Monday we listed some ways to test whether a number is prime. What did we conclude about 13? . . .

   Context can also mean giving new useful data to help answer a question. If the reason a student answers incorrectly is probably due to not understanding a word in the question, you can use the word in a different, related context.

Teacher: What does O. Henry mean by *supercilious* in this paragraph? Della.

Della: Sort of like *delicious*.

Teacher: Whenever I make a joke at home, instead of laughing, my wife gives that *supercilious* look I hate . . .

   A student gives a vague response to each of these questions. How might the teacher provide useful context?

"What does the author mean by *a teal coat*?"

   (*A coat or layer of the bluish color called teal)*

_____

_____

"So, why is Jefferson considered important?"

(Main author of the Declaration of Independence, US. president who made the Louisiana Purchase, founder of the University of Virginia, leader of the opposition to Federalism, and so on)

_____

_____

"Can you show us how to write the letter *y*?"
(Among other criteria, the tail of the y *should extend below the baseline of the word.)*

_____

_____

Supply a Rule

In the next situations, a student stumbles in response to the teacher's question. How might the teacher help *Break It Down* by providing a rule?

Teacher: What part of speech is *angular*?

   (Adjective; descriptor of something; same form as similar, familiar, *and so on)*

Student: It's an adverb?

_____

_____

Teacher: *An* is also a short word. Could it also be a preposition?

   (It's an article, like the. *Prepositions suggest time, belonging, direction, and so on.)*

Student: Plus it comes before a noun.

_____

_____

Teacher: Knowing just that it's very heavy, roughly where would you place uranium on the periodic table of elements—next to helium, here, for example?

   (Helium is a very light element, which places it in the top row of the table. Heavy elements fall in the rows further down. Helium has two protons. Uranium has ninety-two protons.)

Student: Well, helium is a gas, like oxygen, and uranium isn't a gas . . .

_____

_____

Teacher: Unless we're quoting someone else's speech, why can't we write, "She come in the door with a chip on her shoulder"?

   (Standard subject–verb agreement)

Student: It's not good English.

_____

_____

Provide the Missing (or First) Step
What step information could this teacher provide, either in statement or question form?

Teacher: Is this example a complete sentence?

Student: Well, the second word is a noun.

Statement form: _____

_____

Question form: _____

_____

Teacher: Is this example a complete sentence? Tell me how you know.

Student: It has a subject, and *maintains* is a verb word.

Statement form: _____

_____

Question form: _____

_____

Roll Back
Many of us instantly recognize our errors when they're played back for us as if on tape. Try repeating a student's answer back to him or her, or ask the student to repeat it.

"Kim, you said Grant was a great general because his men feared him. [Pause]. That doesn't sound exactly right."

"Kim, you just said that a pilot flying from Boston to Los Angeles would be flying *west* to *east* . . ."

Narrow or Eliminate False Choices
Celia answered incorrectly when you had the class read a paragraph and asked her what it suggested about the author's viewpoint. You might help her focus on the most crucial part.

"Celia, read the first two sentences again for us, aloud . . ."

Model how students might eliminate choices.

"We're trying to recognize elements. Should we include the metal brass? What do we know about how brass came into use—and where it comes from . . . So is brass an element? What do we know about these others—sodium, iron, steel, aluminum?"

Levels of *Break It Down*

You can do this next activity alone or (better) with a partner. Afterward, you can take your results to a group to pick up insights from other teachers as well. Or you can complete the activity as a whole group (see "Practice with Study Group or Partners").

Following are several situations in which a teacher could use *Break It Down*. For each situation, supply four questions that you could ask to *Break It Down* for the student(s) who answered incorrectly.

Then rank each of your questions on a scale from 1 to 4, where 1 means *least broken down* (students doing as much of the work as they can probably manage) and 4 means *most broken down* (students doing the least amount of work). ***Example:***

> **Level: Elementary/Middle**
> **Teacher reads aloud:** *The monarch migrates in the winter.*
> **Teacher asks:** "Why do monarch butterflies migrate in the winter?"
> **Student answers:** "Because they like cold weather."
> **Correct answers:** "They can't survive in cold weather" or "Because they like warm weather."

Four questions that would *Break It Down*:

- What's happening as winter approaches that would cause animals to migrate? (3)
- What does *migration* mean? (1)
- Where does the monarch butterfly start its migration? (2)
- You might want to go to Mexico in the winter, too. Why? Why would birds want to go? (4)

As you work these problems, be sure to consider what you can learn from the student's *incorrect* answer.

> 1. **Level: Elementary/Middle**
> **Teacher asks:** "Use the word *scarce* in a sentence."
> **Student answers:** "It is scarce."
> **Correct answer:** (A sentence that demonstrates the meaning of scarce.)

Four questions that would *Break It Down*:

- _____
  _____ ( )

- _____
  _____ ( )

- _____
  _____ ( )

- _____
  _____ ( )

> 2. **Level: Middle School**
> **Teacher asks:** "What answer did you get for: $3 + 7 + (12 \times 2) = ?$"
> **Student answers:** "44." (The student ignored or forgot that she should resolve parentheses first. Instead, she tried to compute from left to right without noticing the parentheses.)
> **Correct answer:** "34."

Four questions that would *Break It Down*:

- _____

   _____ ( )

- _____

   _____ ( )

- _____

   _____ ( )

- _____

   _____ ( )

3. **Level: Middle School**
   Teacher asks: "What answer did you get for: $3 + 7 + (12 \times 2) = ?$"
   Student answers: "I don't know."
   Correct answer: "34."

Four questions that would *Break It Down*:

- _____

   _____ ( )

- _____

   _____ ( )

- _____

   _____ ( )

- _____

   _____ ( )

4. **Level: Almost Any**
   Teacher asks: "The article says, 'The results were indisputable.' Who can remind us what *indisputable* means?"
   Student answers: "Indisputable means if something cannot be found."
   A correct answer: "Indisputable means impossible to deny or question."

Four questions that would *Break It Down*:

- _____

   _____ ( )

- _____

   _____ ( )

- _____
- _____ (   )

- _____
- _____ (   )

5. **Level: Elementary**
Teacher reads aloud: *The monarch butterfly travels south in the winter.*
Teacher asks: "Why might monarchs travel south?"
Student answers: "Because they can fly."
Correct answers: "They can't survive in cold weather" or "Because they like warm weather."

Four questions that would *Break It Down*:

- _____
- _____ (   )

- _____
- _____ (   )

- _____
- _____ (   )

- _____
- _____ (   )

6. **Level: Middle/High School**
Teacher asks: "What do U.S. historians consider among Theodore Roosevelt's important accomplishments?"
Student answers: "He formed the Rough Riders" or "He got elected."
Possible correct answers: "He steered the country into more effective international policy." "He challenged the trusts." "He oversaw the beginning of the digging of the Panama Canal."

Questions to *Break It Down*:

- _____
- _____ (   )

- _____
- _____ (   )

- _____
- _____ (   )

BREAK IT DOWN

7. **Level: Elementary**
Teacher asks: "What is the moral of 'Goldilocks and the Three Bears'?"
Student answers: "You shouldn't leave your door unlocked."
A correct answer: "Respect others' property and privacy."

Questions to *Break It Down*:

- _____
  _____ (   )

- _____
  _____ (   )

- _____
  _____ (   )

- _____
  _____ (   )

8. **Level: Elementary/Middle**
Teacher asks: "What, if anything, do I need to change to fix the following sentence? *She went to the store and she got some bread afterwards she walked home again*."
Student answers: "You don't have to change anything."
A correct answer: "Possibly break the sentence up into two sentences, because it's a run-on."

Questions to *Break It Down*:

- _____
  _____ (   )

- _____
  _____ (   )

- _____
  _____ (   )

- _____
  _____ (   )

9. **Level: Elementary/Middle**
Teacher asks: "What is the next number in this series: 1, 1, 2, 3, 5, 8, 13, 21 . . . ?"
Student answers: "25."
Correct answer: "34." (This is a Fibonacci series, so you add the two previous numbers to each other to get the next number in the sequence.)

Questions to *Break It Down*:

- _____

  _____ ( )

- _____

  _____ ( )

- _____

  _____ ( )

- _____

  _____ ( )

10. **Level: Elementary**
Teacher asks: "What is the stage of the water cycle called when water changes from a gas into a liquid?"
   Student answers: "Evaporation."
   Correct answer: "Condensation."

Questions to *Break It Down*:

- _____

  _____ ( )

- _____

  _____ ( )

- _____

  _____ ( )

- _____

  _____ ( )

11. **Level: Elementary/Middle**
Teacher reads aloud: *The young boy showed compassion for the elderly woman and helped her to cross the street.*
   Teacher asks: "What does *compassion* mean in that sentence?"
   Student answers: "It means he helped her cross the street."
   A correct answer: "*Compassion* means that he felt sympathy for her and wanted to help her."

Questions to *Break It Down*:

- _____

  _____ ( )

- _____
  _____ (   )
- _____
  _____ (   )
- _____
  _____ (   )

12. **Level: Elementary**
Teacher asks: "I had $5.50. My dad gave me $.75 more. Then I lent my friend $2.00. How much do I have now?"
Student answers: "You have $8.25." (Student added it all.)
Correct answer: "You have $4.25."

Questions to _Break It Down_:

- _____
  _____ (   )
- _____
  _____ (   )
- _____
  _____ (   )
- _____
  _____ (   )

13. **Level: Elementary**
Teacher asks: "Which is worth more: three quarters, three dimes, or three nickels?"
Student answers: "Three nickels are worth more."
Correct answer: "Three quarters are worth more."

Questions to _Break It Down_:

- _____
  _____ (   )
- _____
  _____ (   )
- _____
  _____ (   )

- _____

_____ (   )

Which questions were easier for you to write—the least broken down or the most broken down?

_____

_____

_____

What might this pattern reveal about your questioning in class? Why might you tend to follow this pattern?

_____

_____

_____

In practice, how do you take advantage of what you learned from the exact content of a student's incorrect answer? What steps might you need to take (either in planning or during class) to start to do this more frequently?

_____

_____

_____

How would *planning out* some of your classroom questions in the way that you did in this exercise support your ability to *Break It Down* for students?

_____

_____

_____

_____

_____

PRACTICE WITH STUDY GROUP OR PARTNERS

Revisit the individual work you did in the preceding section to share and compare your responses and see other options.

Partner Breakdown

Two teachers we know practice their questions together in role play. One plays the teacher, asking a question from his lesson. The other plays the student, getting it wrong on purpose with an answer she thinks a real student would be likely to give. The "teacher" then has to react by *Breaking It Down* or using some other technique (such as *No Opt Out*). Afterwards the "student" gives feedback, and they try it again.

Back to Levels

You can do the earlier exercise "Levels of *Break It Down*" as a group, or you can use the group time to process and compare what you did beforehand individually or in pairs.

Reviewing Earlier Work

If the group is reviewing earlier work, members can take turns reading a situation aloud and relating one question they came up with that they are proud of for its precision in addressing the unknown gap.

Then the rest of the group can compare the four questions they wrote in terms of rigor and other factors. For each example, the group should reflect back on these key questions, "How big was the (unknown) 'gap'?" "How much of it does the teacher need to fill?"

Debrief by discussing your responses to the questions at the end of "Levels of *Break It Down*."

Starting from Scratch

If you are starting the exercise from scratch, break a large group into smaller ones. Within each small group, choose one situation to work on and brainstorm together. Then choose another that looks more challenging to the group and repeat. Still in the small group, or reporting back to the large one, share what you wrote and observed.

Debrief by discussing the questions at the end of "Levels of *Break It Down*."

What challenges do you foresee in using *Break It Down*? What useful insights did you gain about *Break It Down* from your independent and group work?

_____

_____

_____

_____

▼ TRY *BREAK IT DOWN* IN THE CLASSROOM

One of the best ways to succeed at *Break It Down* is to prepare for it in the lesson planning process by identifying potential trouble spots and drafting both anticipated wrong answers and possible cues to break them down.

1. Look for places in your lesson where you want to plan out *Break It Down*. Start by identifying potential student errors.

2. Because *Break It Down* is a mainly reactive technique, focus on increasing your awareness of the *Break It Down* methods that don't now readily come to your mind in the moment after a student makes an error. Improve your responses to student errors by planning ahead to intentionally incorporate a variety of methods. Also plan for multiple responses in order to be prepared to give both large and small cues depending on your students' unknown gaps.

3. Set a goal of trying all the methods numerous times.

TROUBLE-SHOOT

Steady On

Keep on yourself to *Break It Down* just enough for the students to raise their *Ratio*; in other words, use *Break it Down* to enable students ultimately to do more rather than less cognitive work.

17 **RATIO**

Other Challenges

Possible Challenge	Possible Solutions

BE CREATIVE

What other options would you add to the six listed in the "Overview" section?

SUSTAIN YOUR PROGRESS

1. Using feedback from your study group or other peers, and reviewing your own lesson notes and observations, monitor your progress on *Break It Down*.

Date	An Effective *Break It Down*	Type of Method	How Well Did It Finesse the Gap?

2. Revisit "Where Am I Now?" Are you ready to build out to some other new technique?

RATIO

OVERVIEW

The aim of *Ratio* is to shift the balance of cognitive effort so that teachers are doing less and students are doing progressively more and more of the speaking, thinking, writing, and analyzing, as soon as they are ready for it. Ultimately, *Ratio* is about raising the level of the *thinking* challenge students are taking on.

3 **STRETCH IT**   Although the following discussion describes several effective ways to up the *Ratio* in your classroom, there are more ways to raise the *Ratio* than any guide can list. Just because it's not here doesn't mean it doesn't work, and we urge you to experiment and invent.

WHERE AM I NOW?

	Proficiency			
Comfort & Confidence	I am brand new to this concept of *Ratio* ...	I'm in the planning and practice stage, though I haven't tried many *Ratio* methods yet in class ...	I'm beginning to try a range of *Ratio* methods in my classroom ...	I use *Ratio* regularly in a wide variety of ways ...
	❑ ... and excited to try it.	❑ ... but know I can make many of them work.	❑ ... and love how they basically work.	❑ ... and am adding my own distinctive touches.
	❑ ... and undecided about my ability to pull it off.	❑ ... because I still have questions about how to apply the specific methods.	❑ ... with mixed results I need to evaluate.	❑ ... but still need to master one or two methods.
	❑ ... and not at all sure it's for me.	❑ ... because, frankly, I still don't really think in terms of the general concept.	❑ ... but several or more don't seem to work or suit me.	❑ ... but when class isn't going well, I do it poorly and it doesn't help.

Work from your strengths. If you find yourself in the bottom left portion, leaf through this technique to locate related ones you might prefer to work on right now.

EXPAND YOUR SKILLS AND REPERTOIRE

Starter Methods

For starters, here are some great *Ratio* methods. Note that some of them overlap with or draw on aspects of other techniques in the book. *Stretch It* questions, for example, inherently up the *Ratio*.

1. *Unbundle.* Break questions up into smaller parts to share the work out to more students.

"How many dimensions to a cylinder, James?"

"Good. What's one dimension, Shayna?"

"And what's another, Diamond?"

"That leaves what, Terrance?"

2. *Make a half statement.* Rather than speaking in complete ideas, give half an idea and ask a student to finish it.

"So the next step is to combine the sentences with a . . . what? John."

Or, better, try reducing the "half" of the sentence you provide over time, so that in this example the statement becomes, "So the next step is to combine . . . John?" and then "So the next step is to . . ."

3. *Ask, What's next?* Ask both what the answer to a step in a problem is and what step comes after that one.

"Okay, what do I do next?"

You can still ask "What's next?" questions even in a class where the specific steps in a process are less clear. For example, in a literature class: "Charles thinks Holden is reacting to the death of his brother. I'm skeptical. What should Charles do now?" After Charles has assembled evidence: "Okay, what now?"

4. *Feign ignorance.* Play dumb and make students narrate what you might otherwise explain.

"So, now can I just add my numerators?"

"That's just a summary I gave of what happens in the story, right?"

5. *Ask why or how.* Such questions demand more rigorous student thinking.

Teacher: "Who's the 'stronger' character, Romeo or Juliet?"

Student: "Juliet."

Teacher: "Why do you say so?"

Student: "Well, she's willing to do anything for love."

Teacher: "Okay, but explain how one could say that indicates strength."

Student: "Well, I just think it does."

Teacher: "Good. I agree. But it only counts if you can tell us why."

6. *Ask about the point of error.* When a student answers incorrectly, ask him or another student to identify the point of error.

Teacher: "Convert this decimal into a percentage for us, Eric."

Eric: ".0037 is 3.7 percent."

Teacher: "How do we go about converting a decimal to a percentage, John?"

John: "We move the decimal point two digits to the right."

Eric: "Oh, I moved it three."

Teacher: "You did."

Eric: "It should be, uh, .37 percent."

Going Deeper

These approaches can also help students go deeper.

7. *Ask for more examples*. Ask students for *another* example after a first that you or they have given. Ask that the next be different from the first (and then how).

"Who gets exploited in *Macbeth*?"

"Good; who gets exploited without knowing it?"

"Can anyone think of an example of a person exploiting and being exploited at the same time?"

8. *Ask students to rephrase or add on*. Ask a student to rephrase and improve an answer she just gave. Or ask another student to revise or improve a peer's answer.

"You are correct, but rephrase that and see if you can make it clearer."

"Who can give Shania a word to use that will help her make her answer better?"

9. *Require supporting evidence*. There's far more cognitive work to be done in supporting an opinion than in holding one. Ask your students to use and explain how evidence supports them. Or give them a position and ask them to assemble evidence in support.

Structural Approaches

The *Ratio* methods described so far essentially focus on your questioning—what you ask and how you frame it. As you progress with students and build their capacity, you'll want to begin changing your role in the discussion. These last two methods help you engineer discussions productively as you begin to "get out of the way."

10. *Batch-process*. As your students show they are ready, strategically step out of the way. Allow for or stimulate a short series of student comments without your mediating from one to the next. By not validating each remark right away, you leave more thinking to be done by the class about how to assess and respond to the remark.

Be cautious with batch processing. It can be nonproductive until students are mature and ready for it. If they are not intellectually prepared through literally years of study, they may go off in every direction. Champion teachers try out the runway in middle school, but high school is where it takes off.

Use batch processing selectively—not as a default—and only after you have taught good habits of discussion (procedures for how to interact). Some champion teachers provide students with starter phrases to begin things in the right direction. With your own class in mind, add several to this list:

"I agree with _____ because . . ."

"I want to say more about what you said . . ."

"That's true because . . ."

"I understand what you're saying, but I have a different opinion [point of view] . . ."

"What evidence can you give to support your opinion?"

_____

_____

_____

_____

The term "batch-process" reminds you that it's still your job to process and respond to student answers. So:

- Structure the discussion so that the ball gets passed back over to you at frequent and regular intervals. You, of course, may pass it back again, controlling its further direction or pace to maximize productivity.

- If the ball doesn't come back soon, intervene before the students dribble it off the court. Decide to intervene, redirect, or conclude.

11. *Establish discussion objectives.* See video clip 30. Getting students to engage with open-ended questions and broad discussions can seem like a goal of learning in itself. Almost by their nature, discussions would seem to increase *Ratio*. But they can just as easily result in students' thinking or talking a lot in haphazard ways or about peripheral or suboptimal topics.

- Before you launch relatively open discussions, know and declare an objective for the students to pursue. Steer your students back toward it as needed.

- Raise students' awareness of what they and students around them can or have contributed: Evidence for some particular claim? Counter evidence? A potentially more productive example? An overlooked consideration? And so on.

Analyze Two Sixth-Grade Sessions

Here are two classroom transcripts.

1. Read each one and then go back and write what *Ratio* method the teacher is using at various points. Keep these in mind:

- Unbundle.
- Make a half statement.
- Ask, What's next?
- Feign ignorance.
- Ask why or how.
- Ask about the point of error.

- Ask for more examples.
- Ask students to rephrase or add on.
- Require supporting evidence.
- Batch-process.
- Establish discussion objectives.

2. Write in anything else you notice that makes for an effective *Ratio*.

Teacher Stephanie Ahn

1	*Ms. Ahn:*	All right, we've got eleven minutes to our name to finish reviewing. I'm just going to step back and I'm like the puppet, and you guys are going to take me through how to solve this problem. So what do you think the first thing you do is? Sidney?	
2	*Sidney:*	First thing you gonna do is split the problem . . . well . . . shape . . . cut the shape up.	
3	*Ms. Ahn:*	Cut the shape up. Why? What's the purpose of doing that, Riniah?	

RATIO

| 4 | *Riniah:* | Find the whole . . . |
| 5 | *Ms. Ahn:* | Find the whole, find the whole . . . |

| 6 | *Riniah:* | Area. |
| 7 | *Ms. Ahn:* | Say it again? |

| 8 | *Riniah:* | Area. |
| 9 | *Ms. Ahn:* | Okay so, to find the whole . . . |

10	*Riniah:*	Area.
11	*Ms. Ahn:*	Excellent. Why are we finding the whole area? You guys are jumping to all of these conclusions; I don't know why. Why are you finding area, Sierra?
12	*Sierra:*	Um . . . well, first you had to read the um . . . problem to see what you're gonna do first.
13	*Ms. Ahn:*	Ohhh, so once we read the problem, what does it tell you you want to find?
14	*Sierra:*	Um . . . I mean . . . Cal needs to cover the pieces with them.
15	*Ms. Ahn:*	Exactly so, if I want to find the tiles, that automatically sets up in your head: *bing,* you want to find the . . .
16	*Class:*	Area.
17	*Ms. Ahn:*	Area, good.

Teacher Sha Reagans

1	*Mr. Reagans:*	Six, five, four, three, two, one. Okay. First one, find the volume. What is volume? The definition of volume? William.
2	*William:*	It's the number of cubic units that occupies a given space.
3	*Mr. Reagans:*	The number of cubic units needed to occupy a given space. That is volume. You are correct. What shape is this? What shape is that, Jabari?
4	*Jabari:*	A cylinder.

5	*Mr. Reagans:*	A cylinder. Okay. What—how many dimensions does a cylinder have? How many dimensions, Olsby?

6	*Olsby:*	Three dimensions.
7	*Mr. Reagans:*	Three dimensions. What are the three dimensions of a cylinder? Amir, tell me one.

8	*Amir:*	Pi.
9	*Mr. Reagans:*	Pi is a dimension. It's actually a dimension of anything that deals with a circle. What's another dimension, Allita?

10	*Allita:*	Radius.
11	*Mr. Reagans:*	Radius is a dimension, and the last, um, Kirah?

12	*Kirah:*	Height.
13	*Mr. Reagans:*	Height is a dimension. Now, what is the formula to find volume of a cylinder? Formula to find volume of a cylinder. Adashiawon.
14	*Adashiawon:*	Pi, *r* squared.
15	*Mr. Reagans:*	What is it, Adashiawon?

16	*Adashiawon:*	V equals pi, *r* squared. Times height.
17	*Mr. Reagans:*	V equals pi, *r* squared. Times height. Give her two claps, one, two, three. And her hand was in the air.

18	*Mr. Reagans:*	Now, let's replace each variable with what we know. Do we know what volume is yet?

	Class:	No.
19	*Mr. Reagans:*	So that's gonna remain a V. Do we know what pi is?

20	*Class:*	Yes.
21	*Mr. Reagans:*	Pi equals what?

22	*Class:*	3 and 14 hundredths.
23	*Mr. Reagans:*	Do we know what radius is?

RATIO

24	*Class:*	Yes.
25	*Mr. Reagans:*	Radius is what?

[ ]

26	*Class:*	3.
27	*Mr. Reagans:*	Put all this to the second power and multiply by height, which is ...

[ ]

28	*Class:*	9.
29	*Mr. Reagans:*	On your fingers, how many operations do we have up here? On your fingers, how many operations up here? How many? Tell me.
30	*Class:*	Three.
31	*Mr. Reagans:*	Of the three operations, which of the three are we going to do first?

[ ]

[ ]

32	*Class:*	Exponents.
33	*Mr. Reagans:*	So we have 3 to the second power, so 3 times 2 is 6, correct?

[ ]

34	*Class:*	No.
35	*Mr. Reagans:*	3 to the second power equals what?

[ ]

36	*Class:*	9.
37	*Mr. Reagans:*	Put your multiplication down, the 3 and the 14 hundredths, the multiplication and the 9. Now we just solve, left to right. So let's multiply pi, which is 3 and 14 hundredths, times 9. Although the decimal is ...
38	*Class:*	There.
39	*Mr. Reagans:*	Pretend that it's not ...

[ ]

[ ]

40	*Class:*	There.
41	*Mr. Reagans:*	But it better be ...

[ ]

42	*Class:*	There.
43	*Mr. Reagans:*	4 times 9 ...

[ ]

| 44 | *Class:* | 36. |
| 45 | *Mr. Reagans:* | 1 times 9 . . . |

| 46 | *Class:* | 9. |
| 47 | *Mr. Reagans:* | Plus 3 . . . |

| 48 | *Class:* | 12. |
| 49 | *Mr. Reagans:* | 9 times 3 . . . |

| 50 | *Class:* | 27. |
| 51 | *Mr. Reagans:* | Plus 1 . . . |

| 52 | *Class:* | 28. |
| 53 | *Mr. Reagans:* | Go back and get our . . . |

| 54 | *Class:* | Decimal. |

3. What other evidence is there in these dialogues that students are doing the cognitive work?

_____

_____

_____

_____

(At the end of this technique are some hints for analyzing the transcripts.)

4. Is there anything else that these teachers have done that you could add to your repertoire to increase *Ratio* in your class?

_____

_____

RATIO

Centering More on the Students

This activity may be most useful for teachers of students in upper grades or high school.

The *Ratio* methods presented earlier were ordered roughly along a continuum that goes from being more teacher centered at the top to more student centered at the bottom. Consider this continuum as you reflect on your own teaching. Do you tend to fall mainly at one or the other end (or in the middle) of the continuum? Or what other pattern do you see in how frequently you use more teacher-centered methods as opposed to student-centered ones?

_____

_____

_____

If you are mainly at the upper, teacher-centered end, what opportunities for more student-centered thinking may you be overlooking?

_____

_____

_____

How might you begin to move more toward the student-centered end? (For example, could methods in the middle become bridges toward the most student-centered methods?)

_____

_____

_____

_____

PEMDAS

You can do this exercise in a group, with a partner, or by yourself.

PEMDAS is an acronym (often remembered with the mnemonic "Please Excuse My Dear Aunt Sally") for the sequence to follow in completing operations in a complex math computation:

Parentheses

Exponents

Multiplication

Division

Addition

Subtraction

Read the transcript here and then tackle the activity that follows it.

Ms. Richard's Transcript

Ms. Richard's fifth-grade math class is reviewing a math problem on the order of operations. The problem students attempted to solve and that they are now reviewing is $6 \times (5^3 + 2)$. Ms. Richard is reviewing the problem at the board via an overhead projector.

| 1 | _Ms. Richard:_ | Number two. Simplify the expression below and show all work in the space provided. Shanaia, what answer did you get, F, G, H, or J? |
| 2 | _Shanaia:_ | I got G. |

RATIO

| 3 | *Ms. Richard:* | You got G? Okay. Two snaps if you got G as well. Two stomps if you did not. One, two. One, two. |

21 **TAKE A STAND**

4	*Students:*	(*Some snap, some stomp.*)
5	*Ms. Richard:*	Okay, a lot of people didn't get G. Let's find out why. Shanaia, where did you start to simplify this expression? What's the first thing you did?
6	*Shanaia:*	Um, the first thing I did was look at the parentheses and the parentheses are first, but then you have an exponent.
7	*Ms. Richard:*	Okay, so you went inside the parentheses first because that's what PEMDAS tells us to do, right? However, inside the parentheses there is an exponent. So, to solve for the exponent first, what did you write?
8	*Shanaia:*	I put 5 to the third power equals 125.
9	*Ms. Richard:*	How do you know? How do you know that 5 to the third power equals 125? What's a good way to simplify an exponent? What did you do, Marcus?
10	*Marcus:*	What I did was 5 times 5 times 5.
11	*Ms. Richard:*	Okay, so 5 times 5 times 5. Okay, is that all you have, though?
12	*Marcus:*	No. After that I did 5 times 5 equals 25. Then I did 25 times 5 equals 125.
13	*Ms. Richard:*	Okay, so that's great, but that doesn't really give me an answer.
14	*Marcus:*	Oh . . . and then . . . you want me to give you the answer?
15	*Ms. Richard:*	Yes, I need to know what you did.
16	*Marcus:*	And then I did 125 plus 2 equals 127.
17	*Ms. Richard:*	Okay, so let's do this. Let's bring everything down, right? We have the 6 and we have the 2 inside the parentheses. 125 plus 2 is 127 . . . times 6, right? I'll bring my arrow up here. So we have 127 times 6. And you got what, Marcus?
18	*Marcus:*	For my answer I got 762.
19	*Ms. Richard:*	762. Let's check it. 7 times 6 is what, Marcus?
20	*Marcus:*	7 times 6 is . . . 24?
21	*Ms. Richard:*	7 times 6?
22	*Marcus:*	I'm sorry, 42?
23	*Ms. Richard:*	42. Good. Bring down the 2, bring up the 4. Now what, Marcus?
24	*Marcus:*	6 times 2 equals 12. Plus 4 equals 16.
25	*Ms. Richard:*	16, good. Drop the 6, pop the 1.
26	*Marcus:*	Then 6 times 1 equals 6, plus 1 equals 7, and the answer is 762.
27	*Ms. Richard:*	Good. 762 is the correct answer. If you need to make any corrections to your *Do Now,* do so now. If not, flip over to the next page and *SLANT*.

32 **SLANT**

RATIO

Directions:

- Underline at least three examples of the effective use of the *Ratio* technique.
- What methods of *Ratio* is the teacher using?

_____

_____

_____

_____

- What is her most effective usage? How so?

_____

_____

_____

- Circle at least two places in the transcript where she could further increase the *Ratio*. For each, how could she do that? Write brief wording she could use to initiate each effort.

1. _____

_____

2. _____

_____

- What insights did you gain about *Ratio* from this activity?

_____

_____

_____

- What questions did it raise for you?

_____

_____

_____

- What do you see as the key to increasing the *Ratio* in your class?

_____

_____

_____

- Are there any specific parts of your regular class period in which you would like to increase the *Ratio*?

_____

_____

PRACTICE WITH STUDY GROUP OR PARTNERS

Revisit the individual work you did in the preceding section to share and compare your responses and see other options.

Group PEMDAS

With a bit of planning by your *Facilitator*, the PEMDAS activity can be done as a group. Or the group can compare work that members did before convening.

Engaging Three Types of Students More Effectively

Will Austin, a champion teacher we have worked with, describes how three types of students engage differently in the review of material:

> When you are reviewing material, almost every student falls into one of three categories: students who already got it (they disassociate unless they are very disciplined), students who think they got it (more dangerous than the first group because they disassociate but need to listen), and students who did not get it (without perseverance, this group tunes out).

With your group, discuss how your use of *Ratio* addresses (or could address) the three types of students Austin describes:

Got it: _____

_____

Think they got it: _____

_____

Didn't get it: _____

_____

Your takeaways:

_____

_____

_____

_____

TRY *RATIO* IN THE CLASSROOM

1. Audio-record your next class session. Later, play it back and count how much of what you recorded is your own voice and how much are the voices of students.

- In most classes, most of the time, teachers say more than the students, but does the participation *Ratio* for your recorded session sound problematic?

- How often in the course of the session are you deliberately eliciting student verbal participation? What happens at these points?

- Whose voices show they are carrying the weight of the active thinking? Where do you seem to be thinking out loud alone? Why aren't you hearing more student thought work?

- As the session went on, did you gradually transition from relatively teacher-centered methods of *Ratio* to more student-centered ones?

2. Apply *Ratio* thinking to your next lesson plan. In this, try to plan *in detail, minute to minute*. Where and how can you shift the *Ratio* and add more rigor? Script what you might say to increase *Ratio* at several different points. As you do so, ask yourself these questions:

- What are the essentials of the objective I am trying to teach?

| 5 **WITHOUT APOLOGY** |

- Are there ways to make my questions more rigorous while still meeting "standards"?

- Are there moments in this planning in which a certain *Ratio* technique will clearly be more effective than another potential choice?

- Are any of the techniques more challenging to use than others?

3. Start with methods you feel most at home with already that fit the *Ratio* perspective. Use them now with *Ratio* firmly in mind. Look for opportunities to

- Move in steps from teacher-centered (what some call "direct instruction") methods of *Ratio* in the early part of the lesson to more student-centered methods toward the end.

| 26 **EVERYBODY WRITES** |

- Build student writing into the plan that shifts the *Ratio* of writing toward the students.

| 14 **BOARD = PAPER** |

- Shift the *Ratio* of thought that will need to go on during any board work or note taking.

| 32 **SLANT** |

4. Before you *batch-process,* consider whether there are any habits of discussion that your students need to learn right now. *SLANT* may be just a beginning. See clip 30.

TROUBLE-SHOOT

Steady On

| 25 **WAIT TIME** |

Are you allowing enough *Wait Time* for *Ratio* to work?

Increase a student's cognitive work *as soon as the student is ready,* but don't jump the gun. Students can do a lot of fishing around (in their minds or in a reference source) trying to solve a complex problem or come up with an answer to a very challenging question, but in that setting, most of their thought and labor isn't likely to be productive, and their actual *cognitive* work may be minimal. Prepare them beginning with what they know now.

Other Challenges

Possible Challenge	Possible Solutions
When I tried it, some *Ratio* method seemed too hard for my class.	Move back to the more teacher-centered end of the *Ratio* continuum? Was it too much of a stretch? How could you have prepared them for it? Is it the difficulty caused by the *Ratio* method you're using or a lack of understanding of content?
I let my kids lead discussion, and it goes off the rails. They just talk about anything.	This is one of the reasons to move slowly with *Ratio*. Model for students how to follow on to a comment with a relevant comment by asking questions that require them to do so as a matter of habit. Focus diligently on how and why and on evidence-based questioning.

BE CREATIVE

Champion sixth-grade teacher Will Austin says that his students have average skills for their grade cohort. In order to increase their skill level, he uses *Ratio* with them and tries to make all review activities rely *completely* on it. See his quote in the "Practice with Study Group or Partners" section. Try planning *your* next review activity with students using *only Ratio* methods.

SUSTAIN YOUR PROGRESS

1. Using feedback from your study group or other peers, and reviewing your own lesson notes and observations, monitor your progress on *Ratio*.

Date	Step Forward	Way to Further Reinforce

2. Revisit "Where Am I Now?" Are you ready to build out to some other technique?

The following are hints for "Analyze Two Sixth-Grade Sessions"

Ms. Ahn

Calls on five-plus students in one minute.

"You want to find the . . ."

"What's the first thing you do?"

"I'm the puppet . . ."

"Why? What's the purpose of doing that?"

"Why are you finding the whole area?"

Mr. Reagans

Calls on more than eight students and uses choral responses and student hand signals.

" . . . height, which is . . ."

"Although the decimal is . . ."

"Go back and get our . . ."

"So we have 3 to the second power, so 3 times 2 is 6, correct?"

CHECK FOR UNDERSTANDING (AND DO SOMETHING ABOUT IT)

15 **CIRCULATE**
20 **EXIT TICKET**
22 **COLD CALL**

OVERVIEW

As most teachers know, checking for student understanding is essential, but the pressures of the daily classroom can make it difficult to do effectively. Following this technique will help you be consistent, thorough, and responsive. *Check for Understanding* is shorthand for two actions:

1. *While you teach, constantly assess what your students understand.* Gather responses from not just one but several students who represent different levels of achievement and performance. Use the data to estimate how many in your class are understanding and what segments of the class you might have left behind.

In this process, ask *Cold Call* questions with the conscious purpose of sampling understanding. Also *Circulate* as students do desk work, with the conscious purpose of sampling levels of mastery in written answers. *Exit Ticket* is yet another technique to *Check for Understanding*.

2. *Respond to misunderstanding by reteaching, and usually reteaching differently.* There's no point to checking unless you also respond—the more promptly the better—to improve understanding. The shorter the delay, the more likely the intervention will work. We will explore many ways to respond.

WHERE AM I NOW?

This is such an essential skill that whether or not you take it on as your main learning goal right now, you may want to begin now to apply some of the methods described in these sections.

	Proficiency			
Comfort & Confidence	I am somewhat new to the mind-set of *Check for Understanding* . . .	I get the idea and do check now and then, but I haven't yet applied it systematically . . .	I'm beginning to try *Check for Understanding* in my classroom . . .	I *Check for Understanding* often . . .
	❑ . . . and excited to try it.	❑ . . . but know with practice I can both check and respond much better.	❑ . . . and love how it basically works.	❑ . . . and am strong on responding quickly.
	❑ . . . and undecided how much I need to do it.	❑ . . . because I still have questions about how to check or respond.	❑ . . . with mixed results I need to evaluate.	❑ . . . but may need to check or respond *more* often.

ANALYZE THE CHAMPIONS

View each video clip, ideally more than once, and answer the following questions. See possible answers for clips 12 and 13 at the end of this technique.

Clip 12. Teacher Bob Zimmerli, Grade 7

1. Name two major ways that Mr. Zimmerli uses *Check for Understanding* in this clip.
2. What practical assumptions might you make about the nature of the separate problem items that Mr. Zimmerli has given the students?
3. Suppose Mr. Zimmerli finds a student totally stumped by the first question. How might he handle that without derailing the overall class process?
4. What other champion techniques does Mr. Zimmerli use?

Clip 13. Teacher Isaac Pollack, Grade 9

How does Mr. Pollack build *Check for Understanding* into the homework?

Clip 14. Teacher Leanna Picard, Grade 8

1. What preparations has Ms. Picard made in order to respond in an efficient way to problems of misunderstanding?
2. As specifically as possible, say how Ms. Picard helps these students improve their responses. Does she provide correct answers? What, if any, questions does she ask?

EXPAND YOUR SKILLS AND REPERTOIRE

Think in terms of data sets.

In the course of instruction, you could pose five different questions to five different students so that their collective answer reviewed a number of steps or distinct bits of knowledge. By contrast, using data-set thinking, you would ask all five students very similar or parallel questions about one step or point. If you included students from your spectrum of typically low, middle, and high performers, you would then be able to judge from their answers the approximate proportion of the class (and who) is understanding that specific point.

| 3 STRETCH IT |

A right answer can be merely a lucky one. To verify its *reliability* as data, when in doubt, you can also follow up with why and how questions.

You want to know whether the class understands what is meant by a "run-on" or "run-together" sentence. Pose the question in five different ways for five different students:

1. _____

_____

2. _____

_____

3. _____

_____

4. _____

_____

5. _____

_____

Design Oral Questions with Understanding in Mind

You can begin *Checking for Understanding* without changing the format of the questions you ask, but more careful thinking about answers *as data* will probably lead you to change your questions when your *goal* is to *Check for Understanding*. For example, you'll

- Recognize that yes-no questions often yield guess answers that happen to be correct even when the student doesn't really understand.

- Be more inclined to follow up on such "self-report" methods as, "How many of you understand?" or "Thumbs up if you get this; thumbs down if you don't."

> 21 **TAKE A STAND**

- Become more aware of "tipping"—giving the answers away in your question, as in this sequence:

  Teacher: Who can tell me what the phrase "off the deep end" means?

  Student: It means someone is upset?

  Teacher: Well, are they a little bit upset or like really, *really* upset?

  Student: Really, *really* upset.

  Teacher: Good.

- Align the questions you ask to *Check for Understanding* more often to the rigor and style of questions your students will ultimately face on actual exams.

Find an exam you've created in the past or might be asked to administer in the future. Pick several question items. Write them here, followed by questions you might ask in teaching before the exam that would match in general content, rigor, and style without asking the identical questions.

Exam item A: _____

_____

Checks for Understanding that match it in rigor and style:

1. _____

_____

2. _____

_____

3. _____

_____

Exam item B: _____

_____

Checks for Understanding that match it in rigor and style:

1. _____

_____

2. _____

_____

3. _____

_____

Use a Quick Quiz

Insert a very short verbal quiz into the fabric of a lesson to increase the amount and usefulness of the data you collect. Format the script of your quiz in a way that lets you quickly tally right and wrong answers and who gave them.

Circulate

| 15 **CIRCULATE** |

Circulating to *Check for Understanding* in students' written work is more immediate and can be more effective than gathering work from everyone for you to go over at home at night.

Following are some tips for increasing your ability to quickly gather useful data. For each, if you're aware of doing something similar now, note briefly what you do. Whatever you do now, what might you do to have more *Checking* power—to *Check for Understanding* more effectively?

1. *Give instructions that will standardize the format of student's written work.*

"Write your final, brief answer in the top right corner."

If you're looking for information in the same place on each student's paper, you'll find it much more quickly and will be able to retain your concentration on comparing answers across students.

Me now: _____

More *Checking* power: _____

_____

_____

2. *Use worksheets or packets.* Worksheets or packets can mark out clear spaces in which to do various steps of a problem or boxes in which to write final answers. Worksheets and packets can be used in all subject areas at all grade levels. Combine with "Show me" (point 3). Worksheets make it easier for students to observe each other's work, which can be positive in some ways; but watch out for copying or piggybacking.

Me now: _____

More *Checking* power: _____

_____

_____

3. *"Show me."* Say "Show me" so that students will know to point to some item or answer on their desk work paper when you *Circulate* to observe.

Me now: _____

More *Checking* power: _____

_____

_____

4. *"One finger up if you think you got question A right . . ."* or *"Two fingers up if you got B," and so on*. This can help direct your path of circulation.

Me now: _____

More *Checking* power: _____

_____

_____

5. *Ask students to underline, circle, or make notes in margins*. In this way students can highlight key aspects of understanding in existing text or at key points in what they themselves are writing.

Me now: _____

More *Checking* power: _____

_____

_____

6. *Use "slates."* Quickly check classwide comprehension by giving your students tools to write down their answers and hold them up to you on cue. You can pass out scrap paper for this or, for example, get enough mini dry-erase boards for the class.

Me now: _____

More *Checking* power: _____

_____

_____

CHECK FOR UNDERSTANDING (AND DO SOMETHING ABOUT IT)

7. *Use a track sheet.* As you focus on the number and types of errors you are seeing, possibly track them on a clipboard so that you can organize and refer back to the data later.

Me now: _____

More *Checking* power: _____

_____

_____

Reteaching Beyond Just Repeating

There are many different ways to act in response to a lack of student understanding. Repeating what you did before in the same or slightly different words might work, but some or all students may respond better to some other form of reteaching. In general,

- Act quickly.
- Inform students of what you generally learned from your data.
- Decide to whom you need to respond: an individual, a group, or the class as a whole.

The following are ways to respond to data. For each, if you're aware of doing something similar now, note briefly what you do. Whatever you do now, what might you do to improve reteaching?

1. *Reteach the topic with a different approach.*
"Let's try visualizing this problem geometrically."

Me now: _____

Possibly stronger: _____

_____

2. *Identify and reteach just the problem step.*
"I think we're struggling over remainders, so let's work on that a little more ..."

Me now: _____

Possibly stronger: _____

_____

3. *Identify and explain difficult terms.*
"I think the term *denominator* is giving us some trouble ..."

Me now: _____

Possibly stronger: _____

_____

4. *Slow the pace*.

"Let's read that list of words again. I'll go really slowly because I want you to make sure you hear me read the suffixes. Then I'm going to ask you to . . ."

Me now: _____

Possibly stronger: _____

5. *Present the information in a different order*.

"This time let's try to put the key events in the story in *reverse* order."

Me now: _____

Possibly stronger: _____

6. *Give more practice* At Bats.

| 19 **AT BATS** |

"It seems like we're able to identify the genre most of the time, but let's try to get a bit more practice. I'm going to read you the first two sentences of ten imaginary stories. For each one, you write down the genre you think it is and one reason why."

Me now: _____

Possibly stronger: _____

7. *Work with students of concern*.

"We're going to push on to the problems in your packet now. I want several of you to come work with me at the front. If I say your name, bring your packet up here . . ."

Me now: _____

Possibly stronger: _____

Analyze Classroom Transcripts

You can do these by yourself or (better) with a partner or group.

Will Austin's Class

1. Read the transcript. Underline examples of *Check for Understanding*. Double-underline three to five places where you see Mr. Austin taking action to address a misunderstanding or checking for further understanding.

2. Go back over your underlining with these questions in mind:

- What effective things does Mr. Austin do in response to student misunderstandings? When and how might you use these actions in your own classroom?

- In what ways is Mr. Austin socializing students to check for and respond to their own misunderstandings?

- Can you identify one other place Mr. Austin might have done an additional *Check for Understanding* or taken additional action in response to data he collected?

3. Go back once more and highlight or star any part of the transcript that might help you as you integrate *Check for Understanding* into a future lesson plan.

1	Mr. Austin:	How many people, show of hands, recognize question two, feel like they've seen it before? That's because it was on a quiz. Be the teacher. Why would I put a question that was on a quiz a week or two ago here on ... Joshua?
2	Joshua:	Because we got it wrong.
3	Mr. Austin:	Yeah, quite a few people not only got it wrong but actually made the same answer. Raise your hand if you have the answer "2" in front of you right now.
4		(*Five students raise their hands.*)
5	Mr. Austin:	Raise your hand. I can see them from here. Raise your hand, raise your hand higher; it's okay to be wrong. Okay, I like that you wanted to divide, Shaqura. Okay, this is a division problem, but a lot of folks jumped into it without really thinking about what they were doing. It is a division problem because we have a total amount and were splitting it into equal groups. The question is which one is the dividend and which one is the divisor. That's the question here. So, Jude, which number is the dividend?
6	Jude:	12?
7	Mr. Austin:	12. Say it without a question mark.
8	Jude:	12.
9	Mr. Austin:	12. Why is 12 the dividend? Christian Salazar?
10	Christian:	Because we're starting with 12 total liters.
11	Mr. Austin:	Yeah, it's our starting quantity. 12 total liters. What number is the divisor? What number is the divisor, Odette?
12	Odette:	24.
13	Mr. Austin:	24. Why is 24 the divisor? Someone else. She knows the answer already. Why is 24 the divisor, Conan?
14	Conan:	Because it's 24 packs?
15	Mr. Austin:	It's not 24 packs, it's just 24 bottles. So we have 12 total liters that are being broken into 24 equal groups. Raise your hand if this looks a little funny to you. Be honest. Raise your hand if this looks a little funny to you. Why does this look a little funny to you? Why, Zatanya?
16	Zatanya:	Because it's switched around.
17	Mr. Austin:	Yeah, usually it's switched around. Usually the smaller number is the divisor. That should be a clue. Is your quotient going to be a whole or a decimal when you look at this? Right away you should be able to say, Norbia?

18	*Norbia:*	A decimal.
19	*Mr. Austin:*	It's going to be a decimal less than one because our divisor is larger than our dividend. Nod your head if you remember doing this with Mr. Armstrong. Okay, so now, what are we going to do here?
20	*Norbia:*	You have to put the decimal and the zero. Then you have to put the zero in the first two … then how many times does 24 go into 120.
21	*Mr. Austin:*	How many times?
22	*Norbia:*	2.
23	*Mr. Austin:*	Higher.
24	*Norbia:*	3.
25	*Mr. Austin:*	Keep going.
26	*Norbia:*	4.
27	*Mr. Austin:*	Keep going.
28	*Norbia:*	5.
29	*Mr. Austin:*	5, good. Okay, let's check that to make sure you're right, Norbia. Yeah, 120, okay? So now I end up with this. So, Norbia thinks the quotient is 5. Who agrees? Disagrees?
30		*(Students raise hands.)*
31	*Mr. Austin:*	*(looks at Norbia)* You disagree with yourself? What did you forget to do?
32	*Norbia:*	I forgot to put the decimal.
33	*Mr. Austin:*	Yes, you sure did. You gotta carry up your decimal into the quotient. So can you read the answer for us, Shetania? How much is that, 5?
34	*Shetania:*	5 tenths.
35	*Mr. Austin:*	What's another way to say 5 tenths? In fact, you just started this with Mr. Armstrong. What's another way you could say 5 tenths, what's a simpler way?
36	*Student:*	One half.
37	*Mr. Austin:*	One half, right? Let's think about this answer for one second; I want to spend a second or two on this. A lot of people wrote 2 liters, right? And there are 24 bottles. That means how many liters are going to be in the package total?
38	*Student:*	48.
39	*Mr. Austin:*	Yeah, that's too big, right? That's why that the answer "2" doesn't hold up. But now think about them each holding a half. If each of them is holding a half, I need how many bottles to make a whole? If each of them hold a half, how many bottles to make a whole? Kristen?
40	*Kristen:*	Another half.
41	*Mr. Austin:*	Yeah, so I need two to make one. So now we can see why, if I drew this out, I'd end up with 24 bottles, but only 12 liters.

Kelli Peterson's Class

In this transcript, Ms. Peterson uses various strategies to respond to student error.

1. Underline as you did in the Mr. Austin exercise. The student errors are numbered and described in the brackets.

2. Find and describe all the different strategies Ms. Peterson uses to reteach in response to student error.

3. Compare her responses to errors (1) and (2). Why does she respond differently? Is one response more effective?

4. Her strategies include isolating an individual as well as calling for whole group repetition. When would you use one or the other, or both in succession?

5. The students make roughly the same error in (3) and (4). Why does the teacher's response change? What is effective about each response?

6. Go back once more and highlight or star any part of the transcript that might help you as you integrate *Check for Understanding* into a future lesson plan.

1	*Ms. Peterson:*	All students, on the page, starting over at the first word, number one. Say it.
2	*Class:*	Climbers.
3	*Ms. Peterson:*	Spell it.
4	*Class:*	C-l-i-m-b-e-r-s.
5	*Ms. Peterson:*	Say it.
6	*Class:*	Climbers.
7	*Ms. Peterson:*	Number two. Say it.
8	*Class:*	Snowballs.
9	*Ms. Peterson:*	Spell it.
10	*Class:*	S-n-o-w-b- *[Letters start to blend together and become garbled.]* (1)
11	*Ms. Peterson:*	Ew no. Number two, try it again slower. Say it.
12	*Class:*	Snowballs.
13	*Ms. Peterson:*	Spell it.
14	*Class:*	S-n-o-w-b-a-l-l-s.
15	*Ms. Peterson:*	Say it.
16	*Class:*	Snowballs.
17	*Ms. Peterson:*	Next word. Say it.
18	*Class:*	Rabbit.
19	*Ms. Peterson:*	Spell it.
20	*Class:*	R-a-b-b-i-t.
21	*Ms. Peterson:*	Say it.
22	*Class:*	Rabbit.
23	*Ms. Peterson:*	Next one. Say it.
24	*Class:*	*[garbled response]* (2)
25	*Ms. Peterson:*	Number four, I want you to just say it. Number four, say it.
26	*Class:*	Danger.
27	*Ms. Peterson:*	Spell it.
28	*Class:*	D-a-n-g-e-r.

29	*Ms. Peterson:*	Say it.
30	*Class:*	Danger.
31	*Ms. Peterson:*	Bottoms up, what word?
32	*Class:*	Danger, rabbit, snowballs, climbers *[not crisply done]* (3)
33	*Ms. Peterson:*	Try it again. Bottoms up, what word?
34	*Class:*	Danger, rabbit *[becoming garbled]* (4)
35	*Ms. Peterson:*	STOP. Number four, finger on four. *(slower)* Bottoms up, what word?
36	*Class:*	Danger, rabbit, snowballs, climbers.
37	*Ms. Peterson:*	Going down, what word?
38	*Class:*	Climbers, snowballs, rabbit, danger.
39	*Ms. Peterson:*	Very good. Next list. Number one, say it.
40	*Class:*	Dud.
41	*Ms. Peterson:*	Spell it.
42	*Class:*	D-u-d.
43	*Ms. Peterson:*	Say it.
44	*Class:*	Dud.
45	*Ms. Peterson:*	Next. Say it.
46	*Class:*	Ham.
47	*Ms. Peterson:*	Spell it.
48	*Class:*	H-a-m. *[One student says e.]* (5)
49	*Ms. Peterson:*	Sa—William, number two, say it.
50	*William:*	Ham.
51	*Ms. Peterson:*	Spell it.
52	*William:*	H-a-m.
53	*Ms. Peterson:*	Say it.
54	*William:*	Ham.
55	*Ms. Peterson:*	All boys, number two, say it.
56	*Class:*	Ham.
57	*Ms. Peterson:*	Spell it.
58	*Class:*	H-a-m.
59	*Ms. Peterson:*	Say it.
60	*Class:*	Ham.

Normalize Error

Facilitate both aspects of *Check for Understanding* (assessing and reteaching) by *Normalizing Error* in your classroom.

49 **NORMALIZE ERROR**

CHECK FOR UNDERSTANDING (AND DO SOMETHING ABOUT IT)

PRACTICE WITH A STUDY GROUP OR PARTNERS

| 49 **NORMALIZE ERROR** | Your group might spend the whole meeting usefully sharing and comparing what you each did earlier in "Expand Your Skills and Repertoire"

and discussing how you can apply that to your next lesson plan. The group may also want to cover *Normalize Error* at this point. The role play requires a small amount of preparation by a *Facilitator*.

Hand Signals Role Play

The *Facilitator* brings a die and may want to arrange to use a different script. The exercise requires at least four participants, but the more the merrier.

One useful way to quickly *Check for Understanding* throughout a lesson is to have students signal nonverbally to show their answers to a series of questions. But results can be misleading. This role play explores some pros and cons of using "thumbs up–thumbs down" hand signals to *Check for Understanding,* but you can substitute any comparable yes-or-no signal. The *Teacher*'s objective is to determine which scholar or scholars definitely need more work on the concept. He or she gets bonus points for also discovering any student who is mimicking others' responses. The role play proceeds as follows:

1.   After one participant is chosen to be the *Teacher,* that person leaves the room, and the rest become *Students,* who roll a die to determine what role they will play. Keep rolling until, among you, you meet the following conditions. If you roll this number . . .

⚀ → Play *Student 1*: Always gets the answer right, as shown in the script. *At least one participant must be a Student 1*.

⚁ → Play *Student 2*: Lacks mastery and gets the answer wrong. *At least one participant must be a Student 2*.

⚂ → Play *Student 3*: Delays responding. Decides how to respond mainly by subtly observing how others have already responded.

⚃ ⚄ ⚅ → Choose any of the other three roles, or display fair mastery by getting most of the answers right.

2.   Allow time for each participant to read over his or her role and the Hand Signals Role Play Script. Then the *Teacher* initiates by following the script. Each *Student* is free to decide how long to wait before responding. Repeat rounds until everyone has played *Teacher* once.

3.   Discuss the following questions after each round, until all participants have played the *Teacher*. (Some possible answers to these questions are shown in "Be Creative." If you've already read them, so be it, but don't cheat by looking at them now!)

Teacher:

● Did you determine who clearly did not have mastery of the concept?

● Did you notice other *Students* who may have been struggling?

All participants:

● How could you prevent *Students* from mimicking the responses of other *Students*?

● What sort of tool (if any) could have helped you keep track of those who did not have mastery?

● How would this exercise have been different with a class of thirty students? What could you have done to narrow your focus?

● What is absolutely necessary in utilizing this strategy?

4.   After the last participant has played the *Teacher* and that round has been discussed, independently reflect in writing for about five minutes on the overall experience, then conclude by discussing how participants might improve their own practice of *Checking for Understanding*. You may also want to talk about how a teacher's tone and manner might affect the quality of data the students will yield.

5.   Consider playing a few more rounds.

What helpful feedback or other insight did you get from this role play?

_____

_____

_____

_____

HAND SIGNALS ROLE PLAY SCRIPT

(In advance, participants can adapt the script to a different grade level or subject by replacing this set of true-false questions with any set that *Checks for Understanding* on a single concept or closely allied ones.)

Teacher: "OK, scholars, you have all been working incredibly hard on solving equations. It is time for a quick *show what you know*! Don't let me trick you! If I say something that is true, give me a thumbs up. If I say something that is false, give me a thumbs down. Show me what you do when something is true. (*Students: Thumbs up*.) Good. And when something's false? (*Students: Thumbs down*.) Good. Let's begin."

(From here on, the *Teacher* reads a true-false item, and *Students* respond according to this continuation of the script. Using whatever means seem effective, the *Teacher* observes and counts responses.)

Teacher Reads Statement:	Student(s) 1 (Correct)	Student(s) 2 (Incorrect)	Student(s) 3 (Tend to Mimic)
"1. In solving an equation with multiple operations, you should always subtract before you divide."	👎	👍	Choose up or down based mainly on what you see others doing.
"2. When solving an equation, you should divide before you multiply."	👎	👍	Choose up or down based mainly on what you see others doing.
"3. Always do what is in the parentheses first."	👍	👎	Choose up or down based mainly on what you see others doing.
"4. When solving math problems with exponents, always solve the exponents first."	👎	👍	Choose up or down based mainly on what you see others doing.
"5. Always add integers before multiplying them."	👎	👍	Choose up or down based mainly on what you see others doing.

TRY *CHECK FOR UNDERSTANDING* IN THE CLASSROOM

1. If you have already audio-recorded yourself teaching, replay all or parts to notice when, how, and how often you used *Check for Understanding*. What changes would you like to make? If you don't yet have a recording, record your next session with this in mind.

11 DRAW THE MAP

2. Select a lesson plan for an upcoming lesson. If you haven't already used *Draw the Map,* do enough of it now to let you *Circulate.*

3. Note in your plan where you will want to *Check for Understanding*. Referring back to your work in "Expand Your Skills and Repertoire," add information about

- What errors students are likely to make. What misunderstandings may they have?
- The method you will use to check. What question(s) will you ask and how? Script your questions in the lesson plan.
- Places where you can use *Circulate* to *Check for Understanding*. Plan (and possibly write down) target student responses. What will you specifically look for in students' work?
- How you can standardize students' work pages so that you can quickly find their work on a particular question (or set of questions).

4. For each instance of checking, ask

- About how long will it take?
- Is it at the appropriate time in the lesson?
- Will it sample my students (and all levels of ability) effectively?
- What data will it yield?

5. For each instance of checking, note what may be your best choice of a way to reteach at the moment.

6. After class, assess your plan and actual performance in class to improve and broaden choices in your next plan and lesson. In your next plan, include any needed reteaching that you couldn't do on the spot.

7. Generally, teachers are better at checking for gaps in student mastery than they are at acting on those gaps. Be realistic about where you are, but do plan to improve at filling gaps well and early.

TROUBLE-SHOOT

Steady On

1. Stay aware of the pattern of answers to data-set questions. Resist the urge to stop *Checking for Understanding* as soon as you get a right response. *Wrong, right, right, right* suggests that students are generally understanding. *Wrong, wrong, wrong, right* suggests only that finally *someone* got it right! Keep asking until the data seem clear.

2. As time weighs on you, remind yourself to monitor how correctly students are responding, not just how close to finished they are.

3. Don't push on to harder material when you know students can't do the preliminary work. Stop, fix it, then move on.

Other Challenges

The table outlines some *Check for Understanding* strategies and their advantages. The middle column mentions common pitfalls and challenges for each. Stick with each strategy long enough to notice where you have trouble. Add other solution ideas to the third column as you continue to work on *Check for Understanding*.

Check for Understanding Strategies: Their Advantages and Challenges

Strategies and Their Advantages	Pitfalls and Challenges	Possible Solutions
Questioning Immediate Done during lesson	Right answers from individual students may not equate with whole-class mastery.	Track students' answers and look for trends.
Observation Immediate Independent work—no copying or piggybacking	Observing students' work at their seats is likely to entail some delay after the moment of actual teaching. To be effective, observing requires consciously targeting a specific skill question and a valid sample of the class.	Pick one question to target; track responses. Observe during *Do Now*. Target specific students.
Quick Oral Quiz Immediate Done during lesson	The teacher needs to be sure to tap the right sample of students.	Intentionally target students who are high, medium, and low on different skills. Track answers. *Cold Call* specific individuals.
Hand Signals Silent Quick Whole class	Students may copy or piggyback.	Ask students to give signals with their eyes closed. Ask for hand signals from smaller subset of class.
Slate Silent Quick Whole class	Students may copy or piggyback.	Explain why piggybacking does not serve the student's own best interest. Signal the moment when everyone should hold up his or her slate. Have students hold up slates at each step of a problem.
Reteaching	As teachers we may tend to delay reteaching, rather than do it right away after data show lack of understanding.	Reteach as soon as possible, even if this requires adjusting objectives and lesson plans.

BE CREATIVE

Read this only after you are finished with the Hand Signals Role Play in the "Practice with a Study Group or Partners" section.

- Use your class roster to track who shows lack of mastery. Next to their name, just write the question number of those questions they missed.

| 21 **TAKE A STAND** |

- If you're asking students to use hand signals for answering yes-no or true-false questions and they are mimicking others' responses, have everyone close his or her eyes during the activity.

- In activities like thumbs up–thumbs down, make it easier to scan responses by asking just the girls or just the boys (or one area of the room or another) to participate in a particular question. Or concentrate only on those students whom you already suspect (from performance on homework, quizzes, participation in class) may struggle with the content.

SUSTAIN YOUR PROGRESS

1. Using feedback from your study group or other peers, and reviewing your own lesson notes and observations, monitor your progress on *Check for Understanding*.

Date	A Great Check	A Great Quick Response!

2. Revisit "Where Am I Now?" Are you ready to build out to some other new technique?

ANALYZE THE CHAMPIONS: SOME OBSERVATIONS

 Clip 12. Teacher Bob Zimmerli, Grade 7

Mr. Zimmerli sets up desk work as a stop-and-go process that requires him to *Circulate* to *Check for Understanding* with each student during the work. He also checks briefly to confirm that the students understand what they are to do. Presumably the answers are short and easy for him to check quickly, and the items are generally similar in terms of what students must do to complete them.

 Clip 13. Teacher Isaac Pollack, Grade 9

| 20 **EXIT TICKET** |

Mr. Pollack requires students to show their work in the homework, which will facilitate *Checking for Understanding* and will also get more students to check it themselves. His use of *Exit Tickets* is another way to *Check for Understanding*.

Technique 19

AT BATS

OVERVIEW

Great lessons should have plenty of *At Bats*. No one masters a new skill on the second go-round or possibly even the tenth. Want to sound real sweet on the violin? Find a good teacher and practice scales ten thousand times. Or, in baseball talk, "Learn to hit by getting as many at bats as you can."

Repeated swings—*At Bats*—ingrain skills in learners' minds, allowing poise and leaving sufficient "working memory" for thinking about where the ball should go, or for learners' remembering now in a way that the memory is still there months later. In class, it's not two or three repetitions to mastery; it's ten or twenty.

Even in a busy lesson, remember repetition. Begin with a few *At Bats* on previous material ("cumulative review"). End with iterations of the skills in your objective so that students reach the point where they can practice further independently—which is where homework comes in.

20 **EXIT TICKET**

WHERE AM I NOW?

	Proficiency			
	I am brand new to *At Bats* . . .	**I'm familiar now with *At Bats* in concept, though I haven't planned it into a lesson . . .**	**I'm beginning to plan and raise the number of *At Bats* in my classroom . . .**	**I give plenty of good *At Bats* . . .**
Comfort & Confidence	❑ . . . and excited to try it.	❑ . . . but know with more practice I'll make it work.	❑ . . . and see their basic value for students.	❑ . . . and balance them well against other time-consuming needs.
	❑ . . . and undecided about my ability to pull it off.	❑ . . . because I still have questions about how to do it right.	❑ . . . but may need to reduce the percentage of strikeouts.	❑ . . . maybe sometimes even more than what students need.
	❑ . . . and not at all sure it's for me.	❑ . . . because, frankly, I still have serious doubts.	❑ . . . but don't feel comfortable with it in some general way.	❑ . . . but when class isn't going well, I do it poorly and it doesn't help.

Work from your strengths. If you find yourself in the bottom left portion, leaf through this technique to locate related ones you might prefer to work on right now.

EXPAND YOUR SKILLS AND REPERTOIRE

Think about how many *At Bats* it has taken you to master *No Opt Out* or some other key technique in this guide. Most likely you had to try the technique many times, in slightly different versions, before you got truly comfortable, found your own natural speaking voice with just the right tone, and were ready and confident in responding to unexpected variations in situation.

What can you take from your own learning process during the study of this book that can help you get your students to mastery?

_____

_____

_____

Mixing It Up

Use multiple variations and formats, so that students can handle changing contexts and variables and look forward to each pitch.

| 22 **COLD CALL** |
| 23 **CALL AND RESPONSE** |
| 24 **PEPPER** |

You probably want your youngsters to know their single-digit addition facts cold. As they become more familiar with them, how many different ways can you pitch the next problem? Add at least five to this set.

"How much is 2 plus 3, Stephen?"

"2 and 6, Darra?"

"I have four pennies and three pennies. How much is that, Shantal?"

"Roger had seven pencils, and Sarah has nine. How many do they have in all?"

"Winnie, you have five fingers on your right hand and five on your left. Don't look! How many is that?"

_____

_____

_____

_____

_____

What "bonus problems" could you add for the students who have these answers down cold?

_____

_____

You want your elementary students to know their parts of speech. Add half a dozen pitches to these:

"What part of speech is this word on the board?"

"What part of speech comes next? (And "Is that surprising?")

"What often comes after a preposition?"

"You need one of these in a predicate . . . Raimundo?"

_____

_____

_____

_____

_____

What "bonus problems" could you add for students who know all the parts?

_____

_____

You want your middle or high school students to know the order of the early presidents because that order tells a lot about what was going on in the first twenty years after independence:

"Who was first? Class."

"The second? Stella."

"Fourth? Mara."

"Who followed Washington?"

"How did that one land the job?"

"When did Jefferson decide he wanted the job? Why?"

"What was Madison before he was president?"

"Who was run out of Washington by the British?"

_____

_____

_____

Bonus problems?

_____

_____

Are Homework Tasks *At Bats*?

We like to think of homework as extended independent practice. It's most useful when

- Students practice further iterations of what *they know how to do,* so it should generally come after plenty of in-class *At Bats.*

- Students get chances to challenge themselves, within limits and by adapting and applying the skills they've mastered.

- It includes independent reading after students have built context in class, assuming you subsequently *Check for Understanding*.

18 CFU

Homework is *not* an effective way to introduce new material or to practice something students don't know how to do well enough to be reliably successful. Homework should let them further practice and consolidate what they already know how to do the right way. If a part of the homework is stretching their abilities, mark it as an extra challenge.

PRACTICE WITH STUDY GROUP OR PARTNERS

Role Play: On the Mound

1. To the group, bring a set of questions that group members really ought to be able to answer cold but might not be entirely sure of. (Your state's traffic laws, for example.) Take turns as *Teacher,* giving twenty or thirty *At Bats* to the rest of the group as *Students*. Vary your pitches. Try to get your group to solid mastery.

2. Discuss the experience from pitchers' and batters' perspectives.

More *At Bats*

With *At Bats* in mind, compare lessons that group members are planning, or discuss what generally happens in your class:

1. How many *At Bats* do students get in your lessons for a given skill?
2. How do you plan where to start pitching?
3. How do you decide when to stop?
4. How might you give them more *At Bats*?

Your takeaways from the group work:

_____

_____

_____

_____

TRY *AT BATS* IN THE CLASSROOM

1. Do the students need more *At Bats* from the previous lesson? How will those *At Bats* pick up from or differ from the ones you pitched last time? Script at least ten pitches.

2. According to your upcoming lesson plan, what's the day's objective? What related skills can be learned and strengthened with *At Bats*?

3. How will you judge whether students have reached the level you require? Be specific about what students will be able to do independently.

AT BATS

4.   At what points in the lesson will students be primed to step up to the plate? Script at least ten pitches for each point.

5.   Script the *At Bats* so that they gradually add variety and greater challenge. Enforce *Format Matters* if your *At Bats* are verbal, but . . .

6.   Written *At Bats* are good in that they cause every student to have to answer each question, which makes the *Ratio* higher. Plus they are the most independent form of work. True *At Bats* mastery may result in your being very quiet and merely *Circulating* and *Checking for Understanding*.

4 **FORMAT MATTERS**
15 **CIRCULATE**
17 **RATIO**
18 **CFU**

7.   At what points may some students be ready for bonus problems? What will those problems be?

8.   How will you end the class with a ton of *At Bats,* getting everyone off the bench and scoring?

9.   Use an *Exit Ticket* as the last *At Bat*.

20 **EXIT TICKET**

TROUBLE-SHOOT

Steady On

Sometimes it's hard to find enough time in the day to get in all the repetition students need; at such moments, homework may seem like a good solution. But homework is just *not* a substitute for *At Bats*. It may be "extra innings," but the umpire went home for supper, and no one's there to call each ball, strike, or homer. Homework is only a means of further independent practice.

Other Challenges

Possible Challenge	Possible Solutions
Students lose interest in the work.	Up the rigor! Increase variations slightly; fold in more challenge.
Too many strikes.	If kids aren't answering with success, it's a good thing; now you know you need to reteach, per *Check for Understanding*.

BE CREATIVE

Batters thrive on positive chatter from the dugout. What succinct chatter can you and the class adopt that the class (or individual students) will appreciate?

AT BATS

AT BATS

SUSTAIN YOUR PROGRESS

1. Keep track of your stats on *At Bats*.

Date	Number of *At Bats* I Gave on This Date, Roughly	At What Moments in the Lesson?

2. Revisit "Where Am I Now?" Are you ready to build out to some other new technique?

EXIT TICKET

OVERVIEW

On the basis of our experience of champion teachers at Uncommon Schools and other top-performing organizations, we recommend that just about every lesson end with an *Exit Ticket*. The "tickets" get passed at the end of class and include three or four questions (in various formats) that assess one or more parts of the objective. Every student receives the same question(s). Each student does the work and writes the answer(s) on his or her sheet, and you collect all sheets as or before students leave. Just after class, or perhaps even while your students are still there, you analyze the results. Did your students master the skills? If not, what parts were thorny for them? Now you know what to focus on in your next lesson plan.

The purpose of an *Exit Ticket* is to gather data on whether your class mastered your daily objective. Next day, having analyzed the data, lead the students in recognizing their own mistakes, reteach (see *Check for Understanding*), and give more *At Bats* as needed.

| 18 **CFU** |
| 19 **AT BATS** |

WHERE AM I NOW?

	Proficiency			
Comfort & Confidence	**I am brand new to *Exit Ticket* . . .**	**I'm in the planning stage . . .**	**I've tried *Exit Ticket* at least once in class . . .**	**I use *Exit Ticket* regularly . . .**
	❑ . . . and excited to try it.	❑ . . . but know I'll make it work.	❑ . . . and see that it can work well.	❑ . . . and regularly replan accordingly.
	❑ . . . and undecided about its value.	❑ . . . but still have questions about how to do it.	❑ . . . with mixed results I need to evaluate.	❑ . . . but need to follow through more consistently or improve in some other respect.

ANALYZE THE CHAMPIONS

View each video clip, ideally more than once, and answer the following questions. See possible answers for clip 13 at the end of this technique.

Clip 13. Teacher Isaac Pollack, Grade 9

1. How does Mr. Pollack's *Exit Ticket* process follow the general guidelines in the "Overview" section?
2. How does Mr. Pollack vary the basic *Exit Ticket* model?
3. What limitations might there be to dismissing students one by one and detaining them briefly at the door?

 Clip 14. Teacher Leanna Picard, Grade 8

1. How does Ms. Picard use *Exit Tickets* to follow up on misunderstandings from the previous session of class?
2. How long does it take her to do it?

| 18 **CFU** |

3. In what additional way not shown here might she be following up?

EXPAND YOUR SKILLS AND REPERTOIRE

Using the Data

| 18 **CFU** |

Exit Tickets ensure solid, classwide data that you can *Check for Understanding*. They enable you to ask,

- What percentage of the class got it right?
- What mistakes were made?
- What does the written work tell you about why those mistakes happened?
- How could the lesson plan be improved?
- How should tomorrow's lesson plan change? For example, what needs to be retaught or practiced more?

Following Up

| 29 **DO NOW** |

Return *Exit Tickets* to students the next day and follow up as needed. You can take a few particular students aside to work with them individually. You can also use the return of the ticket and your analysis (perhaps on the board) as the start of a classwide *Do Now*.

Creating Good Tickets

Great qualities in any *Exit Ticket*:

1. It asks just a *few* questions, numbered. Each is slightly different.

| 6 **BEGIN WITH THE END** |

2. All questions focus on the same basic aspect of the lesson objective.

3. The same basic challenge is posed in more than one way (for example, one multiple choice, another more open ended).

4. The answers required are short so that you can grade them quickly and use the data fast.

5. The layout will make it easy for you to quickly see whether each answer is right or wrong.

6. You can process the lot in ten minutes or less.

Exit Tickets that assess student performance after a reading or English lesson that is heavily focused on comprehending a text can be different from ones that assess skills. Ideally these include two types of question, one about the student's understanding of the reading ("What happened when Jonas tried to take the baby?") and another about some reading or analytical skill that was involved in the reading activity ("How is Jonas changing?"). Sometimes the answers for a reading *Exit Ticket* need to be a bit longer than for other tickets.

Rate the following *Exit Ticket* according to these and other criteria you might apply.

EXIT TICKET

Name _____

Date _____

Class _____

1. Simplify: $\dfrac{m^7}{m^3}$

2. Simplify: $6^5 \times 6^{10}$

3. New York City covers an area of x^7 miles. Minneapolis, Minnesota, covers an area of x^4 miles. How many times greater is the area of NYC than the area of Minneapolis?

   _____

   _____

4. Simplify: $4x \times 7x^3$

5. Simplify: $\dfrac{9c^2}{3c^2}$

PRACTICE WITH STUDY GROUP OR PARTNERS

1. As a group, share and compare your critiques of the *Exit Ticket*.

2. Bring a lesson plan and a corresponding *Exit Ticket* you want to use in class. Exchange tickets and critique them as you did for the *Exit Ticket* here. Also discuss:

   - How the *Exit Ticket* is related to the lesson objective
   - How you might follow up if a number of students answer incorrectly

3. Improve your own plan and *Exit Ticket*.

4. Your takeaways from the group work:

_____

_____

_____

_____

TRY *EXIT TICKET* IN THE CLASSROOM

1. Inform your class about the purpose of *Exit Tickets* and what they and you will do with them. Let them know that these are not graded "tests."

2. Be sure to start from your lesson objective.

TROUBLE-SHOOT

Steady On

Keep your *Exit Tickets* simple and focused on the objective.

Other Challenges

Possible Challenge	Possible Solutions
A student somehow doesn't turn in a completed *Exit Ticket*.	

BE CREATIVE

1. If a lot of students give incorrect answers, let students know, without singling anyone out, the aggregate results for a question. Then involve them in spotting possible sources of error.

3 **STRETCH IT**

2. Rename *Exit Ticket* to fit your own classroom and style.

SUSTAIN YOUR PROGRESS

1. Using feedback from your study group or other peers, and reviewing your own lesson notes and observations, monitor your progress on *Exit Ticket*.

Date	Something Good or Problematic About This Particular Ticket	A Way to Improve

2. Revisit "Where Am I Now?" Are you ready to build out to some other new technique?

ANALYZE THE CHAMPIONS: SOME OBSERVATIONS

 Clip 13. Teacher Isaac Pollack, Grade 9

Mr. Pollack varies the *Exit Ticket* model, maximizing the power of the tickets by reviewing them with his students in real time, as they turn them in, ensuring that they discuss errors (or confirm their mastery) before they leave. This approach may be especially well suited to students in older grades because it puts a premium on their responsibility to "own" errors and because it relies on some flexibility in time of dismissal (students meet him at the door when they believe they are done). Notice the transparency around addressing and remediating errors that this and other clips exemplify: "The rest of the questions will be assessed through your homework tonight."

EXIT TICKET

TAKE A STAND

OVERVIEW

This technique involves getting students to *Take a Stand* (express a judgment) on answers that other students in the class have given. It motivates everyone to do as much mental work as the student who is actually answering the question. It also helps you *Stretch It* and *Check for Understanding*.

| 3 **STRETCH IT** |
| 18 **CFU** |

WHERE AM I NOW?

	Proficiency			
	I am brand new to *Take a Stand* . . .	**I'm in the planning and practice stage, and haven't tried it yet in class . . .**	**I'm beginning to have my students *Take a Stand* in class . . .**	**My students regularly have to *Take a Stand* . . .**
Comfort & Confidence	❏ . . . and excited to try it.	❏ . . . but know with more practice I'll make it work.	❏ . . . and love how it basically works.	❏ . . . and I choose the right moments and ways to probe further.
	❏ . . . and undecided about my ability to pull it off.	❏ . . . because I still have questions about how to do it right.	❏ . . . with mixed results I need to evaluate.	❏ . . . but I could be getting more out of it in terms of boosting their thinking or *Checking for Understanding*.
	❏ . . . and not at all sure it's for me.	❏ . . . because I still have serious doubts.	❏ . . . but it doesn't seem to boost thinking or my own understanding of what they've learned.	❏ . . . but may need to revisit the basic ideas of the technique.

Work from your strengths. If you find yourself in the bottom left portion, leaf through this technique to locate related ones you might prefer to work on right now.

ANALYZE THE CHAMPIONS

View the video clip, ideally more than once, and answer the following questions.

Clip 4. Teacher Stacey Shells, Grade 7

1. How does Ms. Shells prepare the class to *Take a Stand*?

2. How does she help ensure that judgments will be expressed from a constructive frame of mind?

3. What, if anything, does she do to follow up on a judgment and increase the spread of participation?

4. How well is *Take a Stand* established in this classroom? What do you think Ms. Shells may have done in previous sessions to achieve this?

EXPAND YOUR SKILLS AND REPERTOIRE

Take a Stand brings student answers to the forefront of class. It makes them appear to be as fundamental to the work of learning as are teacher-given answers and underscores the value teachers put on student responses.

To maximize the *Ratio* in *Take a Stand,* often (not always) go beyond merely asking whether students agree or disagree, by making sure to follow up on responses—asking students to defend or explain their positions. "Tell me why your thumb is down, David." "Tell me why you gave it a three, Sarah."

Going beyond mere opinion into justification and explanation informs your teaching better and makes students accountable to give engaged rather than perfunctory judgments. One student answers, but every student has to decide if the answer is right, and to do that he or she has to come up with the answer or some criterion for judging it. In this way, in a class of twenty-five students, *Take a Stand* increases your leverage (the amount of gross cognitive work per minute of class) by about twenty-four.

> 17 **RATIO**
> 36 **100%**

Take a Stand also helps *you* see how indicative of the rest of the class an individual student's answer was. For limited-choice questions, you can quickly get data on which *other* wrong answers students chose, and so address a range of misunderstandings.

> 18 **CFU**

Expressing a Stand

You want students to be able to express what they really think, whether they agree or disagree or even possibly feel uncertain. To students, some modes of expression feel riskier than others.

Depending on the current state of your classroom culture and your students' current level of comfort with taking risks and exposing possible error, you can choose different means by which students can indicate they have reached a judgment. Some address the whole class; others single out individuals. Some are verbal, others gestural or related to writing. Some are more or less analytically demanding. Here are some examples:

"Thumbs up, thumbs down, thumbs sideways."

"Two snaps if you agree; two stomps if you don't."

"Stand up if you agree with David."

"One finger up if you also chose answer 1. Two if you choose 2, and so forth."

"How many people think Dashawn is right?"

"Raise your hand when you're ready to respond to what James just said."

TAKE A STAND

"He said New York and New Orleans share the same time zone. How consistent is that with what you know about their longitudes?"

"Score Elisha's answer 1 to 4 on our writing rubric."

"Show me with fingers how many *you* think half a dozen is."

"On your page, write down Sid's answer beside the answer you came up with. Any difference?"

You can also *Cold Call* students to *Take a Stand*.

22 **COLD CALL**

"He said New York and New Orleans share the same time zone. Is that accurate, Jessie?"

Come up with other ways in which you might ask students to *Take a Stand*. Frame each one as a question or statement to your class.

_____

_____

_____

_____

_____

_____

Don't Tip Your Hand

Remember to have students *Take a Stand* at times when the original answer was right *and* at times when it was wrong. Try to keep from revealing, explicitly or implicitly (through your tone of voice, for example), whether the answer was correct or not until you've asked students to figure it out.

"Thank you for stomping, Tarynn. I appreciate that you took the risk of challenging an answer that others showed agreement with. Now let's figure out why you didn't agree."

And, regardless of whether or not Tarynn's minority position was the faulty one,

"Let's have two snaps for Tarynn for pushing us all to think."

PRACTICE WITH STUDY GROUP OR PARTNERS

In a group, describe and compare one or more ways you have gone about getting students to *Take a Stand*.

- What methods have you tried?
- What methods lead to more students *Taking a Stand* and then actually revealing the depth and nature of their judgment?
- Do you need to remind yourself to go behind the stand to engage in questions about how or why students agree or disagree with the substance of the original answer?

TAKE A STAND

What insights do you take away from this discussion?

_____

_____

_____

TRY *TAKE A STAND* IN THE CLASSROOM

1. Mark several places in your next lesson plan where more participation (and *Check for Understanding*) could be achieved with *Take a Stand*. Look for places most closely aligned with the lesson objective.

9 **SHORTEST PATH**

2. If students already do something that can be construed as *Taking a Stand,* plan how you can use that to go behind the stand to explore its depth and expand participation in the moment.

3. Plan when and how you will explain *Take a Stand* and its value to the class. View clip 4 again for ideas.

4. Begin to notice students who may be holding back. Find a way to solicit stands from the class at a level that they will accept. Reward their *Taking a Stand* with praise and other supportive attention to their stand.

TROUBLE-SHOOT

Steady On

To avoid letting *Take a Stand* become a cursory routine, follow up on stands of any sort to elicit more about the judgment and the judgments of others in the class.

39 **DO IT AGAIN**
42 **NO WARNINGS**
49 **NORMALIZE ERROR**

Other Challenges

Possible Challenge	Possible Solutions
Students tend to refrain from *Taking a Stand*.	Praise the act of *Taking a Stand*. In your classroom culture, are students comfortable with exposing and discussing their own errors?
Some students never just voluntarily *Take a Stand*.	Do students know that volunteering is an option? How do you include this as a classroom participation expectation? Script a brief reminder to students, "Since we're all scholars, I'll expect to see everyone's hand. Let's try that again." Reinforce with *Do It Again* or a consequence as necessary.

BE CREATIVE

Invent a different name for *Take a Stand* that resonates with your students and style.

SUSTAIN YOUR PROGRESS

1.   Using feedback from your study group or other peers, and reviewing your own lesson notes and observations, monitor your progress on *Take a Stand*.

Date	Things I'm Doing Well	Ways to Improve

2.   Revisit "Where Am I Now?" Are you ready to build out to some other new technique?

TAKE A STAND

COLD CALL

OVERVIEW

Cold Call means calling on students to answer, regardless of whether their hands are in the air. It trains everyone to pay attention, and pushes *all* students to answer *all* of your questions in their minds.

    Cold Call can help you maintain pacing (the illusion of speed you create in your classroom) and increase the actual rate at which you can cover material. In addition, it can help you maintain both the energy of the students and your own control of the classroom. Finally, you can't *Check for Understanding* reliably without *Cold Calling*, because testing for mastery by relying on the students who think they're doing well guarantees you a skewed sample of your class.

    The following are essential elements of *Cold Calls*:

- Predictable
- Systematic
- Upbeat and positive

- Scaffolded and unbundled (large questions broken into smaller parts, with *Ratio* in mind)

17 **RATIO**

- Focused on curricular substance

Here are some options:

- Allowing "Hands up" versus requesting "Hands down"
- Timing in your naming the student
- Using the *Cold Call* as an initial question or as a follow-on

WHERE AM I NOW?

	Proficiency			
	I am brand new to Cold Call . . .	**I'm in the planning and practice stage, though I haven't tried Cold Call yet in class** . . .	**I'm beginning to try Cold Call in my classroom** . . .	**I Cold Call regularly** . . .
Comfort & Confidence	❏ . . . and excited to try it.	❏ . . . but know with more practice I'll make it work.	❏ . . . and love how it basically works.	❏ . . . and my students answer promptly.
	❏ . . . and undecided about my ability to pull it off.	❏ . . . because I still have questions about how to do it right.	❏ . . . with mixed results I need to evaluate.	❏ . . . but I may be overusing it.
	❏ . . . and not at all sure it's for me.	❏ . . . because, frankly, I still have serious doubts.	❏ . . . but it doesn't seem to work or suit me.	❏ . . . but when class isn't going well, I do it poorly and it doesn't help.

Work from your strengths. If you find yourself in the bottom left portion, leaf through this technique to locate related ones you might prefer to work on right now.

COLD CALL

ANALYZE THE CHAMPIONS

View each video clip, ideally more than once, and answer the following questions. See the end of the technique for some possible answers.

 Clip 16. Teacher Hannah Lofthus, Grade 2

1. How does Ms. Lofthus's way of *Cold Calling* help her achieve effective pacing?
2. How does it promote student engagement?

18 **CFU**

3. How does it support effective *Check for Understanding*?
4. Locate evidence that Ms. Lofthus's *Cold Call* manner is each of these: predictable, systematic, and positive.

 Clip 17. Teacher Summer Payne, Grade K

1. What, if anything, surprises you about the reaction of Ms. Payne's kindergarteners to *Cold Call*?
2. What does Ms. Payne do to make their reaction happen?
3. Develop your answer to question 2 into a brief statement of how you might translate what she is doing to promote their reaction for whatever level of students you teach.

EXPAND YOUR SKILLS AND REPERTOIRE

To review, there are three purposes for *Cold Calling*:

1. Pacing. *Cold Calling* makes your class go faster—no time wasted pleading for answers ("Um, I'm seeing the same three hands. Didn't anyone else do the homework? Do I need to remind you that your participation is being graded?"), and no stultifying perception of slowness from watching the teacher plead for energy.
2. Engagement. When students think they are about to be called on (and expected to participate in a real conversation, one that matters) at any time, they will prepare by engaging in the material.
3. *Checking for Understanding.* Check for mastery by relying on the students who think they know, and you'll always overestimate your students' success. Make it normal to ask any kid what she can do at any time, and you'll begin to see where your students—all of them—really are.

Listen to Yourself in Class

1. Audio-record your next lesson, or listen again to a recent session you recorded. Use a stopwatch to document how much time you spend waiting (and encouraging and cajoling and asking) for volunteers. Then listen to the tape again. What do you notice about the general pacing of the session?

_____

_____

_____

2.   Identify instances you were *Cold Calling* students. In terms of the essential elements of *Cold Calls* noted in the "Overview" section, to what extent were your calls

- Predictably frequent?

_____

If you *Cold Call* for a few minutes of your class almost daily, students will come to expect it and *change their behavior in advance,* preparing to be asked questions at any time by paying attention and readying themselves mentally. At some point in most lessons, students should be asked to participate whether or not they have raised their hands.

- Systematic and calm in tone?

_____

- Spread out around the class in terms of their seating and range of abilities?

_____

- Accomplished without wasting time in "choosing" responders?

_____

- Positive in tone?

_____

An energetic tone of questioning shows your respect and faith in the students' ability to join the conversation. They benefit from the message that *you* thought they could answer the question and that your goal was for them to get it right. They may occasionally surprise themselves with their own capability.

- Focused on the content of the lesson?

_____

Compare this *Cold Call* focused on content . . .

"Do you think Lincoln declared war on the South primarily to eradicate slavery? John?"

. . . to an abrupt question implicitly criticizing student behavior:

"What did I just say, John?"

"Isn't that right, John?"

Team It Up with Other Techniques

Coupled with *No Opt Out, Cold Call* is surely one of the most important techniques in *Teach Like a Champion*. It is also most often the best way to question when you *Check for Understanding*. It lets you control the sample from which you are getting your data for the class as a whole. But make a point of using it *before* you need to check. Normalize it as a natural and upbeat part of your class. Listen to the audio again and notice where you use such techniques.

You can also mix *Cold Call* with *Call and Response*. Move back and forth between whole-group (choral response) and individual responses at a rapid, energetic pace to drive up positive energy. This can also keep students from coasting during *Call and Response*.

| 1 **NO OPT OUT** |
| 16 **BREAK IT DOWN** |
| 18 **CFU** |
| 24 **PEPPER** |

| 23 **CALL AND RESPONSE** |

COLD CALL

Coming out of *Call and Response*, clarify that *Call and Response* has ended by starting your first *Cold Call* name first.

| 26 **EVERYBODY WRITES** | Use *Everybody Writes* to prepare for *Cold Call*, letting everyone think in advance about the topic or questions.

Allow "Hands Up" Versus Requesting "Hands Down"

As you *Cold Call,* you may sometimes allow students to raise their hands if they wish. This lets you to continue encouraging and rewarding students who ask to participate, even while you sometimes call on others. It also allows you to gather data on how many students feel confident and want to participate.

You can also tell students to put their hands down—"Thanks, I'm not taking hands"—and then *Cold Call* whomever you wish. This increases pacing (it's fast when there are no hands) and more forcefully establishes your control of the classroom and makes your *Cold Call* more explicit, predictable, and transparent. "Hands down" also reduces the students' tendency to call out answers and lets you *Check for Understanding* with reticent students in a way that appears less deliberate.

What other advantages can you see for allowing hands ("hands up") or disallowing them ("hands down")?

Advantages of hands up:

_____

_____

_____

Advantages of hands down:

_____

_____

_____

Note that you can move at your discretion between taking hands and *Cold Calling* so that you can scaffold effectively. For example, you could *Cold Call* students for the first three questions in a sequence and then save the last and toughest or most interesting question for a volunteer. How does this compare to what you've generally done in class?

_____

_____

Time the Name

Using the sequence of *question, pause, name* generally keeps the student who will be called on undetermined and causes everyone to come up with an answer during the pause. This gives you the highest possible *Ratio* and so is the default for *Cold Calling*. But there are some cases where you might want to say a student's name first. Can you recall some of them from *Teach Like a Champion*? Can you add some others?

_____

_____

_____

Timing	Effect
"Darren, tell us one cause of World War I, please."	Allows Darren to prepare to hear the question, and may work well also for a student with slow language-processing ability or less strong command of English. But it also lets all others off the hook. They don't even need to catch the question.
"Darren" (pause), "tell us one cause of World War I, please."	May allow Darren more time to get set for the question, but does he even know one is coming? Slows down the class and wastes time for everyone else.
"Tell us one cause of World War I, please, Darren."	May catch Darren short and may fail to give other students sufficient time to think and answer internally.
"Tell us one cause of World War I, please" *(pause)*, "Darren."	*Best general effect: During the pause, all begin to answer the question in their heads, in case they might be called. Darren then gets called on to say his answer aloud. Others mentally (or aloud) add their answer to his.*

You can also *pre-call*: tell a student to expect to be called on later in the lesson. You can pre-call privately before class or publicly during class.

"Latisha, be ready for when we review the stages of the water cycle!"

"Karen knows I'm coming to her when we get to the subject of Lincoln's goals for the proclamation!"

How do these approaches (including the ones in the table) compare to what you've generally done in class?

_____

_____

Use Three Kinds of Follow-On *Cold Calls*

You can follow on to

- *A previous question*. Ask a question via *Cold Call*—often a warmup; then ask the student a short series of further questions (most teachers ask two to four in total) in which her opinions are further developed or her understanding further tested.

- *Another student's comment*. This reinforces the importance of listening to peers as well as the teacher: "James says the setting is 'a dark summer night.' Does that tell us everything we need to know about the setting, Susan?"

- *A student's own earlier comment*. This signals that once you've spoken, you're not done: "But, James, you said earlier that we always multiplied length and width to find area. Why didn't we do that here?"

Follow-ons can help you scaffold. The following is the beginning of a *Cold Call* scaffolding sequence that aims at a fairly complex answer. For each sequence, fill out the blank lines to continue with a possible *Cold Call* process. Try to use different types of follow-on.

The target answer here is an explanation of how the students simplified this equation: $3x + 6y = 36/2$.

1	*Teacher:*	What's the simplified form you've worked out on your sheet—Serena?
2	*Serena:*	$x + 2y = 6$.
3	*Teacher:*	Good. Which side did you first start working on—Gerald?
4	*Gerald:*	The right side.
5	*Teacher:*	_____?
6	*[ ]:*	_____
7	*Teacher:*	_____?
8	*[ ]:*	_____
9	*Teacher:*	_____?
10	*[ ]:*	_____
11	*Teacher:*	_____?
12	*[ ]*	_____
13	*Teacher:*	_____?
14	*[ ]:*	_____

Do the same with this next sequence, whose aim is a brief review of causes of the Civil War. For example, the teacher may want students to mention North–South regional differences regarding industrialization and social life, economic tensions between them, and the Southern perception that Lincoln favored Northern interests.

1	*Teacher:*	So we're agreed that the Civil War wasn't just about the long-standing question of slavery, important as that question was. What other tensions were building up between North and South—Wei-wen?
2	*Wei-wen:*	Well, Lincoln had just been elected.
3	*Teacher:*	Right ... ?
		_____?
4	*[ ]:*	_____
5	*Teacher:*	_____?
6	*[ ]:*	_____
7	*Teacher:*	_____?
8	*[ ]:*	_____
9	*Teacher:*	_____?
10	*[ ]:*	_____
11	*Teacher:*	_____?
12	*[ ]:*	_____

Critique your sequences using the criteria of an effective *Cold Call*.

COLD CALL

Learn Your Students' Names

To *Cold Call* effectively, you need to know your students' names and where they are sitting. If you don't already know their names, make learning their names one of your goals in your *Cold Calls*. For example, consult your roll sheet as you *Cold Call* on as many students as you can in each session until you have all the names at your command.

If classes have already begun, circle any name on your class list you still can't now associate with a face. Then, before or during class, locate faces for which you don't know the name. Ask each one to say his name, thank him, and repeat the name back for yourself.

Consider a class activity in which you allow students to test you. *Cold Call* a student by name and say, "Please point to someone else whose name I need to learn."

Scaffold Cold Calls

Cold Calls should take advantage of *scaffolding*. Draw students in and help them succeed by starting generally with simple questions and progressing to harder ones. Emphasize what they already know and reinforce basic knowledge before challenging them for greater rigor.

You can subtly scaffold by letting students begin answering *Cold Calls* about work they have already done, whose answers they have in front of them. Then follow up with more rigorous questions—for example, asking them to explain how they got that answer.

Consider this sequence as Mr. Williams teaches his third graders strategies for answering multiple-choice questions. The multiple-choice question they are analyzing has required the student to find the "complete sentence."

1	*Mr. Williams:*	We're reading down the set of possible answers. Read the third choice for me, please, Kyrese.
2	*Kyrese:*	*(reading)* "Have you seen a pumpkin seed?"
3	*Mr. Williams:*	Do we have a subject, Japhante?
4	*Japhante:*	Yes.
5	*Mr. Williams:*	What's the subject?
6	*Japhante:*	You.
7	*Mr. Williams:*	You. Excellent. Do we have a predicate, Eric?
8	*Eric:*	Yes.
9	*Mr. Williams:*	What's the predicate?
10	*Eric:*	Seen.
11	*Mr. Williams:*	Seen. Excellent. Is it a complete thought, Rayshawn?
12	*Rayshawn:*	Yes.
13	*Mr. Williams:*	Is that our complete sentence?
14	*Rayshawn:*	Yes.
15	*Mr. Williams:*	So, on to the next page? Or what do we need to do, Shakaye?
16	*Shakaye:*	We need to look at the other two [answer choices] because that might sound right, but one of the other two might sound right, too.

Before you read on, reread the preceding sequence. What evidence do you see of the five main criteria of an effective *Cold Call*?

_____

_____

_____

| 16 **BREAK IT DOWN** | By parceling tasks out to five students, Mr. Williams ensured fuller participation and created the expectation that participation is a predictable and systematic event. He dispensed some opening questions in rapid |

sequence, carefully increasing difficulty. The first, low-difficulty question merely asked a student to read what was in front of him. The second ("Do we have a subject?") was a simple yes-no question designed for the struggling student of whom it was asked to ensure his getting it right. Based on that success and the fact that the student was now engaged in the process of thinking about sentence structure, Mr. Williams came back with a more difficult third question ("What's the subject?"). At question six, he raised the bar again, and his eighth and last question in the series ("Or what do we need to do, Shakaye?") was the hardest.

Analyze Some *Cold Call* Prompts

Read the prompts here and judge whether they satisfy any of the effective keys to *Cold Calling*. Then circle "would" or "would not" to indicate whether or not you would use this as a *Cold Call,* and justify your reasoning. Here are some questions to apply:

- In what ways is the prompt not aligned with the *Cold Call* technique?
- What message about classroom participation does the prompt send to the students?
- Does the prompt seem to be a "gotcha" call, rather than one that aims at success?
- Does the call seem to be based on personal bias? Does the teacher seem to be calling on a student only because the teacher knows that the student knows the material?
- Does the prompt send any strong message about classroom participation? What is the message?

Prompt 1: To a student who is staring out the window: "Do you know the answer, Sara?"

Evaluation of prompt: _____

_____

_____

I would / would not use this as a *Cold Call* prompt because/if:

_____

_____

_____

Prompt 2: "Jamal, earlier you said that snakes are reptiles. Do you still think that after what we've learned?"

Evaluation of prompt: _____

_____

_____

I would / would not use this as a *Cold Call* because/if:

_____

_____

_____

Prompt 3: "Mitch, you love multiplication. What's 16 times 9?"

Evaluation of prompt: _____

_____

_____

I would / would not use this as a *Cold Call* prompt because/if:

_____

_____

_____

Prompt 4: After taking only raised hands from the entire class, "Tell us one cause of the Civil War, Darren."

Evaluation of prompt: _____

_____

_____

I would / would not use this as a *Cold Call* prompt because/if:

_____

_____

_____

Prompt 5: "Who can tell us what the verb is in the sentence 'The elephants were trampling through the jungle'? I see three hands, five hands, ten hands. [To a student whose hand is not raised] Brandy, what do you think?"

Evaluation of prompt: _____

_____

_____

I would / would not use this as a *Cold Call* prompt because/if:

_____

_____

_____

Prompt 6: "Jordan, in about a minute I'm going to ask you to tell me the name of the x-axis on the graph. Be ready!"

Evaluation of prompt: _____

_____

_____

I would / would not use this as a *Cold Call* prompt because/if:

_____

_____

_____

Prompt 7: "Let's see who was listening ..."

Evaluation of prompt: _____

_____

_____

I would / would not use this as a *Cold Call* prompt because/if:

_____

_____

_____

Draft a "Rollout Speech" to Introduce the Class to *Cold Call*

Extend this activity into your group work (see the "Practice with Study Group or Partners" section), but write your own draft before you convene.

Write a brief script that introduces *Cold Call* to your class at the beginning of the school year. Write another you could use midyear.

Consider these challenges:

- *Cold Call* may be new to the students, or they may have experienced surprise calling in the past mainly as a punishment for lapses in participation.

- Students probably want to know the reasoning behind a new routine in class—how it will serve their learning. They may also want to know who will be called on; how they should respond if called; and whether there will be particular times, if any, that they can expect *Cold Call*.

- You want *Cold Call* to become a norm.

- It's good to introduce required behaviors positively, with some element of humor, and to exercise them immediately.

Here's the introductory speech Colleen Driggs gave her fifth graders one year at Rochester Prep.

In some of your classes, your teachers do something called *Cold Calling*. In fact I do it. It's when you don't raise your hand and a teacher calls on you, just to see what you know. And it's not like a "gotcha"; it's really just a way to do a quick review. I don't call it *Cold Calling,* though; I call it "hot calling" because you get a chance to shine and to show that you are *on fire.* So almost every day when we're talking about genre we're going to do hot calling. It's a great way to review all of these definitions and terms that we've learned.

Here's the hardest part about hot calling: you've got to keep your hands down. Your hands are folded, and I will call on a person. When I call on that person, you track just like you normally do and then you track me when you hear my voice again. Nod if you understand. Nod if you are ready for hot calling. Beautiful. Keep your hands down. Please don't call out. Sit up. Remember *SLANT.*

> 32 **SLANT**

What is the definition of genre? Hands down. Robert, what's the definition of genre?

Add Rigor

Part of the power of *Cold Call* lies in students' pride at answering demanding questions on the spot. Although as mentioned, sometimes questions must be simple, others can and should be rigorous and demanding, even without scaffolding.

This transcript of a recent *Pepper* (rapid-fire) *Cold Call* session by teacher Jesse Rector shows you a level of rigor that students can reach. How many of the following *Cold Call* questions, asked in rapid-fire succession, could *you* answer correctly?

> 24 **PEPPER**

1	*Mr. Rector:*	I'm a square field with an area of 169 square feet. What's the length of one of my sides, Janae?
2	*Janae:*	13.
3	*Mr. Rector:*	13 what? [Asking Janae for the units is an example of *Format Matters.*]
4	*Janae:*	13 feet.
5	*Mr. Rector:*	I'm a square field with a perimeter of 48 feet; what's my area, Katrina?
6	*Katrina:*	144 square feet.
7	*Mr. Rector:*	Excellent. I'm a regular octagon with a side that measures $8x$ plus 2; what is my perimeter, Tamisse?
8	*Tamisse:*	$64x$ plus 16.
9	*Mr. Rector:*	Excellent. I am an isosceles triangle with two angles that measure $3x$ each; what is the measure of my third angle, Anaya?
10	*Anaya:*	180 degrees minus $6x$.
11	*Mr. Rector:*	Excellent, 180 degrees minus $6x$. The square root of 400 is .... what, Frank?
12	*Frank:*	100.
13	*Mr. Rector:*	No, the square root of 400 isn't 100; help him out.
14	*David:*	20.
15	*Mr. Rector:*	That's right, it's 20. Tell him why.
16	*David:*	Because if you multiply 20 by 20, you'll get 400.

> 4 **FORMAT MATTERS**

COLD CALL

Considering your work in this chapter and elsewhere, how do you think Mr. Rector brought his students to this level? How might that translate to your own teaching context?

_____

_____

_____

_____

Prepare to Cover the Class Systematically

To address the need to be systematic in your use of *Cold Call,* prepare a reminder and note-making tool (perhaps a simple chart or checklist) you can use next time in class to record evidence of "system," including whom you called on in the session.

PRACTICE WITH STUDY GROUP OR PARTNERS

Together, review and compare your individual work in the "Expand Your Skills and Repertoire" section.

Cold Call Role Play

Cold Call takes nerve the first few times you do it. This activity gets you to break that barrier by practicing it in a supportive group of peers. You need at least four participants.

Well before you meet, your group's *Facilitator* should go over these instructions and remind everyone how to prepare. In the session, the *Facilitator* can use a *Cold Call* to appoint a different participant to play *Teacher* in each round. All other participants are *Students*.

The best topic matter for this exercise is material about which you *all* have already taken notes. In all the rounds, you can use the same topic, such as "How to *Cold Call*," or you can use different topics, such as how to perform some other champion technique that you all have already studied. (The *Facilitator* will help you as a group decide.)

All participants should bring their various notes to the session, and everyone should be informed of what notes or topic the others will be addressing.

In advance, each participant reviews her notes on each topic and plans elements of a *Cold Call* sequence to review the topic when she is in the *Teacher* role.

1. When you convene, for each round appoint one *Student* to also be the *Timer*.

2. In each round, the *Teacher* stands "up front" and leads the session. *Students* answer to the best of their ability.

3. At around ninety seconds, the *Timer* pauses the session, allowing *Students* to give feedback (about a minute total), including

- Something the *Teacher* did well and should continue doing. ("I really like how you are using follow-on questions to keep engagement high.")

- Some way the *Teacher* might have altered what she did at some particular point. ("We might have been helped by some scaffolding when you turned to what's meant by 'predictable.'")

4. The *Timer* asks the *Teacher* to continue for another sixty to ninety seconds. The *Teacher* resumes charge until the *Timer* calls an end.

5. For about thirty seconds, everyone notes down something he or she wants to say or ask later about the round.

6. Go on to the next round until everyone has been *Teacher*.

7. The *Facilitator* leads a discussion about what the group has experienced. Everyone should be free to ask questions, such as these:

To ask of the *Teacher*:

- How did it feel? Were you nervous? Why or why not?
- Did anything surprise you?
- What did you think you did best? Were there any moments you wish you had back?

To ask of *Students*:

- How did it feel to be a student?
- Was anybody nervous? When?
- Was the tension a *good* thing—productive?
- Were all of the questions clear?
- What was one good moment? What was one moment that could have been improved?
- Which rounds seemed most effective in helping us cover the topic? What made them stand out?

For everyone: What's one useful thing you learned from this activity?

_____

_____

Introducing *Cold Call* to the Class

In the group, practice delivering the rollouts you've written (in "Expand Your Skills and Repertoire"). After each has presented, discuss the following points as a group:

- What do you expect will be challenging about introducing *Cold Call* to your students?
- What do you expect will be different about introducing *Cold Call* in the middle of the year?
- Are there any objections from students that you anticipate having to overcome?
- As a group, find good ideas among the introductions you just gave.
- Suggest specific improvements you might make on *your* introduction, and get feedback from the group.

TRY *COLD CALL* IN THE CLASSROOM

1. If *Cold Call* is new to the class, study your lesson plan for a place to explain it. Go directly from that explanation to several actual *Cold Calls*.

2. In the lesson plan, review your objectives and note places you want to be sure to use *Cold Calls*. *Script your questions*. (You only have to try it without scripting to know why; if you're not sure of the answer or if the question is worded poorly and there is no clear answer, your *Cold Call* will be a disaster.) Be sure that some *Cold Call* questions occur early in the session, as part of your strategy of making them the norm and engaging your students *before* they might tune out.

> 6 **BEGIN WITH THE END**

3. Think about which students in your class you would like to see more engaged and what sort of *Cold Call* might work best for them.

COLD CALL

COLD CALL

4. Note where your *Cold Call* goal is to *Check for Understanding* or to enhance some other technique.

5. Considering the range of abilities in your class, where may you need to scaffold?

6. Without feeling that you need to memorize them, review the variety of possibilities described in this chapter and construct a few *Cold Call* questions and sequences that might come in handy. But also *decide* what your first, second, and third *Cold Call* questions could be, and to whom you might put them.

7. Try using *Cold Call* at some moments when you *could* choose from a show of hands.

8. After class, make brief notes based mainly on the "Overview." Look back at this chapter to notice variations you might build into your next lesson plan.

TROUBLE-SHOOT

Steady On

1. "Anyone? . . . Anyone? . . ." laments the comic teacher in the movie *Ferris Bueller's Day Off* (1986) when none of his teenagers raises a helping hand. Use *Cold Call* to banish those tedious, sapping moods and moments.

| 38 **STRONG VOICE** |
| 42 **NO WARNINGS** |
| 45 **WARM/STRICT** |

2. *Cold Calling* is superb preventive medicine, but less effective as a cure. It's an engagement strategy, not a discipline strategy. Once a student is off task, the opportunity to *Cold Call* has passed. Use a *behavioral* technique instead.

3. If your *Cold Call* surprises students, they may learn a lesson ("Darn, I should have been ready"), but unless they know they'll surely be *Cold Called* again *very soon,* they won't have cause to change their behavior *before* you ask your question. They may just feel ambushed and annoyed. Do you need to break a habit of "gotcha" calls? How might you do that?

_____

_____

4. Are you prone to lapsing into any one of these inner thoughts?

"How do I give everyone a chance?"

"Whose turn is it?"

"Who will give me the answer I want?"

| 18 **CFU** |

If so, specify in your lesson plan a systematic method of calling. Also think about what better questions to be asking yourself during the actual *Cold Calls,* in line with *Check for Understanding*.

_____

_____

Other Challenges

Possible Challenge	Possible Solutions
I worded a question unclearly, causing an informed student to have unnecessary trouble with it.	Slow down your delivery of the question. Spend more effort on writing questions into your lesson plan. Deliver a complex question in written form instead. 26 **EVERYBODY WRITES**
Students can't keep up with my pace. I think they know the answers, but the *Cold Call* stresses them out.	Allow for a bit more *Wait Time*: ask the question, pause a bit longer, then say the name. 25 **WAIT TIME** Frame the rollout or the question itself positively. Make your *Cold Calling* a challenge. Ask students to stand for the *Cold Calls* and turn them into *Pepper*. Or ask them if they can, as a class, get ten out of ten in rapid succession. *Break It Down*. 24 **PEPPER** 16 **BREAK IT DOWN**

BE CREATIVE

Some teachers emphasize the systematic nature of their *Cold Calls* by keeping visible charts on which they track who's been called on. It sends a clearer message that everyone gets his or her share.

Ms. Driggs, in her rollout, has renamed *Cold Call* to make it her own. Champion teacher Summer Payne (clip 17) also introduces *Cold Call* to her kindergarteners by renaming it.

SUSTAIN YOUR PROGRESS

1. Using feedback from your study group or other peers, and reviewing your own lesson notes and observations, monitor your progress on *Cold Call*.

Date	Things I'm Doing Well	Ways I Can Sharpen *Cold Call* and Broaden Its Use or Value

2. Revisit "Where Am I Now?" Are you ready to build out to some other new technique?

ANALYZE THE CHAMPIONS: SOME OBSERVATIONS

 Clip 16. Teacher Hannah Lofthus, Grade 2

From a scripted curriculum, Ms. Lofthus asks very short, same-format questions that each child can answer by reading a word. Because each question and answer is so brief, she can poll everyone's understanding and keep them all expecting to be called on not just once but shortly again. She calls on students in rapid succession and in a rhythm, reinforcing engagement by keeping students on their toes. She doesn't just want the answer; she wants it right after the snap. She calls on a student in the front twice in a row—this lets students know that just because they have answered doesn't mean that they won't get another question. She keeps the tone positive with a smile.

 Clip 17. Teacher Summer Payne, Grade K

Many teachers perceive *Cold Calling* to be inherently stress inducing and perhaps too intense for kindergarten. But do the students in this clip even know they're being *Cold Called*? If they do, they're having too much fun to worry.

| 46 **JOY FACTOR** |

Ms. Payne adds a ditty, "Individual tur-urns, listen for your na-ame," and all of a sudden *Cold Call* is a game—one her students are dying to play. The use of the word "turn" (it's your chance) is critical to pulling this off. Making a game of *Cold Call* is doable at any grade level . . . even if it might look different from this game.

COLD CALL

CALL AND RESPONSE

OVERVIEW

Call and Response means using group choral response to build energetic, positive engagement. You ask (call); they answer (respond) in unison. *Call and Response* can be put to three distinct uses:

1. Reinforcing academic review with more *At Bats*
2. Invigorating the class
3. Reinforcing your authority and command

Call and Response may sound simple, but in all its variations, it is a challenging and exceptional tool for helping students engage *and* achieve.

There are at least five types or levels of *Call and Response* and various ways to cue students in about when and how to respond.

WHERE AM I NOW?

<table>
<tr><th colspan="5">Proficiency</th></tr>
<tr><th rowspan="8">Comfort & Confidence</th><th>I am brand new to Call and Response . . .</th><th>I'm in the planning and practice stage, though I haven't tried Call and Response yet in class . . .</th><th>I'm beginning to try Call and Response in my classroom . . .</th><th>I use Call and Response regularly . . .</th></tr>
<tr><td>❑ . . . and excited to try it.</td><td>❑ . . . but know with more practice I'll make it work.</td><td>❑ . . . and love how it basically works.</td><td>❑ . . . and for all three basic purposes.</td></tr>
<tr><td>❑ . . . and undecided about my ability to pull it off.</td><td>❑ . . . because I'm still unsure how to do it right.</td><td>❑ . . . with mixed results I need to evaluate.</td><td>❑ . . . but I may be overusing it.</td></tr>
<tr><td>❑ . . . and not at all sure it's for me.</td><td>❑ . . . because, frankly, I have doubts about using it.</td><td>❑ . . . but it doesn't seem to work or suit me.</td><td>❑ . . . but have work to do on freeloading, looseness, or other issues.</td></tr>
</table>

Work from your strengths. If you find yourself in the bottom left portion, leaf through this technique to locate related ones you might prefer to work on right now.

ANALYZE THE CHAMPIONS

View the video clip, ideally more than once, and answer the following questions.

 Clip 18. Teacher Lauren Whitehead, Grade 1

1. What wording does Ms. Whitehead use in her first *Call and Response*? What academic purposes are served by the *Call and Response*?
2. What other *Call and Response* cue or cues have the students learned?
3. What connection, if any, is there between the first and last *Call and Response*?

EXPAND YOUR SKILLS AND REPERTOIRE

Types of *Call and Response*

Many teachers use only a simplistic form of *Call and Response*—asking students to repeat aphorisms and chants. In fact, there are five levels of *Call and Response* interaction, listed here roughly in order of increasing intellectual rigor.

1. *Repeat*. You heard this in clip 18. Students repeat what their teacher has said or complete a familiar phrase the teacher started. The topic can be behavioral or academic:

"Who are we?!" "Chicago East Prep!"

"What are we here to do?!" "To learn and achieve!"

"When we see a . . ." "Preposition!" "We look for . . ." "Its object!"

---

26 **EVERYBODY WRITES**

2. *Report*. Students are asked to report their answers to problems or questions they've worked out. This method lets you more energetically reinforce academic work once it's been completed.

"On three, tell me your answer to problem number two . . ."

3. *Reinforce*. You reinforce new information or a strong answer by asking the class to repeat it. This method gives everyone additional active interaction with critical new content. And when a student provides the information, he or she sees that "My answer was so important, my teacher asked the whole class to repeat it."

"Can anyone tell me what this part of the expression is called? Yes, Trayvon, that's the exponent. Class, what's this part of the expression called?"

4. *Review*. Students review answers or information from earlier in the class (or unit).

"Who was the first person Theseus met on the road to Athens, class?"

"Who was the second person?"

"And now who's the third?"

"What did we say we did to a number when we multiplied it by itself?"

5. *Solve*. The teacher asks students to solve a problem in real time and call out the answer in unison.

"If the length is 10 inches and the width is 12 inches, the area of our rectangle must be how many square inches, class?!"

This is the most challenging *Call and Response* to do well, but it is also the most rigorous. In order for the class to solve a problem in real time and call out the answer together, there must be (1) a single clear answer and (2) a strong likelihood that all students will know how to solve it. But working at this level of rigor, students often surprise themselves with their ability to solve problems in real time.

Compose three questions that you might ask your students at the level of *solve*:

1. _____

_____

2. _____

_____

3. _____

_____

Types of In-Cues

An *in-cue* allows students to prepare and the teacher to ensure a higher level of precision and maintain the anticipation and fun. For students to participate enthusiastically in *Call and Response,* they must confidently

36 **100%**

and clearly know that when they call out, so will everyone else. A good in-cue is the key to achieving this. Here are five kinds of in-cues.

1. *Count-based in-cues*. Counting is powerful and
   - Gives students time to get ready to answer, including collecting their breath for a shout or a song
   - Helps them answer more exactly on cue
   - Can be cut short if students are not fully attentive or on task in the lead-up to the *Call and Response*
   - Can build suspense and anticipation
   - Can be sped up or slowed down as your pacing requires
   - Lets you save time by gradually truncating it, as students become more familiar with it
   - Can be turned into gesture (see point 3)
     "One, two ..."
     "Ready, set ..."
     "One, two, ready, you ..."
     "One, two ... I don't have everyone ..."
     "One, two ... I love your voices ..."

2. *Group in-cues*. These help foster the class's group identity and remind them that you expect universal participation. If you don't get that participation, repeat the group word slightly more emphatically: "*every*body."

"Who was the main author of the Declaration of Independence? Everybody!"

"Class! What amount can no number be divided by?"

3. *Gestural in-cues.* Nonverbal in-cues can be quick and need not interrupt your flow. If used consistently, they are powerful as well as very efficient. Avoid gestures that may seem excessively schoolmasterish or schoolmarmish. Snapping your fingers isn't inherently so. But think about your expression and other factors as you snap. Here are some garden-variety gestures:

Fingers up

Pointing

Dropping a hand from shoulder height

Looping motion with the finger

A nod

Finger snaps

Finger to ear (for call); hand open to class (for response)

4. *Shift in tone and volume.* Increase the volume in the last few words of a sentence and inflect your tone to imply a question. Teachers who have achieved mastery of *Call and Response* perform this feat seamlessly, effectively, and naturally, but it is the trickiest in-cue and the most prone to error. Try it *after* you master the simpler methods. When you do, expect some miscues to occur and have a simpler in-cue ready as a backup if students miss the cue.

When you want *Call and Response* to end so that you can return to, say, *Cold Calls,* remember that students may still be caught up in the energy of *Call and Response.* For your last *Call and Response,* give them a cue that contrasts with a *Cold Call* and lets them know the fun is over:

"Last time, everyone, all together with feeling! What amount can no number be divided by?"

5. *Specialized in-cue.* To students, a specialized in-cue indicates a specific required response. In many classrooms there are multiple such cues, each indicating a different response. This form of in-cue can be especially fun for teachers and students alike. There's something exciting about a teacher asking a seemingly innocuous question and then, suddenly, having the whole class singing and chanting in unison.

For example, Bob Zimmerli teaches his students songs listing the multiples of all of the numbers up to twelve. After he has taught them these songs, he can prompt them with specialized cues. If he says, "Sevens on two. One, two . . . ," his students will respond by singing, "7, 14, 21, 28, 35, 42 . . . " to the tune of a popular song. If he says, "Eights on two. One, two . . . ," his students will respond with a different song and different numbers.

You might teach your students to always respond to the in-cue "Why are we here?" with the response, "To learn! To achieve!" Once the students have learned that connection, you no longer need to remind them that you are expecting a response (for example, by saying "Ready everyone?"). You suddenly say, "Why are we here?" and your students will chant.

The Purposes of *Call and Response*

As noted in the "Overview" section, there are three primary purposes of *Call and Response*:

| 18 CFU |
| 19 AT BATS |

- *For academic review and reinforcement.* Everyone gives the right answer, increasing the likelihood that he or she will remember it, and everyone in the class simultaneously gets an *At Bat.* When an individual student gives a strong answer, asking the rest of the class to repeat that answer is also a great way to reinforce it—both for the class and for the original student. But *Call and Response* does not suit *Check for Understanding.* Wrong answers can be hard to hear.

- *For energy. Call and Response* is active and spirited. It can make your class invigorating and make students want to be there, as though they are part of a cheering crowd or an exercise class.

- *For command and behavioral reinforcement. Call and Response* makes crisp, active, timely compliance a habit, committing it to muscle memory. This reinforces your authority and command.

For each purpose of *Call and Response,* come up with versions (in at least three forms) that you don't currently use but could use with your students.

1. **Academic review and reinforcement**

    Count-based: _____

    _____

    Group: _____

    _____

    Gesture: _____

    _____

    Tone and volume shift: _____

    _____

    Specialized: _____

    _____

2. **Energy**

    Count-based: _____

    _____

    Group: _____

    _____

    Gesture: _____

    _____

    Tone and volume shift: _____

    _____

    Specialized: _____

    _____

3. **Command and behavioral reinforcement**

Count-based: _____

_____

Group: _____

_____

Gesture: _____

_____

Tone and volume shift: _____

_____

Specialized: _____

_____

Three Ways to Add Value to *Call and Response*

| 22 **COLD CALL** |

1. *Intersperse with Cold Calls*. This varies group and individual accountability to answer, increases students' attention, and adds the unexpected, which makes the class more exciting. If necessary, signal the class to let them know when you're doing a *Call and Response*.

2. *Ask subgroups to respond*. This will jazz up your *Call and Response*. For example, ask the boys a *Call and Response* question and then the girls; ask the left side of the room and then the right; and so on.

3. *Add a physical gesture for students to make as part of their response*. For example, you can prepare students to cross their fingers in a mock addition sign as part of their response as they call out the name for the answer to an addition computation ("The sum!"). When asked where to write the numbers they carry in an addition problem, they can point to the ceiling and say, "On the roof!" Using gestures has at least two advantages:

- They give fidgety students an exciting way to be physically active in class.
- They give you a good way to notice who is holding back while others respond.

Crisp and Sharp

| 39 **DO IT AGAIN** |

Call and Response reinforces the behavioral culture in your classroom only if both components are crisp and sharp. If students sense that they can use their responses to test your expectations—by dragging out their answers, answering in a silly or loud manner, or answering out of sync—they will. In that case, make "sharpening up" a priority. Energetically and positively correct with a phrase like "I like your energy, but I need to hear you respond right on cue. Let's try that again."

Analyze Mr. Klein's Class Transcript

In the boxes to the right of this transcript, briefly comment on these questions:

- How is Mr. Klein effectively delivering the *Call and Response* technique?
- What goal or which of the three purposes is Mr. Klein trying to accomplish in lines 1 through 3?
- What is Mr. Klein trying to accomplish in lines 5 through 13?
- What *Call and Response* in-cues does he use?

Mr. Klein's class is learning about the 3s multiplication table. For this purpose he has written a number pattern on the board. It begins with "3, 6, 9."

1	Mr. Klein:	*(pointing to the pattern on the board)* Is this the 3s multiplication table? Your answer is "yes" or "no" on three. Is this the 3s? One, two, three!	
2	Class:	Yes!	
3	Mr. Klein:	How did we get there? Janaia?	
4	Janaia:	We had to add 3 to each number . . .	
5	Mr. Klein:	*(two minutes later)* What is the next number in the pattern? One, two, three!	
6	Class:	12!	
7	Mr. Klein:	And which number comes *next* in the pattern? This column only *(points to column of students on his right).* One, two three!	
8	Column of students:	15!	
9	Mr. Klein:	Which number comes next, middle column? One, two, three!	
10	Middle column of students:	18!	
11	Mr. Klein:	And what comes after 18? This column *(points to column on his left).* One, two, three!	
12	Column of students:	*(louder than the other two columns)* 21!	
13	Mr. Klein:	They're trying to show you up, middle column . . .	

PRACTICE WITH STUDY GROUP OR PARTNERS

Revisit the individual work you did in the previous section to share and compare your responses and see other options.

Live and in Concert

This activity assumes that everyone has absorbed the elements of *Call and Response* before the group convenes. *Facilitator:* Each participant needs to have a copy of the "Live and in Concert Worksheet."

1. In your group as a whole, one participant leads a review in which you all fill in the worksheet in standard wording you find by consensus.

2. If your group is large, at this point divide into groups of three or four.

3. As a group (or within each subgroup), model the various methods of *Call and Response*. In doing so, formulate numerous *Call and Response* questions that could be used to create a review of *Call and Response*.

Example: "Tell me the first purpose of using *Call and Response* on two. One, two . . . !"

4. Using the fruits of the group work in step 3 and his or her own ingenuity, each participant constructs a set of questions and scripts them into a well-thought-out sequence for review of at least one set of items on the worksheet.

5. By turns, individuals in the group take the role of *Teacher,* and the other participants (or the other members of a small group) become the *Students*. The *Teacher* uses the script he or she created to conduct the review.

6. To the first few questions, the *Students* respond as well as they can. After that, on their own initiative, a few can attempt to "loaf."

7. Reconvene as a whole group and constructively discuss the following questions:

As *Teacher*:

- How did it feel to play the role of *Teacher* conducting the *Call and Response*? Were you nervous? Why or why not?
- Did anything surprise you?
- What do you think you did best? Would you do anything differently?

As *Students*:

- How did it feel to be a *Student*?
- Was it always clear what responses you were expected to give?
- How well did the *Teachers* apply a variety of styles and methods? Specifically, which did you see them try?
- What were the best moments? What were moments for improvement?

Your takeaways:

_____

_____

_____

LIVE AND IN CONCERT WORKSHEET

Review: Call and Response

Primary purposes of *Call and Response*

1. _____

2. _____

3. _____

Types of *Call and Response*

1. _____

2. _____

3. _____

4. _____

5. _____

Types of in-cues

1. _____

2. _____

3. _____

4. _____

5. _____

Ways to add value

1. _____

2. _____

3. _____

Sharpen Up! Role Play

As mentioned earlier, *Call and Response* will only reinforce your behavioral culture and engage all your students if it is kept crisp and sharp, so that students see and hear the whole class responding on cue and in unison. This role play gives you practice in reinforcing that expectation in your classroom. In it *Students* respond to the *Teacher*'s call in various inadequate ways.

This role play requires a *Facilitator* to prepare by photocopying and cutting up the provided Response Cards so that they can be dealt out during the role play. All participants should bring their *Field Guides* so that they can add to their Chart of Responses. Also, they will be using the five sample *Call and Response* exchanges as scripts for the role play and will need the Field Guide for that purpose as well.

When you convene, the *Facilitator* does the following:

1. Ask all participants to add at least one teacher's direction of their own to the Chart of Responses. They can brainstorm this with a partner or in a small group (or you can ask them to do it before the meeting). Then ask participants to share with the whole group.

2. In each round, choose someone to be the *Teacher*. Assign one of the *Call and Response* exchanges to the *Teacher* and ask the *Teacher* to take it out of the room. Promise two or three minutes for *Teachers* to rehearse their lines and prepare for problematic *Student* responses.

(As a variation, you could script or have the group script a different *Call and Response* exchange that might be useful to practice in your particular subject areas or grades.)

3. While the *Teacher* is out, shuffle the Response Cards and ask one participant to choose one and announce it to the group. This card tells the group how it will respond at some point in the exchange.

4. With the *Teacher* still out, decide at which line in the exchange the group will respond in the manner described by the Response Card. Everyone should focus on reacting this way only at one point in the exchange, as this will be less predictable for the teacher.

5. Invite the *Teacher* back into the room. Explain that he should practice the chosen exchange with the group and should ensure crisp, on-cue responses, correcting if necessary. Then allow the *Teacher* to lead the exchange. Give him the opportunity to replay if he'd like (either with the same response manner or a different one).

CHART OF RESPONSES

Student Response	Teacher's Direction to Sharpen Up
Too loud	*Example:* "I love the enthusiasm, but let's do it again in our speaking voice."
Not quite everyone responding	*Example:* "We need the whole team."
Too fast (ahead of in-cue)	*Example:* "Let's do it again in our scholar voices."
Out of sync with one another, dragging it out	*Example:* "On my signal . . ."
Low energy	*Example:* "Match my voice with your voice."
Virtually no response	*Example:* "Let's try again so I can hear your voices."

Call and Response Exchange 1

Teacher: 3 times 3 is what, class?

Students: 9.

Teacher: What do we call the solution to a multiplication problem?

Students: Product.

Teacher: So the product of 3 times 3 is . . . ?

Students: 9.

Teacher: Work backwards. If 3 times 3 is 9, then 9 divided by 3 is . . . ?

Students: 3.

Teacher: And the solution to a division problem is called a . . . ?

Students: Quotient.

Call and Response Exchange 2

Teacher: This is a tough word: *incomprehensible*. Let's all try that on two. One, two . . .

Students: Incomprehensible.

Teacher: Incomprehensible means "impossible to understand." What does it mean?

Students: Impossible to understand.

Teacher: And again the word is . . . ?

Students: Incomprehensible.

Call and Response Exchange 3

Teacher: How many branches does the U.S. government have?

Students: Three.

Teacher: And the branch that makes the laws is the . . . ?

Students: Legislative branch.

Teacher: And the branch that carries out the laws is the . . . ?

Students: Executive branch.

Teacher: And so the last one is the . . . ?

Students: Judicial branch.

Call and Response Exchange 4

Teacher: A synonym for *limited* is *scarce*. What word?

Students: Scarce.

Teacher: For example: if I had fifty pencils but one hundred people needed them, pencils would be scarce. Another example: in our classroom, is air scarce? Class?

Students: No.

Teacher: If you are underwater, is air scarce? Class?

Students: Yes.

Teacher: What is it?

Students: Scarce.

Call and Response Exchange 5

Teacher: A square has four sides of equal . . .

Students: Length.

Teacher: How many sides?

Students: Four.

Teacher: And opposite sides are . . . ?

Students: Parallel.

Teacher: And how many degrees does each corner angle have?

Students: 90.

RESPONSE CARDS

Sharpen Up! Role Play
Student Response Card
Too loud

Sharpen Up! Role Play
Student Response Card
Not quite everyone responding

Sharpen Up! Role Play
Student Response Card
Too fast (ahead of in-cue)

Sharpen Up! Role Play
Student Response Card
Out of sync with one another, dragging it out

Sharpen Up! Role Play
Student Response Card
Low energy

Sharpen Up! Role Play
Student Response Card
Virtually no response

6. Let everyone play a round as *Teacher*.

7. Lead a discussion along these lines:

As *Teacher*:

- What was your best moment?
- What would you do differently next time?

As *Students*:

- What kinds of sharpening responses were most effective? Why?
- What else could *Teachers* have tried?

Whole group:

- What might be challenging about introducing *Call and Response* in your classroom for the first time?
- What are some potential pitfalls of *Call and Response*?
- How might you integrate your takeaways from this exercise into your class next week?

Your takeaways:

_____

_____

_____

_____

TRY *CALL AND RESPONSE* IN THE CLASSROOM

Do this planning with a partner or get feedback from a partner if you can.

1. Integrate *Call and Response* methods into a daily lesson plan.

2. Find at least two places in the lesson where you might use *Call and Response* to increase the level of student engagement and also reinforce academic or behavioral goals.

3. For each place:

- Script the call (what you will say).
- Script the answers you expect students to give.
- Choose the in-cue you will use (for example, "On two. One, two . . ."),
- Label each prompt according to its type: repeat, report, reinforce, review, or solve.

4. After class, review your results. Try to improve your script or calls and your choices of in-cues.

5. Make notes about how to continue trying and possibly extending *Call and Response* in future lessons.

| 22 **COLD CALL** |

6. Revise a future lesson plan to include and coordinate *Call and Response* and *Cold Call*. Consider places where you can alternate or overlap the techniques to further increase the engagement of students. Keep scaffolding in mind.

TROUBLE-SHOOT

Steady On

In using gestures, it's easy to let consistency slip. Keep them complete, consistent, and crisp.

Other Challenges

Possible Challenge	Possible Solutions
Several of my kids just mouth the words of the response.	Add a gesture to signal your expectation that every student speak. Do a *Call and Response* practice using other material to build student comfort with vocalizing.
Many of my kids don't want to participate.	Sharpen up; do it again, frame positively. If necessary, repeat it several times.

BE CREATIVE

Go back and add a possibility to the "Proven ways to add value" list on your Live and in Concert Worksheet. Then test it.

SUSTAIN YOUR PROGRESS

1. Using feedback from your study group or other peers, and reviewing your own lesson notes and observations, monitor your progress on *Call and Response*.

Date	Things I'm Doing Well	Ways to Improve and Expand

2. Revisit "Where Am I Now?" Are you ready to build out to some other new technique?

PEPPER

OVERVIEW

Pepper is cumulative vocal review that builds energy and actively engages the whole class. In effect, the teacher "peppers" the class with a rapid series of questions focusing on quick response. The activity is

- Fast paced
- Inclusive
- Portable (usable outside the classroom as well as during "official" class time)
- Economical in language
- In series, focused on a theme
- Executed without stopping to discuss answers

Pepper often involves *Cold Calls* (but doesn't need to). Often it starts with *Cold Calls* and then proceeds to calling on students whose hands are raised (with increasing eagerness).

22 **COLD CALL**

    Pepper features game-like qualities that usually set it apart from the rest of class and can make it an ideal change of pace, so plan ahead to choose the best time in which to use it.

WHERE AM I NOW?

	Proficiency			
Comfort & Confidence	**I am brand new to *Pepper* . . .**	**I'm in the planning and practice stage, though I haven't tried *Pepper* yet in class . . .**	**I'm beginning to try *Pepper* in my classroom . . .**	**I use *Pepper* regularly . . .**
	❑ . . . and excited to taste it.	❑ . . . but know with more practice I'll get the recipe.	❑ . . . and love how it basically works.	❑ . . . and am adding my own special dashes.
	❑ . . . and a little wary of spices.	❑ . . . because I still have questions about how to add it.	❑ . . . but my delivery isn't quite up to speed yet.	❑ . . . but may be overspicing the class.
	❑ . . . but am not at all sure it's for me or my students.	❑ . . . because, frankly, I still have doubts.	❑ . . . with mixed results I need to evaluate.	❑ . . . but when class isn't going well, *Pepper* goes poorly.

Work from your strengths. If you find yourself in the bottom left portion, leaf through this technique to locate related ones you might prefer to work on right now.

EXPAND YOUR SKILLS AND REPERTOIRE

What's *Pepper* Made Of?

Pepper is fundamentals with lots of repetition. Its ingredients are

- *Rapidity*. It's a *fast* sequence in which a large number of questions get asked.
- *Inclusiveness*. It's a *group* activity. It *can* include *Cold Calling* or hands, and often it progresses from one to the other; but it should engage everyone.
- *Portability*. It can be used anywhere (not just the classroom).
- *Economy*. Everyone's language (question or answer) is economical.
- *Theme and variation*. The series of questions focuses on a theme or skill; or one short sequence works one skill, and the next addresses a closely related one.
- *Constant back-and-forth*. Questions and answers are short and rarely discussed; usually an answer is followed by another question (or the same one if the previous answerer got it wrong.)

When to *Pepper*

Pepper is a great warmup activity. You can use it for daily oral drill at the outset of class or as a way to make review fun. Every minute of school time matters, and *Pepper* can keep the class working while a few students write on the board. It can fill in any stray ten minutes inside or outside the classroom (say, lined up in the hallway) with productive fun.

Mentally review your school day. Identify several short intervals, outside of in-class lesson time, when you might *Pepper* your students. What content could you focus on? What tools (such as a chart or flash cards) might you want to have at hand?

Interval: _____   Content and useful tools: _____

_____

Interval: _____   Content and useful tools: _____

_____

Pepper and *Cold Call*

| 22 COLD CALL |

At first, it's easy to confuse *Pepper* with *Cold Call*, because both can be "hot." This list compares them.

Pepper	Cold Call
Often involves *Cold Call* (and almost always starts with it), but you can ask for hands at times if you wish.	Can happen in a *Pepper* setting but also in various other settings.
Includes quick fundamental questions, often as review.	Includes any question that furthers thought and learning.
Goes at a fast pace, with high energy and no discussion of answers.	Tends to be paced quickly, but discussion of answers is normal.

Pepper	Cold Call
Uses sequences of approximately ten or more questions. *Pepper* implies volume.	Uses no predetermined number of questions.
Sometimes involves game-like features: students standing, class tracking the number it gets correct, a lead-in song, and so on.	Has a wide variety of applications, but less often employs game-like aspects.

You can begin *Cold Calling* at the outset of a session of *Pepper*, then switch to hands as students become more and more engaged and enthusiastic, which is often the case.

Keeping the "G" in *Pepper*

Pepper works best if you keep up your game spirit.

1. *Set up boundaries and work the clock*. Compress *Pepper* in time between a clear end and beginning.

2. *Shift*. In *Pepper* review, move from unit to unit as part of the game. Ask questions about properties of quadrilaterals for two or three minutes and then move on to a series about coordinate geometry. Or shift between topics that may not seem entirely related: in social studies, for example, spend a few minutes on map skills followed by a few minutes on the original colonies.

3. *Employ game gadgets*. Add novel touches:

- Start and end with a ding on a bell.
- Ask all students to stand up.
- Call on students in a unique or unpredictable way.
- Point to students if that's something you don't normally do.

Some neat variations that teachers use:

Pick-sticks. Label popsicle sticks with each student's name to pull at random out of a can. Or generate random numbers on a laptop. Your pick can be random, but with the question tailored to the student. Or, as one teacher pointed out to me, remember that *only you know whose name is really on the popsicle stick!* So call whomever you want to. But be aware that a picking process can slow you down a lot.

Head-to-head. Two students stand up to answer a question. The one who gets the correct answer first remains standing to face a new challenger. But don't get sucked into discussing or arbitrating. You're the ump. Next pitch!

Sit-down. At the beginning of class, all students are standing, and the teacher *Peppers* them so that they can "earn their seats" (sit down) by answering correctly. Use no other engagement than a gesture to signal the student to sit.

Stand-up. *Pepper* to see who's next to join the line for recess.

| 46 **JOY FACTOR** |

Add three game touches you could use:

1. _____

2. _____

3. _____

Practice Scripting

Write a script for a two- to three-minute *Pepper* session in which you would review some of the methods of *Pepper* with your group.

PRACTICE WITH STUDY GROUP OR PARTNERS

Revisit the individual work you did in the previous section to share and compare your responses and see other options.

Discuss a Lesson Plan

Bring a current or past lesson plan to the group. As a group, identify at least three places in your lessons where a round of *Pepper* could apply:

- What would that round cover?
- What would the *Pepper* approach add at this point?
- What scaffolding might be needed and planned in advance?
- What formats (sit-down, stand-up, game, and so on) might work best for the various rounds?

  Mark comments on your own plan, and refer to it later when you plan your next lesson.

Use Your Scripts

With the rest of the group as *Students,* take turns as *Teacher* practicing your scripts from "Practice Scripting" (in the previous section). Time the practice and stop each round at two minutes. After each round, go around the circle noting for

- *Students:* Ways in which that round reflected a good fundamental of *Pepper*
- *Students:* Whether there was "game"
- *Students:* The best moment or question of the round
- *Students:* Whether any questions could have been made more specific or could have been improved in some other way
- *Teacher:* Something you might have done differently

Brainstorm Game

Brainstorm novelty touches. Then vote on all the suggestions. Each voter awards three points among the suggestions: one point for originality, one point for speed and workability, and one point for being most "over the top."

TRY *PEPPER* IN THE CLASSROOM

1. Select a lesson plan for an upcoming class. Study and mark it for one or two times when *Pepper* might add energy and muscle.
2. Identify the content for each round of *Pepper*.

3. Script the questions you will ask. Keep them specific. Plan scaffolds as needed.

4. Decide how you will choose whom to call on. Consider whether you want a chant to introduce it. (For example, "I say salt, you say pepper! Salt!! [*Students:* Pepper!!] Salt!! [*Students:* Pepper!!] What time is it?? [*Students:* It's pepper time!!]")

5. What format or game context will you use to boost the mojo?

6. How will you keep track of and respond to the overall level of student mastery the results of the round suggest?

7. After class, assess results. Make notes about how you will continue *Pepper*.

8. How might you vary or reformulate some of the questions from these rounds in a subsequent round of *Pepper* review—perhaps at the start of the next class session?

9. Consider when you might *Pepper* outside your classroom on the same material you covered in this session.

TROUBLE-SHOOT

Steady On

Pepper takes nerve to try the first time! Practice with a supportive group or partner. Go into class with an actual script and notes about how you will respond if students have too much trouble answering.

Other Challenges

Possible Challenge	Possible Solutions

BE CREATIVE

1.   What are your students' favorite sports and games—online, on TV, on the playground? Pick up spicy "game" ideas from those.

2.   Rename *Pepper* to suit the spirit of your classroom.

SUSTAIN YOUR PROGRESS

1.   Using feedback from your study group or other peers, and reviewing your own lesson notes and observations, monitor your progress on *Pepper*.

Date	*Pepper* Session	Ways to Improve or Do More Often

2.   Revisit "Where Am I Now?" Are you ready to build out to some other new technique?

WAIT TIME

OVERVIEW

Wait Time refers to a few seconds' delay that you can add after your question and before you take a student answer. How much you provide is a critical factor in determining the quality of the answers you get and the number of students who participate. What you do during *Wait Time* can be critical as well, especially when students don't automatically know how to use it productively.

Many teachers hasten to take an answer, but you want the class's best answer, not necessarily the first one. And you want to hear from students who may not be quickest to raise a hand.

Narrated *Wait Time* is often powerful in teaching students how to take full advantage of *Wait Time*. Narrating *Wait Time* means giving guidance about what students should be doing while you wait. Narration and waiting (at least three to five seconds, and often longer) can have these important effects:

1. Increase in the length and correctness of student responses because *Wait Time* methods slow students down when they might be in too much of a rush

2. Increase in the number of students who raise their hands

3. Increase in the use of evidence in answers

Once students have learned to use *Wait Time* effectively, however, be more cautious in narrating, as it can crowd out student thinking.

WHERE AM I NOW?

	Proficiency			
Comfort & Confidence	**I am brand new to this approach to waiting for answers . . .**	**I'm in the planning and practice stage, though I haven's tried *Wait Time* yet in class . . .**	**I'm beginning to try *Wait Time* in my classroom . . .**	**I use *Wait Time* well . . .**
	❑ . . . and excited to try it.	❑ . . . but know with more practice I'll make it work.	❑ . . . and love how narration basically works.	❑ . . . and am adding my own distinctive touches.
	❑ . . . and undecided about my ability to narrate appropriately as I wait.	❑ . . . because I still have questions about how to narrate.	❑ . . . with mixed results I need to evaluate.	❑ . . . but I may be overnarrating.
	❑ . . . and not at all sure it's for me.	❑ . . . because, frankly, I still think maybe I should just wait in silence.	❑ . . . but it doesn't seem to work or suit me.	❑ . . . but when class isn't going well, I do it poorly and it doesn't help.

Work from your strengths. If you find yourself in the bottom left portion, leaf through this technique to locate related ones you might prefer to work on right now.

ANALYZE THE CHAMPIONS

View each video clip, ideally more than once, and answer the following questions. See the end of the technique for some possible answers.

 Clip 19. Teacher Yasmin Vargas, Grade 1

1. How many seconds does Ms. Vargas wait? About how many hands ultimately go up?
2. What pattern do you see in how many hands are up at each point? How does that pattern relate to what Ms. Vargas is saying in her *Wait Time* narrative?
3. Is Ms. Vargas encouraging group effort? How?

 Clip 20. Teacher Katie Bellucci, Grade 5

1. How many seconds does Ms. Bellucci wait?
2. What cueing, if any, does Ms. Bellucci provide in her *Wait Time* narrative?
3. What else is she accomplishing during her *Wait Time*?

 Clip 21. Teacher Christine Ranney, Grade 8

1. How many seconds does Ms. Ranney wait? What pattern do you see in how many hands go up as the *Wait Time* and her narrative continue? How do you explain the pattern?
2. What additional information or cueing does she supply in her narrative?
3. What other champion techniques is she using that support or build on what she accomplishes through her *Wait Time* and its narrative?

EXPAND YOUR SKILLS AND REPERTOIRE

Listening

Use an audio recording of yourself in the classroom to see where you and your students are right now in terms of effective *Wait Time*. Time how long you wait. Note how you narrate the *Wait Time*. Note levels of voluntary student participation. Notice anything else that might be useful to you as feedback, such as signs of your ease or discomfort with extending the wait.

Speaking Words of *Wait Time*

| 43 **POSITIVE FRAMING** | We mentioned three main things that *Wait Time* can do. Here they are again, along with other uses and possible narratives that are based on phrases from one hundred teachers and school leaders from New York, Massachusetts, Washington DC, Pennsylvania, Louisiana, Ohio, Colorado, Tennessee, and the Netherlands at a *Teach Like a Champion* workshop. For each, write in a narrative you already use for the same positive purpose. Then write another narrative you could also try.

1.   Acknowledging and building from the eager

"I see three hands already up."

"I see hands in the front row. I'm looking all over."

"I need to see twelve hands. I'm counting: twelve, eleven, ten . . ."

You say now: _____

_____

You could try: _____

_____

2.   Encouraging more participation

"Everyone has a voice, and I want to hear your thoughts."

"I'm sure that many of you know. Maybe all of you know!"

"Let's bring a few more thinkers into this equation."

"Let's do a countdown for hands. I need twelve. Twelve, eleven, ten . . ."

You say now: _____

_____

You could try: _____

_____

3.   Letting students know they have time to think

"This is hard stuff. Take your time. No hands for ten seconds."

"Step foot in the world for a connection. Come back to share in fifteen seconds."

"This is going to take some big thinking, so I'm going to give you time for that."

"I see you riding thought waves. Keep surfing!"

You say now: _____

_____

You could try: _____

_____

4.   Validating careful, extended thought

"It's good to think it through before you raise your hand."

"Be the tortoise, not the hare. Work smart, not fast."

"Let's all chew on that question before we answer." *(pretends to chew)*

"College-level answers take time."

"Good scholars take time to work out their answer."

"Good mathematicians take time with their calculations."

"It's good to be *slow,* and make sure you *know*."

"Sit with it. It's supposed to be hard."

"Juicy answers take time."

"Push your thinking."

"Rome was not built in a day; take your time to develop sound answers."

"All right, second graders, it's time to take our thinking to the third-grade level!"

You say now: _____

_____

You could try: _____

_____

5. Suggesting what students could be doing in order to arrive at an answer

"What do you see in the [picture, graph, map, and so on]?"

"We're thinking through our thinking. Do I understand this question? What am I doing to solve it?"

"How can you connect your answer to what we were just discussing?"

"Think about the steps involved."

"Remember to use your background knowledge to build current knowledge."

"If you're not sure, think about [hint]."

"How would you explain this to [someone outside the class]?"

You say now: _____

_____

You could try: _____

_____

6. Encouraging paper work

"I see fingers going to work."

"Write the word before you tell us how to spell it."

"Your hand is up or your pencil is moving."

"Take a few minutes to write down your responses to the question."

"This is tricky, so questions are good! Jot them down while you're thinking."

"Write the sentence in your head, then jot it down on paper."

You say now: _____

_____

You could try: _____

_____

7. Encouraging collective focus and enthusiasm

"Rub your temples; get those minds working."

"Tap your brains! Wow, your thoughtful answers are growing bigger and bigger by the second."

"Thinker's pose!" *(Students put hand to chin.)*

"Knowledge stance!" *(Students put hand straight up.)*

"Get those juices flowing!" *(Teacher's hands undulate like fluid.)*

"Can't wait to hear your billion-dollar answer."

"It's so hard to wait because your responses will be brilliant, but I can do it!"

"Brains are on fire. Keep burning!"

"All brains on!"

"Rev up your engines . . . Vroom, vroom, vroom."

"I see hands ready to show off what they've learned."

"I have almost 100 percent; waiting for my first row . . ."

"It's cold over here. I need to go where it's hot and the hands are on fire!"

"I believe that you have the answer. I believe that you will find the way."

You say now: _____

_____

You could try: _____

_____

8.   Encouraging trying, taking risks

"Take a chance even if you might not be right. We learn by risking."

"Where are my risk takers? Life's more fun with a little adventure."

"I love to see scholars take risks to answer challenging questions."

"I don't expect you to get it all the time, but I do expect you to try."

"I want effort, not perfection. We're in this together."

"If you're already there, add a college-level word to your answer."

You say now: _____

_____

You could try: _____

_____

9.   Eliciting more correct responses

"Whisper your answer into your hand before you raise your hand."

"When you think you have your answer, take some mental time to put it in a complete sentence."

"I can't wait to see you use precise vocabulary."

"Even Le Bron practices his shots. Practice the answer in your mind."

You say now: _____

_____

You could try: _____

_____

WAIT TIME

10.   **Normalizing positive behavior**

"I see Serena concentrating."

"I see college-ready scholars pushing their thinking by double-checking their work or finding a different way to solve."

You say now: _____

_____

You could try: _____

11.   **Encouraging use of evidence in answers**

"I see lots of quick hands. I'm going to ask you to prove it. Can you prove it?"

"And we'll want to know why that's correct."

"Evidence, think of your evidence!"

"Point to your evidence."

"I see Wanda using a sticky note to find evidence in the text."

"Take two minutes to mark at least three places where you can find evidence of [fact or idea], using sticky notes."

"What if someone disagrees with your answer? What evidence can prove you're right?"

You say now: _____

_____

You could try: _____

12.   **Encouraging more use of resources**

"I know you can answer, because you know where to look for the answer."

"Are there resources you could use to support or improve your response?"

"As you solve the problem, I should see you looking at your formula sheet for the right formula."

"I spy scholar eyes looking around the room for resources."

"Jamie is looking hard at the picture. Good work, Jamie."

"Earn your detective badges! What clues are on the map?"

"This word is on our word wall. Can you find it there?"

"Scholars are reading the word wall."

"You can go back and use your notes if you need to."

"I'm listening for the sound of notebook pages."

"I see Ezra getting ready for the challenge by checking his notes."

"Good readers take time to look back at the story."

"Find a resource that supports your answer."

"Use resources to test and revise your answer."

"I see Brittany looking at [resource], because it has a problem similar to the one we are working on."

You say now: _____

_____

You could try: _____

_____

13.   Encouraging the double-checking of answers

"How could you check to make sure your answer is correct?"

"This is a tricky question. Think about where a scholar could make a mistake."

"I'll give everyone a minute to double-check with [strategy]."

"Use your resources to check your answer."

You say now: _____

_____

You could try: _____

14.   Encouraging reasoning as part of an answer

"Be ready to explain how you got your answer."

"Be prepared to explain why you set up your equation that way."

"How will you defend your answer?"

"If you've got it, grow it! Build a defense."

"Be ready to prove it!"

"Your answer is ready when you can prove it."

"We'll believe you when you prove it."

"Alex is thinking about how she would prove her idea to us."

"I am going to be contrary, so be ready with your argument. I'm going to try to prove you wrong!"

You say now: _____

_____

You could try: _____

_____

15.   Eliciting alternative possibilities

"There might be more than one explanation."

"I can think of *two* that you could give."

"Your first answer may not be the best one."

"How might another scholar answer?"

"As you come to your answer, list two or three other possibilities on your paper. Then underline the answer you're most confident in."

You say now: _____

_____

You could try: _____

16.   Prompting collective effort

"Let's come up with some ideas to chew on."

"Be ready to listen critically to your classmates' answers if you're not sharing. Think: Are they on track? Are any improvements needed?"

You say now: _____

_____

You could try: _____

_____

PRACTICE WITH STUDY GROUP OR PARTNERS

Revisit the individual work you did in the previous section to share and compare your responses and see other options.

Partner Observation

In lieu of working with the audio recording recommended earlier, have a study partner or other colleague sit in on some portion of a class you are teaching: ask this person to literally time your *Wait Times,* note levels of voluntary student participation, and notice anything else that might be useful to you as feedback, such as signs of your ease or discomfort with extending the wait.

Small Group Video Clip Discussion

Watch each video clip together. Literally time the *Wait Times* by watching the time stamps on the video. Count and record the initial number of hands raised. Count and record the number of hands in the air when a student is called on. Then discuss these numbers and such questions as

- What is each champion teacher doing in the narrative? How do the students react?
- What was the impact of *Wait Time* on the number of hands raised?
- What was the impact of *Wait Time* on the quality of students' responses?
- What did you notice about the mood in the classroom while *Wait Time* was provided?
- How did the teacher balance urgency with the need to wait for students to think?
- Is there evidence that *Wait Time* better allowed the teacher to *Check for Understanding*?

Discuss Your Repertoire

Compare notes about your prior experiences to date, as a teacher or as a student, with *Wait Time*. What aims do you have in mind? What types of narration do you use? What do you actually say?

If your group includes teachers from different grade levels or subjects, talk about how those differences affect *Wait Time* technique.

Revisit "Expand Your Skills and Repertoire" and share ideas for possibly rewording some of the examples or the wording you actually use right now.

How might you expand or otherwise improve your repertoire?

The Waiting Game—a Role Play

For this role play, partner with two or more (up to six) colleagues. You can also recruit friends to fill out your "classroom" of role play *Students*.

In each round, one of you will be the *Teacher*. The rest will be *Students 1, 2, 3,* and so on. In each round, one *Student* will also time the *Wait Time*.

Individual preparation: for your rounds as *Teacher,* prepare some questions based on your curriculum that these *Students* can probably answer, or on other experience and knowledge you generally share. Vary the questions in degree of difficulty.

Collective preparation: on scraps of paper, write the following six roles (or modify to suit your needs). Put them in a container so that the *Students* can draw lots at the start of each new round.

1. Eager beaver, not necessarily correct
2. Slow because meticulous

3. Slow because uncertain

4. Doesn't have a grip on the material, but might eventually raise hand

5. Didn't hear the question, but might eventually raise hand

6. Will not raise hand

In each round, one participant becomes the *Teacher*. The rest are *Students* and draw lots for their roles, which they do not disclose. The *Teacher* establishes any needed context (grade level, expectations), then asks a question. *Students* respond in keeping with their roles. Play out the scenario with *Wait Time* and narrative until the *Teacher* chooses a hand and that *Student* responds.

Repeat so that each *Teacher* gets at least three *Teacher* rounds.

Role play discussion: after each round, *Students* reveal their roles and their reactions to the question and *Wait Time*. The *Teacher* describes the experience from his or her point of view. Continue a general discussion of what went well and what improvements could be tried.

Your takeaways:

_____

_____

_____

_____

TRY WAIT TIME IN THE CLASSROOM

1. Before you lay plans to improve your *Wait Time,* benchmark your current skill by doing the audio-recording activity suggested earlier or by having a colleague time your current waiting times as you teach a class, and share other feedback about what you do with those times.

2. Go over your upcoming lesson plan. Write out several major questions that you plan to ask that will probably benefit by *Wait Time* and narration, including the first question you plan to put to the class. Apply the several planning techniques in this guide, including

In *Wait Time,* you can also circle back to some objective the class may not have entirely mastered in a previous lesson.

| 6 **BEGIN WITH THE END** |

4 Ms. Build enough time into your planned questioning so that you won't feel pressured not to wait.

| 7 **4 MS** |

Plan what your students should be doing in order for them to answer a major question. Note what resources your students will have that

| 10 **DOUBLE PLAN** |

you may want to refer to in your narrative. If paper work is likely to help students answer a question, make a note to suggest or call attention to someone who is modeling that.

3. Besides writing out the questions, write and rehearse *Wait Time* narratives that are likely to be useful for the question.

4. Think about individual students who might benefit most from *Wait Time*. Rehearse some narratives with them in mind.

5. Follow your lesson plan, knowing you will be willing to slow down the question-and-answer process, even if it means you won't cover as much ground as you intended.

6.   After class, go back over your lesson notes and add remarks about where you used or could have used different *Wait Times* and narrative. Apply those notes to your next lesson plan.

7.   After several sessions, record a session again to see what improvements you've made in waiting and in narrating *Wait Time*.

TROUBLE-SHOOT

Steady On

How does silence make you feel while you are waiting for a student to answer or raise a hand? Slow down. Try counting in your head. Think about *Wait Time* as a time to verbally cultivate good student responses. What is more urgent than their responses?

Other Challenges

Possible Challenge	Possible Solutions

BE CREATIVE

1.   Try building *Wait Time* instruction into the question itself, as scaffolding and more.

"Here comes a hard one. I know you'll think carefully before raising your hand. Now: What's the exact value of pi?"

"Here's a thought about pi. We just saw how it was calculated. What do you suspect this might mean regarding a definitive value of pi?"

49 **NORMALIZE ERROR**   2.   How could you be using *Wait Time* to *Normalize Error*?

SUSTAIN YOUR PROGRESS

1. Using feedback from your study group or other peers, and reviewing your own lesson notes and observations, monitor your progress on *Wait Time*.

Date	Good Example of Waiting	Good Narrative Touch

2. Revisit "Where Am I Now?" Are you ready to build out to some other new technique?

ANALYZE THE CHAMPIONS: SOME OBSERVATIONS

 Clip 19. Teacher Yasmin Vargas, Grade 1

The pattern is that the students join in with Ms. Vargas's animated activity of counting hands. They seem eager to become part of the count. Notice how some look around to see how many others are also raising hands. Ms. Vargas encourages group effort by saying "we" and by pointing out how many are "thinking." Also she asks the responder to "talk to your friends."

 Clip 20. Teacher Katie Bellucci, Grade 5

| 18 **CFU** |

Ms. Bellucci cues her students to look at their notes with "You have it all right there." She also seems to be using her *Wait Time* to use *Check for Understanding*.

 Clip 21. Teacher Christine Ranney, Grade 8

| 3 **STRETCH IT** |
| 15 **CIRCULATE** |

Ms. Ranney cues the students with a more concrete definition of "conflict" as a problem facing a character. She also uses *Stretch It* and *Circulate*.

EVERYBODY WRITES

OVERVIEW

Everybody Writes means preparing your students to engage rigorously in classroom discussions by giving them the chance to reflect first in writing. *Everybody Writes* can start in the early grades with simple prompts and stems and short bits of writing—words, phrases, or sentences.

WHERE AM I NOW?

	Proficiency			
	I am brand new to *Everybody Writes* ...	I'm in the planning and practice stage, though I haven't tried *Everybody Writes* yet in class ...	I'm beginning to try *Everybody Writes* in my classroom ...	I use *Everybody Writes* regularly ...
Comfort & Confidence	❑ ...and excited to try it.	❑ ...but know with more practice I'll make it work.	❑ ...and love how it basically works.	❑ ...and am adding my own distinctive touch.
	❑ ...and undecided about my ability to pull it off.	❑ ...because I still have questions about how to do it right.	❑ ...with mixed results I need to evaluate.	❑ ...but I may be overusing it.
	❑ ...and not at all sure it's for me.	❑ ...because, frankly, I still have serious doubts.	❑ ...but it doesn't seem to work or suit me.	❑ ...but when class isn't going well, I do it poorly and it doesn't help.

Work from your strengths. If you find yourself in the bottom left portion, leaf through this technique to locate related ones you might prefer to work on right now.

EXPAND YOUR SKILLS AND REPERTOIRE

Why *Everybody Writes*?

Here are seven of the many virtues of *Everybody Writes*:

1. *Allows a focused starting point for discussion.* *Everybody Writes* allows you to select effective responses with which to begin your discussion because you can review your students' ideas in advance by *Circulating* and reading over shoulders.

> 15 **CIRCULATE**
> 21 **TAKE A STAND**

22 COLD CALL

19 AT BATS

2. *Makes you* Cold Call *ready*. *Everybody Writes* allows you to *Cold Call* students simply and naturally because you know everyone is prepared with thoughts, and you can start merely by asking, "What did you write about, Brittany?"

3. *Enables "Version 2.0."* *Everybody Writes* allows students to refine and improve their thinking before it becomes public. This helps them engage intellectually and improves the quality of their ideas and writing. It also gives them *At Bats* at a skill fundamental to all of their future educational and professional work.

4. *Supplies direction*. The question or prompt you choose steers students right away into thinking that will help to shape meaningful discussion.

"Argue the point of view of someone you don't agree with . . ."

"Write a sentence defining the vocabulary word *imperceptible* that makes it clear that *imperceptible* is different from *invisible*."

"Choose one of these: *What do the Capulets think of the Montagues? Or What do the Montagues think of the Capulets?*"

5. *Upgrades students' memory*. People remember twice as much of what they write as they remember of what they say or hear. Students remember twice as much of what they are learning if they write it down.

17 RATIO

6. *Gets everybody to answer*. *Everybody Writes* raises the *Ratio* because everybody answers, not just those who get called on. It also demands more of students who, in response to an oral question, tend to raise their hands sheerly out of a vague impulse to try to answer.

6 BEGIN WITH THE END
15 CIRCULATE
18 CFU
21 TAKE A STAND
22 COLD CALL

7. *Connects to notes and evidence*. Writing *before* discussion can get students in the habit of sourcing evidence by consulting the text or their notes.

Choose three of the seven virtues whose value grabs you most strongly. For each, give your best concrete example of how adding *Everybody Writes* would benefit a specific class activity you've been thinking about in pursuit of a major lesson objective. (You may find ideas in *Circulate, Check for Understanding, Take a Stand,* and *Cold Call*.)

1. _____

_____

_____

2. _____

_____

_____

3. _____

_____

_____

Making It Work

We just mentioned numerous benefits of *Everybody Writes*. To gain those benefits, keep the following four points in mind:

1. *Keep it tight*. Allow students time to reflect but maintain urgency and manage the clock.

2. *Make the question matter*. Whether your prompt is broad or specific, be sure that it gets students thinking in a direction that prepares them to take a vital, high-*Ratio* part in the discussion that will follow. Write it in advance. Err on the side of clarity.

17 **RATIO**

3. *Set expectations*. Do you want students to write in complete sentences or with attention to other various aspects of grammar, syntax, and spelling? Might you ask students to read aloud what they just wrote? Does the writing need to be neat enough for you, the teacher, to read? Will or might you collect it?

4. *Build the habit of writing*. Request it frequently. As students do more writing, the task becomes easier for them, the quality of expression and thought go up, and the cost in time goes down. Give students a designated place to write (in their packet, in a journal, in their notes with guidelines) to underscore the importance of their writing and to integrate it into their overall process of accumulating learning.

31 **BINDER CONTROL**

Ways to Initiate *Everybody Writes*

The following are various ways and means of launching an *Everybody Writes*. In the empty left column, check any idea you haven't or have rarely tried but that could be appropriate to your classroom. In the empty right column, note a discussion activity that could follow from the work done in that *Everybody Writes* activity. For example, an excellent brief bit of student writing on a formatted "reflections" page in one class session could become the basis for some *Do Now* writing for the entire class at the outset of the next session.

	Writing . . .	Possible Activity
	. . . on a formatted "reflections" page that is sometimes turned in at the end of class	
	. . . on "a piece of scratch paper"	
	. . . in response to teacher-generated questions written on the board or overhead	
	. . . in response to student-generated, teacher-vetted questions	
	. . . in response to a question framed verbally by the teacher at the moment it's assigned	
	. . . a "free write" in response to something the teacher just read aloud	

	Writing . . .	Possible Activity
	. . . a "free write" in response to something students just read	
	. . . in response to one question	
	. . . in response to a series of three or four questions	
	. . . about a question the student has selected from several choices	
	. . . in a "Response Journal" that the teacher rarely sees	
	. . . on sticky notes to paste into the book the student is reading	
	. . . for twenty seconds until the timer goes off	
	. . . "until I give you the signal to stop"	
	. . . for three to five minutes	
	. . . in complete sentences	
	. . . with no format expectations	
	. . . to express one's opinion on a matter	
	. . . to describe the opinion of someone else	
	. . . to assemble evidence to support one of two contrasting opinions	
	. . . in a portion of a packet for which students will be graded	
	. . .	

PRACTICE WITH STUDY GROUP OR PARTNERS

Revisit "Why *Everybody Writes*?"

1. Share your thoughts from "Why *Everybody Writes*?"
2. When someone shares an interesting idea, say aloud, "I'll steal that!" and explain how.

Your takeaways:

_____

_____

_____

Ways to Initiate and Maintain

1. Poll the group to find out how many of you checked each idea in "Ways to Initiate *Everybody Writes*."

2. Discuss several that many of you chose.
   - What value do you see in that idea?
   - What challenges might stand in the way of making it a good path into discussion?

3. Ask the same questions about several that few of you chose.

4. What ways have you already tried, and how did they go?

5. Brainstorm other ways to initiate *Everybody Writes*.

6. Considering your students in particular, what are some things that could go poorly if you used *Everybody Writes*? How could you protect against them?

7. What routines and systems could you put into place to make your *Everybody Writes* more efficient, focused, reflective, and rich?

TRY *EVERYBODY WRITES* IN THE CLASSROOM

1. For a lesson plan in the offing, write an *Everybody Writes* prompt that you want to use to launch a class discussion related to the lesson objective.

6 BEGIN WITH THE END

2. Write the outcomes you would like to see and hear (in the written responses and in the class discussion). Check the question again with *nonneutral prompts* in mind. Consider how this writing might also relate to something students have already learned.

3. Plan the logistics of when and how you will incorporate this into your lesson as well as how long the writing and discussion should take. Keep it tight.

4. Write down what you will say to the students before they begin their task, to clarify your expectation of what they are to do, including where they are to write, the format, and anything else.

5. Anticipate what you will be doing while they write.

6. Anticipate how students will share their responses (for example, read them aloud, share with a partner, turn in to you).

7. Consider having students discuss this latest experience with the process of *Everybody Writes*.

8. Evaluate the process after class.

TROUBLE-SHOOT

Steady On

Don't conflate *Everybody Writes* with "free writing." *Everybody Writes* has a clear question and prepares students for discussion.

Other Challenges

Possible Challenge	Possible Solutions
The students are unable (or unwilling) to sustain writing for the full period I allow.	Did the nonneutral prompt set the students in a clear enough direction? Should the format you require be simpler, quicker to execute? Have students practice writing so that they develop greater stamina for it. Prime the pump: very quickly ask three students what they're going to write about to help generate ideas. Then write.

BE CREATIVE

21 TAKE A STAND

1. Use *Everybody Writes* as a form of *Take a Stand*.
2. For very young students, consider combining the writing with drawing.

SUSTAIN YOUR PROGRESS

1. Using feedback from your study group or other peers, and reviewing your own lesson notes and observations, monitor your progress on *Everybody Writes*.

Date	A New Use or Style of *Everybody Writes*	What Worked, What Didn't	What Next?

2. Revisit "Where Am I Now?" Are you ready to build out to some other new technique?

VEGAS

OVERVIEW

Vegas is the sparkle, the fun that brings students together while progressing toward your learning objective. But the song or dance that gets students going has to reinforce not just academics in general, but the specific learning objective for that day.

For those who wonder: although most if not all *Vegas* is also *Joy Factor,* the latter is a larger category and includes classroom elements devised specifically to induce your students to take an active part in building the room's culture with you.

46 **JOY FACTOR**

WHERE AM I NOW?

	Proficiency			
	I am brand new to *Vegas* . . .	**I'm in the planning and practice stage, though I haven't tried *Vegas* yet in class . . .**	**I'm beginning to try *Vegas* in my classroom . . .**	**We go to *Vegas* often . . .**
Comfort & Confidence	❏ . . . and excited to try it.	❏ . . . but know with more practice I'll make it work.	❏ . . . and love how it basically works.	❏ . . . and with real pizzazz.
	❏ . . . and undecided about my ability to make the magic happen.	❏ . . . because I still have questions about how to devise it or carry it off.	❏ . . . with mixed results I need to evaluate.	❏ . . . but I may be milking it.
	❏ . . . and have never even passed through Reno.	❏ . . . because, frankly, I'm still from Squaresville.	❏ . . . but it doesn't seem to work or suit me.	❏ . . . but the students aren't as with it as I'd like.

Work from your strengths. If you find yourself in the bottom left portion, leaf through this technique to locate related ones you might prefer to work on right now.

ANALYZE THE CHAMPIONS

View each video clip, ideally more than once, and answer the following questions.

Clip 18. Teacher Lauren Whitehead, Grade 1

1. Catch several types of *Vegas* in Ms. Whitehead's energizing introduction of Ben Franklin. What are they?
2. What did you notice about the impact of students' singing during the transition?
3. How challenging was the tune?

 Clip 22. Teacher Laura Palma, Grade 1

1. What is the touch of *Vegas* here? How long does it last?
2. How quickly and clearly is Ms. Palma able to end it? How does she do that?
3. Is this *Vegas* serving a *learning objective*?

EXPAND YOUR SKILLS AND REPERTOIRE

6 BEGIN WITH THE END

Vegas is some added "production value"—music, lights, rhythm, dancing, chanting, singing—that draws students in to a little bit of magic. But it's not sparkle for its own sake. It reinforces academics generally and, at its best, one of the day's learning objectives. It's upbeat but often short, sweet, and on-point.

Vegas Variety

Among other things, *Vegas* can be

- A "carrying song" in addition
- A dance for the vowels
- A game of Jeopardy about certain historical figures or key words to remember
- A competition to be the fifth-grade squaring champ or high school "economist of the week"
- A theatrical heightening of the story you just read aloud or that the students just read in silence

What could *Vegas* be for some objectives in your unit, in line with your own talents and for your age of students?

Objective: _____

Vegas idea: _____

Objective: _____

Vegas idea: _____

Objective: _____

Vegas idea: _____

VEGAS

Storytelling Production Values

Add "production values" to any narrative you tell.

- Be dramatic.
- Vary tone and pace.
- Sometimes whisper for emphasis, then speak in a booming voice.
- Sometimes speak very slowly; sometimes race crisply.
- Let students literally "ooh" and "ahh" on cue.

End It Cleanly

When it's over, it's over, like a turned-off faucet. A game that lingers on distracts students from the work of class. If it crops up again when your back is turned, crack down quickly.

The Chorus Line

Don't allow *Vegas* to spiral out of control. You own it and set the rules and limits for the activity. Students must know when to stand, how to play, what to do if they lose, and so on. If they don't, you risk allowing the activity to undercut instead of enhance achievement.

If students subtly express disdain for the *Vegas,* for example by singing deliberately off-key, use behavior management techniques to correct immediately.

| 36 **100%** |

| 37 **WHAT TO DO** |
| 38 **STRONG VOICE** |
| 39 **DO IT AGAIN** |
| 43 **POSITIVE FRAMING** |

VEGAS

PRACTICE WITH STUDY GROUP OR PARTNERS

1. Before the meeting, members can prepare (ideally with a partner) some *Vegas* appropriate to the group itself. After members teach it to the group, the group can decide to adopt it or not. Get group feedback about

- The activity's relatedness to a group's broad objective for that week's meeting
- Ease of learning and execution of the *Vegas*
- Brevity
- A crisp way to end the activity

2. Demonstrate for the group the *Vegas* that you have created in the "Try *Vegas* in the Classroom" section following. Get group feedback on these questions:

- Was the activity clearly related to the class session learning objective?
- Was the students' part of the *Vegas* easy to learn and execute?
- Was the activity brief?
- Was the ending crisp?

3. For those still too shy to boogie, brainstorm and discuss what very simple starters of *Vegas* might still feel manageable and useful.

Spice It Up!

In this activity, pairs of group members create *Vegas* songs that support and energize the class through a transition. As a starting option, the group can watch and comment on clips 18 and 22. The *Facilitator* can bring Internet access so that group members can hear the original "Indiana Fight Song" on YouTube or similar service.

1.   In pairs, consider some transitional moments in the day or lesson when student engagement might be improved by a song. Using the models included here or any other source, take about twenty minutes to create two songs—one for each member of the pair.

"Planets Song" supporting academic content (to the tune of "Twinkle Twinkle Little Star"):

I know the planets one by one

Starting with the one that's closest to the sun.

Mercury, Venus, Earth, and Mars,

Are the first four among the stars.

Jupiter, Saturn, Uranus, Neptune

Are the next planets in my tune.

Pluto's the farthest one from the sun.

I know the planets one by one.

"Indiana Fight Song" supporting classroom culture and shared values in a classroom that has been named after Indiana University:

Indiana, Our Indiana

Indiana, we're all for you

We will sit up straight

track the speaker,

do our homework for Old IU (IU)

Never quitting, we cannot give up

When it gets hard, we persevere

Indiana, Our Indiana

Indiana, we're all for you!

"Transition Song" supporting instructions during a physical transition:

Scholars are transitioning, transitioning, transitioning

Scholars are transitioning and following directions

"Core Song," by teacher Katie Melcher

I wanna learn about Brooklyn, Brooklyn

I wanna learn about my community,

I wanna learn about Earth's resources,

Plus there's more *(clap, clap)*

IT'S CORE

I wanna learn about planets, planets,

I wanna learn about my whole universe,

I wanna learn about bugs and butterflies,

Plus there's more *(clap, clap)*

IT'S CORE

2. At the twenty-minute mark, the *Facilitator* lets the group know they have five more minutes to plan how they would introduce their songs to a classroom of students.

3. In pairs, sing your songs to the group and describe how you will introduce them to a class. You can also share your work with members of the group on paper, via e-mail, or with an audio recording.

TRY *VEGAS* IN THE CLASSROOM

1. What's the objective?
2. Where in the lesson plan would be a good moment for *Vegas*?
3. What will you do, and how will the students respond with voices, bodies, and so on?
4. What will you say to instruct the students on their part? What will they do to practice it for chorus-line precision?
5. How will you end it clearly and crisply?
6. Considering your students' response, how might you use that *Vegas* again in the next session?
7. How can you add more *Vegas*?

TROUBLE-SHOOT

Steady On

Put yourself out. Willingness to embarrass yourself is okay if students see you're doing this for them, not just for yourself.

Other Challenges

Possible Challenge	Possible Solutions
My *Vegas* gets my kids a little out of control.	Watch clip 18 again.

VEGAS

BE CREATIVE

1. A touch of costume or a simple prop (or even a hand puppet) could be part of *Vegas*.

2. Team up outside the group. Gilbert, Sullivan, May, Nichols, Lerner, Lowe, Rogers, Hammerstein, Sondheim, and Bernstein all worked with partners of complementary creative leanings.

3. Write another simple *Vegas* song, set to a tune your students already know.

| 12 **HOOK** |

4. Connect your *Vegas* to your *Hook,* remembering that they serve different motivational moments.

SUSTAIN YOUR PROGRESS

1. Using feedback from your study group or other peers, and reviewing your own lesson notes and observations, monitor your progress on *Vegas*.

Date	Our Latest, Greatest *Vegas*	Our Next Production

2. Revisit "Where Am I Now?" Are you ready to build out to some other new technique?

VEGAS

THE IMPORTANCE OF ROUTINES

Creating a strong classroom culture largely comes down to creating strong, positive daily classroom routines that the students embrace as their own. Established effective routines signal that you are prepared, know what you expect, and have high standards. They set a tone of order in your classroom, reduce off-task student behaviors, and engage students in accomplishing tasks as a team.

Each technique in this section (numbers 28 through 35) is about creating, honing, and maintaining a different, important type of routine. In this overview are some routine-building principles and methods that apply across all eight types, along with activities to get you started in deciding which routines you are most interested in establishing. In the long run, making these routine tasks automatic can free amazing new amounts of time for teaching.

Even if doing so seems like taking a leap, we recommend you find at least one procedure to routinize in your classroom, as early as possible in the school year. For example, are you losing time during class moving people from place to place or getting from one activity to another? Ask yourself what routines you have right now. Do students know exactly how to do them? Could they do them well even without you?

HALLMARKS OF GOOD ROUTINES

Good routines are consistent and efficient. They minimize disruptions and maximize instructional time by embodying all these characteristics:

1. *Quick.* The goal is the *fastest possible right version* of the routine. That means you make sure that your students practice the correct version and do it right, and then you work to speed things up.

2. *Low narration.* Once taught, the routine should require only short prompts and reminders, not extensive narration or instruction. This will make the routine more efficient and allow you to do and think about other things (like your upcoming lesson!).

3. *Well planned.* In advance, plan exactly what you want during each step of the procedure: what students will do, where, in what order, and with what cues to tell them. Consider likely pitfalls.

| 10 **DOUBLE PLAN** |

4. *Without interruptions.* If you allow for students' interruptions during routines (for example, "When is the test?" "Will we be able to go to the bathroom before math?"), you show that interruptions are a permissible part of the routine. Ask students to hold their questions and keep hands down while you are in transition. Don't warn students who deviate from a planned routine:

| 39 **DO IT AGAIN** |
| 43 **POSITIVE FRAMING** |

provide a consequence. *Do It Again,* positively framed repractice, is an ideal choice.

5. *Shared ownership.* Routines will symbolize your classroom culture, so students should feel as though those routines belong to everyone in the culture. Find ways to let students "own" them—by assisting or leading, by timing one another, by adding their own unique variations to them, class by class.

CREATING STRONG AUTOMATIC ROUTINES

These are basic practices for establishing any routine that you want to have become automatic:

1. *Invest up front.* If you're worried you're spending too much time getting your routines right at the beginning of the year (or at the beginning of your rollout of the routine), that's probably a good sign. Routines require a lot of initial investment, but they pay you back many-fold over the long haul. Make the up-front investment even if it seems as though you're putting too much into it. First plan the routine carefully, then continue to invest.

13 NAME THE STEPS

2. *Number the steps.* For younger students especially, break your routines into steps that you can teach one at a time. Give each step a number and add sequential cues that allow you to pace the routine verbally or nonverbally—for example, holding up three fingers to show it's time for the third step. Gradually remove instructions as the students internalize the process.

3. *Model and describe.* Show your students what the routine and its steps look like, at least as much as you tell. Do walk-throughs, modeling what students will be doing. Or get students to show one another how to do it right while you describe what they are doing that's so good.

4. *Pretend practice.* Practice early on in a simplified form (for example, doing a brush cleanup routine without any brushes in anyone's hands; passing out imaginary materials first, then real materials). Practice in focused chunks: "Let's just master what we're going to do when we arrive at our desks." This lets students get feedback quickly and concentrate on doing fewer things better the first time around. Then connect the chunks.

5. *Transfer ownership.* Give students the chance to "own" more and more of the process. Or let students "captain" the routine.

"Who can tell us what's next?"

"Show me that you can do it on your own."

In this case, the class has taken on the name "Homeroom Harvard" so that, in effect, the students are encouraged to "own" not just a classroom but a long-term academic ambition.

"Let me see a transition, Homeroom Harvard–style."

6. *Maintain.* Once your class has mastered a routine, practice and reaffirm expectations regularly to keep it in shape all year. Set new goals for quickness. Challenge students to "sharpen up."

ESSENTIAL ROUTINES

1. What have you turned into an efficient routine in your own life (for example, your routine for waking up in the morning or for a workout)? How did you establish that routine? What are the benefits of having the routine in place?

_____

_____

_____

_____

_____

_____

2.   Here are some routines that other teachers recommend:

- How to enter class (*Entry Routine*)
- How to raise hands
- How to disagree with a peer during discussion
- How to head your paper
- How to walk down the hall

| 28 **ENTRY ROUTINE** |

What is something that you do not have a routine for in your classroom that you wish you did? How would it help you make your teaching more efficient?

_____

_____

_____

_____

3.   Many experienced, successful teachers take care to establish an efficient *Entry Routine* right away with a new class of students. In addition to an *Entry Routine* and other suggestions mentioned earlier, you may want to plan routines for these:

| 30 **TIGHT TRANSITIONS** |
| 31 **BINDER CONTROL** |
| 32 **SLANT** |
| 34 **SEAT SIGNALS** |

- Transitions within the building or classroom
- Distribution and collection of materials
- Classroom participation (how to sit, raise hand, and so on)
- How you and students can use hand signals to "interrupt" without interrupting
- How to read like a college-bound student (with pencil in hand marking up text, underlining key passages, circling key terms)

4.   What may interfere with effective routines in your classroom right now? Do other teachers in your school also "routinize" things? Do parents and students understand the "why" behind your routines? Does the layout of the room create obstacles to the execution of quick, efficient routines?

| 11 **DRAW THE MAP** |
| 36 **100%** |
| 48 **EXPLAIN EVERYTHING** |

_____

_____

_____

CORRECT STEADILY AND POSITIVELY

When students deviate from a critical routine, practice again, framing it as an opportunity for success. Kids get stuff wrong. Act as though you knew that would happen, but also fix it. If you keep it positive,

| 37 **WHAT TO DO** |
| 38 **STRONG VOICE** |

THE IMPORTANCE OF ROUTINES

| 39 **DO IT AGAIN** |
| 42 **NO WARNINGS** |
| 43 **POSITIVE FRAMING** |

you're unlikely to encounter defiance; if you do, provide a predictable consequence. Consequences here come not for good-faith mistakes but for defiance or unwillingness to try.

QUESTIONS FOR REFLECTION OR GROUP DISCUSSION

1. How do you build routines?

2. How do you know when a routine is broken down or missing?

3. What improvements in routine does your classroom need? What could save time in the long run?

4. How can you recognize students for appropriate behavior during a routine at the beginning of the year? Middle of the year? End of the year?

5. What should be the consequence for students if they do not meet the expectation of a routine that has clearly been taught and practiced, at the beginning of the year? Middle? End?

6. What brings joy to routines? What could work for your classroom?

- Sing a song or give a challenge problem to solve during the routine?

- Give students who "star" at transitions something to honor them (for example, a crown for younger students)?

- Take and post pictures of your students during transition?

- Ask them to walk like kings, queens, or admired historical figures?

- _____

- _____

- _____

- _____

- _____

- _____

- _____

- _____

- _____

- _____

- _____

- _____

- _____

ENTRY ROUTINE

OVERVIEW

Your *Entry Routine* describes how you expect students to enter the classroom and how the classroom session begins. In the absence of a conscious *Entry Routine,* an unconscious, often inefficient one takes over by default.

As the overview to Section Five says about all classroom routines, a good *Entry Routine* is planned to proceed quickly and automatically with little or no narration by the teacher. It becomes part of the classroom culture in which students take pride and ownership.

WHERE AM I NOW?

	Proficiency			
Comfort & Confidence	**I'm brand new to *Entry Routine* . . .**	**I've identified the default routine for entry that's in place right now, but I haven't shaped it with this technique . . .**	**I've introduced a deliberate *Entry Routine* in my classroom . . .**	**We have a good *Entry Routine* . . .**
	❑ . . . and want to try it.	❑ . . . but am planning an *Entry Routine*.	❑ . . . and see the benefits.	❑ . . . that I consciously maintain.
	❑ . . . and not sure we need it.	❑ . . . but it seems to be okay.	❑ . . . but it's not really clicking yet.	❑ . . . but it lapses.

Usually we encourage you to work from your strengths if you're not confident. You can do that here, too, but often this routine is the starting point.

EXPAND YOUR SKILLS AND REPERTOIRE

For your *Entry Routine,* follow the general guidelines for creating strong routines:

1. Invest up front.
2. Number the steps.
3. Model and describe.
4. Pretend practice.
5. Transfer ownership.
6. Maintain.

ENTRY ROUTINE

Analyze Your Current *Entry Routine*

| 26 **EVERYBODY WRITES** |
| 29 **DO NOW** |

A significant amount of time often transpires between when students enter the room and the moment a teacher begins formal instruction. *Entry Routine* aims at getting students to use that time productively—for example, by including a *Do Now* that has them write and reflect. Whatever tasks the *Entry Routine* includes, manage the time so that your expectations are clear and students do not gradually pressure you into expanding to an ever larger amount of unproductive time.

Your students should know where to deposit any homework materials, where to sit, what to do (and what not to do), and what materials to get out when they sit down. The planned routine often begins with students entering the room and picking up a packet of materials (for example, all of the reading and handouts for the lesson, prepped in advance in a single batch) from a small table just inside the door. Or, especially at the lower grades, packets might already be at students' desks.

| 10 **DOUBLE PLAN** |

1. In a table similar to the one here (Current Entry Routine Template), write down your current intended *Entry Routine,* if any. Also write down what you believe actually happens during this time.

Current Entry Routine Template

Current Steps as Intended		What Really Happens	
What I do	*What they do*	*What I do*	*What they do*
1.			
2.			
3.			
4.			
5.			
6.			

Any gaps? _____

_____

_____

_____

2. In your next teaching session, consciously note what is actually happening as students enter the class to see whether what you believed was happening is in fact the case. Then modify your table as needed.

- Is there a clear *Entry Routine* in your mind and the students'?

_____

_____

- How efficient is the routine in terms of time spent, and how well does it get students on task?

  _____

  _____

  _____

- Is there downtime in that routine that could be turned to better use?

  _____

  _____

  _____

- What is happening by default that you might want to change?

  _____

  _____

  _____

3. If you can, record in audio or video your current de facto entry events, or have a peer observe them and take notes. Then revisit the previous questions.

Script an *Entry Routine*

Write a step-by-step *Entry Routine* describing what students are to do in your classroom from the moment they shake your hand at the *Threshold* to the point where you may want them to be working on a *Do Now*.

Write a paragraph-long script you would use to instruct them on the routine.

> 29 **DO NOW**
> 41 **THRESHOLD**

PRACTICE WITH STUDY GROUP OR PARTNERS

Discuss and Compare

1. Revisit the individual work you did in the previous section to share and compare your responses and see other options.
2. What's the current state of your *Entry Routine*?
3. Is there downtime at the outset of class? How could you capture that time and use it to address your objective for each day?

Deliver Your *Entry Routine*

This activity lets you practice delivering the script you began to prepare in the "Script an *Entry Routine*" section. It works best with four or more participants. If you have fewer, the *Facilitator* can adapt however it makes sense for your number.

| 29 **DO NOW** |

To prepare, each participant has already done "Script an *Entry Routine*" and has brought copies to share. Ideally, each has also prepared a brief *Do Now* as part of the *Entry Routine.*

1. Exchange and mutually discuss your scripts with other members of the group. Share what you notice about interesting elements in others' scripts.

2. Take turns as *Teacher*. As *Teacher,* deliver your script. Then take your *Students* to the threshold and role-play the entry until all are seated and ready for you to begin the lesson. Then briefly begin an appropriate lesson.

3. If you have prepared a *Do Now,* have the *Students* do it. Then continue briefly into the lesson based on that.

4. At the end of each round, discuss these questions as a group:

As *Students*:

- How did the *Teacher*'s choices reflect good *Entry Routine* technique?
- Were any moments or directions unclear? Did you ever fail to do it right even when you were trying to? If so, why?
- What loopholes did you notice in any particular step?
- How could the directions have been improved?
- What was most useful for you about observing this *Entry Routine*?

As *Teacher*:

| 43 **POSITIVE FRAMING** |

- How would you deal with any student mistakes? *Positive Framing* is a great tool for responding.

- In your next *Entry Routine* design, how would you address any issues raised by your experience and the *Student* feedback about it?

Your takeaways:

_____

_____

_____

_____

TRY *ENTRY ROUTINE* IN THE CLASSROOM

1. Plan some improvements you can make in your class's current de facto *Entry Routine*. Integrate them into your next lesson plan. This checklist may be useful:

- ❑ Materials for the lesson (packets, books, pencils or pens, rulers, and so on)
- ❑ Materials not needed for this lesson (binders, home folders, pencils)
- ❑ Seating (Assigned seats? How will you assign?)

❑   Traffic flow to seating

❑   Materials to pass in (including homework)

❑   *Do Now*—immediate work for students to engage in with no instruction

❑   Board configuration—objectives, agenda, homework

❑   Sound level: What should the class sound like during the *Entry Routine*?

❑   Timing and pacing of each part: How quickly do you expect everything to happen?

❑   _____

❑   _____

2. List each step the students need to take and what you will be doing then.

3. Review (with a partner if you can) the steps to confirm that they are specific, concrete, sequential, and observable.

4. Revisit *Draw the Map* to see how well the "map" supports your proposed *Entry Routine*.

5. Prepare an introductory script (exactly what you will say and model). Include five specific praises you can offer to students who demonstrate the behaviors you henceforth expect.

6. Allow time in the session for needed practice or questions from students.

7. Remind the class of tomorrow's session by giving brief positive feedback at the end of class. Make notes about what further feedback or practice you can give the class next time. Inform your students about any adjustments you expect in their entry behaviors.

8. Maintain through subsequent sessions, noticing how you might improve on

- Students getting it right
- Reducing the need for narration or prompts
- Reducing interruptions
- Increasing speed
- Increasing joy
- Increasing shared ownership

| 10 **DOUBLE PLAN** |
| 11 **DRAW THE MAP** |
| 44 **PRECISE PRAISE** |
| 32 **SLANT** |
| 46 **JOY FACTOR** |

ENTRY ROUTINE

TROUBLE-SHOOT

Steady On

Monitor how much time elapses during your *Entry Routine*. Avoid allowing it to expand.

Other Challenges

Possible Challenge	Possible Solutions

BE CREATIVE

11 DRAW THE MAP   Create a friendly visual to post to teach and maintain your *Entry Routine*.

SUSTAIN YOUR PROGRESS

1. Using feedback from your study group or other peers, and reviewing your own lesson notes and observations, monitor your progress on *Entry Routine*.

Date	Total Time	How Well Used?

2. Revisit "Where Am I Now?" Are you ready to build out to some other new technique?

DO NOW

OVERVIEW

Do Now is a short activity you have written on the board or placed on students' desks for them to do as soon as they enter the classroom, as part of an *Entry Routine*.

28 **ENTRY ROUTINE**

Students should be able to enter and begin *Do Now* without any specific instruction to do so and using materials they have at hand.

WHERE AM I NOW?

	Proficiency			
Comfort & Confidence	I am brand new to *Do Now* ...	I'm in the planning stage, though I haven't tried *Do Now* yet in class ...	I'm beginning to try *Do Now* in my classroom ...	My students often do *Do Now* ...
	❏ ... and eager to try it.	❏ ... but know with more practice I'll make it work.	❏ ... and like how it bascially works.	❏ ... and from it we move into my overall lesson plan.
	❏ ... and not sure my class ever needs it.	❏ ... because I still have questions about how to make it serve the day's lesson objective.	❏ ... with mixed results I need to evaluate.	❏ ... but I may still be learning when and how to use it to best advantage.

Work from your strengths. If you find yourself in the bottom left portion, leaf through this technique to locate related ones you might prefer to work on right now.

EXPAND YOUR SKILLS AND REPERTOIRE

Past Approximations

1. Review five previous lessons. If they did not include a *Do Now*, might the lessons have benefited from it? Script one retroactively.

_____

_____

_____

2.   Wherever you included something like *Do Now* in a previous lesson, what did it contribute toward the day's objective?

_____

_____

_____

3.   The biggest challenge in using *Do Now* is preventing it from going on too long. If you're currently using *Do Nows,* time yourself. Are you done with it in three to five minutes? If not, try "sampling"—that is, discussing answers to only some of the questions you asked rather than every one. Working with a timer may also help you complete the activity faster.

Necessary Process

Do Nows can include brief review, reading, writing, analysis of math or graphs, answering questions, and the like. Their content usually serves to get the ensuing lesson plan rolling as soon as the teacher starts the class. Whatever the content and connection, students need to know, without having to ask,

- What to do, from written instructions or prompts
- How much time they have to do it
- How to signal when they're done
- How to dispose of any handout materials that aren't intended to be kept

Devise a plan for a *Do Now* routine that you can use on a regular basis. Write a script that explains *Do Now* to the class. In addition to the four preceding points, you may want to include

- Where students should routinely look to find the *Do Now*
- Your expectations: what they should do if they have a question (for example, "Sit, get working, raise your hand briefly so I know, and then work until I come to you"); whether they can be talking to each other (hint: no); what they should do if they find the work confusing or too hard
- How *Do Now* benefits the learning

PRACTICE WITH STUDY GROUP OR PARTNERS

1.   Revisit the individual work you did in the previous section to share and compare your responses and see other options.

2.   You will probably cover *Do Now* briefly in a meeting of your group in which most of the time is spent on some other technique. Consider appointing a *Facilitator* to prepare and conduct a *Do Now* that will lead into that larger topic. Begin the session with the *Do Now.* Discuss how effective it was at bridging into your main topic.

6 BEGIN WITH THE END

3.   Share and compare your planning for a *Do Now* that you could use in an upcoming lesson. Be sure the planning began with the lesson objective.

TRY *DO NOW* IN THE CLASSROOM

1. Make *Do Now* a part of an upcoming lesson plan. Evaluate and perfect the activity in terms of
   - The purpose of the *Do Now* in relation to a lesson objective
   - How you will use the students' *Do Now* to launch the next step in the lesson
   - Brevity
   - Giving short, clear instructions about what to do, how long to take, and what students should have achieved in the *Do Now*
   - Setting a level of difficulty that enables everyone in class to make an honest attempt
   - How the format will make the results convenient for you to process with the class

2. Reviewing the script you prepared as part of "Necessary Process," plan how and when you will explain aspects of *Do Now* however much as necessary.

3. Remember that this or the next day's *Do Now* can include review, but also build into it something that will launch today's lesson wherever you want it to start.

TROUBLE-SHOOT

Steady On

Keep *Do Now* simple. Aim it to launch discussion of a particular problem or question that ties in with what they did in the *Do Now*.

Other Challenges

Possible Challenge	Possible Solutions
Some students don't get right down to it.	Do they know what to do? Have you practiced intentionally? Is the task something they can focus on and do right now, at the start of class?
I run out of ideas.	Use *Do Now* to ensure ongoing mastery of skills. Practice a previous skill with the *Do Now,* or make it a challenge problem or a short reading. Example: Students read a passage and are asked to identify the author or text and how they can tell.

BE CREATIVE

Create *Do Nows* that get all the students looking at the same picture or graph on the wall at the front of the class, or teaming up as a class to solve one hundred problems in, say, three minutes.

DO NOW

SUSTAIN YOUR PROGRESS

1. Using feedback from your study group or other peers, and reviewing your own lesson notes and observations, monitor your progress on *Do Now*.

Date	One Thing *Do Now* Did Well	A Needed Improvement?

2. Revisit "Where Am I Now?" Are you ready to build out to some other new technique?

TIGHT TRANSITIONS

OVERVIEW

To maximize time and energy for learning, champion classrooms have *Tight Transitions* that students can execute without extensive narration by the teacher.

Teachers need to envision what the transition will look like and sound like, and how long it will take to execute. Once you have routinized a transition (see the overview to Section Five for general methods of creating *any* strong routine), you can add a touch of joy—for example, a song that ends as the transition draws to a close.

46 **JOY FACTOR**

WHERE AM I NOW?

	Proficiency			
	I'm brand new to *Tight Transitions* ...	**I'm becoming familiar with *Tight Transitions*, but haven't yet put it to work ...**	**I'm beginning to create *Tight Transitions* in class ...**	**Our transitions are consistently tight ...**
Comfort & Confidence	❑ ... and excited to try it.	❑ ... however, I know I can.	❑ ... and love how they basically work.	❑ ... and I've added or am adding joy.
	❑ ... and undecided about my ability to pull it off.	❑ ... because I still have questions about how to do it right.	❑ ... with mixed results I need to evaluate.	❑ ... but haven't got around to the joy.
	❑ ... and not sure they're needed.	❑ ... because I still have hesitations.	❑ ... but they don't seem to work.	❑ ... except on bad days.

Work from your strengths. If you find yourself in the bottom left portion, leaf through this technique to locate related ones you might prefer to work on right now.

ANALYZE THE CHAMPIONS

View each video clip, ideally more than once, and answer the following questions. See the end of the technique for some possible answers.

 Clip 18. Teacher Lauren Whitehead, Grade 1

1. What's involved in Ms. Whitehead's *Tight Transition* routine besides a song that may promote the students' quick, orderly movement?

2. What else do you notice in this rich clip?

Clip 22. Teacher Laura Palma, Grade 1

1. How long do Ms. Palma's transitional routines here take?
2. What individual subroutines do you see in this clip? Are their purposes different? How so?
3. What's the net effect of these routines on the students, as of the moment when Ms. Palma says, "Thank you, Tarri, title of story?"

 Clip 23. Teacher Lauren Whitehead, Grade 2

1. Including the hands ritual at the beginning, how long does it take Ms. Whitehead's entire class to move from the desks to the reading area?
2. What details support this *Tight Transition*?

 Clip 24. Teacher Marisa Segel, Grade 6

1. Here Ms. Segel gathers seat work from an entire class. How long, typically, does it take you or other teachers you've observed to do so? What else tends to go on while the students are doing that?
2. Obviously Ms. Segel has invested some time during previous sessions in preparing her students for this stopwatch routine. Do you think the time was well spent? What other dividends does the routine earn besides the seconds of teaching time it adds?

EXPAND YOUR SKILLS AND REPERTOIRE

Tight Transitions as Routines

| 28 **ENTRY ROUTINE** |

1. Consult "Creating Strong Automatic Routines" in the overview to Section Five about these keys to establishing any routine:

- Invest up front
- Number the steps
- Pretend practice
- Model and describe
- Transfer ownership
- Maintain

| 10 **DOUBLE PLAN** |

2. Consult also the "Hallmarks of Good Routines" section in the overview for discussion of these characteristics of good routines:

- Quick
- Low narration
- Well planned
- No interruptions
- Shared ownership

Analyzing Transitions

1. If you have or can make an audio or video recording of a class you have taught, review it to notice what went on during transitions between activities and how much time those transitions took. (With audio you can tune in to sounds of students talking, paper shuffling, furniture scraping . . .) For later reference back to the audio or video, note the times on the recording at which the transitions began.

2. In the recording or on a lesson plan you've prepared, try to notice at least five transitional moments. What were they? Briefly describe what happens in each.

If you are using a recording or a remembered experience, also try to quickly evaluate each transition by the criteria provided here.

Transition 1: _____

_____

    Quick? _____

    Low narration? _____

    Upbeat? _____

    Interruptions? _____

Transition 2: _____

_____

    Quick? _____

    Low narration? _____

    Upbeat? _____

    Interruptions? _____

Transition 3: _____

_____

    Quick? _____

    Low narration? _____

    Upbeat? _____

    Interruptions? _____

Transition 4: _____

_____

    Quick? _____

TIGHT TRANSITIONS

Low narration? _____

Upbeat? _____

Interruptions? _____

Transition 5: _____

_____

Quick? _____

Low narration? _____

Upbeat? _____

Interruptions? _____

To what extent are your current routine transitions *Tight Transitions*? What do you need to work on?

_____

_____

_____

_____

Perfecting Narratives

If you meet with a group, your *Facilitator* for *Tight Transitions* might want to designate several of the following narratives for group review, brainstorming, and rewriting. Otherwise, you can do them yourself or with a partner.

1. Read all of the following transitional narratives. Which are likely to be most or least effective? Why?

_____

_____

_____

2. Rewrite or edit each one as much as it needs.

Narrative 1: First-grade reading class of twenty to thirty students sitting on mats in front of the teacher. Teacher says to students,

"Okay, scholars, when you're ready, put away your books and line up by the door."

Possible rewrite: _____

_____

_____

_____

Narrative 2: Fourth-grade math class sitting at desks after finishing their *Exit Ticket,* getting ready to dismiss to lunch. Teacher says,

"In just a moment we are going to: on one, get up from our seat quickly and quietly, push in our chairs. On two, we are going to walk to the door and line up behind the person in front of you with your hands by your sides and feet both on the floor. On three, we will walk in a silent line out the door to lunch. One . . . two . . . three."

Possible rewrite: _____

_____

_____

_____

Narrative 3: Sixth-grade English class. Teacher says,

"Okay, sixth graders, this is it, we are done with our reading books. So what I need you to do in just a moment is put a bookmark on the page we finished with, pass your book to the left to be collected, and take out your vocabulary notebooks and have your pencil in hand. Yesterday you were really fast at this, but I think you can beat that time today. So I have my stopwatch—let's see if you can beat yesterday's fifteen seconds. Ready, set, go."

Possible rewrite: _____

_____

_____

_____

_____

_____

Narrative 4: Tenth-grade science class, about to start an experiment. Teacher says,

"Okay, guys, this is super important because we don't want to lose our lab privileges, so let's make this move to get materials clean. Remember, I'm looking for one lab partner, I don't care which one, to quietly gather the materials you will need for this experiment and come back to your desk and begin working from page one of the lab instructions. Go."

Possible rewrite: _____

_____

_____

_____

Basic Resources

Here are a few techniques and resources that might help you establish *Tight Transitions* at numerous times during the day. What others might help?

| 31 **BINDER CONTROL** |
| 32 **SLANT** |
| 43 **POSITIVE FRAMING** |
| 44 **PRECISE PRAISE** |

Poster

Stopwatch

Consistent cues

A dismountable wall clock—or, better, a clock you can project on an overhead when you want students to manage the time for themselves

_____

_____

SLANT

Binder Control

Positive Framing

Precise Praise

_____

_____

Create a *Tight Transition*

| 11 **DRAW THE MAP** |

Consider your recent experiences conducting transitions and pick the loosest one—the one that wastes the most time and generally least resembles a *Tight Transition*. If you don't have a recent experience to choose from, use a transition point in a lesson plan you are working on. Use the resources mentioned in the previous section to script the steps students will take, and identify any pedestrian routes.

_____

_____

_____

_____

_____

_____

_____

_____

Also record how you will:

1. Cue and minimally narrate the transition: _____

_____

2. Teach and model behaviors or praise student models: _____

_____

_____

3. Conduct practice: _____

_____

_____

4. Enforce 100 percent compliance during the transition: _____

_____

_____

5. Limit student attempts to distract (for example, "Hands down"): _____

_____

_____

6. Increase the speed: _____

_____

_____

7. Get students to internalize, embrace, and enjoy it: _____

_____

_____

PRACTICE WITH STUDY GROUP OR PARTNERS

Revisit the individual work you did in the previous section to share and compare your responses and see other options.

Compare Work and Discuss

1. If your group chose a *Facilitator* for this technique, he or she may ask the group to work together on completing one or more of the "Perfecting Narratives" items in the previous section. If not, discuss and compare your rewrites.

2. Share and discuss your discoveries in "Analyzing Transitions."

3. Brainstorm more ideas for basic resources.

4. Discuss your plans to create or improve a transition in your respective classrooms.

5. Discuss what your consequence would be for students if they did not meet the expectation of an established *Tight Transition* at the beginning of the year, at the middle, and at the end.

TIGHT TRANSITIONS

TIGHT TRANSITIONS

| 27 **VEGAS** |
| 46 **JOY FACTOR** |

6. Discuss how you would recognize students for appropriate behavior during a *Tight Transition* at the beginning, middle, or end of the year.

7. Talk about building joy into *Tight Transitions.*

As You Would Do Unto Yourselves

Identify and tighten some loose transition that occurs in your group.

Your takeaways:

_____

_____

_____

_____

TRY *TIGHT TRANSITIONS* IN THE CLASSROOM

| 39 **DO IT AGAIN** |

1. In past and upcoming lesson plans, spot and mark transitions.
2. Then apply the process in "Create a *Tight Transition.*"
3. Maintain with praise and practice.

TROUBLE-SHOOT

Steady On

Keep them tight.

Other Challenges

| 28 **ENTRY ROUTINE** |

See also your challenges from *Entry Routine.*

Possible Challenge	Possible Solutions

BE CREATIVE

Stop by *Vegas* for some examples of *Tight Transition* joy.

27 **VEGAS**

SUSTAIN YOUR PROGRESS

1. Using feedback from your study group or other peers, and reviewing your own lesson notes and observations, monitor your progress on *Tight Transitions*.

Date	*Tight Transition!*	Just Noticed Some Looseness

2. Revisit "Where Am I Now?" Are you ready to build out to some other new technique?

ANALYZE THE CHAMPIONS: SOME OBSERVATIONS

 Clip 18. Teacher Lauren Whitehead, Grade 1

The students are moving on to a new topic (Ben Franklin) and a different physical space in the room. In addition to a topic-related song, Ms. Whitehead's transition routine includes an understanding of moving by rows. It also includes a hand gesture that may be intended to keep hands occupied (and not wandering to other students) as they move.

TIGHT TRANSITIONS

Clip 23. Teacher Lauren Whitehead, Grade 2

| 23 **CALL AND RESPONSE** | Ms. Whitehead's class transitions tightly in part because everyone knows exactly what to do in response to her simple finger signals. Even more than that, at least some of the students enjoy the quick |

precision. Ms. Whitehead keeps the transition brisk by being at the head of the students right away in the new setting and launching immediately into a routinized *Call and Response* about the activity they're about to start. Also notice the rectangle pattern on the seating mat, which probably helps get students seated with the right amount of spacing between each other and a clear sense of boundaries.

 Clip 22. Teacher Laura Palma, Grade 1

Ms. Palma's first subroutine might be called "You can get ready!" It seems to involve pronouncing several words (that may be in the story the students are about to read). A second routine is "S-T-O-R-Y." A third routine involves her finger signals and apparently tells the students to dip and pick up their packets containing the story. "Title of our story?" may be yet another routine transitional phrase.

 Clip 24. Teacher Marisa Segel, Grade 6

Ms. Segel instills student ownership in the transition by making it a class effort (a team effort) to reach the goal. She lets students serve as timers and shows her excitement at their success—while also noting that she will hold them to this standard of excellence.

TIGHT TRANSITIONS

BINDER CONTROL

OVERVIEW

Most experienced teachers have discovered that their classroom work is much more enjoyable and productive when their students are able to keep track of their own previous work and are able to retrieve it when needed. Require students to compile their notes in a binder that you manage actively and protect from loss, damage, or disorganization.

Consider letting your students take home what they need each night in a homework *folder,* which can be color coded so that you and parents can readily identify it. Each night, students can put everything they need in the folder and leave the binder in the classroom.

WHERE AM I NOW?

	Proficiency			
	I am brand new to *Binder Control* . . .	I'm in the preparation stage . . .	I'm beginning to institute *Binder Control* in my classroom . . .	I use *Binder Control* consistently . . .
Comfort & Confidence	❏ . . . but already see its value for me.	❏ . . . and have a target date for starting *Binder Control.*	❏ . . . and see its benefits.	❏ . . . and am adding my own distinctive touch.
	❏ . . . but already have something similar and fairly workable.	❏ . . . but am still working on how it improves on what I do now, or some other question.	❏ . . . with mixed results I need to evaluate.	❏ . . . and my students follow the system.

EXPAND YOUR SKILLS AND REPERTOIRE

1. Demonstrate the importance of what you teach by building a system for the storage, organization, and recall of what your students have learned.

2. Have a required format for organizing papers within the binder (for example, chronological, front to back) so that everybody is using the same system, and you can check to make sure everyone has (and can find) everything he or she needs. The following are some useful ideas:

    *   Assign a number to everything you expect your students to keep in the binders.

    *   Assign a title or have students title their work in a way that allows them and you to immediately see the purpose and relevance of each piece of work.

| 14 **BOARD = PAPER** |

- As students place items inside the binder, have them also enter the numbers and titles into a table of contents at the front. Ideas from *Board = Paper* may help you train younger students to do so.
- Partition the binder if you teach various subjects.

3. Before you start *Binder Control* with your students, experiment with the practicalities by making and trying a binder system for yourself.

| 10 **DOUBLE PLAN** |

4. Consider what routine you want to follow about whether and when students should retrieve their binders at the outset of class.

5. Practice the basics. It sounds silly, but if you want students to use the binders consistently and effectively, you may have to practice, using all of your tools for building routines.

"Let's practice putting these notes away. Binder out on three ... Good. Let's open to the section for class notes. These'll go at the front. I want to hear those rings popping open on two. One, two ..."

| 1 **NO OPT OUT** |

6. *Binder Control* makes it easy for you to say, "If you don't remember, check your notes," because you know every student has the notes, and you can even tell students where in their binders to find them.

7. Use *Binder Control* to ensure that students have a full and complete packet when reviewing for tests:

"You'll need to take home items 25 to 30 from your binder to prepare for this test."

8. To ensure that students follow through, leave time for them to put their materials away during class.

"Please add 'number 24 Notes on the Civil War' to your table of contents and file these notes away on my signal."

PRACTICE WITH STUDY GROUP OR PARTNERS

1. As a group, discuss these points:
   - How you currently address the basic problems that *Binder Control* addresses
   - How *Binder Control* might improve your practice if you don't currently use it
2. Share examples of the binders and homework folders you use. Compare their virtues.

TRY BINDER CONTROL IN THE CLASSROOM

1. Consider how *Binder Control* might serve *Tight Transitions* or strengthen your *Entry Routine*.

| 28 **ENTRY ROUTINE** |
| 30 **TIGHT TRANSITIONS** |

2. Create a short list of expectations for students about how the binders and homework folders are to be treated and used.

3. Plan how you will introduce *Binder Control* and the actual materials to the class.

| 11 **DRAW THE MAP** |

4. Revisit *Draw the Map* to decide where binders should be stored.

TROUBLE-SHOOT

Steady On

Don't overrate student freedom that leads them to lose papers or take notes on a scrap that gets buried in a pile of stuff.

Other Challenges

Possible Challenge	Possible Solutions
I don't have money to supply student binders.	Ask students to bring a specific binder or type. If you can't require it, allow bonus points for bringing one. Mention to parents or require at parent conferences.
The students use up too much time finding, opening, searching in the binders, and so forth.	Simplify if necessary, but remember that putting things in the binder is a transitional routine. Practice and get faster at it, treating *Binder Control* as a *Tight Transition*.

SUSTAIN YOUR PROGRESS

Using feedback from your study group or other peers, and reviewing your own lesson notes and observations, monitor your progress on *Binder Control*.

Date	Things I'm Doing Well	Ways to Improve

SLANT

OVERVIEW

SLANT is an acronym for five student behaviors that boost their ability to pay attention:

*S*it up straight.

*L*isten.

*A*sk and answer questions.

*N*od your head (to show you understand and are listening).

*T*rack the speaker.

SLANT is a one-word reminder you can use to get all students to instantly tune in to any one of its parts.

36 **100%**

SLANT can be a strong contributor to *100%* participation and can increase your awareness of students who may be giving something less at the moment.

WHERE AM I NOW?

	Proficiency			
Comfort & Confidence	**I am brand new to *SLANT* . . .**	**I'm familiar enough with *SLANT* now to try it . . .**	**I'm beginning to try *SLANT* in my classroom . . .**	**I use *SLANT* or something like it regularly . . .**
	❑ . . . and may try it.	❑ . . . and am preparing to introduce it to the class as it is or in some variation.	❑ . . . and like how it works.	❑ . . . and my classroom culture reflects its essence.
	❑ . . . and use something similar to which I can compare it.	❑ . . . but need to sort out how it fits with something I already use.	❑ . . . but not yet all five aspects of it.	❑ . . . but want to make my students even quicker to use it with minimal signals from me.

Work from your strengths. If you find yourself in the bottom left portion, leaf through this technique to locate related ones you might prefer to work on right now.

ANALYZE THE CHAMPIONS

View each video clip, ideally more than once, and answer the following questions.

 Clip 4. Teacher Stacey Shells, Grade 7

1. What do you hear or see in this clip that shows the presence of *SLANT*?
2. Where are Ms. Shells's eyes while the first student reads?

 Clip 8. Teacher Patrick Pastore, Grade 8

What do you hear or see in this clip that shows the presence of *SLANT*? If you have difficulty spotting more than one piece of evidence now, come back and view the clip again after you've done more work on this technique.

EXPAND YOUR SKILLS AND REPERTOIRE

*S*it up straight.

*L*isten.

*A*sk and answer questions.

*N*od your head.

*T*rack the speaker.

"SLANT." The acronym is a simple, positive instruction you can give in an instant and that students readily understand. A poster on the front wall

42 **NO WARNINGS**

can also remind them of what it means. When individual behaviors drift, you can use *SLANT* as a consequence, directing it in a noninvasive way to the whole class, in line with the advice in *No Warnings*.

To teach your class to *SLANT*, also see the general methods of creating *any* strong routine that are discussed in the overview to Section Five.

Explain to your students how *SLANT* improves their ability to learn by attending to the words of others—yours as well as those of classmates. It is a set of focusing behaviors many students need to learn about and to perfect through practice.

As a set of five different reminders, *SLANT* can be broken apart when necessary. Teachers can remind their students about the "S in *SLANT*" or the "T in *SLANT*," or use a punchy phrase like "Turn and track."

In the most effective classrooms, the word in various forms is deeply embedded in the vocabulary of learning:

"Where's my SLANT?"

"Make sure you are SLANTing."

Nonverbal Signals

Use nonverbal signals to reinforce or correct *SLANT* behaviors without interrupting whatever else you are doing. For example, folding your hands in front of you can mean *Sit up straight;* pointing to your eyes with two fingers can mean *Track the speaker.*

SLANT

Variations

The acronym SLANT was originally used by the first KIPP schools, but other schools have over time developed effective variations—for example, STAR (Sit up. Track the speaker. Ask and answer questions like a scholar. Respect those around you.) or S-SLANT (which adds Smile). The most essential parts of any version may be "Sit up" and "Track."

TRY *SLANT* IN THE CLASSROOM

11 DRAW THE MAP

1. On the day you introduce *SLANT,* post a sign about it at the front of the room that shows the acronym and what each letter stands for.

2. Just as you may practice other routines, plan to lead your class in learning and practicing each part of *SLANT* before you begin to require it. Model what you mean by *S* and check each student's attempt. Also model and check the students' *T*. This will help make students aware of what to do and that it applies to everyone.

3. With the sign in place, you can name individual letters ("Give me the *L* in SLANT!") and have students practice that component. Later, as part of class routine you can use these phrases again, or you can just say "SLANT" or "I need SLANTing" when you want some part of it. Still later, often you can just establish eye contact with a deviating student and point to the sign or trace the letter in the air.

39 DO IT AGAIN

4. Occasionally you may need to take the class back to practicing *S* and *T*.

TROUBLE-SHOOT

Possible Challenge		Possible Solutions
43 POSITIVE FRAMING	I feel too militant.	Explain the "why" to your students—and yourself—always in terms of purpose, not power: "We do this so you can be stars" rather than " . . . because when I ask you to do something I want it done." Keep it positive.
My kids are too grown up.		Rewrite your acronym around professionalism. "We're going to *WORK:* Watch who's talking. Observe the rules of active listening (in other words, nod). Respect the speaker by not interrupting. Keep sharp with good posture energy. Let's make sure we look like we're at WORK."

SLANT

BE CREATIVE

Some teachers make it *SLANTS*—with the "Smile" at the end. Change *SLANT* to suit your and your students' needs, but keep a good acronym quality. Begin some notes to get yourself started.

_____

_____

_____

SUSTAIN YOUR PROGRESS

1. Using feedback from your study group or other peers, and reviewing your own lesson notes and observations, monitor your progress on *SLANT*.

Date	Some Part of *SLANT* We Should Practice Again	A Particularly Successful Use of *SLANT*

2. Revisit "Where Am I Now?" Are you ready to build out to some other new technique?

SLANT

ON YOUR MARK

OVERVIEW

On Your Mark refers to the simple but essential idea that everyone in class should be ready at the "starting line" when you begin the class. A coach doesn't start practice by telling kids to get their shoes on; kids show up with their shoes on. That's the expectation, and because you know kids can do it for sports, you know they can do it in the classroom. Don't ask kids to get ready as class begins, *show them how to prepare before it begins and then expect them to do so every day.*

On Your Mark can mean that every student starts class with books and paper out and pen or pencil in hand—and that this is the expectation in every class, every day.

WHERE AM I NOW?

	Proficiency			
	I am brand new to *On Your Mark* . . .	**I'm planning but haven't tried *On Your Mark* in class . . .**	**I'm now requiring *On Your Mark* . . .**	**My class is on its mark . . .**
Comfort & Confidence	❑ . . . and excited to try it.	❑ . . . but know I'll make it work.	❑ . . . and love how it basically works.	❑ . . . and I remind the class and enact individual consequences when needed.
	❑ . . . and as yet undecided about using it.	❑ . . . and am still not sure exactly what *On Your Mark* should consist of in my classroom.	❑ . . . with mixed results I need to evaluate.	❑ . . . I'm pretty sure, but may need to notice more carefully.

Work from your strengths. If you find yourself in the bottom left portion, leaf through this technique to locate related ones you might prefer to work on right now.

EXPAND YOUR SKILLS AND REPERTOIRE

To teach *On Your Mark,* also see the general methods of creating *any* strong routine that are discussed in the overview to Section Five.

1. *Be explicit about what students need to have to start class.* Make it a small and finite list (fewer than five things) that doesn't change. You can also let students know how their desk or "station" should be set up:

- Paper out
- Desk clear (of everything else)
- Pencil sharp and ready ("in the pencil tray")
- Homework out (in the upper right hand corner of your desk)
- Nothing else out

For your class that list is:

_____

_____

_____

_____

2. Be explicit about where students need to be and what they need to be doing:

_____

_____

_____

3. *Set a time limit.* Be specific about when students need to have the listed items ready. This heads off nonaccountable student protests, such as "I was doing it" or "I was about to." What's your limit?

_____

4. *Use a standard consequence.* Have a small and appropriate consequence that you can administer without hesitation, such as loss of some privilege or doing some work to help the class stay prepared. Students not on their marks can lose points in a token economy, be directed to sharpen all pencils in the pencil box at lunch time, or be required to arrive earlier for a week to set up. Per *No Warnings,* what will your standard consequence be?

| 42 **NO WARNINGS** |

_____

5. *Provide tools without consequence (pencils, paper) to those who recognize the need before class.* A student can suddenly find that a pencil tip is broken. Her responsibility is to notice that *before* you start class. You could have a can of sharpened pencils where students can trade in their old one, or a stack of unused loose-leaf paper on the corner of your desk. Students can take them as part of your *Entry Routine.* Once class starts, apply the consequence for anyone still not on his or her mark. List here what you will supply:

| 28 **ENTRY ROUTINE** |

_____

ON YOUR MARK

6. *Don't leave homework to chance.* Make being prepared to process homework or checking homework for completeness and turning it in part of *On Your Mark*. Have a separate consequence for not doing it, such as coming to "homework club" outside the normal class time. Write out your homework expectation regarding *On Your Mark*:

_____

_____

_____

_____

PRACTICE WITH STUDY GROUP OR PARTNERS

1.   Share and compare your responses to "Expand Your Skills and Repertoire." Be sure to discuss how you are handling homework as part of your *Entry Routine*.

| 29 **DO NOW** |
| 31 **BINDER CONTROL** |

| 11 **DRAW THE MAP** |

2.   Discuss how you plan to introduce *On Your Mark* to the class.

3.   Discuss other techniques that might tie in with *On Your Mark*.

4.   If you have a poster or poster concept for *On Your Mark,* share it.

Your takeaways:

_____

_____

_____

_____

TRY *ON YOUR MARK* IN THE CLASSROOM

| 13 **NAME THE STEPS** |
| 29 **DO NOW** |
| 31 **BINDER CONTROL** |

| 28 **ENTRY ROUTINE** |
| 41 **THRESHOLD** |

1.   Whether or not you worked with a group on this technique, read through "Practice with Study Group or Partners." Add its ideas to the ones in "Expand Your Skills and Repertoire."

2.   Make your *On Your Mark* list "sticky" with ideas from *Name the Steps.*

3.   Early on, work reminders about *On Your Mark* into your *Threshold* and *Entry Routine.*

"Good morning, Keera. On your mark?!"

SUSTAIN YOUR PROGRESS

Using feedback from your study group or other peers, and reviewing your own lesson notes and observations, monitor your maintenance of *On Your Mark*.

Date	Slight Flaw in *On Your Mark* Execution	My Response

ON YOUR MARK

Technique 34

SEAT SIGNALS

OVERVIEW

Seat Signals let students attend to necessary business (being excused to use the bathroom, sharpening pencils, and so on) without distracting the class or taking up its learning time. Students should be able to signal their requests

- Nonverbally
- From their seats
- Unambiguously
- Without becoming a distraction

Be explicit and consistent about the signals you expect students to use and the signals with which you may respond. The right set of signals will enable you to manage both their requests and your response without interrupting instruction.

WHERE AM I NOW?

Proficiency			
❑ I am brand new to *Seat Signals*.	❑ I'm in the planning and practice stage, though I haven't tried *Seat Signals* yet in class.	❑ I'm beginning to try *Seat Signals* in my classroom.	❑ We're using the right set of *Signals*.

EXPAND YOUR SKILLS AND REPERTOIRE

To introduce *Seat Signals* to your class, also see the general methods of creating *any* strong routine that are discussed in the overview to Section Five.

A main goal is to prevent problems with students leaving their seats without permission, sauntering in the classroom, or making unnecessary trips to the bathroom. You'll want it to meet these criteria:

- The signals should be specific and unambiguous but subtle enough so that the signals themselves don't become a distraction.
- Students must be able to signal their request from their seats, nonverbally.
- You should be able to manage their requests and your response nonverbally without interrupting instruction.

These student signals have proven their worth in outstanding classrooms:

"I need . . .	Signal
. . . to use the bathroom."	Hand up; two fingers crossed.
. . . a new pencil."	Hold pencil up, wait for exchange.
. . . a tissue."	Left hand pinching nose.
. . . to get out of my seat." (for example, to get something that dropped on the floor)	One finger held up and rotated in a circular motion.

Assisting the System

- Establish conventions that students must follow, such as allowing only one person out at a time to use a bathroom.
- Establish *when* students can signal certain requests. Possibly rule out bathroom requests until relatively late in the classroom session.
- Tie the signals in with a larger behavior management system. Many schools use green, yellow, and red cards for each student to track his or her level of behavior. You might offer anyone on green the right to ask for the bathroom anytime after the first fifteen minutes of class, whereas those on yellow can go only during the last ten minutes.
- If you limit access to the bathroom, have a separate signal for "bathroom emergency."
- If bathroom requests get out of hand, use a token economy of "scholar dollars" for students to "buy" an occasional second trip. Students can be expected to earn some of their dollars through some form of classroom "service."
- Rather than letting students sharpen pencils, have presharpened ones for which they can exchange a dull one.
- Have tissues where students can get them.

PRACTICE WITH STUDY GROUP OR PARTNERS

1. In the group, compare the *Seat Signals* you each use now.

2. Agree on *Seat Signals* the group can use in this and future meetings. When someone is "in charge" as *Facilitator* or *Teacher,* the signal can be flashed to her, and she can respond. At other times, the signal can be flashed to the group, and everyone can field it.

TRY *SEAT SIGNALS* IN THE CLASSROOM

1. Decide what signals you need to have in place.
2. Teach your *Seat Signals* to the whole class and have students practice them in unison.
3. Also teach students how to interpret your signaled responses—"In three minutes," "After the person ahead of you has returned to their seat," and so on.
4. Post the signals.
5. Accept no substitutes.

SEAT SIGNALS

SEAT SIGNALS

BE CREATIVE?

In general, no. Keep *Seat Signals* few, essential, unmistakable, and nondistracting.

In a token economy, find creative ways to award good prosocial or learning-supportive behaviors with "scholar dollars."

SUSTAIN YOUR PROGRESS

Monitor your *Seat Signals.*

Date	A Signal I Need to Change, Add, or Reteach	Date Done

PROPS

OVERVIEW

Props—a.k.a. "shout outs" and "ups"—are public praise for students who demonstrate excellence or other virtues. Everyone responds to praise, and most of us love to hear rooters cheer us on.

Classroom *Props* are engineered by the teacher. Make sure they happen in your classroom. By equipping classmates to consistently deliver quick resounding praise, you build a culture of effort without sacrificing order or precious learning time.

WHERE AM I NOW?

	Proficiency			
Comfort & Confidence	I am brand new at *Props* . . .	I'm in the planning and practice stage, though I haven's tried *Props* yet in class . . .	I'm beginning to try *Props* in my classroom . . .	I use *Props* . . .
	❑ . . . and excited to try it.	❑ . . . but know with more practice I'll make it work.	❑ . . . and love how it basically works.	❑ . . . creatively, often, and at the right moment of hard work.
	❑ . . . and undecided about my ability to pull it off.	❑ . . . because I still have questions about how to do it right.	❑ . . . with mixed results I need to evaluate.	❑ . . . and continue to learn about timing.
	❑ . . . and not sure it's my style.	❑ . . . because, frankly, I still have serious doubts.	❑ . . . but it doesn't seem to work or suit me.	❑ . . . but the class needs more training or something.

Work from your strengths. If you find yourself in the bottom left portion, leaf through this technique to locate related ones you might prefer to work on right now.

EXPAND YOUR SKILLS AND REPERTOIRE

To create *Props,* see also the routine-building advice discussed in the overview to Section Five.

Effective *Props*

You say: "Two stomps for Cassy!"

Your students respond automatically and thunderously: every foot stomping twice (and only twice!) in unison before it's back to learning.

Invest the time up front to teach students to give the *Props* crisply, quickly, and enthusiastically. The routine should begin and end in less than five seconds. When it's done, it's done, and the transition back to task is immediate. Aim for

- *Quick.* Fast is energizing. Be able to cue a *Prop* in one second. Teach your students and have them practice so that their response is equally quick and sharp, and almost as short.
- *Visceral, too.* Props can be verbal, of course. But the students' role isn't to name or identify the behavior so worthy of praise. That's your job, if it's not obvious. Few-or-no-word *Props* are less likely to wear out. "On the way to college!" will age pretty quickly. Get the muscular fun of group percussion, noise, and rhythm. Some students will drum on anything in your class if given the chance. Use controlled but emphatic movement and noise.

36 **100%**

- *Universal.* When you give *Props,* everybody does it. Set and enforce this expectation.
- *Enthusiastic. Props* are a fun, lively, brief break from hard work—an exclamation point, not the sentence.
- *Evolving.* Abandon *Props* that have grown stale. Students can enjoy dreaming them up and will then take a more vigorous part. And if they are forever thinking of new ones, giving *Props* won't get tired, boring, and obligatory.

Seven *Props* Plus Three

We've stolen these starter ideas from great teachers who probably stole them, too, or invented them with the help of students. Add at least three (stealing is good) that would resonate with your kids.

"The Hitter"

You: "Let's give Clarice a Hitter."

Class: Pretend to toss a ball and swing a bat at it. They shield their eyes as if to glimpse its distance flight. Then they mimic crowd noise suitable for a home run for exactly 3 seconds.

"Lawnmower"

You: "Let's give Jason a Lawnmower."

Class: Reach down to pull the cord to start the mower and yank upward twice. They make an engine sound, grip the imaginary handles, and smile for exactly 2 seconds.

"Roller Coaster"

You: "Oh, man, that answer deserves a Roller Coaster."

Class: They put their open hands in front of them pointing upwards at 45 degrees, palms down. They "chug, chug, chug" (three times only) with their hands mimicking a roller coaster slugging its way up the last steep hill. Then they shout "Woo, woo, woo" three times as their hands mimic a coaster speeding over three steep hills after the big drop.

"Two Hands"

You: "Jimmie, lead us in a Two Hands."

Jimmie: "Two hands!"

Class: Snap twice with both hands while chanting "Ay, ay!"

Jimmie: "One hand!"

Class: Snap twice with one hand while chanting "Ay, ay!"

Jimmie: "No hands!"

Class: Dance a funky impromptu for exactly 1.75 seconds.

"Hot Pepper"

You: "An answer like that deserves a Hot Pepper."

Class: Hold up an imaginary hot pepper, dangling it above their mouths. They take a bite and make a sizzle sound "tssssss" for exactly 1 second.

"The Cheese Grater"

You: "Oh, man, let's give Daekwan some cheese!"

Class: Hold up right hand with the cheese, left hand with the grater. Scrape three times and say in unison, "You're great, great, great!"

"Two Snaps, Two Stomps"

You: "Two snaps, two stomps for Jimmie P!" (Or "two stomps, two claps," or "two snaps and one stomp," and so on)

Class: Two snaps and two thundering stomps that end perfectly on cue.

Add three for your classroom:

Prop name: _____

    Me: _____

    _____

    Class: _____

    _____

    _____

Prop name: _____

    Me: _____

    _____

    Class: _____

    _____

    _____

PROPS

Prop name: _____

    Me: _____

    _____

    Class: _____

    _____

    _____

PRACTICE WITH STUDY GROUP OR PARTNERS

You will probably do group work on *Props* in a session that includes some other techniques. If so, begin with *Props*. Then each member of the group can choose one to use in the group at least once as you work on the other techniques.

    1. Take turns leading the group through practicing and performing the seven examples of *Props* in "Seven *Props* Plus Three."

    2. Take turns leading the group through at least one other *Prop* (invented, adapted, or stolen!) by each member of the group.

    3. Discuss any challenges you have encountered using *Props* in the classroom.

TRY PROPS IN THE CLASSROOM

    1. Listen in class for ideas about *Props* that will resonate with your students.

    2. Use the routines advice from the overview to Section Five to launch a set of classroom *Props*.

    3. Call *Props* when students are already attentive, in the midst of hard work.

    4. As you try out *Props,* listen for moments when *Props* will come off quickly and direct the whole class energy as you want to see it go.

    5. Work on and convey pride in speed. Six seconds? Five? Four?

TROUBLE-SHOOT

Steady On

You may enjoy praising students at length. When you feel that urge, focus just on identifying in six words what you want to praise. Then call a *Prop.*

Other Challenges

Possible Challenge	Possible Solutions

BE CREATIVE

1. Props can wear out. Keep coming up with new ones.
2. For variety, let students choose the *Prop* by name. Practice instantaneous choosing.
   You: "Jason, *Prop* for Melissa!"
   Jason: "Lawnmower! Let's give Melissa a Lawnmower!"
3. Is there a fun *silent* (but *physical*) *Prop* that could be your students' ultimate homage?

SUSTAIN YOUR PROGRESS

1. Using feedback from your study group or other peers, and reviewing your own lesson notes and observations, monitor your progress on *Props*.

Date	New Prop	Prop Additions or Changes Well Done

2. Revisit "Where Am I Now?" Are you ready to build out to some other new technique?

100%

OVERVIEW

Expect *100%* of students to do what you ask *100%* of the time, *100%* of the way. But know that you win this battle with finesse far more often than with brute force. The three principles of *100%* compliance are as follows:

1. Use the least invasive form of intervention.
2. Rely on firm, calm finesse.
3. Invent ways to make compliance visible.

In order from least invasive to most, here are the six types of intervention discussed in *Teach Like a Champion*:

1. Nonverbal intervention
2. Positive group correction
3. Anonymous individual correction
4. Private individual correction
5. Lightning-quick public correction
6. Consequences (with a scaled series thereof)

In intervening, firm, calm finesse is a must:

- Make compliance an exercise in purpose, not power.
- Use universal language.
- Catch it early!
- Say "Thank you" (a powerful phrase).

Emphasize compliance you can see:

- Invent ways to make compliance visible.
- Be seen looking.
- Intervene at marginal compliance.

Be a stickler for *100%*. If you accept 90%, then you may already be on your way to 80% or 70%. Students also notice when their peers aren't expected to do as you've asked and will respond accordingly.

WHERE AM I NOW?

	Proficiency			
Comfort & Confidence	**I am brand new to 100%** ...	**I'm in the planning and learning stage, but I haven't tried 100% yet in class** ...	**I'm beginning to try 100% in my classroom** ...	**I use 100% regularly** ...
	❏ ... and excited to try it.	❏ ... but know with more practice I'll make it work.	❏ ... and love how it basically works.	❏ ... and get to it consistently.
	❏ ... and undecided about my ability to pull it off.	❏ ... because I still have questions about how to do it right.	❏ ... with mixed results I need to evaluate.	❏ ... but still get slightly less.
	❏ ... and not at all sure it's for me.	❏ ... because, frankly, I still have serious doubts.	❏ ... but it doesn't seem to work or suit me.	❏ ... but need to focus on it more.

Work from your strengths. If you find yourself in the bottom left portion, leaf through this technique to locate related ones you might prefer to work on right now.

EXPAND YOUR SKILLS AND REPERTOIRE

As soon as you realize that students are off task, make the least invasive correction possible—ideally nonverbally—so that your teaching is not interrupted. If you stop teaching—to lecture or explain or emphasize—you risk entering the "death spiral," in which the time it takes you to reset one student allows (or causes!) another to become off task, and stopping to correct that student causes another. In the end, you risk never catching up. Thus correct without stopping your teaching whenever you can—make your corrections *fast, positive, confident,* and *as invisible as possible.*

The Needed (Least Invasive) Intervention

From the list in the "Overview" section, choose an intervention from as near the top as you can. But don't regard the six levels as implying a step-by-step process. The idea isn't necessarily to progress methodically through each level—champion teachers use the tools with discretion and flexibility. That can mean starting with visible intervention or even with a consequence. Simply be aware that the goal is to be as near the top as possible, when possible.

However, stay aware of this rule of thumb: levels 1 through 5 apply especially to students whom you believe are (or may be) making a good-faith effort to comply and for students who are distracted or perhaps even benignly silly. *When misbehavior is defiant, you should be more inclined to move straight to a consequence.*

On some recent occasion inside or outside a classroom, did you see trouble have time to brew, either because someone overlooked it early on or because the teacher wasn't confident about how to respond decisively? Describe that occasion. What were the consequences?

_____

_____

_____

Likewise, have you seen someone intervene too forcefully and visibly when something simple and unobtrusive would have done? Describe that occasion. What were the consequences?

_____

_____

_____

Discuss these occasions with a partner or take them to your working group.
Here we discuss each level of intervention, beginning at the top.

Level 1: Nonverbal Intervention
You can use gestures, eye contact, or both—sometimes with a bit of proximity mixed in—to address off-task students *while doing something else, preferably teaching.* By many measures, teachers interrupt their own lessons more than students do; using nonverbal correction *while teaching* keeps your own

| 15 **CIRCULATE** |
| 38 **STRONG VOICE** |

interruptions to a minimum and your lesson on the rails. A quieter tone of voice—for example, a whisper—also can be more effective than a loud one because it sends a signal that your correction is private and does not warrant any response.

Come up with a simple, unambiguous, nonverbal intervention for each of these student behaviors. The first example is done for you.

1. Student slouching in his chair

| 32 **SLANT** |

Intervention: *Make "hands folded" gesture (hands folded in front of you with elbows bent ninety degrees and fingers intertwined) to signal SLANT.*

2. Student with her head down on her desk (eyes up)

Intervention: _____

_____

3. Student with her head down on her desk (eyes hidden)

Intervention: _____

_____

| 34 **SEAT SIGNALS** |

4. Student sending the bathroom signal at critical time during lesson

Intervention: _____

_____

5. Frequent struggler doing well and working hard today

Intervention: _____

_____

6. Student persistently raising hand (for reasons unrelated to your questions)

Intervention: _____

_____

7. Student engaged in sustained looking under desk for "something"

Intervention: _____

_____

8. Student gazing out window

Intervention: _____

_____

Level 2: Positive Group Correction

Positive group corrections are quick verbal reminders given *to an entire group* that describe what students *should be doing* and not what they shouldn't be doing. They describe the solution, not the problem.

37 **WHAT TO DO**

"Scholars, you should be following along in your books."

"Check yourself. You should be tracking the speaker."

You can often supplement this with nonverbal modeling that demonstrates how all students should look at the moment; for example, you ask students to check their *SLANT*s, and model straight posture yourself as you ask. A quick nod to a slow-to-comply student can also help.

Level 3: Anonymous Individual Correction

An anonymous individual correction offers a verbal reminder to the group, similar to a positive group correction except that the anonymous individual correction makes it explicit that not everyone is meeting expectations.

"I'm waiting for two more pairs of eyes."

"We're ready to go when we get one more person with his pencil at the ready."

Consider for a moment the difference between level 1 and levels 2 and 3. Note some reasons why you might elect to use a level 2 positive group correction or level 3 anonymous individual correction instead of a level 1 nonverbal intervention.

_____

_____

_____

_____

_____

Script an effective *positive group correction* or *anonymous individual correction* for each of these situations. The first one is done for you.

1. Student slouching in his chair

Intervention type: *Positive group correction*

"Class, show me your best SLANT!"

2.   Student with her head down on her desk (eyes up)

Intervention type: _____

_____

_____

3.   Student with her head down on her desk (eyes hidden)

Intervention type: _____

_____

_____

4.   Student gazing out window while peer is talking

Intervention type: _____

_____

_____

5.   Student engaged in sustained looking under desk for "something"

Intervention type: _____

_____

_____

6.   Student persistently raising hand (for reasons unrelated to your questions)

Intervention type: _____

_____

_____

7.   Student writing when it's "pencils down"

Intervention type: _____

_____

_____

8.   Student sending the bathroom signal at critical time during lesson

Intervention type: _____

| 34 **SEAT SIGNALS** |

_____

_____

9. Frequent struggler doing well and working hard today

Intervention type: _____

_____

_____

10. Student demonstrating one of your own "favorite" behaviors

Behavior: _____

Intervention type: _____

_____

_____

Level 4: Private Individual Correction

Try to correct privately and quietly if possible. Walk by the off-task student's desk, for example. Lean down confidently and, using a voice that preserves as much privacy as possible, quickly and calmly tell the corrected student what to do.

First private individual correction: "Quentin, I've asked everyone to track me, and I need to see you doing it too."

Second private individual correction (including a *consequence*): "Quentin, I need you to track me so you can learn. I'm going to have to [move your card to yellow, take two scholar dollars (see *Seat Signals*), ask you to come in and practice at recess, and so on]. Now please show me your best."

| 34 **SEAT SIGNALS** |

Level 5: Lightning-Quick Public Correction

Private or anonymous corrections are not always possible. Sometimes (ideally not often) you are forced to correct individual students during public moments. Train yourself to do this confidently and without hesitation. Your goals:

- Minimize the time a student whose behavior has been negative is "on stage."
- Tell him what to do right rather than scolding or saying what he did wrong.

| 43 **POSITIVE FRAMING** |

- Divert students' attention to a student whose behavior is worthy of attention.

    "Quentin, I need your eyes. Just like Corales and just like Paula."

    "Quentin, I need your eyes. Looking sharp, Corales. Thank you, Paula."

On occasion, you may wish to circle back to emphasize (to Quentin and to his classmates) his accountability.

"Quentin, I need your eyes. Looking sharp, back row! Thank you, Quentin. Much better."

Level 6: Consequences (Scaled Series)

Consequences are a necessary part of managing behavior. However, many teachers use consequences in an unproductive way.

Some teachers mistakenly wait until a behavior becomes truly disruptive—and they have become angry—before giving a consequence. It's better to act earlier using a smaller consequence than to wait until the issue has grown large and requires a much more significant consequence. If you're angry, it means you probably waited too long. Try giving a smaller consequence earlier in the process.

Other teachers overadminister consequences—they use a huge disincentive when a smaller one will do. Often this can be remedied by planning out a series of incrementally larger consequences that feel appropriate and fair and that you can administer without hesitation. One of the most useful consequences is doing a task over again. It's also important to note that a consequence can be administered with *Positive Framing*. "Five minutes of detention, John. Show me your best so we can leave it at that."

Consequences, like other interventions, are best given so that instruction is not interrupted. Delivery should be quick, decisive, unwavering, and unemotional—private is effective, too, when possible.

When you must intervene several times in sequence, try to emphasize that things are getting better.

> 39 **DO IT AGAIN**
> 43 **POSITIVE FRAMING**

> 38 **STRONG VOICE**
> 42 **NO WARNINGS**

> 37 **WHAT TO DO**

"Quentin, I need to see your SLANT."

"Two dollars. Off task. Show me your legs under your desk. Thank you."

"Much better."

Calm Finesse

- Make *100%* an exercise in purpose, not power.
- Use universal language.
- Catch it early!
- Say "Thank you."

Be About Purpose, Not Power

Some teachers get compliance at the start of the school year and forget to emphasize its purpose. After three weeks, the students begin to fight back against what they perceive as arbitrary power. Students need to know that their behavior is ultimately about their success and not about your power, your job being easier, or some other reason. That means that at the start of the year, you have a limited window of time (about two or three weeks) to convince your students that when you ask them to comply it's not about you; it's about them and their path to a successful future, including college. Command obedience not because you can or because it feels good but because it serves your students. Make that distinction evident in your language, tone, and demeanor.

Not So Good	Good	Better	Best
"I asked for your eyes on me. When I ask you to do something, I expect you to do it."	"I need your eyes on me so you can learn."	"It's going to take your best to get to college. Show it to me now."	(Script your own with a partner)

What happens if you get compliance but fail to convince your students that their compliance serves their own best interests? How will they react? Then what happens?

Often teachers "lose" their classes when they fail to focus enough on purpose. How can you prevent this? Script five phrases that you can use to emphasize the purposefulness of your interventions:

1. _____

_____

2. _____

_____

3. _____

_____

4. _____

_____

5. _____

_____

Use Universal (and Often Impersonal) Language to Correct

Many teachers try to individualize every response to student behavior. They feel it should reflect the specific needs and people involved in each situation. In contrast, *100%* teachers are strategically *impersonal*. When it comes to behavioral expectations, individualizing decisions is as likely to result in students' feeling misunderstood and unfairly handled as it is their feeling cared about, especially when they don't like the teacher's decisions. Reinforcing expectations with a bit of impersonality reminds students that it's about expectations, not about them personally.

Consider how "I need your eyes, Trevor" is made stronger by the universal language (we and us) in "We need everyone with us." Note also how statements like "That's not how we do it here" and "In this classroom we respond respectfully to peers" make the universal not only a shared goal (we) but a shared expectation (how we do it).

Or compare these two interventions:

"We're always on time for class. You know that's two demerits, Trevor."	"Trevor I'm really disappointed in you. I'm going to take two demerits."

The second intervention seems more personal, but is actually less productive. The point is that late equals demerit for every student; here the individualization only makes the consequence sound more personally motivated.

Catch It Early

Catch misbehavior before the rest of the class (maybe even the student in question) know it's an "it." Catch it as students appear *ready* to stray, not after they've strayed. As *No Warnings* explains, if you're mad, you have

| 42 **NO WARNINGS** |

probably waited too long to deal with problematic behavior. Spend some time doing or revisiting the activities in that technique to equip yourself for a new term or year.

Say "Thank You"

After a student meets your request for the correction, end with a firm, quick "Thank you," often accompanied by a nod, as in, "I'm still waiting for one set of eyes ..." (shifting your look to Makalia) " ... and ... thank you." This reinforces civility, and graciously and respectfully points out to the rest of the class in the most politic manner that you won: that you got the behavior you asked for and that students are back on the path to success.

100%

Visible Compliance

Take advantage of ways of making your expectations and the tasks you ask students to do visible. This allows you to manage them more clearly and makes it more evident to students that you can see whether or not they have done as asked.

Invent Ways to Make Compliance Visible

Great teachers find ways to make it easier to see who's followed their directions by asking students to do things the teacher can see. This also makes it far harder for students not to comply and so discourages them from willfully trying to resist. The three directions that follow are listed in order of "observability": the first one is entirely nonobservable; the next, slightly observable; and the last, explicitly visible. Add a couple more examples like the third one in the space provided.

"I need everyone's attention." (But what is it you want to see?)

"All eyes on me." (A visible behavior, but subtle to recognize)

"Pencils down and eyes on me." (More visible on any quick scan of the room)

_____

_____

Be Seen Looking

Champion teacher Colleen Driggs says,

> My eyes are rarely on the student who is asking the question; instead, they are looking all around the rest of the room making sure everyone else is _SLANT_ing, not looking out the window or trying to poke someone else in the back. I hope to send the message that I will accept nothing less than their very best behavior. I think that paying attention to the small details prevents some more problematic misbehavior that could occur.
>
> I believe this can be one of the most difficult things for new teachers. The more you need to have a lesson plan right in front of you, the more you get caught off guard with an unexpected question, the more you get rattled by a behavior that you were not expecting, the more [you miss] the nonacademic warning signs that are going on all around you at the same time.
>
> I play out my lesson in my head from the time I am in the shower that morning, during my ride in to school, and continually until I actually am teaching it. It kind of gives me a "been there, done that" approach even if it is my first time teaching to that objective. I have already thought of the potential pitfalls, the areas where the pacing might be a bit slower, the questions the students will have at each segment of the lesson.... This allows my mind to not get bogged down during the delivery of the lesson.

Every few minutes, scan the room with a calm smile to ensure that all is as it should be. When you give a direction, pause and scan the room. Narrating your scan shows that your "radar" is on.

"Thank you, Peter. Thank you, Marissa. Eyes right on me, front row."

Can you be seen looking? How do you let students know, positively, that your radar is on?

_____

_____

Intervene at Marginal Compliance

If the correct class percentage of follow-through is *100%*, so is the correct *extent* of follow-through. Marginal compliance, especially when public, corrodes.

A certain number of students will complete a task only as fully as you show them you expect it to be completed. They'll rightly want to know what exactly "Raise your hands" means. They think,

- "Is it okay just to raise my hand halfway?"

- "Can't I rest my elbow on the desk?"

- "Is there some way to do this and not look like I am trying to be her pet?"

- "Is it okay to 'raise' my hand the minimum conceivable amount (say, with a slight articulation of the wrist) and demonstrate to my peers that I am only humoring this teacher because I have graciously decided it is not worth my time to disrespect her publicly?"

The answer to these questions should be no. The message should be, "What we do, we do right because it helps us on the path to college." Excellence is *the* habit; the easiest way to do something well is to do it well every time. Once you set the meaning of an instruction like "Raise your hands," insist on that standard.

In *Call and Response,* you are telling everyone to respond. Keep this technique working with *100%* compliance. (Actually, *Call and Response* is a great way to give students enjoyable practice at complying fully.)

In what ways do students in your class tend to comply but only marginally? What *100%* phrasing can you use to address that?

> **23 CALL AND RESPONSE**

Instance: _____

100%: _____

_____

Instance: _____

100%: _____

_____

Instance: _____

100%: _____

_____

PRACTICE WITH STUDY GROUP OR PARTNERS

Share and Compare

Share and compare your phrasings from the activities in "Expand Your Skills and Repertoire." Demonstrate nonverbal ideas you can add to stares and proximity.

310

100%

Read and Reflect

Let someone in the group read this statement aloud. Then reflect on it together.

> At times I simply tell them that I am very jealous of their attention and I don't want to share it with anyone. I think this lends itself to *Strong Voice* as well. From the minute I step into that classroom, I want the students to feel a shift in the atmosphere. I know it sounds hokey, but I want them to know I've arrived and mean business. I don't mean in a hostile or negative way, but in my mind a very effective teacher is a performer. Not a "dog and pony show," but someone who uses the classroom as his or her stage and has an agenda that will be accomplished and a set script already in mind. It has been rehearsed many times already leading up to my walking in there. [Now] they need to feel like they don't want to miss a minute of anything that happens ... like waiting for a movie to start.

Teacher Colleen Driggs

"Pledge" Intervention Role Play

This role play can improve your abilities to reinforce *100%* expectations using the least invasive means: nonverbal interventions. It uses the Pledge of Allegiance, but with advance agreement from the group, the *Facilitator* can substitute any short choral text that's somewhat familiar to everyone. If group members don't all know it by heart, the *Facilitator* should distribute copies (in advance if possible) to everyone.

Pledge of Allegiance

I pledge allegiance to the flag of the United States of America,

and to the Republic for which it stands:

one Nation under God,

indivisible, with Liberty and Justice for all.

Using the same text, play as many rounds as needed to give each member a chance to be *Teacher*. Everyone else is a *Student*.

1. Before each round, the *Facilitator* reminds the group that the goal is to address behavior without stopping the lesson, and that the best interventions are

- Simple—you want to use 'em fast
- Unambiguous—reliability of interpretation is critical
- Positive—call attention to the solution rather than the problem

Nonverbal interventions aren't limited to gestures.

2. For each round, the *Facilitator* chooses a *Teacher*. While the *Teacher* momentarily steps outside, the *Facilitator* designates several *Students* to give less than *100%* during the round by each exhibiting several of the following behaviors:

Head down on desk

Not tracking

Talking

Hand up at the wrong moment

Calling out

Other of *Student*'s own invention

These *Students* position themselves in disparate locations within the "class." During the lesson (see point 3), they will more or less alternate the behaviors, about fifteen to twenty seconds apart.

3. The *Teacher* returns and leads a lesson whose objective is that the class will *memorize* the text. At the same time, without stopping the lesson, he or she must intervene with gestures and other nonverbal responses to the deviant behaviors.

4. The purpose of the role play is to force the *Teacher* to use effective gestures and nonverbal interventions while teaching. Thus the deviant *Students* should correct their behavior in a compliant manner if they feel that a simple, unambiguous, and relatively positive nonverbal intervention has been made.

5. Proceed until the *Facilitator* calls a halt. At the end of all rounds, discuss questions like these:

For those who played *Teacher*:

- What was most difficult about the activity?
- What were your most effective interventions? Why?
- What helped you manage the situation effectively?

For participants as *Students*:

- What did you notice about the *Teacher*'s interactions with you or your peers?
- As a student who was doing what was asked, did you feel engaged in and important to the lesson? Were you able to focus on the lesson?

As a group, discuss practical takeaways about using effective nonverbal interventions (for example, the importance, when making a gesture, of moving into a student's line of sight).

Your own takeaways:

_____

_____

_____

_____

_____

_____

"Peter and the Wolf" Role Play

This activity uses the story "Peter and the Wolf," but the *Facilitator* can substitute another of similar length. This role play requires a small bit of preparation: the *Facilitator* needs to photocopy and cut up the provided Student Role Cards so that they can be distributed during the role play. Group members should already be acquainted with the six levels of correction.

The game requires minimally about six participants, but more is much better. Four group members will have a chance to rotate through the role of *Teacher,* each covering one of the four parts of the story. Anyone not currently a *Teacher* is a *Student.* The group should decide in advance the grade level of the *Students.*

1. Each *Student* picks a role card. The *Facilitator* needs to ensure a balance between "*100%* students" and others who are less in line.

STUDENT ROLE CARDS

"Peter and the Wolf" Student Card
You're a 100% student. You will track; you will raise your hand when appropriate; you will do as you are told.

"Peter and the Wolf" Student Card
You're a 100% student. You will track; you will raise your hand when appropriate; you will do as you are told.

"Peter and the Wolf" Student Card
You're a 100% student. You will track; you will raise your hand when appropriate; you will do as you are told.

"Peter and the Wolf" Student Card
You're a 100% student. You will track; you will raise your hand when appropriate; you will do as you are told.

"Peter and the Wolf" Student Card
You're a 100% student. You will track; you will raise your hand when appropriate; you will do as you are told.

"Peter and the Wolf" Student Card
You're a 100% student. You will track; you will raise your hand when appropriate; you will do as you are told.

"Peter and the Wolf" Student Card
You're the hand raiser. Raise your hand consistently until you get attention or are told to put it down.

"Peter and the Wolf" Student Card
You're a nontracker. Put your attention elsewhere. Gaze out the window until you are corrected. Maintain your tracking for thirty seconds and then stray again.

"Peter and the Wolf" Student Card
You're the interrupter. You will interrupt instruction by calling out questions to the speaker until you are corrected.

"Peter and the Wolf" Student Card
You will do anything the speaker reminds or asks you to do ... the second time.

"Peter and the Wolf" Student Card
You're a nontracker. You will put your head down on your desk sideways. Correct the first time you are asked, count to ten, and do it again.

"Peter and the Wolf" Student Card
You're a nontracker. Slouch down in your chair progressively until you are corrected.

"Peter and the Wolf" Student Card
You are completely enamored of the person sitting next to you. Your goal is to get his or her attention and to avoid being ashamed at all costs. Remember, you are cool!

"Peter and the Wolf" Student Card
Two minutes after class begins, you have a headache. You'll make a basic effort to do what you're told, but you can't get your mind off your head. If you're asked to speak, end every statement with "my head hurts."

"Peter and the Wolf" Student Card
Two minutes after class begins, you have a headache. You'll make a basic effort to do what you're told, but you can't get your mind off your head. If you're asked to speak, end every statement with "my head hurts."

"Peter and the Wolf" Student Card
You're a 100% student. You will track; you will raise your hand when appropriate; you will do as you are told.

"Peter and the Wolf" Student Card
You remember two minutes into class that you have a question about last night's homework. You feel like it's the most pressing issue of the day. Raise your hand eagerly and if you're not called on, call out.

"Peter and the Wolf" Student Card
You are completely enamored of the person sitting next to you. Your goal is to get his or her attention and to avoid being ashamed at all costs. Remember, you are cool!

"Peter and the Wolf" Student Card
You're a 100% student. You will track; you will raise your hand when appropriate; you will do as you are told.

"Peter and the Wolf" Student Card
You're a 100% student. You will track; you will raise your hand when appropriate; you will do as you are told.

"Peter and the Wolf" Student Card
You're a 100% student. You will track; you will raise your hand when appropriate; you will do as you are told.

2. The first *Teacher* begins by reading aloud part 1 of the story, then stops and poses the part 1 questions here (or others along these lines). After about three to five minutes, the second *Teacher* takes over with part 2, and so on until all four parts have been covered.

Part 1 Questions

- Which two characters were having an argument in the meadow by the pond? (The bird and the duck were arguing.)
- What does it mean to be sly?
- Who thought to grab the little bird while he was arguing with the duck? (The cat thought to grab it—but failed.)

Part 2 Questions

- What does it mean that the cat walked "on her little velvet paws"? (She walked very quietly.)
- How did Peter's grandfather feel about his being in the meadow by himself? (He was upset.)
- Why doesn't Peter's grandfather want him in the meadow by himself? (If a wolf should come out of the forest, Peter would be in great danger.)
- How does Peter feel about wolves? (He is not afraid of wolves.)

Part 3 Questions

- How did the wolf eat the duck? (He grabbed her with his teeth and swallowed her with one gulp.)
- What does it mean that Peter stood behind the closed gate "without the slightest fear"? (He had no fear at all, not even a little bit.)
- What does *distract* mean? (To take someone's attention away from what he is doing)
- Who was supposed to distract the wolf? (The little bird)
- What does it mean that the wolf snapped angrily at the bird? (He was mad and quickly biting down, trying to eat the bird.)

Part 4 Questions

- What does it mean to annoy someone? (To make someone angry or irritated)
- If you are "pulling on a rope with all your might," how are you pulling? (You are pulling very hard, with all your strength.)
- What did Peter want to do with the wolf? (He wanted to put the wolf in the zoo.)
- What does it mean to triumph? (To win or succeed)
- What kinds of processions can you think of? (Weddings, graduation, parades)
- Why was Peter's grandfather shaking his head discontentedly? (He was wondering what would have happened if Peter had not caught the wolf.)
- If you are discontented, are you happy? (No, you are unhappy.)
- What happened to the duck in the end? (It was in the stomach of the wolf; it had been eaten alive.)

3. As each *Teacher* conducts one part of the lesson, *Students* either listen or follow along on the printed text, depending on the grade level the group decides to simulate. During the reading and the questions, the *Students* behave in keeping with the role on their card.

The *Teacher*'s challenge is to identify the off-task students and correct them using *100%* techniques, without disrupting the flow of the lesson. The *Teacher* should use at least one nonverbal signal.

4. Between *Teacher* turns, the *Facilitator* can issue new role cards to the *Students*.

5. Once the whole story has been covered, the group turns to discussion.

As *Teachers*:

- What off-task behavior did you notice?
- Which was more effective as an intervention, verbal or nonverbal?
- What was most difficult about the activity?
- What were your most effective interventions? Why?
- What helped you manage the situation effectively?
- How did verbal interventions affect the lesson in comparison to nonverbal interventions?

As *Students*:

- What did you notice about the *Teacher*'s interactions with you?
- As a *Student* who was doing what was asked, did you feel engaged in and important to the lesson?
- What did your *Teacher*'s action make you think about your less engaged peers?
- As a *Student* who was either engaged or disengaged, were there any distracting interventions?
- As a *Student* who was off task, did your *Teacher*'s actions help you reengage? How did you feel afterwards?

All participants:

- How could you integrate any of these verbal or nonverbal cues in your classroom to facilitate full participation?

Your takeaways:

_____

_____

_____

_____

Peter and the Wolf

Part 1

One morning, a young boy named Peter opened his gate and walked out into the big green meadow that was beyond it. On a branch of a big tree in the meadow sat a little bird that was Peter's friend.

"All is quiet!" the bird chirped.

A duck came waddling around. She was glad that Peter had not closed the gate and, seeing that it was open, decided to take a nice swim in the deep pond in the meadow. The little bird saw the duck and flew down upon the grass. The bird settled next to the duck and shrugged his shoulders.

"What kind of bird are you if you can't fly?" said the bird.

The duck replied, "What kind of bird are you if you can't swim?" and dove into the pond.

The bird and the duck kept arguing, and the duck swam around the pond while the little bird hopped along the edge of the pond. Suddenly, something caught Peter's attention. He looked around and noticed a sly cat crawling through the grass.

The cat thought: "That little bird is busy arguing with the duck; I'll just grab him while he is busy!"

Part 2

Very carefully, on her little velvet paws, she crept toward the bird.

"Look out!" shouted Peter, and the little bird flew up into the tree for safety, while the duck quacked as loud as she could at the cat, from the middle of the pond.

The cat walked around the tree and thought, "Is it worth using up so much energy and climbing up so high into the tree? By the time I get there, the bird will have flown away."

Just then, Peter's grandfather came out of their house. He was upset because Peter had gone into the meadow without his permission.

"The meadow is a dangerous place! If a wolf should come out of the forest, then what would you do? You would be in great danger!"

But Peter paid no attention to his grandfather's words. Boys like him are not afraid of wolves. So Grandfather took Peter by the hand, led him back inside the gate, and locked it.

Part 3

No sooner was Peter locked inside the yard than a big gray wolf came out of the forest. In a second, the cat climbed up the tree. The duck quacked, and leapt out of the pond. But no matter how hard the duck tried to run, she just couldn't outrun the wolf. He was getting closer and closer and catching up with her! Then he grabbed her with his teeth and with one gulp, swallowed her.

And now, this is how things stood: the cat was sitting on one branch, the bird on another, not too close to the cat. And the wolf walked around and around the tree, looking at the cat and the bird with very hungry eyes.

In the meantime, Peter, without the slightest fear, stood behind the closed gate and watched everything that was happening. Then he ran into the house, came out again with a good, strong rope, and climbed up the high stone wall that divided his yard from the meadow. One of the branches of the tree around which the wolf was walking stretched out way beyond the stone wall. Grabbing hold of the branch, Peter carefully and quietly climbed onto the tree.

Peter said to the bird, "Fly down and circle over the wolf's head. Try to distract him! But be careful that he doesn't catch you."

The bird flew around the wolf and almost touched the wolf's head with his wings while the wolf snapped angrily at him with his jaws, from this side and that.

Part 4

Oh, how the bird annoyed the wolf—how he wanted to catch him! But the bird was clever and very quick, and the wolf simply couldn't do anything about it.

Meanwhile, Peter made a lasso with the rope and carefully let it down from the tree, catching the wolf by the tail. Peter pulled on the rope with all his might! Feeling himself caught by the rope, the wolf began to jump wildly, trying to get loose. But Peter tied the other end of rope to the strong tree, and the wolf's jumping only made the rope round his tail tighter.

Just then, two hunters came out of the woods, following the wolf's trail and shooting their guns as they went.

But Peter, sitting in the tree, said, "Don't shoot! Birdie and I have caught the wolf. Now help us take him to the zoo."

Then came the triumphant procession. Peter was at the head. After him came the two hunters leading the wolf. And winding up the procession were Grandfather and the cat. Grandfather shook his head discontentedly.

"Well, what would have happened if Peter hadn't caught the wolf? What then?"

Above them flew Birdie chirping merrily. "My, what brave fellows we are, Peter and I! Look what we have caught! A giant wolf!"

And perhaps, if you listen very carefully, you will hear the duck quacking inside the wolf, because the wolf, in his hurry to eat her, had swallowed her alive.

TRY *100%* IN CLASS

1. Next time you teach, without interrupting your teaching allow yourself to notice

   - Behaviors that are less than *100%*
   - Moments when you needed to preplan what students should be doing
   - Moments when you don't notice what students are doing around the class

If you can manage to do so, try responding. After class, record the data and
use them to plan how you can *visibly* notice more often.

2. Remove barriers to noticing (for example, sight lines) or to intervening at the least distracting level. Notice whether you need to post "SLANT" or similar routine instructions.

3. In your general routines, identify several that the class does not yet do acceptably or could do better; plan to reteach and practice them.

4. In a coming lesson plan, identify several points where you definitely want *100%* because these moments are key to the learning objective. (Hint: the beginning of class is the most critical moment.) Use your work in the previous sections to anticipate and plan for less than full participation and compliance.

5. Script and plan to deliver any brief explanation of *100%* you think will benefit the class.

10 **DOUBLE PLAN**

| 11 **DRAW THE MAP** |
| 15 **CIRCULATE** |
| 32 **SLANT** |

| 28 **ENTRY ROUTINE** |
| 30 **TIGHT TRANSITIONS** |
| 39 **DO IT AGAIN** |

| 6 **BEGIN WITH THE END** |
| 37 **WHAT TO DO** |
| 38 **STRONG VOICE** |

| 48 **EXPLAIN EVERYTHING** |
| 49 **NORMALIZE ERROR** |

TROUBLE-SHOOT

Steady On

Resist the urge to ignore misbehavior, which equals countenancing.

Other Challenges

Possible Challenge	Possible Solutions

BE CREATIVE

| 34 **SEAT SIGNALS** |

Swiping a bill from a student's "scholar dollar" pile can be a quick, soundless, and impressive nonverbal, consequential intervention (see *Seat Signals*).

SUSTAIN YOUR PROGRESS

1. Using feedback from your study group or other peers, and reviewing your own lesson notes and observations, monitor your progress on *100%* participation and compliance.

Date	Today's Percentage	How Can I Raise It?

2. Revisit "Where Am I Now?" Are you ready to build out to some other new technique?

WHAT TO DO

OVERVIEW

What to Do denotes giving directions that tell students what to do, as opposed to what *not* to do. A *What to Do* direction is

- Specific: what Aaron should adjust (his legs, his hands, and his eyes)
- Concrete: how Aaron should accomplish this (legs *under* the desk, hands *folded, tracking me* with your eyes)
- Sequential: breaking complex tasks into a series of simple actions and directions
- Observable: easily observed and therefore maximally accountable

Because such directions are clear and practicable, they allow teachers to respond in different ways to off-task behavior, depending on which of the following three causes underlie that behavior:

- Incompetence (Student doesn't understand or know how to do what you expect.)
- Opportunistic misbehavior (Student is exploiting a gray area or lack of clarity.)

  Teacher: "I thought I told you to pay attention."

  Student: "I *was* paying attention."

- Defiance (Student is trying to demonstrate that you cannot control him.)

WHERE AM I NOW?

	Proficiency			
	I'm brand new to *What to Do* . . .	I'm learning about *What to Do,* but haven't yet started focusing on it in the classroom . . .	I'm beginning to focus on *What to Do* in my classroom . . .	I say or show *What to Do* when it's needed . . .
Comfort & Confidence	❑ . . . and excited to try it.	❑ . . . but know that with more practice I'll make it work.	❑ . . . and love how it basically works.	❑ . . . and am adding my own distinctive touch.
	❑ . . . and undecided about my ability to pull it off.	❑ . . . because I'm still not sure how.	❑ . . . with mixed results I need to evaluate.	❑ . . . but slip into what *not* to do more than I might.
	❑ . . . and not at all sure it's for me.	❑ . . . because I still have doubts.	❑ . . . but it doesn't seem to work or suit me.	❑ . . . but often can't pull it off completely.

Work from your strengths. If you find yourself in the bottom left portion, leaf through this technique to locate related ones you might prefer to work on right now.

WHAT TO DO

EXPAND YOUR SKILLS AND REPERTOIRE

We waste a lot of school time defining the behavior we want by the negative: "Don't get distracted." "Stop fooling around." "Cut it out." Such statements force students to guess what you want them to do. But you can turn that around by telling students what you want them *to do,* an action that refocuses you, in turn, on *teaching*—even in moments that are about behavior—because, in the end, it shows that you're willing to teach students how to meet behavioral expectations, such as what it means to "pay attention."

Specific directions focus on manageable and precisely described actions that students can take. Instead of advising John to "pay attention," for example, the teacher can say,

"Put your pencil on your desk."

"Keep your eyes on me."

Concrete directions emphasize an action John knows how to do, or they say how to do it, with no gray area:

"Put your feet under your desk."

Sequential directions help make directions ultra-concrete, which is useful both when directions are more complex and need to be broken down and when students are slow to respond. Suppose you ask a student to *SLANT,* and she fails to respond fully, making only a minimal effort. You could reply with

"Turn your shoulders to face me."

"Bring your legs around."

"Put them under your desk."

"Pull in your chair."

"Good. That's what SLANT looks like."

For each of these directions, you can *observe* whether the student performs these acts or not, and you leave little wiggle room about whether she is behaving accountably. Knowing perfectly well that you can see whether she is obeying or not, she is more likely to comply.

Revising Insufficient Directions

You can do this activity by yourself or (better) with a partner. For each scenario, note any ways in which the *What to Do* statement is insufficiently specific, concrete, sequential, or observable, and write a better *What to Do* statement that addresses the misbehavior.

Scenario 1: Walking with your fourth graders to PE, you hear several students start talking in line.

Teacher: "Shhhhhh . . ."

Specific, concrete, sequential, or observable? _____

_____

Better *What to Do*: _____

_____

Note: To develop the best possible response to this situation, you first have to decide what you want: no talking at all, or quiet talking only. You might script a response for both situations.

_____

_____

_____

_____

Scenario 2: You are about to begin your second-period tenth-grade chemistry class. Several students are talking to each other (turned around in their seats and across the aisles), and one student is playing with his pencil.

Teacher: "I'd like to begin. Please get ready for class."

Specific, concrete, sequential, or observable? _____

_____

Better *What to Do*: _____

_____

Scenario 3: Your fifth graders are taking a practice state exam. Three seventh graders whom you do not know are talking loudly and goofing off outside your classroom.

Teacher: "Stop fooling around."

Specific, concrete, sequential, or observable? _____

_____

Better *What to Do*: _____

_____

Scenario 4: You have outlined the major characters in *To Kill a Mockingbird* for your ninth graders, and you notice that only half of the class is taking notes.

Teacher: "You should be writing this down."

Specific, concrete, sequential, or observable? _____

_____

Better *What to Do*: _____

_____

Scenario 5: It is September in your kindergarten class. You notice that Denise and Elise have been talking to each other on the carpet during your read-aloud.

Teacher: "Elise, please stop talking to Denise."

Specific, concrete, sequential, or observable? _____

_____

Better *What to Do*: _____

_____

WHAT TO DO

Scenario 6: You are trying to distribute social studies materials to your second graders. The first students in the row are playing with materials from the previous lesson.

Teacher: "Please take a packet and pass it."

Specific, concrete, sequential, or observable? _____

_____

Better *What to Do*: _____

_____

Scenario 7: Your third-grade students have just finished their math assignment. You are late for lunch, and half of your class still has their materials out on their desks.

Teacher: "Line up for lunch."

Specific, concrete, sequential, or observable? _____

_____

Better *What to Do*: _____

_____

Case Studies

If you are working with a group, consider using these cases for group discussion rather than individual work. Read and analyze each case; all are based on real dialogues.

Case Study 1. Mr. Jones

Mr. Jones is reading a story with his reading group. About six students are situated around a small table, Mr. Jones sitting opposite them. The students are all generally excited and engaged in the book. During the entire class, one student, James, has spoken out of turn, gotten out of his seat without permission, and fidgeted in his chair, making him a source of distraction to Mr. Jones and the other students.

1	*Mr. Jones:*	*(begins reading from the text and then looks for a student reader)* Oh, I need someone to read this . . . *(looks around the table)*
2	*James:*	*(stretches his hand high into the air)* Oh!
3	*Mr. Jones:*	*(notices James out of the corner of his eye, but consciously looks straight ahead at a student who is raising his hand without vocalizing)* Emmet, you read!
4	*James:*	*(dramatically plops down head and hand on desk)*
5	*Mr. Jones:*	*(turns to James and leans into him across the table, putting his hand on James's arm)* I can't let you read until you are calmer.
6	*James:*	*(no overt reaction)*
7	*Mr. Jones:*	*(sternly)* Sit up.
8	*James:*	*(sits up)*

1. When was Mr. Jones precise or imprecise with his direction?

_____

_____

_____

2. What does it mean to be calm?

_____

_____

_____

3. Why was James more willing or able to comply with Mr. Jones when he said, "Sit up" rather than when he said, "I can't let you read until you are calmer"?

_____

_____

_____

4. How is "Sit up" a more effective *What to Do* than "I can't let you read until you are calmer"?

_____

_____

_____

5. How could you have reacted differently to James? Consider both named and anonymous interventions.

_____

_____

_____

Case Study 2. Ms. Clark

Ms. Clark is about to transition to a new reading activity. Before she does that, she wants her class to tear off the top sheet of the paper they have been working on and pass it to the left. Her students are chattering and active, though not completely unruly.

Ms. Clark: I need everyone to appropriately pass their work to the left. Jared, that means no distracting Marissa. We are going to begin our in-class reading in a moment, and when we do, I need everyone to pay attention. That means no goofing around. Okay, I hear some talking. I'll wait.

1. Find three errors in the approach that Ms. Clark takes to making this transition.

_____

_____

_____

WHAT TO DO

2. How could Ms. Clark have been clearer with her directions? Address what constitutes an effective *What to Do* in your answer.

_____

_____

_____

3. What is a possible outcome of proposing to wait until students' behavior settles down?

_____

_____

_____

WHAT TO DO

Case Study 3. Ms. Walker

Ms. Walker is leading a reading group of seven fourth-grade students. The students are sitting in a circle, all facing Ms. Walker and the easel tablet. The students have chairs but do not have desks, so they are holding their books on their laps as they read and discuss. One student, Reggie, won't answer the question he has been asked.

1	Ms. Walker:	*(to Reggie)* He lets the tiger take his what? *(She touches the student's nose with a stuffed animal. Reggie bats it away and buries his head behind his clipboard.)* Back on track. He lets the tiger take his what? Come on. He lets him take his what? Don't get shy, come on. I know you have the right answer down. Okay, everybody, let's be the voice. He has it written down. Everybody, what's the right answer? *(snaps her fingers)*
2	Students:	*(slightly high pitched)* Eggs.
3	Ms. Walker:	Noo, use your right voices. *(snaps her fingers)*
4	Students:	*(Some students respond.)* Eggs.
5	Ms. Walker:	*(pauses, appears unsatisfied with response)* One person.
6	Zachary:	It's eggs! *(Shannon begins giggling.)*
7	Ms. Walker:	*(looking at Zachary)* Oh, no. Heads down. *(begins a countdown)* Three. I'm disappointed right now. *(to Shannon)* Fix your body. It went from funny, to now, not funny. I said, "Heads down." *(Zachary is still sitting up.)* I said, "Head down." Oh, no ... This is problematic ... Shannon, I thought I was very clear about my expectations. Reggie, I thought I was very clear. When I say "Sit up," we're going to have respect. Sit up. *(begins countdown again)* Three. Two. *(Reggie is still sitting, slightly turned with his head down.)* I'm at one now. Your body needs to be respectful. I was very clear about my expectations. It was to sit the right way. *(Reggie drops his clipboard to the ground. Ms. Walker picks it up.)* You do not usually sit without a table; however, you can figure it out because you are in fourth grade. If you cannot, we can practice later. *(She begins countdown again.)* Three. Two. *(Reggie doesn't move.)* It went from fun to now just rude. *(She repositions Reggie in his chair, but he continues to stare down at the ground.)* Okay, just rude. You can prac—*(Reggie repositions himself but has his head down, pouting.)* Okay, good, you fixed yourself. Good job. The word was *eggs,* Zach. What did the tiger take?
8	Zachary:	*(mumbles)* Eggs.
9	Ms. Walker:	*(continues with the lesson)*

1. Ms. Walker mentions her clear expectations several times. Was she in fact clear about her expectations? In what way?

_____

_____

_____

2. Ms. Walker's communication with her students breaks down in numerous places, resulting in a power struggle. Select two or three and discuss more effective alternatives.

_____

_____

_____

_____

_____

3. Consider "fix your body," "we're going to have respect," and "sit the right way" in the context of this case. How were they ineffective as a *What to Do*? How did they contribute to Ms. Walker's breakdown in communication?

_____

_____

_____

4. What is one possibility that could have been said in place of these commands?

_____

_____

5. How could a more effective *What to Do* have yielded a better result?

_____

_____

_____

Key Moments in Your Classroom

Working alone or with a partner, what are some specific moments in your own classroom when a *What to Do* is essential? Think about how effectively you deliver these, and about any improvements you might be able to make.

1. _____

Improvement: _____

_____

2. _____

Improvement: _____

_____

3. _____

Improvement: _____

_____

4. _____

Improvement: _____

_____

Incompetence, Opportunism, and Defiance

To be truly his or her best, a teacher needs to distinguish between the three possible causes of off-task behavior: incompetence, opportunism, and defiance.

Briefly, when incompetence is the cause, students fail to follow directions because they don't know how to complete the task proficiently. You say, "Pay attention," and a student doesn't do it because he doesn't know *how* to pay attention—or what *you* mean by paying attention—or has never practiced it enough to be consistent at it. Incompetence, which can also include students' tuning out in a moment of benign distraction, is probably the cause of far more off-task behavior than many of us suppose.

When opportunism is the cause, students fail to follow directions because they take advantage of a lack of clarity that presents itself to them. They don't set out to disobey, but find themselves presented with a case where there isn't clarity about expectations—or where they can claim there isn't clarity—and where quite possibly there is social status pressure to be earned by exposing it. You say, "Line up," and a student lines up facing backwards, thinking or saying, "But you didn't say which way we had to face."

When defiance is the cause, students fail to follow directions because they don't want to: they want to test you or establish their own power in the classroom, or are processing anger, frustration, or some other emotion.

Understanding these distinctions is critical to strong classroom culture—and relationships—because teachers should respond to behavior in a manner that fits the cause.

- If the issue is incompetence, your obligation is to teach. If you punish students for not complying when they are unable to do so, the consequence will seem unjust or random and will erode your relationship.

- If the issue is opportunism, your goal should be to close the window of ambiguity. You say "Line up facing the door" or "Line up at the door." Or practice lining up "like falcons" (at and facing the door) and say, "This is what I expect whenever I ask the falcons to line up. Line up, falcons."

- If the issue is defiance, your best option is to provide a prompt, clear consequence. If you don't, the impunity will likely persist and grow throughout the term.

Specific, concrete, and observable commands help you not only to eliminate ambiguity and incompetence but also to know clearly when you are dealing with defiance so that you can respond decisively.

Assume for a moment that a second-grade student, Andre, is off task, dancing at his desk when you are giving directions for an activity to the class. You are not sure whether Andre's behavior is incompetent, opportunistic, or defiant. Compare how well each of the following statements will address Andre's behavior, describing in each case how you think Andre is likely to respond.

| 36 **100%** |
| 38 **STRONG VOICE** |
| 39 **DO IT AGAIN** |
| 42 **NO WARNINGS** |

	"Andre, stop fooling around."	"Andre, pay attention."	"Andre, legs under your desk, hands folded; track me."
Effect if the cause is incompetence			
Effect if the cause is opportunism			
Effect if the cause is defiance			

Compare your notes here to some possible responses provided at the end of the technique.

| 36 **100%** |

PRACTICE WITH STUDY GROUP OR PARTNERS

Faulty Directions Role Play

This activity can be done in a group of three; more is better. Its purpose is to give you a student's perspective on vague directions from a teacher. Only the *Facilitator* needs to read these instructions before the group convenes. *Facilitator:* Because the directions within the activity ask *Students* to get paper, you want to ensure that paper is available.

In the activity, the *Facilitator* will be the *Teacher* and will be delivering a set of directions to the other participants, who are all *Students*. Before the session, the *Facilitator* does one of these:

- Make enough copies of the "vague directions" (listed in point 2) for each participant to have one.
- Set up an overhead projector on which to show the directions.
- Prepare to read the directions aloud.

1. The *Facilitator* begins by standing and saying she is the *Teacher* and everyone else is a *Student*. Rearrange seating so that all *Students* face the *Teacher*.

2. The *Teacher* shares the following vague directions with the *Students*:

Get some paper.

On half of it, write your name and contact information.

On the top, write the date.

When you are done, wait quietly.

3.   The *Teacher* directs the *Students* to read the directions, saying, "Please follow the directions as quickly as possible." She refuses to either take questions or answer them.

4.   The *Students* follow the directions.

5.   When the *Teacher* decides they are done, she tells the *Students* to exchange their paper with someone else and poses the following questions and instructions, one by one. The *Students* comply.

"How many of you took out one piece of paper? Hands, please."

"How many of you kept your paper in a notebook? Hands, please."

"Show me where the person whose paper you're holding wrote the date."

"Did the person write a phone number? Show me where."

"Pass your papers forward, please."

6.   As a group, discuss

- What happened generally
- How well the directions were conveyed
- The general orderly quiet (or not) with which the *Students* proceeded and ended
- Any problems *Students* encountered in following the directions
- Any problems the *Teacher* encountered
- Any problems the *Teacher* may have later with the *Students'* completed hand-ins
- Any problems that arose or might now arise with the general flow of classroom work

7.   In pairs or as a group, rewrite the directions in line with *What to Do* (specific, concrete, sequential, observable). As a group, discuss your results.

Your takeaways:

_____

_____

_____

Transition Role Play

30 TIGHT TRANSITIONS

This activity needs three or more participants. Ideally, the group has already worked on *Tight Transitions*. If not, the *Facilitator* should suggest that members visit that technique before the session. Also before the session, the *Facilitator* and group members should look over the suggested situations and consider any modifications they may want to make based on the group's general grade-level focus or other needs.

Participants can also prepare in advance by looking at the situations the *Teacher* will face and plan what they may want to say, but they should *not* script their *Teacher* lines in advance.

In each of four rounds, the *Facilitator* assigns one participant as *Teacher*; the rest are *Students*. The following describes round 1. For additional rounds, use a different *What to Do* situation. (See the suggestions at the end of the activity.) Allow a little time before each round for the *Teacher* to prepare.

Round 1 situation: *Students* are transitioning from reading novels to writing in journals.

1.   Begin at the point at which *Students* have cleared their desks of all things except for a novel they are pretending to read. (Any book will work for a prop.)

2. The *Teacher* gives instructions for the *Students* to transition from reading novels to writing in journals. The instructions should be as *What to Do*-ish as possible—in other words, specific, concrete, sequential, and observable. (However, error is normal, and even a very experienced *Teacher's* instructions may or may not be perfectly chosen. Participants will probably not need to be deliberately less than perfect here in order for the activity to be informative and fun.)

3. The *Students* try in good faith to comply. But where they have difficulty complying, they can respond either out of simple ignorance or with defiance.

4. The *Facilitator* decides when to end each round.

5. After the round, call on the *Teacher* first to discuss these questions:

- Did the instructions follow the *What to Do* format? Were the instructions specific? Concrete? Sequential? Observable?

- Did any *Students* have difficulty following the instructions? Why or why not?

- How did you feel while giving the instructions? What was difficult? What should you have done differently?

- Do you think your instructions helped you determine the difference between incompetence and defiance?

6. Then the *Students* discuss the following:

- Did the instructions follow the *What to Do* format? Were the instructions specific? Concrete? Sequential? Observable?

- Did you have difficulty following the instructions? Why or why not?

- How did you feel while attempting to complete the instructions? What was difficult? What should the teacher have done differently?

- Do you think the instructions helped the teacher determine the difference between incompetence and defiance?

Situations for additional rounds:

Round 2: Students are transitioning from gym class to reading class.

Round 3: Students are at the threshold of a classroom, preparing to enter.

Round 4: Students are transitioning from their desks to a small group reading area.

After all rounds are completed, air and discuss suggestions for improved directions.

Your takeaways:

_____

_____

_____

_____

TRY *WHAT TO DO* IN THE CLASSROOM

1. You can't plan out *all* the directions you give in class, but you can examine your next lesson plan for places where you know you'll need to give directions.

2. Sketch them out (specific, concrete, observable, sequential). Think about how *you* would want to hear those directions. This will free more "brain power" to devote to *100%* compliance.

38 **STRONG VOICE**

39 **DO IT AGAIN**

3. Consider what *Strong Voice* or *Do It Again* you may need to use to make sure that your directions get across.

4. Note any directions that you want to condense or solidify further into a regular classroom routine. Build something into the lesson plan to move in that direction.

5. Carry over what you learn to subsequent lesson planning.

TROUBLE-SHOOT

Steady On

When you are tempted to tell a student to "pay attention," ask yourself:

- Does she know my specific expectations for paying attention (having her eyes on the speaker, say)?
- What outward sign of inattention did I observe? How can I focus on that?
- Does she *know* how to pay attention? Can I teach her?
- Has anyone ever helped her learn to avoid and control distractions and distractedness?

Other Challenges

Possible Challenge	Possible Solutions
Students don't follow my directions.	Are you allowing enough time? How specific and concrete were your directions? Have you practiced them? How quickly or slowly did you deliver them? Did students know you were about to give directions? Can you make more use of the visuals to remind students and reinforce what you want them to do? Are you acknowledging positive behaviors sufficiently (but genuinely—reinforcing only that which is truly positive)? Helping students take pride in their success?

BE CREATIVE

1.   Jocelyn Goodwin teaches grade 2. She noticed that the boys thrived on directions that told them exactly what to do. If they knew what they were supposed to do, they felt more comfortable and less anxious. They liked feeling successful and constantly worked for the positive feedback that told them that they indeed *were* successful. They wanted to please her and knew they could do so by following directions the first time they were given.

What do you notice in your class that makes particular students or clusters of students more comfortable and less anxious? What role can *What to Do* or other techniques play in that regard?

2.   Where might there be more opportunities to *model* the behavior you expect from your students?

SUSTAIN YOUR PROGRESS

1.   Using feedback from your study group or other peers, and reviewing your own lesson notes and observations, monitor your progress on *What to Do*.

Date	Good *What to Do*	A Place I Could Have Used One

2.   Revisit "Where Am I Now?" Are you ready to build out to some other new technique?

WHAT TO DO

The following are possible responses to the "Andre ..." activity in the "Incompetence, Opportunism, and Defiance" section.

	"Andre, stop fooling around."	"Andre, pay attention."	"Andre, legs under your desk, hands folded; track me."
Effect if the cause is incompetence	Doesn't teach the student (that is, tell him how to solve the problem).	Too vague to be useful.	Teaches; describes the solution in a way that helps student succeed.
Effect if the cause is opportunism	Allows gray area to persist.	Allows gray area to persist.	Removes ambiguity so that it cannot be exploited.
Effect if the cause is defiance	Calls attention to negativity. Hard to hold Andre accountable. Doesn't ask him to do anything productive.	Easily manipulated or ignored; leaves degree of defiance ambiguous.	Clearly delineates degree to which student is defying. Allows you to respond appropriately.

WHAT TO DO

STRONG VOICE

OVERVIEW

Some teachers enter a room and are instantly in command, even in the trickiest of situations. We have no way of bottling the skills and attributes that let them bring order to a frenzied cafeteria or scholarly focus to a notorious class that gets the better of their peers. Still, any teacher can use five concrete and easily applied rules to capture much of the authority and confidence those teachers exude, especially at critical moments:

- *Use economical language.* When you need control, fewer words are better. Additional words merely distract students from the most important thing they need to attend to. Show that you are calm and know clearly what you want by dropping every unnecessary word.

- *Do not talk over.* Show that your words matter by not talking if students are talking or making noise.

- *Do not engage.* When you've asked for compliance on a given topic, don't allow the subject to be changed until the issue is resolved.

- *Square up; stand still.* Face difficulty with both shoulders. Stand stock-still to show that there's nothing else on *your* mind.

- *Exude quiet power.* Quieter and slower: when you're under pressure, these signal that you're calm, composed, and in control.

    Operate in the "formal" register. Manage behavior formally rather than casually and without being urgent when urgent action is not required.

WHERE AM I NOW?

	Proficiency			
Comfort & Confidence	**I am brand new to *Strong Voice* . . .**	**I'm gearing up but haven't yet deliberately tried *Strong Voice* in class . . .**	**I'm beginning to use *Strong Voice* . . .**	**I use *Strong Voice* regularly . . .**
	❏ . . . and look forward to adopting it.	❏ . . . but know with practice I'll make it work.	❏ . . . and love how it basically works.	❏ . . . and mine is distinctive.
	❏ . . . and undecided about my ability to pull it off.	❏ . . . because I still have questions about how to do it.	❏ . . . with mixed results I need to evaluate.	❏ . . . but may be overusing it.
	❏ . . . and not at all sure it's for me.	❏ . . . because I still have serious doubts.	❏ . . . but it doesn't seem to work or suit me.	❏ . . . but when class isn't going well, it doesn't help.

Work from your strengths. If you find yourself in the bottom left portion, leaf through this technique to locate related ones you might prefer to work on right now.

EXPAND YOUR SKILLS AND REPERTOIRE

Use Economical Language

When you need to be all business, be clear and crisp and then stop talking. Fewer words are stronger than more, and show that you are prepared and purposeful. Chattiness or verbosity can suggest nervousness, indecision, flippancy—and that your words can be ignored.

When students need to follow your directions, say what is most important *and no more*. Make one brief priority point at a time.

The following transcripts were derived from real-world situations. Read each one. Underscore examples of the effective economy of language. Double-underscore examples of uneconomical language. Then rewrite the uneconomical language.

For group work later, prepare to discuss your rewrites and the strengths and weaknesses of the teacher's *Strong Voice,* particularly in terms of economy of language.

Case Study 1. Ms. Ryan

On a Wednesday afternoon, part of Ms. Ryan's first-grade class is in a small reading group. The class is learning how to decode words by breaking them into chunks.

1	Ms. Ryan:	Sometimes we're going to find chunks of letters that can make more than one sound. We know all of our chunks so well from our wall cards! That's where we write what we learn about all of our words.	
2	Class:	*(Several students start rocking back and forth, talking to each other, looking around the room, and rising to their knees.)*	
3	Ms. Ryan:	Okay, I know that we've been on the rug for a while because the principal changed my schedule, but I need to see my scholars focus right now.	
4	Class:	*(four-second pause)*	
5	Ms. Ryan:	So, Marianni, where's your seat?	
6	Marianni:	*(Marianni points.)*	
7	Ms. Ryan:	Move there. Kylee, are you having trouble, too? Where's your seat?	
8	Kylee:	*(Kylee points and moves to her spot.)*	
9	Ms. Ryan:	Very good, and that's how you should be sitting. Edward, how should you be sitting?	

| 10 | *Edward:* | *(Edward shifts slightly; teacher waits. Edward shifts again.)* | |

| 11 | *Ms. Ryan:* | Sasha, how should you be sitting? | |

| 12 | *Sasha:* | *(Sasha sits up straight. Marianni starts fanning herself with her hand.)* | |

| 13 | *Ms. Ryan:* | Marianni, do you remember how we talked about if you do this *(imitates Marianni's fanning),* it actually makes you hotter because you're actually moving your body? So that's why your hands should be still in your lap. *(Teacher models folded hands.)* | |

| 14 | *Class:* | *(ten-second pause as teacher scans group of students)* | |

| 15 | *Ms. Ryan:* | So, I want to read the pages where we've already found chunks . . . | |

Case Study 2. Mr. Jackson

Mr. Jackson's class is reading The Diary of Anne Frank *and reviewing the previous day's chapter. Mr. Jackson is asking questions about the characters and the nature of the Nazi occupation described in the book.*

| 1 | *Mr. Jackson:* | Tell me what other characters in the book say or think about the Nazis. *(Mr. Jackson calls on a few students.)* | |

| 2 | *Class:* | *(The students give answers about people feeling afraid and suspicious of the Nazis. Mr. Jackson appears disappointed that more students don't have responses to his questions.)* | |

| 3 | *Mr. Jackson:* | I don't get the sense that everyone is looking and trying to answer. I get the sense that a couple of people have an idea in their head and the rest of you are just sort of sitting there. | |

| 4 | *Class:* | *(Mr. Jackson notices Tyreese, who is holding his book and fanning the pages.)* | |

STRONG VOICE

5	*Mr. Jackson:*	Okay, and when you're playing with your book like that when I'm standing right next to you, to me that doesn't look like someone who's trying to answer the question, does it? Does it? Okay, take a hint. Put your book down. I don't think it's a very scholarly look. Sit up the right way. *(three-second pause)* Anything else, Nageray?
6	*Class:*	*(More discussion of yesterday's reading ensues. Mr. Jackson tells the students that they need to "move along," and he begins reading aloud. Students are still off task.)*
7	*Mr. Jackson:*	I am not sensing all of the energy I would like to see in this room right now. There are some people right here *(motions to a small group of students to his left)* who seem to be actively thinking, but I'm looking around at other people, and I'm seeing that not everyone is sitting up like Thomas is sitting up, and not everyone is shooting their hand up the way Gladys is shooting her hand up. If you can't answer the question I just asked, you should tell yourself, "Well, I better pay attention from now on because that was really embarrassing when I didn't know where I was or I couldn't answer the question," okay? Can everybody do that?
8	*Class:*	*(students nod)*
9	*Mr. Jackson:*	Okay, loudly and proudly . . . Marcus.

Case Study 3. Ms. Davis

Ms. Davis has just started her Friday afternoon third-grade art class. She is distributing cotton balls for a project they are working on.

1	*Ms. Davis:*	We're going to each get one cotton ball. You may not take more than one cotton ball. How many cotton balls do you get, everybody?

2	*Class:*	One!
3	*Ms. Davis:*	Because if you took two, then not everybody would have one. There wouldn't be enough in your bin to give to your friends. So, it's not nice to take more than one cotton ball, and if you take more than one, you will be in trouble. You're good kids, so I know you're not going to take more than one. *(Ms. Davis begins passing around a bin of cotton balls.)*

4	*Class:*	*(Some children get out of their seats.)*
5	*Ms. Davis:*	*(with hands on hips)* I'm not putting up this Scholar Star because some of you got out of your seats. I'm not putting it up. I believe in you, and I believe we can get this star. But I said, "bottoms in the seat," and three of you decided not to follow my direction. I'm not putting that star up there now. And now *four* children are out of their seats, and one scholar is talking while Teacher is talking, my goodness!

6	*Ms. Davis:*	Eyes over here! This is important, Shauna. Eyes over here, Nigel. I'm over here, Edgar. Now watch this … Red table, put the markers down! Yellow table, I notice that you are still coloring and two are out of their seats. Yellow table, if you don't start paying attention, you're not getting any cotton balls.

Don't Engage Distractions

Once you have set the topic of conversation, avoid engaging in other topics until you have satisfactorily resolved the topic you initiated, especially when the topic is behavioral follow-through. Suppose you have an encounter with David, who is pushing Margaret's chair with his foot. Your best instruction would tell David where to put his foot:

"David, please put your feet under your desk and face me."

David, however, might seek to change the subject: "But she's always bugging me" or "Her chair's in my space" or "It's not bothering her." In any of those cases, your best move would be to make sure he follows through on what you asked him to do:

| 37 **WHAT TO DO** |

"I asked you to put your foot under your desk and to face me. Let me see you do that now."

Take a moment to reflect on how David would likely respond to these two less advantageous responses:

"Margaret, were you doing that?"

"I'm not really concerned with what Margaret was doing."

Now consider these responses:

"David, I asked you to take your foot off of Margaret's chair."

"Right now I need you to follow my direction and take your foot off Margaret's chair."

How are the latter responses better?

- They explicitly refer to the fact that you initiated a topic of conversation and expect it to be addressed.

- They don't require you to announce that you "don't care" what Margaret did, which isn't exactly the message you want to convey.

If you have any doubt that David *did* have his foot on Margaret's chair, an effective response would be:

"David, make sure your foot is under your own desk and that it stays there."

If he distracts with "But she was . . . ," you might merely repeat your request that he remove it. If he says, "It wasn't on her chair," simply respond:

"Good. Then let me see it under your desk for the duration of class."

If you think David's likely to test you, you could add,

"I'll keep an eye on it so that I can help you practice that at recess if you need the help."

Suppose David responded to your initial order by saying, "But I wasn't doing anything!"
Again, the best strategy is not to engage his topic. Your best reply:

"I asked you to take your foot off Margaret's chair. Once you've done that, you don't need to say anything more."

Note that wherever your command begins, *your aim is for David to follow your directions with no change of topic.* In refusing to engage, you ensure David's accountability. This is especially important because students in the process of protesting their but-I-wasn't-ness often convince *themselves* that they were not behaving in a negative manner. By refusing to engage with David, you also establish a tone of focused accountability for the class as a whole. Students must "do" first and discuss later.

You also allow yourself to delay a possibly complex issue of who is bugging whom until a time when instruction is not happening. Here's another useful example, in which the "yellow card" is part of a behavioral self-monitoring system:

Teacher (to James, who was talking out of turn): "James, you are talking. Please move your card to yellow."

James: "It wasn't me!"

Teacher: "Please move your card to yellow."

James: "Shanice was talking! Not me!"

Teacher: "I asked you to move your card. Please get up and move your card to yellow."

It *might* be reasonable for the teacher to discuss who was talking *with* James, but the expectation must be that the latter conversation doesn't happen until James has first done what his teacher asked. Only after James has obeyed the initial request can he dissent or seek redress. Until then, the topic does not change.

The Defiant and the Benign

Remember that students can get you off task not only through defiance but through more benign distractions, sometimes deliberately and sometimes without ill intent. These, too, can be addressed with a slightly gentler version of *Do not engage,* as in

You: "Okay, please get going on your problem sets."

Student (raising a hand): "Are we going to do our oral reports soon?"

You: "Right now we're working on our problem sets. Let me see you get started, please."

Though these situations pose less of a challenge to your stewardship of the classroom, they can be just as corrosive to productivity, so it's important to practice deflecting them.

First, do some reflecting. What are some of the things students say that get you off the topic or task you have announced? Add to the list we've started:

"My stomach hurts!"

"That dress [shirt] looks so pretty [cool] on you!"

"Do you really *like* this book?"

_____

_____

_____

_____

Which topics or types of topic shifts are you most vulnerable to? When you engage but should not, what catches you, and why?

_____

_____

_____

_____

_____

As noted earlier, students can take various emotional approaches and attitudes when they attempt to shift the topic away from the one you initiated, such as:

STRONG VOICE

Argumentative:

>   *Teacher:* "Please take your foot off David's chair."

>   *Student:* "But he keeps bumping me."

Benign:

>   *Teacher:* "So as you can see, Lincoln's greatness stems from his response to crisis."

>   *Student:* "How do you think President Obama responds to crisis?"

What student tones are likely to distract you into changing topic?

_____

_____

_____

_____

What criteria do you want to use in deciding whether to engage a change of topic when a student initiates a topic in response to your question or instruction? ("My stomach hurts." "This book is so boring." "I love this book—has the author written anything else?!")

_____

_____

_____

_____

_____

Don't Engage When Answers Are Called Out

Engaging with a called-out answer, even with "Right, but please don't call out," sends the message that your rules don't apply if what the student calls out is interesting enough or is the right answer when no one can seem to get it or is said loud enough or repeated often enough. Engaging will rapidly lead to students' constantly calling out. Without engaging with the answer, you can say,

"In this class, we raise our hands when we want to speak."

Less Engagement, Please!

Following each scenario here, write a short reflection about where the teacher may have gone wrong. Then rewrite line 3.

Scenario 1. Achy Stomach

1. *Teacher:* You have five minutes to finish your worksheets.
2. *Student:* But my stomach hurts. I think I might throw up.
3. *Teacher:* Do you want to go to the nurse?
4. *Student:* I don't know. I just really don't feel well. I think it was the lunch. That pudding stuff is *nasty. (Class laughs.)*

    Reflection: _____

    _____

Rewrite of line 3: _____

_____

Scenario 2. *Of Mice and Men*

1. *Teacher:* We are starting our essay on *Of Mice and Men* today. Please get out your novels.
2. *Student:* Man, when are we going to do something fun?
3. *Teacher:* Stop complaining. Please get out your novel.
4. *Student:* I do not complain! When do I complain? Why are you always calling people complainers!?

Reflection: _____

_____

Rewrite of line 3: _____

_____

Scenario 3. More *Mice*

1. *Teacher:* We are starting our essay on *Of Mice and Men* today. Please get out your novels.
2. *Student:* I still don't understand why they had to go and kill Lennie! Everywhere you look, the Man gets you. Right, Mr. P?
3. *Teacher:* I'm not sure it's all that simple, Jason.
4. *Student:* Aw, come on, Mr. P. You know what happens if you get out of line. Look at Rodney King!

Reflection: _____

_____

Rewrite of line 3: _____

_____

Reducing Engagement

Here are several teacher-student interactions. Note that in each set the teacher response varies at line 3. Reflect on that line in terms of its likely effectiveness, tone, and possible risk.

   Setting: Sitting next to each other, Peter tries to wrench Marnie's book out of her hands.

1. *Teacher:* Peter, please let go of Marnie's book.
2. *Student:* But she's always got her stuff on my desk.
3. *Teacher:* I understand. Please let go of Marnie's book.

Reflection: _____

_____

_____

_____

Setting: The same.

1. *Teacher:* Peter, please let go of Marnie's book.
2. *Student:* But she's always got her stuff on my desk.
3. *Teacher:* I asked you to let go of Marnie's book.

Reflection: _____

_____

_____

_____

Setting: The same.

1. *Teacher:* Peter, please let go of Marnie's book.
2. *Student:* But she's always got her stuff on my desk.
3. *Teacher:* We can discuss that later. Right now I need you to let go of her book.

Reflection: _____

_____

_____

_____

Setting: Early afternoon in March; a tenth-grade English class, a smart but mercurial bunch.

1. *Teacher:* The book we're going to begin today, *1984,* is a twentieth-century classic. You will discuss it and read it again in college. Does anyone know the name of the author?
2. *Student:* Did *you* read *1984* in college?
3. *Teacher:* That is not, in fact, the name of the author. Who else would like to try?

Reflection: _____

_____

_____

_____

Setting: The same.

1. *Teacher:* The book we're going to begin today, *1984,* is a twentieth-century classic. You will discuss it and read it again in college. Does anyone know the name of the author?
2. *Student:* Did *you* read *1984* in college?
3. *Teacher:* The question, again, was, Does anyone know the name of the author? Would you like to try again?

Reflection: _____

_____

_____

_____

Setting: The same.

1. *Teacher:* The book we're going to begin today, *1984,* is a twentieth-century classic. You will discuss it and read it again in college. Does anyone know the name of the author?

2. *Student:* Did *you* read *1984* in college?

3. *Teacher: (ignoring student)* Does anyone know the name of the author?

Reflection: _____

_____

_____

_____

Setting: The same.

1. *Teacher:* The book we're going to begin today, *1984,* is a twentieth-century classic. You will discuss it and read it again in college. Does anyone know the name of the author?

2. *Student:* Did *you* read *1984* in college?

3. *Teacher:* I did. Now, does anyone know the name of the author?

Reflection: _____

_____

_____

_____

Formal: The Default Register of *Strong Voice* Teachers

"Register" refers to the tenor of a conversation, encompassing eye contact, body position, gestures, facial expression, and rhythm of language.

Distinguish the Three Registers: Casual, Formal, Urgent

Imagine three interactions between colleagues in some workplace setting:

Casual register. In the lunchroom, in a *casual* register, a woman tells her colleague about her recent weekend trip with friends to a nearby city:

> "Oh my gosh, it was such a great weekend," she begins. As she speaks, her eye contact drifts away from and comes back to her colleague, as if she were gazing out at some latent image of the weekend projected on a nearby wall. Her hands also move as she speaks. "We were in this funky coffee shop with old records on the walls," she says with a sweeping gesture. She stands with her hips to the side, reclining against a wall, perhaps. She's squinting slightly. Her weight is on one foot. Her words run together in a pitter-patter rhythm.

All of these behaviors—inconsistent eye contact; gestures; asymmetrical, relaxed posture; words running into one another—suggest casualness, informality, a sense of ease. They also seem to say,

We're just talking here. You can interrupt me any time. If you have to walk away in the middle to do something else, that's okay too.

Many teachers use something like this casual register in the classroom. It's fine to do so if you're aware of what it signals. But teachers often deliver an important message in a casual register that ultimately undercuts it. And in any contest between register and actual words, the register is likely to win.

Formal register. The photocopy toner has run out, and someone feels strongly about a need for better office management.

> She suddenly stands up straight and holds her body in a symmetrical position. She looks right at her colleague. Her chin rises slightly. She puts her hands behind her back—no sweeping gestures; you can't even *see* her hands. "Every day, we depend on that machine," she says, each word a distinct and important part of the solemn ritual. Her articulation of the syllables is clearer. She doesn't ask her colleague to strike the formal hands-behind-the-back pose she's using, but when the colleague sees it, she knows something important is being expressed, and she's likely to stand up straight herself; she may even put her own hands behind her back in unconscious mimicry.

The person's formal register bespeaks the importance of the message and causes a purposeful attentiveness in the listener. Champion teachers tend to use the formal register for the great majority of their statements in which they seek control. Watch them in action and you'll see them standing straight and symmetrically, choosing words carefully, allowing for brief pauses between words, and holding their eyes steady. If they make a hand gesture, it's very controlled and simple, involving one movement and ending crisply. This formal register is the wrapping that makes *Strong Voice* especially effective.

Urgent register. The building is on fire. A worker enters the lunch area and places her hands firmly on the shoulders of a colleague:

> "Listen," she says. "There's an emergency. I need you to come with me right away. I need you to put everything down and follow me. Do you understand? I need you to follow right away. Let's go." She's leaning in closer than she would in a mere formal pose, and she's punching her words. The pauses are actually more noticeable, though you might have expected her to rush. Her eyes are locked more than steady. She makes a gesture toward the fire exit with a crisp, truncated chopping motion. She is not panicked, not blathering and rushed, just very, very focused.

Is urgency the register you want to use in your classroom to ensure compliance? Maybe or maybe not. When the chips are truly down, an urgent message will get through if and only if it is *delivered* as urgent (calm, focused, and very insistent) and not panicked (emotional, hurried, and anxious). But speaking with urgency can also be like crying wolf. It has to be saved for truly urgent situations. Overused, it shows weakness and lack of control.

Emphasize Formal

If you watch champion teachers for long enough you will see that they most often choose the formal register when they need control. At other moments they may choose other registers. Like the five *Strong Voice* principles generally, the formal register is not for the moments when you're discussing the Civil War, but for the moments in between when students need to become attentive and ready. In the formal register you are likely to demonstrate

- Symmetrical posture
- Squared-up pose, facing students directly
- Standing straight up or leaning in very slightly, perhaps five or ten degrees
- Feet squarely set
- Simple, nonrepeated gestures
- Steady eye contact
- Enunciate words clearly and separately

Use Video (and Audio) Recordings

A video recording is ideal for analyzing your nonverbal behaviors, but an audio recording of a teaching session can reveal your speech patterns under pressure. Or a peer can observe and give you notes on these behaviors. Drawing on these and your own observations, what do you notice about your behaviors?

What is your default register in the classroom?

_____

What behaviors do you exhibit in your urgent register (when you are nervous, for example)?

_____

_____

_____

What conditions lead you into a register you'd rather not enter?

_____

_____

_____

What specific behaviors do you want to improve?

_____

_____

_____

Synthesizing *Strong Voice* Principles

In his third-grade classroom, Darryl Williams's *Strong Voice* drives a clear and compelling culture. On a recent morning, he demonstrated all five techniques within just a few seconds to bring his class to order. Having completed a study of prefixes and suffixes at the board, Mr. Williams turns to explain what's next on the agenda.

"Okay," he begins, "let's see who's . . . " His voice pulls up abruptly, demonstrating a refusal to talk over students. Two or three boys have their hands in the air while he is talking. Two others are talking to a classmate. Someone's head is on a desk.

"Well," he says, dropping his voice to just above a whisper, "most of us are doing an excellent job today."

He puts down the book he was carrying. He turns to face the class and places his arms behind his back in a formal "Square up" pose.

Quietly, slowly, firmly he says, "Please put your hands down," focusing their attention on the request with strict economy of language. His refusal to take hands is yet another way to avoid engaging in a topic other than the one of his own choosing. The distractions are gone now.

The room is silent. All eyes are on him. For Mr. Williams, though, there's one more step—the task of making his actions transparent and benign.

"Thank you," he says, showing his appreciation for their rapid return to full attentiveness. "The reason I can't answer all your questions right now ... I would like to and I love it when you tell me intelligent things. But we don't have a lot of time. We still need to read our story and then ..."

For Mr. Williams, the strength is not just in the control but in the caring. His explanation of the rationale behind his authority ensures that he will be able to sustain that control—with students' buy-in—for the long haul.

PRACTICE WITH STUDY GROUP OR PARTNERS

With a partner take turns trying the behaviors in the "Emphasize Formal" section. Also see "Use Video (and Audio) Recordings."

Case Studies

Discuss the rewrites from your work in the "Case Study" section earlier. What parts of the teacher dialogue did you rewrite? Why? Did others in the group notice problems or possible solutions that you admire? What were they?

_____

_____

_____

Body Language Role Plays

These two activities focus on the register and body language aspects of *Strong Voice*.

Body Language Threesome
This requires three participants. If the group is large, work in groups of three; if small, in each round one participant is the *Speaker,* one is the *Addressee,* and the third or more participants are *Observers*.

In each round, the *Speaker* stands up and speaks to the *Addressee* three times. In the *Speaker* role, proceed along the following lines:

1. Describe what you did this weekend.
2. Recite the Pledge of Allegiance.
3. Pretend the building is on fire. Talking to the *Addressee* as if he were a child you don't know, tell him what to do.

The *Observer(s)* take notes, paying particular attention to what is different about the person's body language in each register. After all three conversations are finished, *Observer(s)* describe the body language they observed and what it signals about the *Speaker*'s intent, level of commitment, and so forth.

Body Language Double Deck
Before the group convenes, the *Facilitator* photocopies and cuts out the sets of Statement and Register cards provided and compiles them as two separate decks.

BODY LANGUAGE DOUBLE DECK
Statement Cards

Body Language Double Deck Statement "Please go back and try that again."	Body Language Double Deck Statement "We don't use that word in this classroom."	Body Language Double Deck Statement "Track the speaker."
Body Language Double Deck Statement "Pick up reading from there."	Body Language Double Deck Statement "Please sit down and get started."	Body Language Double Deck Statement "You may use the bathroom after you've completed the first two pages."
Body Language Double Deck Statement "Hands down."	Body Language Double Deck Statement "If you have something to contribute, raise your hand."	Body Language Double Deck Statement "I'd like you to be more respectful to your classmates."
Body Language Double Deck Statement "Turn over your paper."	Body Language Double Deck Statement "This row line up at the door, quickly."	Body Language Double Deck Statement "Sit up."
Body Language Double Deck Statement "Put your pencils in their trays."	Body Language Double Deck Statement "I want to see your best work on this."	Body Language Double Deck Statement "Your effort is really impressing me today."
Body Language Double Deck Statement "You're going to have to work together."	Body Language Double Deck Statement "Take your seat."	Body Language Double Deck Statement "Close your books; track me."

REGISTER CARDS

Body Language Double Deck

Register: Urgent

Body Language Double Deck

Register: Casual

Body Language Double Deck

Register: Formal

Body Language Double Deck

Register: Urgent

Body Language Double Deck

Register: Casual

Body Language Double Deck

Register: Formal

1. Place the Statement deck face down.

2. Participants take turns drawing a Statement card. Each participant then tries to say the statement on the card in each of the three registers, announcing beforehand which register is intended this time: casual, formal, or urgent. The participant keeps trying until the rest of the group confirms that the effort captures the intended register in both verbal and nonverbal respects.

3. Shuffle the cards back into the deck. Place the Register deck face down beside the Statement deck.

4. In turn, each participant draws a card from each deck. Without revealing what either card says, the participant silently delivers the gist of the statement *nonverbally* (in body language and gestures) in accordance with the register stated on the card.

5. The other participants each separately record their decisions about what register was intended. As a group, share your conclusions in a positive way and discuss your evidence.

6. The speaker announces what register was intended. If the group does not agree that this register came across well, allow the speaker to try again, with more constructive feedback from the group.

7. Repeat the process with more draws from the decks until everyone has mastered each register.

Situational Envelopes Role Play

This exercise puts the *Teacher* in a difficult situation in which *Strong Voice* can be very effective. It requires at least three participants (more would be better), and the materials allow for up to five experiences as *Teacher*.

Before the group convenes, the *Facilitator* needs to photocopy and cut out these five situations and put them in five envelopes. Label the envelopes "Situation 1" through "Situation 5."

1. When the group convenes, the *Facilitator* gives out the envelopes to participants playing *Teacher* in the five different situations.

2. The *Teacher* for situation 1 opens that envelope and reads the description aloud to the group. Allow the *Teacher* a minute or so to think of how to handle the situation while the *Students* decide privately among themselves who will perform the *Student* behaviors mentioned in the situation. Physically arrange yourselves according to the situation.

3. When everyone is ready, the *Facilitator* says, "Let's begin." The group carries out the role play. In the course of it, the *Teacher* responds to the scenario. If additional *Student* behavior or exchanges seem warranted, continue the role play. The *Facilitator* decides when to stop.

4. Group discussion:

For *Students*:

- How did the reaction of the *Teacher* in this case affect your behavior?
- Were there any moments that you would consider ineffective or to which you reacted negatively?
- What were the most positive and effective moments?

For the *Teacher*:

- How effective was your economy of language?
- Discuss the ease or difficulty of refusing to engage with students in your situation.
- How did squaring up or other gestural behavior change your use of language and the impact you think it had on the students?

5. Proceed to the next *Teacher*'s situation.

6. As a group, discuss what you observed and learned.

STRONG VOICE

SITUATIONAL ENVELOPES ROLE PLAY

Strong Voice Situation 1
You are going over double-digit multiplication problems. As you do, you begin *Cold Calling* students to talk about both the process and the answers to each step. Some students are repeatedly calling out the answers to your questions. They giggle when you first ask them to desist.

Strong Voice Situation 2
While you are going over the rules of subject–verb agreement, several of your students raise their hands with questions about both the current lesson and whether the class will later be reading *Harry Potter and the Sorcerer's Stone.* They then begin to discuss their favorite parts of the movie.

Strong Voice Situation 3
You are in the middle of a lesson when a group of three students perch themselves outside your classroom talking loudly about a scuffle they witnessed in the lunchroom. They are recalcitrant but not belligerent when confronted.

Strong Voice Situation 4
You are giving directions for how to transition to your next activity (going over yesterday's homework—order of operations examples) when two students in your class begin discussing the previous night's *American Idol* results. One of the students adamantly claims that she wasn't talking.

Strong Voice Situation 5
You are waiting outside with students for parents at the end of the day, when one of your students is accosted by a teenager who is not from your school. Intervene on his behalf. Note: Although it is true that you might choose not to intervene in this situation, your aim is to test your abilities in the most challenging situations. Give it a try in this safe environment.

Taken from *Teach Like a Champion Field Guide: A Practical Resource to Make the 49 Techniques Your Own.* Copyright © 2012 by Doug Lemov.

Your takeaways:

_____

_____

_____

_____

TRY *STRONG VOICE* IN THE CLASSROOM

1. Some people come to teaching with most aspects of *Strong Voice* already theirs. If that's not you, start wherever you feel you are strongest and expand from there. Be patient with yourself. It takes effort, time, and experience to develop.

2. Look around for another teacher who may be more advanced in *Strong Voice* and is willing to advise you about specific behaviors he or she employs. Or partner with a peer and serve as mutual sounding boards and supports.

3. Do you already *Circulate* well? If not, look for places in the lesson plan that you can mark to *Circulate*. (A habit of *Circulating* will make it easier for you to subtly *move toward trouble* when the need arises.) Mark places where you intend to *Circulate* as part of maintaining control (for instance, during student desk work).

15 **CIRCULATE**

4. Stay with the idea that *Strong Voice* really comes down to five deliberate behaviors, each of which you can work on independently: using economical language, not talking over, not engaging, squaring up and standing still, and exuding quiet power. Break down the challenge by deciding which of the five to focus on first in the classroom. We recommend you choose two: one in which you have some skill and confidence already that you can solidify, another in which you need to improve more dramatically. Practice to improve those two behaviors until you have made some progress on both, then shift your focus to a third, and so on.

5. Mark places in the lesson plan where you want to ensure good control with *Strong Voice*. Script and rehearse brief wording and body language with those points in mind.

6. If you still need to let students know your expectations about what they should be doing when you are talking, be sure to inform them.

48 **EXPLAIN EVERYTHING**

7. Prepare a short "note-to-self" reminder card for reference during future sessions about *Strong Voice* phrasing and nonverbal language you want to use but tend to forget.

TROUBLE-SHOOT

Steady On

1. To reduce openings for students to change topic or go off task, champion teachers discipline themselves generally not to frame directions as questions. Early in the year they may explain the difference between a question and a direction and how students are to respond to each.

STRONG VOICE

2.   Don't slip into talking too much, then noticing that students are restless or fidgety. Work on exuding quiet power. Stop, take a deep breath and a more formal pose. Give yourself (and the students) five seconds before moving on.

3.   A pencil in a student's hand may be tempting for him or her to play with. Modify your routines and established expectations to ensure that pencils are down at moments when you need students' full attention.

Other Challenges

Possible Challenge	Possible Solutions

BE CREATIVE

1. Devise and try out a small hand gesture or other nonverbal signal to go with each economical phrase you use often to control the class. Also, as practicable, plan to show students what you expect by explicitly modeling the proper behavior.

2. Try connecting several of your economical directions with some form of countdown that is formal but positive in spirit.

SUSTAIN YOUR PROGRESS

1. Using feedback from your study group or other peers, and reviewing your own lesson notes and observations, monitor your progress on *Strong Voice*. On a given date, award yourself a point for each type of *Strong Voice* you used in class:

- Employ economical language
- Do not talk over
- Do not engage

- Square up; stand still
- Exude quiet power

Date	Points	Date	Points

2. Revisit "Where Am I Now?" Are you ready to build out to some other new technique?

DO IT AGAIN

OVERVIEW

Asking students to *Do It Again* is the perfect response when they're not up to speed at a simple task and could use more practice. And the frame of mind is positive: "Good, better, best." It is ideal for times when students do something acceptably but could do it better. In fact, at least one champion teacher calls this technique "Do it better"!

Do It Again is also useful when compliance is the issue. In *100%, Do It Again* is often the right intervention: an immediate consequence that does not require you to brief administrators, fill out forms, speak with parents, or keep a student from joining the recess line. What a blessing! *Do It Again* is almost completely freestanding and can be used in any classroom.

Here are four key pointers:

- Cut the task short.
- Think good, better, best.
- Manage affect as well as behavior.
- Give specific feedback.

WHERE AM I NOW?

	Proficiency			
Comfort & Confidence	**I am brand new to Do It Again ...**	**I'm a bit familiar with Do It Again, but haven't yet planned and done it in class ...**	**I'm beginning to try Do It Again in my classroom ...**	**We Do It Again for compliance and improvement of routines and skills ...**
	❑ ... and excited to try it.	❑ ... but know I can learn to make it work.	❑ ... and like what it accomplishes for classroom learning.	❑ ... and I'm rarely at a loss for words or positivity.
	❑ ... and undecided about my ability to pull it off.	❑ ... because I'm still not sure what to say or when.	❑ ... with mixed results I need to evaluate.	❑ ... but I might need to be more systematic.
	❑ ... and not at all sure it's for me.	❑ ... because I still have doubts.	❑ ... but it doesn't seem to work or suit me.	❑ ... but when class isn't going well, I do it poorly.

Work from your strengths. If you find yourself in the bottom left portion, leaf through this technique to locate related ones you might prefer to work on right now.

ANALYZE THE CHAMPIONS

View each video clip, ideally more than once, and answer the following questions.

 Clip 4. Teacher Stacey Shells, Grade 7

1. What does Ms. Shells insist that a student do again, aloud?
2. What is the value of having him do that?
3. How does he react to the request?

 Clip 15. Teacher Lauren Whitehead, Grade 2

What's the *Do It Again* moment in this clip? In what ways does it conform with the four pointers listed in the "Overview" section?

 Clip 25. Teacher Katie Bellucci, Grade 5

What is Ms. Bellucci after with her *Do It Again*?

 Clip 26. Teacher Alexandra Bronson, Grade 5

1. What part of *SLANT* is Ms. Bronson training her students to use?
2. How is what she is doing aimed at increasing her *Strong Voice*?
3. What rewards or consequences is Ms. Bronson using?
4. What's her emotional tenor?
5. How do her students appear to feel about Ms. Bronson's *Do It Again*?

EXPAND YOUR SKILLS AND REPERTOIRE

Why *Do It Again*?

Do It Again is not punishment. It's a sound way to teach and learn. Consider these five reasons why.

1. It shortens the feedback loop. Behavioral science has shown that the shorter the time lag between an action (behavior) and a response, the more effective the response will be in changing the behavior. If the reaction comes immediately after, while the original action is fresh in a student's mind, the two will be more deeply associated in his or her memory. When you say "*Do It Again*," the lag time is only three words long.

2. It can set a standard of *excellence* beyond compliance and a culture in which students replace acceptable with excellent, first in the *small* things, then in *all* things.

"That was good, but I want great."

"In this class we do everything as well as we can—including lining up."

19 **AT BATS**

3. Not just individuals but groups can *Do It Again*, which adds *At Bats,* and it is especially effective as a group consequence.

"I heard one or two talking as you were lining up. Let's all try it again."

This holds the group accountable in a reasonable, nonpunitive way for the behavior of all of its individuals. It builds incentives for individuals to behave positively because it makes them accountable to their peers as well as to their teacher.

4. *Do It Again* ends in success, and the last thing you remembers of an event often shapes your perception of it more broadly. Through *Do It Again,* the last thing students do in a sequence is do an activity the right way. This helps engrain the perception and memory of what right looks like. It also helps build muscle memory.

5. Ideal consequences are those that are logically related to the behavior that precedes them, and this connection helps students understand what they did wrong or indifferently and what is expected of them in terms of doing it right or better. (That's one of the strengths of *Do It Again.*)

Which of these reasons impress you most? Why? Do any not seem convincing?

_____

_____

_____

_____

The Four Pointers

1. *Cut the task short.* Don't wait for the entire task to be completed. Restart once you know you're going to *Do It Again.* Begin the redo as close as you can to the part of the task that didn't measure up.

43 **POSITIVE FRAMING**

2. *Think good, better, best.* Set a powerfully positive tone: "That was good. But I want great."

3. *Manage affect (and with affect) as well as behavior.* Students often change from the outside in. In *Do It Again,* if you tell them you want to see something done with more spirit or enthusiasm, you are using an effective tool for managing their *affect.* Especially if you *model enthusiasm yourself,* asking a low-energy class to repeat something with enthusiasm can start a self-fulfilling cycle.

| 37 **WHAT TO DO** |
| 38 **STRONG VOICE** |

4. *Give specific feedback.* This doesn't necessarily mean identifying what someone did incorrectly. Use *Strong Voice* to tell students *What to Do* that you and they can visibly see they are doing.

"I want to see those eyes up so you look like scholars. Let's do it one more time."

Apply the Pointers

Which of these is likely to be a more effective *Do It Again*? Why?

"Oooh, let's line up again and prove why we're the best reading group in the school."

"Class, that was very sloppy. We're going to do it again until we get it exactly right."

The best wording for *Do It Again* is often as a challenge, though the word "challenge" need not appear.

"Let's try that again, Superman." (A nickname)

"Let's do that like we did this morning." (Praise for past action)

"Today I need your very best." (The expectation for the day)

"I know we can do better." (A call to improve)

"This *is* the world-famous Fairfax fourth grade, right? I wanna see it!" (Another nickname and training in pride)

Conjure up some moments when you've been in class (as a teacher or student) and not everyone has done their best to comply in some coordinated task (lining up, turning in papers, *Call and Response*) and, looking back, you think *Do It Again* could have applied. Assume you could have stopped the activity as soon as you noticed the problem.

Name the moment and task. Name what behaviors could have been better. Phrase a *Do It Again* for each that takes off from the point when you halted the task and is consistent with the four pointers.

23 CALL AND RESPONSE

Moment: _____

Improvable behavior(s): _____

_____

Do It Again: _____

_____

Moment: _____

Improvable behavior(s): _____

_____

Do It Again: _____

_____

Moment: _____

Improvable behavior(s): _____

_____

Do It Again: _____

_____

DO IT AGAIN

Go "Green"

Do It Again is entirely recyclable, repeatable, and harmless to the ozone. You don't need to keep inventing new consequences. You can *Do It Again* and again right away, and you can still be positive in administering the third iteration.

"I still think we can do this even better. Let's give it one more shot!"

You can also have a class or individual again *Do It Again* ten minutes later or in the last moments of class so that they walk out on a high note.

PRACTICE WITH STUDY GROUP OR PARTNERS

| 43 **POSITIVE FRAMING** |

Note to *Facilitator*: The group work in *Positive Framing* includes "*Do It Again* Using *Positive Framing*." You could do that exercise now if the group has already worked on *Positive Framing* and *Do It Again*.

Group Discussion

A whiteboard or flipchart paper will be helpful.

1. Share and compare the tasks and solutions from the activity in "Apply the Pointers."

2. Discuss how you've had students or others do things again in a way that follows one or more of the pointers. How can you incorporate more of the essence of *Do It Again*? Share obstacles and solutions.

3. From the individual work, as a group choose and write out three or four phrasings of *Do It Again* where everyone can see them. Brainstorm more possible rephrasing, and discuss the harvest of possibilities.

Insights?

_____

_____

_____

_____

Positive Correction Role Play

| 43 **POSITIVE FRAMING** |

This role play needs at least four participants—the more the better. It lets the group practice *Do It Again* techniques in a way that emphasizes the positive.

The *Facilitator* can prepare in advance by copying and cutting out the Role Play Scenario and Student Role cards. The group can also invent scenarios based on their classroom experience and interests.

POSITIVE CORRECTION ROLE PLAY
Role Play Scenario Cards

Positive Correction Role Play Scenario Dismissing students for lunch	**Positive Correction Role Play Scenario** Greeting students at the door as they enter the classroom at the beginning of class	**Positive Correction Role Play Scenario** Transitioning from carpet to desks
Positive Correction Role Play Scenario Passing out papers for the next in-class assignment	**Positive Correction Role Play Scenario** Passing out books to read in class	**Positive Correction Role Play Scenario** Greeting students at the beginning of class (all the students are already in their seats)

Student Role Cards

Positive Correction Student Role You are passively distracted by thoughts of tonight's *Dancing with the Stars* finale. You will correct the first time you are asked.	**Positive Correction Student Role** You are aggressively trying to distract the person next to you because you have a crush on him or her and you want them to like you. You correct the third time you are asked.	**Positive Correction Student Role** You are dreaming about the new bike you just got. Although you do not get it right the first time, you will if corrected.
Positive Correction Student Role You're bored, but you are not a troublemaker. You will correct the second time you are asked.	**Positive Correction Student Role** You are timid. You don't actively try to make mistakes, but somehow your lack of confidence gets in your way. You can usually get things right the second time.	**Positive Correction Student Role** You are bored, and you want everyone to know it. You will comply the third time you are asked.
Positive Correction Student Role You do it right the first time, with a smile.	**Positive Correction Student Role** You do it right the first time, with a smile.	**Positive Correction Student Role** You do it right the first time.
Positive Correction Student Role You do it right the first time, enthusiastically.	**Positive Correction Student Role** You do it right the first time.	**Positive Correction Student Role** You do it right the first time, energetically.
Positive Correction Student Role You do it right the first time, with a smile.	**Positive Correction Student Role** You do it right the first time, with a smile.	**Positive Correction Student Role** You do it right the first time.
Positive Correction Student Role You do it right the first time, enthusiastically.	**Positive Correction Student Role** You do it right the first time.	**Positive Correction Student Role** You do it right the first time, energetically.

1. In each round, one participant plays the *Teacher* and chooses (randomly for added drama) a scenario card and makes any desired change in the setup of the working space.

2. The other participants are *Students.* Out of view of the *Teacher,* each selects a student role card. The *Facilitator* will want to have enough cards for everyone such that there is a 2-to-1 ratio of compliant versus noncompliant behavior. In each round, limit the number of difficult students to roughly that ratio.

3. The *Teacher* starts the round by asking the *Students* to perform the task. After that try, the *Teacher* asks them to *Do It Again,* and can continue asking and interacting until all *Students* get it "better" or even "best." The *Teacher* can incorporate other appropriate techniques as well, and any routines with which the "class" is already familiar, such as *SLANT.*

If the group is large enough, one or more members can play *Observer* instead of *Student,* watching and assisting as needed by suggesting positive language.

4. During the round, the noncompliant *Students* do not simultaneously erupt into chaos but choose their moments, and improve as the *Teacher*'s guidance and instruction warrant.

5. The round ends when the *Teacher* is satisfied or after roughly one to three minutes.

6. After each round, discuss these questions.

For the *Teacher*:

- What off-task behavior did you notice?
- What were your most effective interventions? Why?
- What was most difficult about the activity? How did you attempt to overcome that?
- What's the biggest challenge you might face when introducing this to your classroom?

For the *Students*:

- What did you notice about the *Teacher*'s interactions with you?
- If you had to do it again, how did that change the expectation of the class?
- What did your *Teacher*'s action make you think about your less attentive peers?
- As a *Student* who was either engaged or disengaged, were there any distracting interventions? Did your *Teacher*'s actions help you to reengage, and how did you feel afterwards?
- How did this round differ from any previous one?

For all, after all rounds:

- What is your main takeaway from this activity?

Your takeaways:

_____

_____

_____

_____

TRY *DO IT AGAIN* IN THE CLASSROOM

Remember that *Do It Again* can be reused, right away or later in the session regarding the same earlier task.

1.   In your lesson plan or general routines, identify several that the class does not yet do acceptably or could do better.

2.   Prepare for those moments by anticipating how you will cut off a task if it's not up to snuff and scripting and rehearsing your *Do It Again* in advance. In your script, anticipate that one *Do It Again* may not be enough.

3.   Also script and practice any explanation of *Do It Again* that you think will benefit the class.

4.   Try *Do It Again* in the classroom.

5.   After the session, briefly note how you might want to *Do It Again* next time.

> 28 **ENTRY ROUTINE**
> 30 **TIGHT TRANSITIONS**

> 38 **STRONG VOICE**

> 5 **WITHOUT APOLOGY**
> 48 **EXPLAIN EVERYTHING**
> 49 **NORMALIZE ERROR**

TROUBLE-SHOOT

Steady On

Don't explain before *Do It Again*. If you explain, do so after students have done well.

Other Challenges

Possible Challenge	Possible Solutions

BE CREATIVE

1.   Adding a stopwatch to some routines will make the challenge of *Doing It Again* and better only more powerful.

2.   You can sometimes turn *Do It Again* into a friendly competition between different sections of the class.

> 46 **JOY FACTOR**

DO IT AGAIN

SUSTAIN YOUR PROGRESS

1. Using feedback from your study group or other peers, and reviewing your own lesson notes and observations, monitor your progress on *Do It Again*.

Date	What Needs *Do It Again*?

2. Revisit "Where Am I Now?" Are you ready to build out to some other new technique?

DO IT AGAIN

SWEAT THE DETAILS

OVERVIEW

Sweat the Details aims at being sure that even minor aspects of what your classroom and its occupants look like signal the right expectations for student conduct and behavior, without students necessarily being aware of them.

In your classroom, through preparation, create the physical, visual perception of order. Lay out expectations for how students "detail" the class and themselves as well.

Sweat the Details is preventive. In an orderly, organized place, it's harder for individuals to imagine and initiate disorder.

WHERE AM I NOW?

	Proficiency			
Comfort & Confidence	**I am brand new to *Sweat the Details* . . .**	**I'm planning but not yet *Sweating* much . . .**	**I'm beginning to *Sweat the Details* of my classroom . . .**	**I *Sweat the Details* regularly . . .**
	❏ . . . and determined to try it.	❏ . . . but see the value.	❏ . . . and like what I see.	❏ . . . and notice new details now and then.
	❏ . . . but not sure I'm enough of a neat freak to buy in.	❏ . . . because it doesn't suit me.	❏ . . . whether I really like them or not.	❏ . . . and everything looks fine.

EXPAND YOUR SKILLS AND REPERTOIRE

Some Orderly Details

Some details you can attend to; some you can expect your students to take care of or assist at:

- Clutter removed.
- Desk rows tidy.
- Shirts tucked in, hats off. Uniform guidelines add to a productive sense of order.
- Room repairs and windows looked after.
- Teacher properly attired.
- Outside hallway unlittered.

Add others you would like to see:

_____

_____

_____

_____

The Key Is Preparation

Put systems in place in advance that make it quick and easy for you or students to accomplish the goal.

1. To get students' desks in neat, crisp rows, try putting tape marks on the floor so you can instruct students to "check their desks" and move them onto their marks.

2. For neater, tidier homework, give students a homework standards rubric and sometimes collect assignments one at a time from each student's desk.

> **4 FORMAT MATTERS**
> **15 CIRCULATE**

3. As you *Circulate* during desk work, give brief feedback about details and neatness: "I don't see a name on this, Charles." "Is this your best work, Tani?" "You know I won't accept this with fringe on the paper, Danny." Also offer brief corrections, such as, "Check your punctuation here, Rhonda." "Are your columns lined up well enough to be sure you're adding down each one?"

> **31 BINDER CONTROL**

> **39 DO IT AGAIN**

> **30 TIGHT TRANSITIONS**

4. To train students not to lose materials and to keep them neatly in their binders, the first fifty times they put things in binders, have them do it together on cue, with cues: "We're going to put these at the front of your vocabulary section. Get ready and we'll open our binders on three. Ready?"

5. Want your students to raise their hands quietly and crisply to foster orderly participation? Teach them how to raise their hands and remind them "how we raise our hands here" frequently.

6. Keep transitions tight.

What other aspects of neatness and order do your students need to think of more than they do?

_____

_____

_____

PRACTICE WITH STUDY GROUP OR PARTNERS

1. In the group, who really agrees or disagrees with the basic premise of *Sweat the Details*? What is the source of any disagreement?

2. With the group, share your own list of details that matter. For the ones you generally agree on, discuss what you do or could do. For ones you don't agree on, figure out why and adjust your own list and practice as you see fit.

Useful ideas from the group:

_____

_____

_____

_____

TRY *SWEAT THE DETAILS* IN THE CLASSROOM

1. Take on one or two small issues at a time. If it's a big issue, tackle it separately.
2. If problems recur, post expectations.

SUSTAIN YOUR PROGRESS

Using feedback from your study group or other peers, and reviewing your own lesson notes and observations, monitor your progress on *Sweat the Details*.

Date	Details Mainly for My Attention	Details for Student Attention

SWEAT THE DETAILS

THRESHOLD

OVERVIEW

Threshold means meeting students at the door, setting your classroom culture expectations before they even enter the room. This is the single most important moment for setting those expectations. *Threshold* technique is part of establishing and maintaining strong positive, disciplined systems and routines in your classroom. These are the basic elements:

- *See both sides.* Stand where you can see the room and the hall.
- *Control the flow.* Stand where you control movement in and out as much as possible; it's your right and responsibility to control how quickly and when students enter.
- *Shake hands!* This builds a tone of civility and should cause each student to pause and make eye contact.
- *Reset expectations.* Use *Threshold* as an opportunity to remind and reset students who are in danger of slipping. A gentle reminder of your expectations will go a long way for students struggling to improve.
- *Use positive chatter.* Build positive rapport and connections to students with brief personalized comments—"Looking sharp, Devon!"

| 28 **ENTRY ROUTINE** |

View your *Threshold* as part of your broader *Entry Routine.* If you don't already have a conscious, effective *Entry Routine,* visit that technique at least briefly before you tackle *Threshold.*

WHERE AM I NOW?

	Proficiency			
	I am brand new to these ideas of *Threshold* . . .	I'm in the planning and practice stage, though I haven't tried *Threshold* yet in class . . .	I'm beginning to use *Threshold* . . .	I use *Threshold* regularly . . .
Comfort & Confidence	❑ . . . and excited to try it.	❑ . . . but know I can make it work.	❑ . . . and love how it works.	❑ . . . and add touches that my students love.
	❑ . . . and undecided about my ability to pull it off.	❑ . . . because I still have questions about how to do it right.	❑ . . . with mixed results I need to evaluate.	❑ . . . but I may be overdoing it or taking too long.
	❑ . . . and not sure it's for me.	❑ . . . because I still doubt its value for my classroom.	❑ . . . but it doesn't seem to work or suit me and my students.	❑ . . . but at times I let it slide.

Work from your strengths. If you find yourself in the bottom left portion, leaf through this technique to locate related ones you might prefer to work on right now.

ANALYZE THE CHAMPIONS

View the video clip, ideally more than once, and answer the following questions.

 Clip 27. Teacher Shadell Noel, Grade K

1. What does Ms. Noel do and say in the course of each greeting?
2. How much do the greetings vary in tone or other respects?
3. What has Ms. Noel noticed in her greeting with the last student? How does she respond?

EXPAND YOUR SKILLS AND REPERTOIRE

Your Current *Threshold* Practice

1. Which of these have you already incorporated into a *Threshold* routine? For those you now incorporate, how well do they seem to work? What might do with improvement? For those you don't yet incorporate, what benefit might you derive from adopting them?

   See both sides   ☐ Yes   ☐ No _____

   _____

   Control the flow   ☐ Yes   ☐ No _____

   _____

   Shake hands!   ☐ Yes   ☐ No _____

   _____

   Reset expectations   ☐ Yes   ☐ No _____

   _____

   Use positive chatter   ☐ Yes   ☐ No _____

   _____

2. Do you currently coordinate a *Threshold* routine with a broader *Entry Routine*? How so?

   | 28 **ENTRY ROUTINE** |

   _____

   _____

   _____

THRESHOLD

THRESHOLD

3. Do you notice any problems of coordination between *Threshold* and your launch of the actual lesson?

_____

_____

_____

Observe Others

Notice the behaviors of students entering other classrooms where teachers have or don't have *Threshold* down. What do you notice about the students' behaviors and about the overall efficiency with which they enter?

_____

_____

_____

Threshold Greetings

Here are various aims your greetings can serve. Which of these have you used? For each, write some wording of your own that you could use.

1. Remind students where they are or where they are going: "Ready for college today?"

_____

_____

2. Remind students what you expect of them: "I'm ready to see your best!"

_____

_____

3. Build relationships and rapport with students: "Great shot in yesterday's game!"

_____

_____

4. Tell students what is coming next: "Are you ready for today's quiz?"

_____

_____

39 DO IT AGAIN

5. Correct behavior: "You can give a stronger handshake than that!"

_____

_____

6. Recognize good behavior: "Excellent patience from you yesterday."

_____

_____

7. Reinforce academic material: "What's 15 divided by 3?"

_____

_____

PRACTICE WITH STUDY GROUP OR PARTNERS

Compare Notes

1. Discuss a *Threshold* routine you've used. What is it intended to accomplish? What do you do? How do students respond?

2. Discuss what's easy or more challenging for you in *seeing both sides, controlling the flow, shaking hands, resetting expectations,* and *using positive chatter.* What useful comments do you hear from the group?

_____

_____

_____

3. Share your ideas from "*Threshold* Greetings." Brainstorm others and write down new ones you could use.

_____

_____

_____

Threshold Role Play

This role play can work with four participants; the more the merrier. In each round, one participant is the *Teacher* and the rest are *Students.*

Facilitator: Prepare labels like the ones shown that about half the *Students* will draw from a hat each round. Use sticky name labels or provide some way to clip the label to *Students'* clothing. The rest of the *Students* do not draw labels; they politely greet the *Teacher* and comply with any directions.

THRESHOLD ROLE PLAY CLOTHING LABELS

Threshold role play **Melts down**	Threshold role play **Sneaky**
Threshold role play **New Hairstyle**	Threshold role play **Off-task**
Threshold role play **Absent Yesterday**	Threshold role play **Enthusiastic**
Threshold role play **Instigator**	Threshold role play **Struggles academically**
Threshold role play **Defiant**	Threshold role play **Absent yesterday**

Optional for *Teachers*: Choose a specific time of year when your *Threshold* is taking place—for example,

- Opening day of the school year—the first time you have ever greeted your students
- First day back from Thanksgiving break
- A sunny day in the beginning of June

1. *Students* stand "outside" the classroom, *Teacher* at the "door."

2. The *Teacher* initiates *Threshold* greetings with the idea of getting all students into the classroom quickly while at the same time building relationships, enforcing expectations, and setting the tone for the classroom. *Students*: Do *not* act out the role on your sticker. The information on the sticker is about behavior you have shown in the past. Just respond and pass on through.

3. When everyone has had a turn as *Teacher* (or periodically if the group is large), take a few minutes to reflect and take notes. Then debrief:

As *Teacher*:

- What went well for you in creating a *Threshold*? What was particularly challenging? For example, were some of the labels more challenging than others?
- What would you do differently in order to expedite your *Threshold*?
- What did students respond particularly well to?
- How did this prepare you as a teacher to create a classroom with strong academic and behavioral expectations?

As *Students*:

- What did the *Teacher* do that was effective?
- How did you feel when he or she built rapport with you?
- What messages were conveyed to you about the classroom that you were entering?
- What feedback do you have for the *Teacher* that could help him or her improve the *Threshold*?

Your takeaways:

_____

_____

_____

_____

TRY *THRESHOLD* IN THE CLASSROOM

1. In your next lesson plan, incorporate a note about *Threshold* that can strengthen its usefulness as part of your overall *Entry Routine*.

2. Look over your work in *Threshold* greetings and mentally rehearse:

Two greetings that relate back to the previous session:

_____

_____

THRESHOLD

Two greetings that connect to some activity or expectation for today:

_____

_____

3. Are any students likely to slip into the room before you've posted yourself at the door? How will you include them in the greeting and make that less likely to happen next time?

_____

_____

_____

TROUBLE-SHOOT

Steady On

| 43 **POSITIVE FRAMING** |
| 45 **WARM/STRICT** |

It's best to maintain a consistent positive tone. It can be tempting to greet some students with a smile and positive words and others with subtle verbal or nonverbal chastisements, or not to greet them at all. Are there any individuals you greet less supportively than others? Who are they? What can you do to maintain a positive tone for everyone in the class?

Other Challenges

Possible Challenge	Possible Solutions
A student... • Avoids eye contact • Responds with a silly greeting • Fails to respond to the greeting • Offers a greeting that is barely audible • Offers a weak handshake 39 **DO IT AGAIN**	*Do It Again.* Insist on (and model) desired behavior. Ensure that expectations are known and met.

THRESHOLD

BE CREATIVE

1. What greetings could you use that reflect your school's or your classroom's overall climate? Is there a phrase that, if you say it, students will be proud to say back to you?

_____

_____

2. What's the current de facto routine that takes place when the class session is over and students leave the classroom? Could that be improved by methods similar to *Threshold*?

| 20 **EXIT TICKET** |

_____

_____

SUSTAIN YOUR PROGRESS

1. Using feedback from your study group or other peers, and reviewing your own lesson notes and observations, monitor your progress on *Threshold*.

Date	Things I'm Doing Well	Ways to Improve

2. Revisit "Where Am I Now?" Are you ready to build out to some other new technique?

THRESHOLD

NO WARNINGS

OVERVIEW

"Warning" students can send a mixed message: "I'll put up with some of this, but at some point I'll react." In that case you give students the incentive to figure out how much of the behavior they can get away with.

36 **100%**

No Warnings focuses on preserving relationships through consistency and small, composed consequences rather than angry overreactions or mixed messages about partial tolerance. Strive to be

- Early in responding
- Reliable, predictable, and consistent
- Proportionate to the misbehavior

- Calm, poised, and nonjudgmental
- Private when possible, public if necessary

WHERE AM I NOW?

	Proficiency			
Comfort & Confidence	I am brand new to *No Warnings* . . .	I'm in the planning and practice stage, though I haven't tried *No Warnings* yet in class . . .	I'm beginning to try *No Warnings* in my classroom . . .	I act early, using *No Warnings* when and how it works best . . .
	❑ . . . and excited to try it.	❑ . . . but know with more practice I'll make it work.	❑ . . . and love how it basically works.	❑ . . . and am adding my own useful subtleties.
	❑ . . . and undecided about my ability to pull it off.	❑ . . . because I still have questions about how to do it right.	❑ . . . with mixed results I need to evaluate.	❑ . . . but still have wrinkles to iron out.
	❑ . . . and nervous about it.	❑ . . . because I'm still nervous.	❑ . . . but it doesn't seem to work or suit me.	❑ . . . but when a challenge is large, what I do doesn't work as well as I need it to.

Work from your strengths. If you find yourself in the bottom left portion, leaf through this technique to locate related ones you might prefer to work on right now.

ANALYZE THE CHAMPIONS

View the video clip, ideally more than once, and answer the following questions.

Clip 11. Teacher Nikki Frame, Grade 6

1. Ms. Frame has a *No Warnings* moment with Brett. What is it? What's the consequence?
2. She also returns to Brett shortly after. How and why?

EXPAND YOUR SKILLS AND REPERTOIRE

Students will take advantage of as many free passes they think you'll give them. Champion teachers address deliberate flouting of rules the first time so that the rule still *rules*.

A warning is not taking such action; it is *threatening* that you *might* take it. This is counterproductive and often gets in the way of taking action.

Teacher says: "I don't want to see you do that again."

Students think: "It's okay if we disobey, just not too much or doing the same thing too many times."

"We can play around, just not too much. It's okay if each of us does something bad only once."

You *never* want to punish incompetence. Your response to incompetence should always teach or direct a student how to comply:

"Amy, try that again, and pay attention to how you . . ."

"We don't have more time now, but let's you and I practice a little more after class."

> 37 **WHAT TO DO**
> 39 **DO IT AGAIN**

"Put your legs under your desk, put your pencil down, and keep your eyes on me."

Proactively Remind

A reminder is not the same thing as a warning: it does not directly follow a flagrant violation, and it can be framed as a positive expectation. It's given at a different moment when you choose to remind everyone in the room about some behavior that may have slid but can be brought back in line.

> 43 **POSITIVE FRAMING**

Sometimes misbehaviors arise because a student is acting in good faith but has run out of stamina and is (not very consciously) slipping off task. At those times, give the benefit of the doubt and remind him individually about *100%*.

> 36 **100%**

Effective Interventions

Effective interventions are all of the following.

Early
Acting early is a favor to your students. With a minor consequence, you are heading off the need for a major one later.

Reliable, Predictable, and Consistent
Be predictable and consistent so that students won't stray into guessing or even testing how you might react. Focus their attention on whatever it was that they did or didn't do that compelled you to act. Giving consequences right when needed will make future misbehaviors less frequent.

> 37 **WHAT TO DO**

What allows you to consistently extinguish misbehaviors is having a scaled system of incrementally larger consequences that you can deliver fairly and without hesitation.

What tempts you away from being predictable and consistent about correcting misbehaviors?

_____

_____

_____

Proportionate to the Misbehavior

If you play your biggest consequence card right away, students will know you have nothing left in your hand, and they will have no further incentive to change behavior. Start small when the misbehavior is small.

| 34 **SEAT SIGNALS** |

Keep incentives in play if you can. When possible, take things away in pieces. Some great teachers scale their responses using a consequence system—for example, colored behavior cards (with elementary school students), "scholar dollars" (with middle school students), or demerits (with high school students).

What's one student behavior you need to extinguish? What scaled incremental system of consequences do you or could you use?

_____

_____

_____

_____

If you already have a proportional system of incentives, such as tokens or merits and demerits, that you can bestow or withdraw in varying amounts proportional to what the student deserves, how much and how effectively does your system serve to foster and maintain correct behaviors? If you don't have such a system, how might one support your *No Warnings*?

_____

_____

_____

_____

Calm, Poised, and Impersonal

| 38 **STRONG VOICE** |
| 47 **EMOTIONAL CONSTANCY** |

Avoid signaling anger or vindictiveness. Focus on the now ("I'm hoping you'll show us your best from here on out"). Move quickly back to your academic objective.

If you can, identify a recent classroom teaching moment when you were aware of some personal anger when you were dealing with a misbehavior. In retrospect, what was the likely source of that anger? How did the anger affect your reaction to the misbehavior?

_____

_____

_____

_____

Are there any misbehaviors that have happened in your classroom or that you foresee happening, for which you don't have in mind a set of scaled responses from which you can easily choose? What specific actions could the set consist of?

_____

_____

_____

_____

Private When Possible, Public If Necessary

If a behavior doesn't affect anyone else, deal with it privately. But if a student has appeared to get away with something in front of the class, the class needs to know that there was accountability—that you acted.

PRACTICE WITH STUDY GROUP OR PARTNERS

Compare Experience

In breakout groups, or the group as a whole share, discuss, and compare:

1. The type of anger, frozen calm, or other states of mind that challenge you when misbehaviors occur
2. What works for you to free your choice and use of actions from whatever negative thoughts or feelings might be going on inside you
3. How you do or could maintain *Strong Voice* at these times

> 38 **STRONG VOICE**

Sequential Consequences

For the situations listed here (or other situations you have needed to address), as a group, brainstorm and create sequences of consequences through which you can advance as far as warranted, reliably, fairly, and without hesitation. For example, if two students were jostling each other at some task, the set might be as follows:

1. Require the two to repeat that moment of the task without jostling.
2. Require them to apologize.
3. Take away a small piece of a privilege, such as part of recess.
4. Take away an entire privilege for a period of time and make a phone call to the parents.

Situation 1: At a moment when quiet is clearly expected, a student begins a low grumbling chant.

Situation 2: The class is instructed to stand. One student remains seated, slouching, arms folded.

Situation 3: No hats are allowed in class. You call that to a student's attention as he enters, but when you begin to teach, the student puts the hat back on.

Situation 4: You called for *SLANT* and got it from everyone except someone in the middle of the class.

Situation 5: Two students begin to argue across the room while you're teaching.

NO WARNINGS

Your takeaways:

_____

_____

_____

_____

TRY *NO WARNINGS* IN THE CLASSROOM

| 11 **DRAW THE MAP** |
| 15 **CIRCULATE** |

1. Draw or revisit your map with *No Warnings* in mind. Be sure that the layout of seating and passage space allows you to *Circulate* and oversee consequences with the least possible disruption to your teaching or to other students.

2. Is there any behavioral standard or expectation for which your class may need more explanation or a fresh reminder?

3. List any small misbehaviors you are likely to encounter in your next classroom session. Write down the set of responses you may want to draw on. Note which response is likely to be your best choice for each. Then do the same for larger misbehaviors.

4. For at least one potential deliberate violation, come up with a sequence of consequences that you can deliver reliably, fairly, and without hesitation. Follow the general advice in "Sequential Consequences" in the previous section, such as this set of steps:

- Require student(s) to repeat an action more appropriately.
- Require them to apologize.
- Take away a small piece of a privilege.
- Take away an entire privilege for a period of time and make a phone call to a parent.

5. Rehearse the sequence in *Strong Voice*.

6. If there's any ambiguity about what consequences you can administer or call on from other school officials, clear it up now.

TROUBLE-SHOOT

Steady On

1. The name *No Warnings* might suggest that this whole technique is about resisting an urge to warn, chastise, or otherwise be controlled by frustration. Really though, it's about being proactive with many other techniques for controlling classroom culture. Use *No Warnings* as a springboard into (or back into) the other techniques.

2. Resist allowing your positive relations with certain class members to lead you to "warn" them in a friendly way. In the classroom, where compliance is the issue, be equally calm, impersonal, and proactive with everyone.

Other Challenges

Possible Challenge	Possible Solutions

SUSTAIN YOUR PROGRESS

1. Using your own classroom observations, monitor your progress on *No Warnings*.

Date	How I Handled a Deliberate Misbehavior	Possible Improvement

2. Revisit "Where Am I Now?" Are you ready to build out to some other technique?

POSITIVE FRAMING

OVERVIEW

Positive Framing means narrating the world you want your students to see even while you are relentlessly improving it, making corrections consistently and positively. It depends also on intervening when student behavior requires it. To frame positively,

- Live in the now. Talk about what should happen next.
- Assume the best.
- Allow plausible anonymity.

- Build momentum by narrating the positive.
- Challenge your students.
- Talk expectations and aspiration.

| 45 **WARM/STRICT** |

Please do not misinterpret this technique. It is not suggesting that you avoid correcting nonproductive behavior. *Positive Framing* is about the hard work of *correcting* consistently and positively in a way that shows your abiding faith in students.

WHERE AM I NOW?

	Proficiency			
Comfort & Confidence	I am brand new to some aspects of *Positive Framing* . . .	I'm in the planning and practice stage, though I haven't tried *Positive Framing* yet in class . . .	I'm beginning to try *Positive Framing* in my classroom . . .	I use *Positive Framing* . . .
	❑ . . . and excited to try the technique.	❑ . . . but know with more practice I'll make it work.	❑ . . . and love how it basically works.	❑ . . . and am adding my own distinctive positivity.
	❑ . . . and undecided about my ability to pull them off.	❑ . . . because I still have questions about how to do it right.	❑ . . . with mixed results I need to evaluate.	❑ . . . but I may need to intervene more than I do.
	❑ . . . and not at all sure they're for me.	❑ . . . because, frankly, I still have doubts.	❑ . . . but it doesn't seem to work or suit me.	❑ . . . but am still absorbing some of its methods.

Work from your strengths. If you find yourself in the bottom left portion, leaf through this technique to locate related ones you might prefer to work on right now.

EXPAND YOUR SKILLS AND REPERTOIRE

Using *Positive Framing* means intervening to correct student behavior in a positive and constructive way. *Positive Framing* is based on evidence that people are motivated by the positive far more than the negative and by a vision of a positive outcome more than by a vision of avoiding a negative one.

Positive Framing does *not* mean avoiding interventions or talking only about the positive behaviors you see. You do need to respond to off-task or nonconstructive behaviors, and you need to fix and improve them consistently and with clear and firm consequences when necessary. But *as you do these things,* your interventions will be far more effective if you can frame them positively.

Precise Praise can be used to reinforce behaviors that were already correct.

> 44 **PRECISE PRAISE**

Live in the Now

Positive Framing can help you eliminate nagging—harping on what students have already done wrong. Talk about what should or even must happen next. Focus corrective interactions on the things students should do *right now* to succeed from this point forward. There's a different time and place for processing what went wrong—not in the midst of a lesson. Give instructions describing what the next move on the path to success is. If necessary, you can do so very firmly and forcefully.

> 37 **WHAT TO DO**
> 38 **STRONG VOICE**

"Show me SLANT!"

"Keira, I need your eyes forward."

"Show me your eyes, fifth grade."

"Charles, Tina is describing the setting. Your eyes should be on the speaker."

"Third grade, Tina is describing the setting. Our eyes should be on the speaker."

Not: ~~"You weren't SLANTing."~~

Not: ~~"Keira, stop looking back at Tanya."~~

Not: ~~"Fifth grade, some of us are looking out the window."~~

Not: ~~"Charles, I'm tired of asking you to track the speaker.~~

Not: ~~"Third grade, you're not on the speaker."~~

Assume the Best

Show that you assume your students will obey you. Don't attribute to ill intent what could be the result of distraction, lack of practice, or genuine misunderstanding.

Until you know a poor action was intentional, your public discussion of it should remain positive, showing that you assume your students have tried (and will try) to do as you've asked.

"Just a minute, class; some people seem to have forgotten to push in their chairs."

"Whoops. The chair part seems to have slipped our minds, so let's go back and get it just right."

"Just a minute, fourth grade. A couple of people were so excited to write about Ronald Dahl that they went ahead before I told them to start."

"I hope we didn't forget our rules about tracking, Tina. Give us a second before you start."

Not:
~~"Just a minute, class; some people don't seem to think they have to push in their chairs when we line up."~~

Not: ~~"Just a minute, class; I asked for chairs pushed in, and some people decided not to do it."~~

Not: ~~"Fourth grade, none of us should be trying to sneak ahead of the rest of the class."~~

Not: ~~"Tina, please wait to answer until Jeffrey decides to join us."~~

Framing positively as shown in the left column costs you nothing, because *you can still proceed from there to deliver any consequence you choose.* And even while you deliver it, you can and should still assume the best. By removing any judgment about student intentionality from the discussion, you also remove much emotion from the consequence. The message is

"We do things a certain way, and we fix it when we fail to do that."

Not: ~~"You did this on purpose, and now you have to take the consequences."~~

Assuming the worst makes you appear weak—as though you're waiting for deliberate misbehavior because you expect it! By contrast, showing that you assume your students are always trying to comply with your wishes demonstrates that you're in charge. Which of these two reveals your suspicion that Charles will disobey you? Cross that one out.

"If you can't sit up, Charles, I'll have to keep you in from recess."

"Show me your best SLANT, Charles."

Make your first intervention the one on the right, then walk away (for the moment) as if you couldn't imagine a world in which he wouldn't do it. Or say something like, "Charles, I need your eyes," which also asserts nothing about Charles's intention, only what he needs to do.

Thank you can be strong language. Show that you assume the best by thanking students as you give them a command. You can still apply a consequence if needed.

"Thank you for taking your seats in three, two, one . . ."

Allow Plausible Anonymity

When students need behavioral correction, allow them to remain plausibly anonymous *as long as they are making a good-faith effort.* When possible, begin by correcting them without using their names. Don't immediately identify them as posing a problem. In most cases this will yield the fastest results.

"Straighten the line."

Not: ~~"Tony's out of line."~~

"Check yourself to make sure you've done exactly what I've asked."

Not: ~~"Rhondesia, make sure you did what I said."~~

"Fourth grade, check yourself to make sure you're in your best SLANT with your notes page in front of you."

Not: ~~"Jason, I want to see you in SLANT with your notes page in front of you."~~

"Stop. Some people aren't managing to follow directions the whole way, so let's try that again."

42 **NO WARNINGS**

Even when good faith is missing, don't generally make "naming names" your first move. You can still deliver *consequences* anonymously, stressing shared responsibility for maintaining a culture of order and excellence.

Build Momentum by Narrating the Positive

Narrate your strength, not your weakness. Narrate the evidence that students are doing as they're asked—of things getting better, of momentum building in your favor. Call your students' attention to this and then normalize it.

Narrating the positive: "I see lots of hands. The left side of the room is really with it!"

Adding momentum: "I see five, six, seven hands. Now ten hands ready to start reading *Hatchet*!"

Narrating the Positive	Narrating the Negative
"I need three people to fix it. Make sure you fix it if that's you! Now I need two. We're almost there. Ah, thank you, ladies and gentlemen; let's get right into it!"	~~"I need three people to fix it. And one more student doesn't seem to be ready, so now I need four. Some people don't appear to be listening. I am waiting, gentlemen. If I have to give detentions, I will."~~

In the right column, the teacher tells a story that no one wants to hear, and the "gentlemen" right away smell fear, weakness, and the inevitable unhappy ending because everything is wrong and getting worse and unlikely to result in any consequences. It's a narration normalizing student impunity. Never litanize your woes. Consider the next two examples. Circle the positive one and cross out the negative.

"Okay, here we go! I see pencils journaling. I see those ideas rolling out. Jamie's ready to roll. Keep it up, Marcus!"

"Okay, here we go . . . Not everyone has begun yet. Do you need me to help you think of a topic, Jamie? Marcus, I asked you not to stop. Let me remind you, class, that this is not an optional activity."

The narration on the left creates positive momentum. Supply this next scene with a narration that is positive and builds momentum:

You've just told the class of twenty-five to put away their books. About half the class does so quickly and gives you the usual *SLANT*. Another handful are slower. One sighs as she does it. Several poke around in their packs before straightening up. One is slower than all the rest because he's still looking at a picture in the book. The person next to him asks him a quiet question.

_____

_____

_____

_____

Challenge!

Challenge students. They love it. They love to prove they can do things and to compete, even against themselves and friends. They love to win. In a classroom, you'll find that challenging them as groups is usually better than challenging them as individuals.

"You guys have been doing a great job this week. Let's see if you can take it up a notch."

Build competition into the day—again, usually as groups—by asking them to compete against:

- Other groups within the class
- Other groups outside the class (the other homeroom)
- An impersonal foe: the clock
- How well they might do it better than "acceptably" a year or grade from now
- An abstract standard
- New circumstances

POSITIVE FRAMING

"You've got the idea, but let me hear you use the word 'elusive' in your answer. Can you do it?!"

"The sixth-grade girls are *killing* it, boys. Can you keep up?"

"You guys have been doing a great job this week. Let's see if you can take it up a notch."

"I love the tracking I see. I wonder what happens when I move back here."

"Ms. Austin said she didn't think you guys could knock out your math tables louder than her class. And they're sitting across the hall right now. Let's show 'em what we've got . . ."

Write three challenges you could lay down the next time you teach.

1. _____

_____

2. _____

_____

3. _____

_____

Talk Expectations and Aspiration

Talk about who your students are becoming and where they can be going. Frame praise in those terms: "Make sure you get 100% today."

When your class looks great, tell them they look "college," that they look like "scholars," that you feel as though you're sitting in the room with future presidents and doctors and executives.

Let them know that the goal is not for them to please you but to leave you behind on a long journey toward a more distant dream and success of their own. Let your praise set a goal larger than your own opinion.

"If you finish early, great; check your work. Make sure you get 100% today. Every week, college gets closer."

(To a fourth grader) "Good, Juan. Now let me hear you make it a fifth-grade answer by using the word 'product'."

"Can you answer that in the words of a scientist [historian/editor/manager]?"

"When you get to college, your thesis statements are going to blow your professors away. Let's see if we can do this one more time so you really take the campus by storm."

Write three challenges tailored to a subject and grade level you teach or plan to teach.

1. _____

_____

2. _____

_____

3. _____

_____

Avoid Rhetorical Questions and Contingencies

Don't ask questions that you don't want answered. Don't pretend to be asking a question when you aren't. Don't make a charade by asking "Would you like to join us, David?" Just say, "Thank you for joining us on the rug, David."

Don't say "I'll wait" unless you intend to do that regardless of what the student does. Saying you'll wait is handing power to students by making your actions contingent on theirs. If you'll wait, say how long, and wait that full time. But this would be stronger, more positive, and productive:

"We [or I] need you with us."

Analyze These Transcripts

As you may notice, each of these transcripts is a series of moments excerpted from a classroom session, rather than one continuous moment. In each transcript, underline the key words of each example of *Positive Framing*. On the right, note briefly what positive feelings the framing evokes—excited, motivated, cared about, and so on.

Teacher Emily Volpe

1	*Ms. Volpe:*	Wow, I see everyone getting started right away; excellent . . . Joshua is perfect right now. I see one, two, three perfect SLANTS, four, five, six . . .	
2	*Ms. Volpe:*	*(shortly thereafter, timing)* One minute . . .	
3	*Ms. Volpe:*	*(later)* I was really pleased with your transition; you should be very proud of yourselves.	
4	*Ms. Volpe:*	*(later)* Four, everything down in three, two, one . . . Melanie, pencils down now, everything away.	
5	*Ms. Volpe:*	*(later)* All right, students of Rochester Prep, you're showing me excellence right now; I'm very proud of you.	
6	*Ms. Volpe:*	*(later)* Who can help me with the *Do Now* by reading me the directions? Look at all those hands; excellent. Trinity, go ahead.	
7	*Trinity:*	*(reading from the overhead)* "Answer the following questions, using complete sentences where appropriate."	

8	*Ms. Volpe:*	Good, and I noted complete sentences because some of you are forgetting to write in complete sentences on your homework, and I know that you know here at Rochester Prep we should answer in a complete sentence.	
9	*Ms. Volpe:*	*(later)* Number one, What part or parts of a cell are only found in plant cells? Awesome. I like how I see all those hands. Natalia, help me out.	

Teacher Janelle Austin, Part 1

In this math lesson about bar graphs, Ms. Austin is using a countdown while the students prepare for class.

1	*Ms. Austin:*	. . . and now, Imarius, I am on one. Good afternoon, Harvard.	
2	*Class:*	Good afternoon, Ms. Austin!	
3	*Ms. Austin:*	What is our objective for today? *(Nearly all students raise hands.)* Oooo, look at those hands.	
4	*Ms. Austin:*	*(later in the lesson)* Okay, here we go. Let's go with A first. What did we do a long time ago when we first did patterns? It was a while ago, I know. It was a while ago. When we first did patterns . . . I *love* the track that I'm seeing now. I wonder what happens if I move around the room. *(walks to the back of the room and takes a pencil from an empty desk)*	
5	*Ms. Austin:*	What is that first step—oh, second step, sorry . . . that we do after we circle the rule? We need to draw them. Brookleen, track her.	
6	*Ms. Austin:*	*(later)* I see hands up there that are ready to read. We only have three choices left, so, let's see. All right! I need someone with voice. *(looks around the room)* Allison, do you have voice for me?	
7	*Allison:*	Yes.	

8	*Ms. Austin:*	You sure? All right, hands down; Allison's reading.	
9	*Allison:*	*(reading)* "August has four more birthdays than June."	
10	*Ms. Austin:*	All right, don't say anything because I need to see my fingers. True . . . for Jasmine . . . true or false? Let's see 'em. Now you can't do this, 'cause I can't tell. *(holds two fingers together instead of spread as a V)* Looks like one big finger. *(She waves first one finger in the air and then two, indicating that students should use one finger to indicate that they think the answer is true and two fingers to indicate that the answer is false.)*	
11	*Ms. Austin:*	True or false? I like how Brookleen took her time quickly to read and make sure she knew *her* answer. She didn't look around the room to look at anybody else's fingers; she wanted to make sure that *she* knew *her* answer.	
12	*Ms. Austin:*	*(later)* Oh, boy, we're down to the last two. I hope one of these works. That wouldn't be good if it didn't. Oh well, we'll see. Here we go. I need someone to read C. I need voice though. Kayla, we're going to work on your voice, okay?	
13	*Kayla:*	Okay.	
14	*Ms. Austin:*	Oh, yeah, because I know you have it. I want to hear it. C, read it—I really like the enthusiasm that I'm seeing. This column right here *(points to column)* is really grabbing; hold to it. Jordan, I know you're trying to persevere today; keep on trying, okay? All right, let's hear C . . . Summer, use your voice!	
15	*Summer:*	*(begins to read C)*	

POSITIVE FRAMING

Teacher Janelle Austin, Part 2

Part 2 takes place later in the period.

1	Ms. Austin:	*(pointing to graph on the board)* What is this scale counting by right now? What is that scale counting by? Obsession, what is that scale counting by? *(Entire class tracks Obsession as she reads the answer.)*	
2	Obsession:	Two.	
3	Ms. Austin:	Oooo, look at that track. I didn't even have to say it. It's counting by two.	
4	Ms. Austin:	*(later)* What do we have to do for each one of those things?	
5	Class:	Draw four lines.	
6	Ms. Austin:	Draw four lines. So for A and C, let's draw our four lines. Bryesha, make sure you're drawing your four lines and nothing else. Draw your four lines. Draw your four lines. Oh! Shantay has it. *(gives Shantay a high five)*	
7	Ms. Austin:	*(later in the class period)* Where's my SLANT? *(waits for students to SLANT)* Jordan, I see you trying to keep it together, sir. All right, turn your page.	
8	Ms. Austin:	*(later in the class period; leaning over Jordan's desk)* I know you're having a hard day. Let's see how you do, okay? *(Ms. Austin straightens up and begins to move around the room.)* Emmarius is done. Don't slam your pencil. I'll know you're done when I see your track. Pencils down in five … four … three … I just saw Bryesha go from the top of the bar that way over here *(points to a bar on the bar graph)* so she could make sure she had the right number. Two … pencils down, and one.	

| 9 | *Ms. Austin:* | *(later)* When we do heads down, eyes closed, what do we do? We take a what? | |

| 10 | *Student:* | Vote? |
| 11 | *Ms. Austin:* | A vote. Very good. How come we didn't choose B, "crackers and candy"? Why not? Why not, Tiantay? I like you just tracked, Deonte, without even a word. | |

| 12 | *Ms. Austin:* | *(later)* Now, it's not enough to just tell me that you chose that answer. Here are Ms. Austin's questions. Here we go. Show me SLANT. Don't lose it. You guys have been doing an awesome job persevering. Here we go! | |

Rewrite Positively

Rewrite the statements in this exercise as directed, reframing key phrases and sentences in a more positive light to ensure that students are fully respected and challenged, while avoiding rhetorical questions and contingencies. Here are good examples.

Live in the now:	"Keenan, I need your eyes forward." "James, put your pencil down."
Assume the best:	"Ooops, it looks like we forgot to push in our chairs; let's go back and try that again."
Allow plausible anonymity:	"Check yourself to make sure you did exactly what I asked." "Tigers, let's raise our hands again with no calling out."
Narrate the positive; build momentum:	"I need four people to put their pencils down; now I'm only missing one, and now we're ready to start our oral drill."
Challenge:	"Let's see if we can get our homework out silently in ten seconds. Ready, set, go!"
Talk expectations and aspiration:	"The Titans always track." "Who has a college-level answer?"

Rewrite this statement in each way:

"Just a minute, Cindy; absolutely nobody is tracking right now except Winston and Beth."

Live in the now: _____

_____

Assume the best: _____

_____

Allow plausible anonymity: _____

_____

Narrate the positive; build momentum: _____

_____

Challenge: _____

_____

Talk expectations and aspiration: _____

_____

Reframe each of the next statements twice, changing types (*Live in the now, Challenge,* and so on) between the first and second. Write the type name in the parentheses.

1. "Kea, stop fooling around."

   (_____): _____

   _____

   (_____): _____

   _____

2. "Maria still isn't ready."

   (_____): _____

   _____

   (_____): _____

   _____

3. "I don't see everyone SLANTing."

   (_____): _____

   _____

   (_____): _____

   _____

4. "Tyrone, Jamal can't hear you."

(_____): _____

_____

(_____): _____

_____

5. "You can't participate until you behave."

(_____): _____

_____

(_____): _____

_____

6. "I see Lester, Robby, and Ana still talking."

(_____): _____

_____

(_____): _____

_____

7. "Are you ready to get started, Jennifer?"

(_____): _____

_____

(_____): _____

_____

8. "We're going to have a better day today, right, David?"

(_____): _____

_____

(_____): _____

_____

PRACTICE WITH STUDY GROUP OR PARTNERS

Group Discussion

1.   Referring to your individual work on "Analyze These Transcripts," compare Emily Volpe's use of *Positive Framing* to Janelle Austin's. What do they have in common, and what's different? Why are the differences important?

2.   Compare your work in "Rewrite Positively." Did members of the group choose some types of *Positive Framing* very often or avoid other types? Talk about why.

3.   How does Ms. Austin's use of *Positive Framing* impact the behavioral expectations in her classroom?

4.   How might your *Positive Framing* need to differ (or not) from that of other members of the group who teach at a different grade level or in some different setting?

5.   Share and compare your responses to the other exercises in "Expand Your Skills and Repertoire."

Do It Again Using *Positive Framing*

The group *Facilitator* may want to prepare for this competitive activity by creating or soliciting original scenarios from members of the group, to use in addition to or instead of the ones provided here.

If your group is large enough to divide into smaller groups of about four, divide and use these instructions in a competition. If not large enough to divide, give everyone a chance to play the role of *Teacher,* and vote as a group on who did it best, including a discussion of how.

1.   In each round, a subgroup chooses one of its members to be *Teacher.*

2.   Everyone else (all groups combined) mingle as *Students. Students* from the *Teacher*'s subgroup do their best to live up to the *Teacher*'s expectations. *Students* from outside that subgroup may do less than their best, to varying degrees, but no one purposely does the defiantly "wrong" thing.

3.   The *Teacher* conducts the *Students* through a straightforward set of behaviors, such as a procedure for classroom dismissal using *Positive Framing* and *Do It Again.*

4.   Insofar as the *Teacher*'s techniques are effective, the outside-subgroup *Students* improve.

5.   Anticipate letting each round run for a minute or two. In practice, either the *Teacher* or the group *Facilitator* can let the round continue longer or stop it at any point.

6.   After each subgroup has had at least one chance for a member to be *Teacher,* as a whole group discuss the challenges that each *Teacher* faced, and vote on "Teacher of the Day."

You can use these scenarios more than once.

Scenario 1. Elementary or Middle School, Dismissal for Lunch
In your classroom, the procedure for dismissal is (1) stand up, (2) push in your chairs, and (3) line up at the door.

Now it's just before lunch. You're wrapping up a successful math class that modeled exactly what you expect from your students. The expectation is that the lining up should be quick and quiet.

Scenario 2. Middle or High School, In-Class Transition
In your classroom, the procedure is as follows: (1) each student places his or her book under the chair; (2) the teacher passes a stack of paper, and the students take one and pass the rest down the row; (3) the students put their heading on the paper and then put their pen or pencil down.

The class has just finished using its books, which now need to be put away, and you need students each to have out one sheet of blank paper that you will provide. The expectation is that the transition will be silent and quick.

TRY *POSITIVE FRAMING* IN THE CLASSROOM

1. By reviewing a recording of your teaching, having a supportive peer observe, or recalling your memories, review your experience in previous teaching with moments when you know you were framing negatively or more publicly than may have been necessary. Also notice where you used rhetorical questions or got tangled by a contingency statement. Try reframing some things you've said in the past.

2. Where in your next lesson plan do you need to be most ready to keep things positively framed? Prepare what you can say to frame and narrate the positive.

3. In your classroom, after employing *Positive Framing* and other techniques like *What to Do* and *Break It Down*, what consequences will you be prepared to assign, including and beyond *Do It Again*?

> 16 **BREAK IT DOWN**
> 39 **DO IT AGAIN**
> 45 **WARM/STRICT**

4. For moments when a consequence is your best first response, what consequences will you likely lead with?

> 42 **NO WARNINGS**
> 47 **EMOTIONAL CONSTANCY**

TROUBLE-SHOOT

Steady On

Positive Framing takes long practice to perfect. Rather than dismiss it as "idealistic," recognize that it in no way reduces your options for effectively controlling the class and individual students, or for administering a consequence.

Other Challenges

Possible Challenge	Possible Solutions

POSITIVE FRAMING

BE CREATIVE

Spend a while reflecting on the aspirations you most want to foster in your students.

SUSTAIN YOUR PROGRESS

1. Using feedback from your study group or other peers, and reviewing your own lesson notes and observations, monitor your progress on *Positive Framing*.

Date	Smart *Positive Framing*	A Frame to Improve On

2. Revisit "Where Am I Now?" Are you ready to build out to some other new technique?

PRECISE PRAISE

OVERVIEW

Precise Praise brings a high degree of strategy and intentionality to positive reinforcement—one of the strongest tools available to teachers. The following are some key ideas:

- Giving plenty of acknowledgment in response to students' meeting your expectations and saving praise for when students have exceeded expectations
- Using the power of public praise when appropriate
- Using praise to reinforce actions, as specifically as possible, especially behaviors and actions that students can choose to do
- Using praise to reinforce both behavioral and academic skills
- Maintaining sincerity and honesty in giving positive reinforcement

> 43 **POSITIVE FRAMING**

WHERE AM I NOW?

	Proficiency			
Comfort & Confidence	**I am brand new to *Precise Praise* . . .**	**I'm familiar now with the concepts of *Precise Praise* but haven't applied them yet in class . . .**	**I'm beginning to try *Precise Praise* in my classroom . . .**	**I employ *Precise Praise* for both academic and supportive behaviors . . .**
	❏ . . . and excited to try it.	❏ . . . but know with practice I'll make them work.	❏ . . . and love how it basically works.	❏ . . . choosing well between praise, acknowledgment, and criticism.
	❏ . . . and undecided about my ability to pull it off.	❏ . . . because I still have questions about how to do it right.	❏ . . . but need to get more precise.	❏ . . . but I'm still working on distinctions.
	❏ . . . and not at all sure it's for me.	❏ . . . because I still have serious doubts.	❏ . . . but it doesn't seem to work or suit me.	❏ . . . but when class isn't going well, I do it poorly.

Work from your strengths. If you find yourself in the bottom left portion, leaf through this technique to locate related ones you might prefer to work on right now.

ANALYZE THE CHAMPIONS

View the video clip, ideally more than once, and answer the following question. See the end of the technique for some observations about the clip.

Clip 11. Teacher Nikki Frame, Grade 6

What does Ms. Frame say after a student misreads a word and tries again?

EXPAND YOUR SKILLS AND REPERTOIRE

Positive reinforcement is one of the most powerful tools in a classroom, and many experts say that it should be given three times as often as criticism and correction. However, any powerful tool can be used poorly or for naught. Poorly implemented positive reinforcement is no exception.

Rules of Thumb

Differentiate Acknowledgment from Praise

Acknowledge when expectations have been met. An acknowledgment describes what a student has done, often with explicit thanks, often with positivity, but without value judgment and exaggeration.

Save praise for remarkable effort or performance beyond expectation.

Praising when expectations have merely been met undercuts those expectations—as if you were surprised they were met.

Acknowledgment does not have to be bland or dull. Develop a repertoire of enthusiastic acknowledgments.

"Johnny B! Bringing his tools to work today!"

Reinforce Loudly; Criticize Quietly

Positive reinforcement is often most powerful when public (there are exceptions). Public reinforcement motivates others to strive and gives the recipient attention that can make him or her feel proud and honored.

As will be discussed in "Keep It Real," the best form of reinforcement is honest and real. Sometimes quiet reinforcement has advantages; for example, a whispered moment of praise can have a strong effect on a student who's not expecting it: "You're really impressing me today. Keep it up." Or you can make it memorable by delivering a very formal request ("Mr. Ramirez, may I speak with you please") that leads to quiet and entirely unexpected reinforcement ("Your essay was truly outstanding. You should be very proud of your work.")

| 43 **POSITIVE FRAMING** |
| 45 **WARM/STRICT** |
| 47 **EMOTIONAL CONSTANCY** |

Giving criticism does not mean being negative. It means providing more guidance or correction in a positive, *Warm/Strict*, emotionally constant manner. Whispered (or even nonverbal) corrections allow students to self-correct without being "called out" in public. Even when behavior is clearly defiant, quiet criticism is best; it keeps the student "off stage" as much as possible and makes you appear to be in control.

Reinforce Actions, Not Traits

Reinforce as specifically as possible, and focus on behaviors and actions that students can choose to do. A student can't decide to be "smart," but a student can decide to "work hard and persevere." When you praise the latter, you make it more likely that the student will choose to do it again and brave future constructive risk.

| 3 **STRETCH IT** |

Praising students as "smart"—especially for doing something they might not be able to repeat every time—can incline them to take fewer risks and *Stretch It* less; because they believe they are already "smart," they choose not to risk that reputation by going a step beyond. They learn to fear challenge rather than loving it—and seeing it as a reward.

Keep It Real

Students who meet expectations deserve to be noticed and acknowledged as frequently as possible, but even young students learn to listen for and discount insincere praise, often as an indication that their work is inferior. Most insincere praise is meant to bolster self-esteem. It's fine to bolster self-esteem with

"Nice job getting ready, Bill."

"You did it just like I asked, Shayna. Thank you."

But say these kinds of things only if Bill or Shayna really did do it, and not as a roundabout message to Sally, sitting next to Shayna, who has gotten sidetracked. Correct Sally more directly so that you jeopardize neither your relationship with either student nor the relationship between them.

Students who do something truly exceptional also deserve to be told (praised) that what they did was above and beyond. Praising usually adds a judgment to a mere description:

"Fantastic work, John!"

"That's really great, Niles."

"Great job, Brian. Thanks."

But keep the distinction clear about acknowledging met expectations and praising what exceeds them. Confusing the two is, in the long run, both ineffective and destructive. Consider this statement that praises a student for meeting but not exceeding expectations: "Great job bringing a pencil to class today, John!" Why, thinks the rest of the class, is John being praised for doing what they've been doing all along? Are the rules different for him because he hasn't been bringing his pencil? Has he really been "great"? Is the teacher's praise that cheap to come by?

Recent research by Carol Dweck demonstrates that students have come to interpret frequent praise as a sign that they are doing poorly and need encouragement from their teacher. They see cheap praise—often rightly—as a marker of failure. In many teachers' experience, for students who easily do things worthy of some degree of praise, continuous praise trivializes its value.

If you suspect you overpraise, review a recording of yourself in the classroom. How often does it happen? When and why?

_____

_____

Acknowledge, Praise, or Criticize

These common classroom occurrences warrant a response. Following the example in the first, write what type of response is called for (acknowledge, praise, or criticize) and what you would say.

1. A student who struggles to track catches herself looking out the window, and tracks the speaker.

Response: *Acknowledgment*

You say: *"Thank you for tracking, Mahogany. You're really getting it now."*

2. A chronically unprepared student brings in her pencil and begins class correctly.

Response: _____

You say: _____

_____

3.   A student answers your question with a complete sentence, as you expect.

Response: _____

You say: _____

_____

4.   Students get to work immediately at the beginning of class.

Response: _____

You say: _____

_____

5.   Students are enthusiastically participating in class, raising hands, smiling, and tracking.

Response: _____

You say: _____

_____

6.   A student delivers a well-thought-out complete answer of unusually high quality.

Response: _____

You say: _____

_____

7.   A student uses the proper *Seat Signal* in September.

Response: _____

You say: _____

_____

8.   A student uses proper *Seat Signals* in February.

Response: _____

You say: _____

_____

9.   A student turns a negative attitude around since the morning.

Response: _____

You say: _____

_____

10. A student who normally shouts out the answer raises her hand.

Response: _____

You say: _____

_____

11. A student who is normally very well disciplined in class shouts out an answer.

Response: _____

You say: _____

_____

Precise Rewrite

Here are some statements commonly made by teachers in the classroom. Some are praise statements that need to be rewritten as acknowledgments, and some are acknowledgments that need to be rewritten as praise.

What message does the statement send to students? How conducive to creating effective and positive classroom culture is it? Rewrite each statement as precisely as possible.

1. "I love the way you tracked the speaker just now. Amazing job!"

_____

_____

2. "Thank you for answering in a complete sentence. I appreciate it."

_____

_____

3. "Everybody followed my directions. Good."

_____

_____

4. "Wow! That was an amazing complete sentence. Excellent job using a complete sentence to answer my question."

_____

_____

5. "You read that with great expression. Thank you."

_____

_____

6.   "Jamal, you've turned yourself around since this morning."

_____

_____

7.   "I absolutely love the SLANT I am seeing; now can you fix your shoe?"

_____

_____

8.   "Can you please pick up your pencil that you dropped? Excellent!"

_____

_____

9.   "I couldn't be happier with the way you read that, Mahogany."

_____

_____

10.   "I appreciate that you guys came in so orderly."

_____

_____

What to Praise?

Be thoughtful in deciding what to praise so that you praise the right behaviors for the right reasons. This exercise could be useful for planning praise in your current classroom. It calls attention to various classroom routines. For each, identify one or two behaviors or actions as specifically as you can that you'd love to see from every student. For example:

As students enter the classroom

Behaviors you want: _Entering the classroom and moving swiftly and professionally to their seats._

Why you want them: _Reflects a sense of urgency about getting started learning._

Phrasing: _"I love seeing how [Sayvion, for example] is moving quickly to his seat showing me he is eager and ready to learn!"_

In the following, address the named routine, or substitute others you use.

1.   As you introduce new material to the class (or other routine: _____)

Behaviors you want: _____

Why you want them: _____

Phrasing: _____

_____

2. Independent practice (or other routine: _____)

Behaviors you want: _____

Why you want them: _____

Phrasing: _____

3. A lesson wrap-up (or other routine: _____)

Behaviors you want: _____

Why you want them: _____

Phrasing: _____

Printable Praise

Here are some ideas for fortifying spoken praise. Reflect on the pros and cons for you as you see them.

1. Post praisable (not merely expected) behaviors on the board, and write the names of students who do them.

Pros: _____

Cons: _____

2. Write into lesson plans or student materials the kinds of behaviors you are most eager to praise on that day ("Today I'm looking to see who can even ... "). Then devote a part of your bulletin board to naming students in praise.

Pros: _____

Cons: _____

3. Prewrite notes to pass out to students every day commending or encouraging them.

Pros: _____

Cons: _____

4. In student material, include opportunities for students to praise each other's work. For example, in a *Do Now,* include a portion where everyone in the class writes down the name of the "most professional" student. Announce the results to the class.

Pros: _____

Cons: _____

"Situational Praise Role Play" as Individual Work

The group activities in the next section include a situational praise role play. If you are working on your own, read the five scenarios it includes and write down what you would say.

PRACTICE WITH STUDY GROUP OR PARTNERS

Go Over Individual Work

1. Share and compare your individual work and thoughts from the previous section.

2. To get used to saying aloud the phrases you came up with in "Acknowledge, Praise, or Criticize," practice them out loud with a partner or small group acting as *Students*.

Situational Praise Role Play

This activity gives you practice in choosing to acknowledge or praise and then doing so precisely.

Before the meeting, the *Facilitator* makes two copies of the five scenarios, and cuts each set of five apart. One set of copies goes in five envelopes, labeled 1 through 5 to correspond with the situation number. The *Facilitator* keeps the other set to be used during the role play.

1. In each of the rounds, a different member of the group becomes the *Teacher*; all others will be *Students*. There is no intended progression in the scenarios; they can be done in any order.

2. Decide who will play the *Teachers* in the various scenarios. The first *Teacher* then opens the envelope and reads the description inside. The *Teacher* has one minute to think of how to handle the situation. Meanwhile, the *Facilitator* shows the matching remaining copy of the scenario to the group and assigns any *Student* roles the scenario mentions to specific *Students*.

3. *Students* and *Teacher* take starting positions appropriate to the scenario and act it out from there. The *Teacher*'s task is to conduct the routine, including making and acting on appropriate choices of acknowledgment or praise.

4. After each role play, discuss the following questions:

For *Students*: How did the response(s) of the *Teacher* in this case affect you?

For the *Teacher*:
- Why did you make a certain choice?
- How effective was it?
- How did deciding on acknowledgment or praise affect your use of language or tone?

5. If you don't have enough time for the role play, just ask the *Teachers* to identify and demonstrate what they would say in each situation. Then proceed to questions like the ones in point 4.

SCENARIOS FOR SITUATIONAL ACKNOWLEDGMENT OR PRAISE

Situational *Precise Praise* scenario 1

A *Student* in your class uses a well-thought-out complete sentence in answer to a question you have asked, but gives an incomplete or wrong answer. Do you respond with acknowledgment or praise?

Situational *Precise Praise* scenario 2

A *Student* who has been continually problematic for several days in a row (acting out, disrupting, generally not focusing on assignments in class) comes in, sits down quietly, puts his bag in its proper place, picks up his pencil, and immediately begins working on a *Do Now*, like everyone else. Do you respond with acknowledgment or praise?

Situational *Precise Praise* scenario 3

A normally unruly class of *Students* all come in to the room on time, sit down, and begin working—except that three of them, who normally do not act up, are sitting at their desks but look to be discussing the problem. Do you respond with acknowledgment or praise for the rest of the class?

Situational *Precise Praise* scenario 4

A *Student* is tracking the speaker in the second week of class, whereas the whole class is tracking at the end of January. How would you respond differently in each of those different circumstances? Do you respond with acknowledgment or praise?

Situational *Precise Praise* scenario 5

A *Student* follows all the directions you have given her, but still falls short of your expectation behaviorally—for example, she still has her feet stretched out in front of her when the directions you have given are ''Sit up, hands folded in front of you, and eyes on me.'' Do you respond with acknowledgment or praise?

PRECISE PRAISE

The Soaring Power of Praise

Do this with a large group or break up into smaller ones (no fewer than four or five). The *Facilitator* should bring enough sheets of letter-size paper so that each member of the group will have twice as many sheets as the number of rounds the *Facilitator* intends to conduct.

This role play aims to improve the ability to deliver specific and genuine *Precise Praise* by practicing its delivery. There are two *Teacher* scripts. Whoever is *Teacher* will run through both, and the rest of the group will be *Students*. The *Facilitator* or group can decide how many *Teacher* rounds there will be (each round including both scripts). (The visual summary of the script is for the *Teacher*'s reference and benefit, and is not shared with the *Students*.)

1. Starting with script 1, the *Teacher* teaches and models how to fold a paper airplane, praising the *Students* for successful completion of the steps.

2. At this point each *Student* can take notes on (1) What specific phrases the *Teacher* used to praise the group, and (2) What behaviors the *Student* would show if she wanted to receive praise from her *Teacher*. Review *Students'* responses with the group.

3. The *Teacher* teaches and models again, this time following script 2.

4. After script 2 is finished, the *Students* take notes again as they did in step 2.

5. At the end of the round or of several rounds, the group discusses the experience, based on the *Student* notes.

Your takeaways:

_____

_____

_____

_____

Script 1

(Teacher: *You can alter the directions a little, but be sure to include the phrases that are bolded throughout and do not attempt more precise or individual praise.*)

Today you are going to learn the important skill of making paper airplanes. You may already know how to do this; however, today I want you to follow my directions carefully. I will model this as we go along.

1. Take a regular piece of paper and fold it in half.

   Everyone is doing a great job on this.

2. Fold the short edge of one side down to the first fold. It should make a forty-five-degree angle. *(Pause while* Students *fold.)* Do this for the other side too.

   I like seeing the good work.

3. Fold down the new fold you have created to the original fold you made in step 1. Repeat for the other side.

   Keep up the good work!

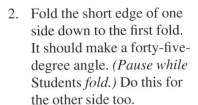

4. Repeat this again for both sides.

5. Hold the center and open the wings out.

Script 2

(Teacher: *This time you may choose to alter the directions a bit, watching out for behaviors at each step that merit genuine praise.*)

Today you are going to learn the important skill of making paper airplanes. You may already know how to do this; however, today I want you to follow my directions carefully. I will model this as we go along.

1. Take a regular piece of paper and fold it in half.

   I like seeing how

   _____ is

   making really crisp creases on the edges.

2. Fold the short edge of one side down to the first fold. It should make a forty-five-degree angle. *(Pause while* Students *fold.)* Do this for the other side too.

   Good job carefully folding each side so they're the same,

   _____.

3. Fold down the new fold you have created to the original fold you made in step 1. Repeat for the other side.

   I like seeing how

   _____

   has only looked up at me and then looks back down at his/her airplane. He/she isn't distracted by class-mates!

4. Repeat this again for both sides.

5. Hold the center and open the wings out.

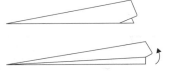

TRY *PRECISE PRAISE* IN THE CLASSROOM

1.   Survey what you've done in the previous sections that you can use in the classroom, including "Printable Praise."

2.   While you are still learning *Precise Praise,* commit to a realistic system by which you can recognize and track your pattern of praise.

3.   To be intentional about making your classroom as productive as possible, decide what you most want to reinforce. For key parts of your lesson or day, identify the behaviors you most want to have met and exceed expectations. Script the language you could use to either critique or reinforce by acknowledgment or *Precise Praise.*

TROUBLE-SHOOT

Steady On

Some people are reluctant to praise. Becoming more precise about praising will make it come more easily.

Other Challenges

Possible Challenge	Possible Solutions

BE CREATIVE

What genuine, deserved praise can you give that might surprise the class or individual students?

SUSTAIN YOUR PROGRESS

1. Using feedback from your study group or other peers, and reviewing your own lesson notes and observations, monitor your progress on *Precise Praise*.

Date	Right Choice of Acknowledgment or Praise	Good Precision

2. Revisit "Where Am I Now?" Are you ready to build out to some other new technique?

ANALYZE THE CHAMPIONS: SOME OBSERVATIONS

 Clip 11. Teacher Nikki Frame, Grade 6

When the student self-corrects his misreading of a word, Ms. Frame is right there with "Good self-correction." This demonstrates the principle of reinforcing replicable actions and academic skills.

WARM/STRICT

OVERVIEW

"Warm" and "strict" are not opposites. Although many of us are socialized to think otherwise, you can and should seek to be both—*Warm/Strict*—at exactly the same time. When you are simultaneously clear, consistent, firm, and unrelenting *and* positive, enthusiastic, caring, and thoughtful, you send the powerful message that having high expectations is part of caring for and respecting someone. To make *Warm/Strict* effective,

- Explain to students why you're doing what you're doing.

- Distinguish between behavior and people.

- Demonstrate that consequences are temporary. Get over it quickly yourself.

- Use warm nonverbal behavior.

WHERE AM I NOW?

	Proficiency			
	I am brand new to *Warm/Strict* . . .	I haven't tried *Warm/Strict* yet in class . . .	I'm beginning to try *Warm/Strict* in my classroom . . .	I use *Warm/Strict* regularly . . .
Comfort & Confidence	❑ . . . but feel I have a clear sense of it already.	❑ . . . but know with practice I'll make it work.	❑ . . . and love how it basically works.	❑ . . . and my students get what I mean.
	❑ . . . and undecided about my ability to pull it off.	❑ . . . because I still have questions about how to do it right.	❑ . . . with mixed results I need to evaluate.	❑ . . . but the message sometimes seems to confuse them.
	❑ . . . and not at all sure it's for me.	❑ . . . because I still have doubts.	❑ . . . but it doesn't seem to work or suit me.	❑ . . . but sometimes the two still feel strange to me.

Work from your strengths. If you find yourself in the bottom left portion, leaf through this technique to locate related ones you might prefer to work on right now.

ANALYZE THE CHAMPIONS

What evidence of *Warm/Strict*, if any, do you see in these clips as the technique is summarized in the "Overview" section? With the same question in mind, view the clips again after you've expanded your skills.

Clip 5. Teacher Alexandra Bronson, Grade 5

 Clip 11. Teacher Nikki Frame, Grade 6

EXPAND YOUR SKILLS AND REPERTOIRE

We're socialized to believe that warmth and strictness are opposites: if you're enough of one, you must be not enough of the other. That false conviction will undercut your teaching. The degree to which you are warm has no bearing on the degree to which you are strict, and vice versa.

Warm = positive, enthusiastic, caring, and thoughtful.

Strict = clear, consistent, firm, and unrelenting.

How to Make It Work

Explain what you do. Tell students why you're doing what you're doing and how it will help them.

"Sweetheart, we don't do that in this classroom because it keeps us from making the most of our learning time. I'm going to have to try to help you remember that."

| 48 **EXPLAIN EVERYTHING** |

| 47 **EMOTIONAL CONSTANCY** |

Distinguish between behavior and people.

"Your behavior is inconsiderate."   Not: ~~"You're inconsiderate."~~

Translate the following into observations about behavior:

1. "You're evidently lazy today."

   _____

2. "Who's the troublemaker right now?"

   _____

3. "You're in one of your hyperactive states."

   _____

4. "Why are you so mean to everyone?"

   _____

5. "You're not very generous."

   _____

6. "You're an average student—no shame in that."

   _____

7. "You're stubborn, aren't you!"

   _____

WARM/STRICT

8. "You're unhappy."

    _____

9. "Now you're one of my smart ones!"

    _____

Show that consequences are temporary. Once you give a consequence, your next task is to forgive. You use a consequence so you won't have to hold a grudge. Get over it quickly. Model for students that when they've fulfilled the consequences of a mistake, it is immediately in the past. Be sincere, but try to make your modeling include smiling and greeting them naturally. Show that the slate is clean.

"After you're done, I can't wait to have you come back and show us your best."

Use warm nonverbal behavior. Put your arm on a student's shoulder and use facial expression to convey your sympathy that he'll have to redo the homework, but you know he's capable of better.

| 5 WITHOUT APOLOGY |

Bend down to a third grader's eye level and explain firmly that she won't be allowed to talk to her classmates that way. But don't apologize because you care.

Warm/Strict:	Apology:
"Because I care about you, you must serve the consequence for being late."	"~~I care about you, but you still must serve the consequence for being late.~~"

Overcome "the tyranny of the 'or'." In balanced combination, *Warm/Strict* can even help students resolve apparent contradictions and realize that many of the either-or choices in their lives are false constructs. It helps students realize that they can be hip and successful, have fun and work hard, be happy and say no to self-indulgence.

Compose *Warm/Strict*

Read through these situations. Compose a *Warm/Strict* response for at least three of them. Responses can include verbal and nonverbal elements.

1. The student is a gifted, amiable comic, but you've just had to issue a light consequence because a one-liner that you, too, found funny has caused a distraction.

    _____

    _____

    _____

2. A six-year-old with a seriously ill parent balks and complains about arithmetic.

    _____

    _____

    _____

3. You've just had to issue a consequence to a sensitive student who tries hard but burst out in frustrated anger when it looked as though someone had stolen his eraser.

_____

_____

_____

4. As you begin to instruct, three athletes at the back of the room begin to muse together quietly over a moment in which their team lost a varsity game.

_____

_____

_____

5. You've just had to separate two genuine friends because, sitting together, they can't refrain from talking and giggling.

_____

_____

_____

6. You've just had to issue a consequence to a student who genuinely often isn't aware of her humming.

_____

_____

_____

7. A lonely student in a funk slumps at a desk, probably at least in part because he has no idea how to tackle a *Do Now*.

29 **DO NOW**

_____

_____

_____

8. A struggling student in a funk harmlessly (fortunately) tosses a pencil, probably in part because she has no idea how to tackle a *Do Now*.

_____

_____

_____

How You Come Across

You know how you really are, but choose one response to this prompt: "In general, my students consider me . . ."

1. Warm
2. Strict
3. Warm and strict by turns
4. *Warm/Strict*

5. _____ but not warm or strict, particularly. (For example, you might say students find you "Funny, but not warm or strict" or "Intellectual, but not warm or strict.")

6. Other: _____

What existing evidence might support their view or mislead them in their thinking?

_____

_____

_____

Are their sentiments divided—one group seeing you in one way and another in a different way? Who are the groups? Why might they differ? Is that a problem you need to address?

_____

_____

_____

PRACTICE WITH STUDY GROUP OR PARTNERS

Take a Stand on *Warm/Strict*

| 21 **TAKE A STAND** |

| 44 **PRECISE PRAISE** |

Before the group meets, the *Facilitator* should become familiar with the directions to read aloud (point 1).

1. With the group standing in a circle, the *Facilitator* reads these directions, adding touches of *Precise Praise* if needed:

Please close your eyes. (*Pause to see that eyes are closed.*)

I'm going to ask you to *Take a Stand.* I'll offer two choices. Raise one hand as soon as I finish—right hand for the first choice, left hand for the second.

Eyes closed. Show me you can do right for the first. (*Pause for show.*)

Good. Hands down. Show me left for the second. (*Pause for show.*)

Good. Hands down. You must choose without thinking and raise only one hand. Here goes: In the classroom, if you could only be one, would you be warm? . . . or strict?

Up and keep them up, sweethearts! (*Pause.*)

Open your eyes and count. *(Group members open their eyes and count.)*

Thank you. Let's all sit.

2.   In a *Warm/Strict* manner, the *Facilitator* leads a thoughtful discussion of what just happened in the *Take a Stand*. In any order as opportunities arise, solicit thoughts about challenges members face in

- Distinguishing between behavior and person
- Conveying to students that there is no either-or
- Showing students that consequences are temporary
- Themselves putting classroom incidents behind
- Using warm nonverbal behavior

Try to cover all the questions.

3.   Solicit a summary from several members of the groups.

4.   If members have not already done so, invite them to say how they go about being *Warm/Strict*.

More Discussion Ideas

1.   Share and compare your efforts in the "How to Make It Work" activity to translate from comments that address the personal to those that address behavior.

2.   Compare your thoughts in response to "How You Come Across." Is it a problem if different segments of the class see you differently in terms of *Warm/Strict*? If so, what are some solutions?

3.   From the student's point of view, evaluate the message in the *Warm/Strict* responses you created in the "Compose *Warm/Strict*" activity.

Your takeaways:

_____

_____

_____

_____

TRY *WARM/STRICT* IN THE CLASSROOM

There's no need to try to do all these at once. Plan and try one (maybe two) in your next session. Retry and expand from there.

1.   Is there any class routine or activity in which you are strictly strict, without some outward sign of warmth? Would you gain anything by changing that? What *Warm/Strict* language can you prepare?

2.   Is there any extended moment in class when you are totally warm? Would you gain anything by changing that? What *Warm/Strict* language can you prepare?

3.   Look at an upcoming lesson plan. Note any points in the lesson where you may feel cornered into being just plain strict. Even if strictness must rule right then, how can you liberate yourself from feeling forced?

4.   Are there any individuals in the class toward whom you feel compelled to be consistently either warm or strict? With those individuals in mind, prepare and practice some *Warm/Strict* language.

5. What false either-or perceptions might be holding your students back? Is there an appropriate moment to reveal and discuss your perception with them?

TROUBLE-SHOOT

Steady On

At school inside or outside the classroom, if you tend to separate *Warm/Strict,* write down three things you might do to be able to join them more.

1. _____

2. _____

3. _____

Other Challenges

Possible Challenge	Possible Solutions

BE CREATIVE

Of people you have known, who has best exemplified *Warm/Strict*? Is there something of theirs that you can apply in the classroom?

SUSTAIN YOUR PROGRESS

1. Using feedback from your study group or other peers, and reviewing your own lesson notes and observations, monitor your progress on *Warm/Strict.*

Date	Good Combo	Particular Type of Moment to Work On

WARM/STRICT

2. Revisit "Where Am I Now?" Are you ready to build out to some other new technique?

JOY FACTOR

OVERVIEW

A *Joy Factor* is an activity for celebrating joy in the work of learning as members of a high-achieving class. Joy can be loud or quiet; it can be individual, small group, or large group oriented.

Five Kinds of *Joy*

- Games including challenge, play, and competition
- Drama, song, and dance
- Us and Them (activities that make students feel like part of something)
- Humor
- Suspense and surprise

Reminders About *Joy Factor*

- You turn it on and turn it off, like a faucet.
- It means students whistle *while* they work.
- The best ones serve the objective.

27 VEGAS

Vegas is one kind of *Joy Factor* in being an instructional tool that explicitly reinforces the lesson objective and draws students into the content. Other kinds of *Joy Factor* also aim more clearly at inducting and including everyone in the classroom's culture and sense of group.

WHERE AM I NOW?

	Proficiency			
Comfort & Confidence	I'm brand new to *Joy Factor* . . .	I'm on the edge of thinking and creating this way, though I haven't yet brought *Joy Factor* into the classroom . . .	I'm beginning to try *Joy Factor* in my classroom . . .	I use *Joy* often . . .
	❑ . . . and excited to try it.	❑ . . . but know with more practice I'll make it work.	❑ . . . and love how it basically works.	❑ . . . with focus and playful gusto.
	❑ . . . and undecided how joyful I can be.	❑ . . . because I still have questions about how to do it right.	❑ . . . with mixed results I need to evaluate.	❑ . . . but occasionally my timing is off.
	❑ . . . and not at all sure it's for me.	❑ . . . because, frankly, I still have serious doubts.	❑ . . . but it doesn't seem to work or suit me.	❑ . . . but have more work to do in making it *100%*.

Work from your strengths. If you find yourself in the bottom left portion, leaf through this technique to locate related ones you might prefer to work on right now.

ANALYZE THE CHAMPIONS

View each video clip, ideally more than once, and answer the following questions.

 Clip 28. Teacher Kelli Ragin, Grade 5

1. What's the name of the bit of joy in this clip? Is it also *Vegas*?
2. What academic *and* social purposes does it serve?
3. How long is it? Is so much time well spent?

> 27 **VEGAS**

 Clip 29. Teacher Tamika Boykin, Grade K

1. What are the rules of the delightful game that Ms. Boykin's class plays?
2. What subtleties of situations and her directions keep her youngsters' excitement within bounds and under her control?

EXPAND YOUR SKILLS AND REPERTOIRE

Finding joy in the work of learning—the *Joy Factor*—is a key driver not just of a happy classroom but of a high-achieving one. As Disney's Snow White was aware, people work harder when they enjoy working on something and punctuate the work with moments of joy (whistling, for example).

The Faucet Whistles and Waters

"The faucet whistles and waters" could be a mnemonic for the three main hallmarks of *Joy Factor* beyond its obvious joy:

1. Like a faucet, you need to be able to turn it quickly on and off.
2. We whistle *while* we work, not as a break from work.
3. As a faucet waters the person or plant, so the best *Joy Factor* serves the objective.

> 6 **BEGIN WITH THE END**

Quiet Joys

Joy is for every age of child, adolescent, or adult and, as I mentioned in the "Overview," can be loud or quiet; it isn't necessarily antic. The best of teachers find a way to let their own genuine version of joy shine through in subtle and quiet ways. Even touches of positive teasing can express it, as such touches often do in loving families. So a teacher whose student Micah has expressed some annoyance about studying C. S. Lewis's *The Lion, the Witch, and the Wardrobe* ("Aren't we too old to be reading a book about talking animals?") might open the lesson by reading a bit from this classic work and saying to the class:

"The lion Aslan says, 'Do not cite the Deep Magic to me, Witch. I was there when it was written.' Hmm. You know, Micah was telling me just yesterday how she *loves* the talking animals and all that fantasy stuff. Micah, help us understand what Aslan means here."

Games

| 18 **CFU** |
| 19 **AT BATS** |

Games take advantage of young people's love of challenges, competition, and play. They also give more *At Bats,* and kids like chances to one-up their teacher. You may want to *Check for Understanding* of the rules before you launch the game. If points are involved, explain how (for what behaviors) they will be awarded. Here are some game examples:

- Contests to see who can "roll their numbers" (that is, do repeated addition) the fastest or who can put the midwestern states in alphabetical order by last letter the fastest
- "Bees" in spelling, geography, math, and so forth
- Relay races
- Jeopardies

Kindergarten teacher George Davis does more teacher-versus-student games when students get distracted easily and have trouble remaining engaged. The tone is nonconfrontational, and the format gives them space to make mistakes and participate without fear because "it's just a game."

For the first few weeks he also models appropriate "winner" and "loser" behavior and narrates relevant thoughts, saying, "I can't believe I lost—I'm so angry—no, I shouldn't be angry—I should be happy for my teammates who won."

Later, when he says, "I can't believe I lost—I'm so angry—no, I shouldn't be angry . . . ," students will often complete the thought with a helpful, "No, you should be happy for your teammates who won."

See if you can come up with two other game scenario ideas; think about how they might be adapted to make them true *Joy Factors* in your classroom:

1. _____

_____

_____

2. _____

_____

_____

Us and Them

You want your class to feel that they belong to an important "Us." You can increase this sense through the use of unique language, names, rituals, traditions, imaginary presences, songs, and so forth. In many cases, the more inscrutable these rituals are to outsiders, the better. Some examples:

- Pleasing nicknames for all the students in your class, which you use in and outside class. Nicknames show you care and that you notice individualities.
- Secret signals and special words.
- A song everyone knows and sings.
- A "secret" song that everyone knows but whose tune is just hummed.

- A myth or story shared by the teacher that the teacher invokes again later to prove a point or teach a lesson. For example, before every test, refer back to a funny story you've told them about your diffident cousin Martha:

  > "Remember my cousin Martha, who gives up when the going gets tough. Don't go pulling a Martha!"

Drama, Song, Movement, and Dance

"Stand up!" is often a good way to begin *Joy Factor*. Group song, dramatic play, and movement raise spirits and also reinforce belonging. Acting things out and singing about them are great ways to remember information. For example:

- Songs in foreign languages. Any song (and added gestures) in the language students are learning can let them practice, enjoy, and remember vocabulary and expressions for the rest of their lives.

- Songs that mark sequences or processes like "Do-Re-Mi" from *The Sound of Music*. See also the *Joy Factor* songs in *Vegas*.

  > **27 VEGAS**

- A short, scripted enactment of how Hawaii rose from volcanic sources under the Pacific and became a haven for life on reefs and land, with students narrating and acting out the movements of these natural forces.

- Chant and movement or dance, as shown in clip 28.

Teaching Chant and Song

Call and repeat (one variation of *Call and Response*) can be used as a way of teaching students a fairly long song or chant. Champion kindergarten teacher George Davis discovered his students' "amazing ability to pick up new things when connected to music and melody. For whatever reason they get it in song better than in conversation."

> **23 CALL AND RESPONSE**

1. Teach a phrase at a time. As you call out the phrase, point to your ear or collar bones to signal students to listen. Then point to them to repeat. Gradually combine phrases.

2. Teach a song the same way. In teaching a song, you can cue students that the next note goes up or down (and about how far) by holding your hand in front of you flat and parallel to the floor, raising or lowering the hand sharply as the pitch goes up or down. At the same time, slide the same hand a small distance sharply front to mark the beat.

3. Get tips and coaching from a nearby cheer or song leader.

4. What simple chants or songs do you want to try? Record a few ideas right here. Expand them on separate paper or computer. Then practice teaching one to a mirror.

Ideas: _____

_____

_____

Humor

Shared laughter can strengthen and spread an environment in which happy and fulfilled students and teachers can thrive! If you're not sure how to create shared positive laughter, steal material from someone who knows!

JOY FACTOR

Suspense and Surprise

Your strong classroom routines make occasional variations all the more fun, surprising, and memorable. Some examples:

- Hide the next lesson in a box or a mystery envelope.

- Wrap something you plan to show the class (art, a map, a specimen for study) as a gift. Then build anticipation by playing at "deciding" when to open it or by involving the students in some "Open Sesame" ritual.

- "Oh, man, you're gonna love the last verse of this addition song. It's really funny. And if we keep working, we'll get to hear it soon . . ."

- "The mystery pointer only chooses scholars who are sitting up and looking up at me . . ."

- Occasionally hand out varied material (such as vocabulary words) to individual students in sealed envelopes. Whisper, "Don't open them yet! Not till I say."

Idea for surprise or suspense: _____

_____

How to extend it or intensify it even further: _____

_____

Precisely how it will end: _____

_____

A Caseful of Joy

Creating *Joy Factor* takes thought and rethought to make it really sing in class. For each case here, identify two ways in which it is effective *Joy Factor*. Also identify two areas in which it bears improving. Then come up with an idea or two for specific improvements.

Mutually evaluate your answers with a partner or group.

Case 1. Ms. Green

The students are focused and working on their grammar lesson for the day—the difference between the subject and object of a sentence. Students turn in their desk work, and Ms. Green says, "That was great diligence you displayed today, University of Chicago. Let's all stand up and sing one of our favorite songs before moving on to math."

The students are all smiling and stand up quickly and silently. They sing "I Like Big Books," a song based on a popular one whose lyrics Ms. Green modified to make it about how much students love reading. They sing in unison, loud and proud, and it goes on for a couple minutes. When they finish the song, Ms. Green silently counts to three on her fingers, and the students sit down, still grinning, and immediately get started on their math.

Effective features:

1. _____

2. _____

Improvable areas:

1. _____

2. _____

Specific improvements? _____

_____

_____

_____

Case 2. Miss Violet

Miss Violet created an incentive that seemed to make her students happier and more focused. She knew they loved to compete against each other, so with good behavior, they could earn minutes at the end of class for playing Heads Up, Seven Up, or a math facts game.

Effective features:

1. _____

2. _____

Improvable areas:

1. _____

2. _____

Specific improvements? _____

_____

_____

_____

Case 3. Mr. Gold

Mr. Gold welcomes his students one by one at the *Threshold*. With some, he bumps fists; with others, he gives high fives and back slaps. He asks one about his girlfriend. He gives one a serious stare-down until the student

| 41 **THRESHOLD** |

laughs and then smiles. He asks a student who is visibly upset, "What's up?" They talk for a minute and then he continues. As one student approaches, he tips his head and says, "Yo." The student smiles and enters the class.

Effective features:

1. _____

2. _____

Improvable areas:

1. _____

2. _____

Specific improvements? _____

_____

_____

_____

Case 4. Mrs. Rose

In Mrs. Rose's class, a student is expected to answer her questions thoroughly and with a complete sentence. When Josh does so today, she tells the students, "We are going to give Josh a Roller Coaster Cheer—ready?" They do the cheer with big smiles and giggles, not in unison, but they generally finish around the same time. They are laughing and giggling, and some students sitting next to Josh also give him a high five or a pat on the back. Mrs. Rose begins the next part of the lesson while some students are giggling, or talking quietly. She stops and says, "If we can't handle celebrating in this class, we won't be able to do it anymore. We will just work, work, work."

Effective features:

1. _____

2. _____

Improvable areas:

1. _____

2. _____

Specific improvements? _____

_____

_____

_____

PRACTICE WITH STUDY GROUP OR PARTNERS

Build on Individual Work

1. Share and compare your work in "A Caseful of Joy." For any needed improvement on which the group agrees, brainstorm more solutions.

2. Share and compare (or even try out) your work in "Suspense and Surprise."

JOY FACTOR

Practice Teaching a Song

As an optional preparation, the *Facilitator* and team members can look for a nearby music teacher, cheerleading coach, or other individual (perhaps a member of the group) to assist with this activity. If the music teacher or coach can't attend, the *Facilitator* can spend fifteen minutes with her ahead of time and impart her advice and modeling to the group.

Team members who would like to be *Teacher* come with a short song or chant and teach it to the group. (*Teachers* can also consult ahead of time with the music teacher or coach.) You can use any song or chant. Simple songs will work best here and in the classroom.

Brainstorm and Plan *Joy Factor(s)*

The goal here is to discover new *Joy Factors* members could do, not to go over ones they or someone they know already does (but of course members can use new ideas they thought up in other exercises). The *Facilitator* appoints a *Recorder* and *Timer* and makes sure there's a means to write down ideas.

1. The *Facilitator* reminds the group of the general brainstorming process. (See the Introduction.)

2. Give the group a minute to think. Then begin going around the group, asking each person to "Suggest one idea for an activity that would increase the *Joy Factor* in your classroom."

3. Number the resulting list. Each participant then chooses and shares the numbers of his or her top three choices. The *Recorder* keeps a count with hash marks next to the numbered item. From this, arrive at the two to four most popular activities.

4. If the group is large, the *Facilitator* can divide it here into smaller ones and assign an activity to each group, or the existing group can settle on one choice.

5. The group(s) create a detailed activity plan based on the assigned or chosen idea, including

   • Name of activity

   • Objective

   • Step-by-step instructions: What the activity looks and sounds like (if a song, write out the song; if a game, script the rules of the game; and so on), how you will present the activity or teach it to students, and when you will use it

   • Estimated time

   • Materials needed

6. Try other selections if you have time.

7. Then discuss the plans as a whole group, allowing praise and constructive criticism. Some useful questions include

   • How does this activity help reinforce the *Joy Factor* technique?

   • How would this activity best be used?

TRY *JOY FACTOR* IN THE CLASSROOM

1. For your own students, design a *Joy Factor* "faucet that whistles and waters." Also decide on a quick way to cue students to start (and end, if needed).

> 6 **BEGIN WITH THE END**

2. Rehearse it outside class—with a partner or group if you can.

3. Plan where you'll teach and try it out in your lesson plan.

4. Teach it to the class.

5.   Try it during a working moment.

6.   If you want to use nicknames, privately annotate your roll with ideas as they come to you. When you have one for everyone, check them again and start trying them out. You can also involve the students themselves in helping you select the nicknames you will use.

TROUBLE-SHOOT

Steady On

Great performers perfect their scripts. For most teachers, when they are teaching, it's best not to try to conceive of or pull off *Joy Factor* on the fly. Jot down the idea whenever it comes to you, then take it home to plan, rehearse, and sharpen before you open on Broadway.

Other Challenges

Possible Challenge	Possible Solutions
A *Joy Factor* causes one student to get so excited that she starts to distract other students. 48 **EXPLAIN EVERYTHING**	More mindfully set up expectations for the *Joy Factor* moment, what it should look like, and how students should come back when you end it. A gentle "SLANT" can be a good way to come down quietly from on high.
I lose class control and time. 32 **SLANT**	Rethink the *Joy Factor* and reset expectations. Be more detailed in planning so that *Joy Factor* balances time between fun and academics. Keep *Joy Factor* activities short and embedded in the instruction.
Kids don't find my *Joy* ideas to be very fun. 42 **NO WARNINGS**	See what your peers and partners do. Start small ... try for little lively moments rather than massive fun-fests while you're still learning what works. Or try to sell it a little more. Sometimes your own doubts can be self-fulfilling prophecies.

BE CREATIVE?

Yes, but remember "the faucet whistles and waters."

At one school, students play their teachers in math baseball. To hit a single, the batter must solve the problem faster than the teacher who's covering first base.

Enlist any cheerleaders in your class (or a previous class) in a *Joy Factor* project. Involve them at all points of the process.

SUSTAIN YOUR PROGRESS

1. Using feedback from your study group or other peers, and reviewing your own lesson notes and observations, monitor your progress on *Joy Factor*.

Date	*Joy Factor*	Refinement

2. Revisit "Where Am I Now?" Are you ready to build out to some other new technique?

EMOTIONAL CONSTANCY

OVERVIEW

A teacher's *Emotional Constancy* is a source of students' steadiness in academic work. *Emotional Constancy* does not mean withholding all emotions. It means you express emotions as a way of consistently promoting student learning and achievement. Emotionally constant teachers

- Control their own emotions rather than let students experiment in controlling them.
- Use their outward show of emotions to keep the learning moving forward
- Tie their language to achievement and positive behavioral expectations.
- Earn students' trust that the teacher is always in control of self and of the room, and will use that control respectfully to help students cope with emotional trials that interfere with learning.

WHERE AM I NOW?

	Proficiency			
	I am brand new to *Emotional Constancy* . . .	I understand though I haven't tried this approach yet in class . . .	I'm beginning to try *Emotional Constancy* in my classroom . . .	I use *Emotional Constancy* regularly . . .
Comfort & Confidence	❑ . . . and excited to try it.	❑ . . . but see the practical value of it and am planning to try it.	❑ . . . and love how it basically works.	❑ . . . and with relative ease by now.
	❑ . . . and undecided about my ability to pull it off.	❑ . . . because I still have questions about how to do it right.	❑ . . . with mixed results I need to evaluate.	❑ . . . but it's often still a stretch.
	❑ . . . and would rather not get into emotions in my professional life.	❑ . . . because, frankly, I still have serious doubts.	❑ . . . but it doesn't seem to work or suit me.	❑ . . . but when class isn't going well, I can lose it.

Work from your strengths. If you find yourself in the bottom left portion, leaf through this technique to locate related ones you might prefer to work on right now.

EXPAND YOUR SKILLS AND REPERTOIRE

Control and Temper Your Emotions

School is a laboratory for students; they need to be able to figure out how to behave without seeing you explode. You should expect almost anything, so act as though you expect it and have a plan to deal with it and with whatever internal emotions you need to manage.

Expect their emotions to rise and fall; control your own to compensate. Expects students to occasionally get upset, and train yourself to respond calmly. Part of adolescence is experimenting with exaggerated emotions; don't fuel theirs by letting your own become inflamed.

Harness Your Outward Emotion to Keep the Learning Moving Forward

View the end of a consequence as a fresh start. After all, you chose that consequence because you considered it a sufficient disincentive. Once the student has acquiesced, the consequence has done its job and the cycle is over. Go back to teaching in a positive manner. If the consequence wasn't sufficient, use a stronger one rather than getting angry.

Tie Your Language to Achievement

Don't tie your language to your own emotional needs, nor mainly to those of the students. An emotionally constant teacher treads cautiously around such language as "I'm really disappointed in you" when a class has behaved poorly. After all, the whole point of the rule or expectation isn't really just to please the teacher.

At rare times, the teacher's personal sense of connection and approval are something students should be concerned about, but almost always the teacher's best option is to remove his or her personal emotions from the equation and focus the conversation on what kids did (or didn't) do in relation to the ultimate goal.

"You can do better, and I expect that."

"The expectation in this class is that you give your best."

Take the Helm

Emotionally constant teachers earn students' trust in part by ensuring that students know that the teachers themselves are always under control. These teachers know that success is in the long run about a student's consistent relationship with productive behaviors. The affect they show and require from students is productive, respectful, and orderly. Students need to know that when emotions run hot, the teacher will de-escalate them. They need to be able to trust your hand on the rudder that steers them back to calm and productivity by the shortest route.

Rephrase

Edit or replace these feeling statements with words (and possibly nonverbal suggestions) that disconnect from an individual's grief and connect instead to expectations that underlie future achievement.

1.   "You've really let me down this time."

2. "Why aren't you even willing to try?"

_____

_____

3. "You have no idea what teaching is like."

_____

_____

4. "Is this how you reward me?"

_____

_____

5. "Do you disappoint your parents?"

_____

_____

6. "I can see you're not in the mood, but . . ."

_____

_____

7. "This behavior makes me sad."

_____

_____

8. "Don't you feel embarrassed?"

_____

_____

9. "You need to control your emotions, mister!"

_____

_____

10. "After all I've said, none of you listened."

_____

_____

11.   "There's no excuse for disrespect."

_____

_____

12.   "Don't think you can push me around."

_____

_____

13.   "Calvin, who are you really angry at?"

_____

_____

PRACTICE WITH STUDY GROUP OR PARTNERS

Discuss these and similar questions.

1.   Have you ever been angry or frightened as a student in the classroom? Was the teacher aware of that? What emotional steadying or needed control was the teacher able to give? What would have benefited you most?

2.   What student behaviors push your buttons? To what extent can you change their behaviors? What helps you reestablish your own calm?

3.   What consequences have you used or witnessed that give students space to cool down and regain self-control?

4.   How do *Strong Voice* techniques tie in with *Emotional Constancy*?

5.   Does a current class of yours pose particular challenges to *Emotional Constancy*? Invite others to describe what they might do.

Your takeaways:

_____

_____

_____

_____

TRY *EMOTIONAL CONSTANCY* IN THE CLASSROOM

1.   Check and possibly improve the strength of your routines for orderly behavior when students must be out of their seats (for example, when moving to another room) or are following some instruction that requires them to interact directly with each other.

28 **ENTRY ROUTINE**

EMOTIONAL CONSTANCY

| 15 **CIRCULATE** |
| 41 **THRESHOLD** |

| 48 **EXPLAIN EVERYTHING** |

2. Consider how *Circulate* can serve *Emotional Constancy* and how *Threshold* might help you assess and address students' emotional states.

3. What reminders of your *Emotional Constancy* might younger students appreciate hearing from you?

4. Have there been moments recently at school when a student especially needed *Emotional Constancy* from you? What language or steps can you rehearse by yourself to prepare for a recurrence?

5. Including playground duty or other tasks outside the classroom, what activities or moments during your school week are most likely to challenge your students' own emotional control? If you share responsibility with other school staff at these times, talk with them about needs for routine control or calming you might handle better with collaboration.

TROUBLE-SHOOT

Possible Challenge	Possible Solutions

BE CREATIVE

Is there a phrase you can rehearse and memorize to announce to yourself and share privately with an individual or to the class at large that some emotional steadying is needed—something that you can follow directly with a further intervention?

SUSTAIN YOUR PROGRESS

1. Using feedback from your study group or other peers, and reviewing your own lesson notes and observations, monitor your progress on *Emotional Constancy*.

Date	Things I'm Doing Well	Ways to Improve

2. Revisit "Where Am I Now?" Are you ready to build out to some other new technique?

EMOTIONAL CONSTANCY

EXPLAIN EVERYTHING

OVERVIEW

Champion teachers *Explain Everything.* They share the big picture with their students and ground their explanations in the missions of the classroom—helping the student get to college or to be more responsible. They constantly remind students why they do what they do. Students in a high-performing classroom understand

- The logic behind the rules and expectations designed for their betterment
- The dynamics of personal and group accountability
- That group success depends on everyone's participation

| 38 **STRONG VOICE** |
| 42 **NO WARNINGS** |

The purpose of explaining is not to acquire control. When control is the issue, you will want to bring other techniques into play.

WHERE AM I NOW?

	Proficiency			
Comfort & Confidence	I am brand new to *Explain Everything* . . .	I've learned about but haven't yet tried *Explain Everything* in class . . .	I'm beginning to *Explain Everything* in my classroom . . .	I *Explain Everything* . . .
	❑ . . . and excited to try it.	❑ . . . but know with practice I'll make it work.	❑ . . . and love how it basically works.	❑ . . . and know my students get it.
	❑ . . . and undecided about my ability to pull it off.	❑ . . . because I still have questions about how to do it right.	❑ . . . with mixed results I need to evaluate.	❑ . . . but would like more of the message to get across.
	❑ . . . and not at all sure it's necessary or useful.	❑ . . . because, frankly, I still don't think it's crucial.	❑ . . . but it doesn't seem to work or suit me.	❑ . . . but sometimes I explain when I need to exercise control.

Work from your strengths. If you find yourself in the bottom left portion, leaf through this technique to locate related ones you might prefer to work on right now.

ANALYZE THE CHAMPIONS

View the video clip, ideally more than once, and answer the following questions.

Clip 4. Teacher Stacey Shells, Grade 7

1. When does Ms. Shells explain in response to an error?
2. What's at the heart of her explanatory criticism of the error?

EXPAND YOUR SKILLS AND REPERTOIRE

Clarify Events and Logic

Students are helped by knowing rules of conduct that you will apply and how they better the class or the student.

"Shelly, if you're too sick to learn right now, then I'm sure you're also too sick to play. Do you understand that if you go to the nurse, when we have recess you're not going to participate?"

If a certain pace needs to be maintained in order to achieve the day's objective, the *Explain Everything* teacher says so.

"I'd love to spend more time talking about this, but there's a lot we've got to do."

"Hands down. I know that you all have questions, and I love it when you say intelligent things, but we have a lot to do, and right now there's not time. We still need to read our story and do workshop."

Explain Dynamics of Personal and Group Accountability

Couch conversations about misbehavior in language that explains to students how one action or behavior affects another and why improving behavior matters. Understanding the logic behind your decisions regarding routine and control will make students more apt both to believe that the systems are in their best interests and to make rational choices on their own.

"When we SLANT, we invest our incredible energy in every one of your futures. You SLANT for me, and I and everyone else in this room will SLANT for you. You'll have our full attention and support."

Explain how everyone is a model—maybe even a mentor—to those around him or her. Clarify how small, immediate corrections benefit everyone.

> 42 **NO WARNINGS**

Explain How Group Success Depends on *100%*

100% is one of your key techniques and might be a useful phrase in class. Explain how it benefits everyone, in terms of what teachers and students are trying to do together. If you want young students to understand the term, you may need to tell them something about what "%" and "percent" mean and what "100%" means. Or is there a better way to name the idea for them? Older students may also need some brief, classwide explanation of percentages.

> 36 **100%**

EXPLAIN EVERYTHING

Separate Explanation from Control

| 37 **WHAT TO DO** |
| 38 **STRONG VOICE** |
| 45 **WARM/STRICT** |

Explaining is not an effective part of regaining control in the classroom: it is too easily heard as pleading. When students have just behaved in some detrimental way is not the time to explain why they should do differently. Don't mix explanation into your methods to assert control. Control first. Rely on *Warm/Strict, Strong Voice,* and *What to Do.*

If you suspect that students don't know why a certain behavior is required or that they need to be reminded, explain later, only after you have restored control. Better yet, explain *before* a moment arises when you need to actively control.

| 5 **WITHOUT APOLOGY** |

Imagine that in the moment each of the following statements is made by the teacher, something is going on that requires control. Is the teacher attempting to explain? If the statement needs to be revised, do so in a way that best addresses the immediate problem of control. Also write down what the teacher may need to explain at a moment when the class is under control.

1. "Remember, when I call on one student to answer, we're all looking and listening. *(sternly)* Charles, we're all looking and listening because we're learning from our friends, even if it's not our turn."

_____

_____

At some other (controlled) time: _____

_____

2. "I hate to see hands flapping in the air. I can see a hand without any flapping."

_____

_____

At some other (controlled) time: _____

_____

3. "If you're looking at what someone else's writing right now, you're not doing your own work. Please, no looking during a test."

_____

_____

At some other (controlled) time: _____

_____

EXPLAIN EVERYTHING

4. "Serena, SLANT. All eyes on the speaker."

_____

_____

At some other (controlled) time: _____

_____

5. "People are talking at the back. How does that make the rest of the class feel right now? How does that make _me_ feel?"

_____

_____

At some other (controlled) time: _____

_____

6. "Hands down. It's a fascinating issue. We'll try to come back to it later."

_____

_____

At some other (controlled) time: _____

_____

7. "I need silence ... Thank you. Now we can hear you, Serena."

_____

_____

At some other (controlled) time: _____

_____

PRACTICE WITH STUDY GROUP OR PARTNERS

1. Share and compare your individual work and thoughts from the previous section.

2. In your respective classrooms, how aware are students of the effect their positive and negative behaviors have on others? How aware are they of their ability to control those behaviors?

- What accounts for those levels of awareness?
- If you have tried to raise those levels, what happened?
- What other options might work?

3. What issues of trust or mistrust arise among your students? How do they explain their trust or mistrust? Are there ways to help them improve their beliefs and explanations?

Your takeaways:

_____

_____

_____

_____

TRY *EXPLAIN EVERYTHING* IN THE CLASSROOM

1. Especially if you are having mixed success with maintaining control of the classroom, listen to an audio recording of a recent session. Do you notice any tendency to mix explanation with control? Transcribe several of those moments and rescript them in a way that would have focused exclusively on control as long as control was at stake.

18 **CFU**

2. Do your students already know the following things? What further explanations of them might they need? Plan times for those soon in coming sessions. Also, how will you *Check for Understanding*?

- The logic behind rules and expectations designed for their betterment
- The dynamics of personal and group accountability
- That group success depends on everyone's participation

TROUBLE-SHOOT

Steady On

Short positive explanations and reminders are generally better than long ones. Ahead of time if possible, distill the few things you need to say.

Other Challenges

Possible Challenge	Possible Solutions

BE CREATIVE

Make your explanations "stickier" (see *Name the Steps*).

> 13 **NAME THE STEPS**

SUSTAIN YOUR PROGRESS

1. Using feedback from your study group or other peers, and reviewing your own lesson notes and observations, monitor your progress on *Explain Everything.*

Date	I Explained It	Evidence They Got It

2. Revisit "Where Am I Now?" Are you ready to build out to some other new technique?

EXPLAIN EVERYTHING

NORMALIZE ERROR

OVERVIEW

Normalize Error recognizes that instruction followed by error followed by correction is the fundamental process of schooling. Getting it wrong before getting it right should be an acceptable, normal order of events. *Normalize Error* has several implications:

- Let students' errors be a normal, unremarkable, anxiety-free part of their learning process.
- Neither chasten nor make excuses for error.
- With minimal talk about the wrongness, quickly get the student to fix the error.
- Don't normally praise or fuss over right answers.
- Acknowledge students' work of correction.

WHERE AM I NOW?

	Proficiency			
	I'm brand new to *Normalize Error* . . .	**I haven't tried *Normalize Error* yet in class . . .**	**I'm beginning to try *Normalize Error* in my classroom . . .**	**I use *Normalize Error* regularly . . .**
Comfort & Confidence	❏ . . . and eager to make error a respected step in the learning process.	❏ . . . but understand the methods and think I can learn to apply them.	❏ . . . and love how it basically works.	❏ . . . and have made it part of our culture.
	❏ . . . and undecided about my ability to pull it off.	❏ . . . because I still have questions about how to do it right.	❏ . . . with mixed results I need to evaluate.	❏ . . . but my students still get disturbed by their earnest errors.
	❏ . . . and not at all sure it's for me.	❏ . . . because I'm still skeptical.	❏ . . . but it doesn't seem to work or suit me.	❏ . . . but when errors are frequent and flat wrong, I tend to suspend the technique.

Work from your strengths. If you find yourself in the bottom left portion, leaf through this technique to locate related ones you might prefer to work on right now.

.

ANALYZE THE CHAMPIONS

View the video clip, ideally more than once, and answer the following questions.

Clip 11. Teacher Nikki Frame, Grade 6

1. How do the students react to having their errors pointed out?
2. Did any student make an error that Ms. Frame did not promptly and simply help them correct?
3. How else does Ms. Frame's teaching show the hallmarks of *Normalize Error* mentioned in the "Overview" section?

EXPAND YOUR SKILLS AND REPERTOIRE

If all students are getting all questions right, the work you're giving them isn't hard enough.

Provide Students a Three-Legged Stool

Let your entire classroom sit on a stool of normal, unremarkable, anxiety-free error. The legs for this stool are *No Opt Out, Right Is Right,* and *Format Matters.* Each helps students turn wrong or incomplete answers into entirely right and complete ones. All three also emphasize that understanding is not neatly divided into "right" and "wrong" and that real understanding of anything is an effortful, gradual process of mastery.

> 1 **NO OPT OUT**
> 2 **RIGHT IS RIGHT**
> 4 **FORMAT MATTERS**

Strip Out Rebukes and Excuses

Line out any explicit or implicit chastisement or excuses for wrong answers in these examples.

1. "Kenny, our brightest, I'm surprised that out of everyone you missed that! What was it we said about carrying in addition?"
2. "No one should get this next one wrong if you're paying attention."
3. "No, we talked about this. You have to flip the sign, James."
4. "Oh, that's okay, honey. That was a really hard one. You needed to think about what happens when we form plurals for words ending in *y*."
5. "Where in the world did you get that?"
6. "Didn't I see your hand up when I asked how many had memorized these last night as homework?"

> 47 **EMOTIONAL CONSTANCY**

Fix Rather Than Study Wrongness

Rather than spend much talking about the wrongness, get down to helping the student to fix an error. Many teachers feel obligated to name every answer as right or wrong, but usually you can skip even that. Suppose you just say,

"What's the first thing we have to do in solving this kind of problem, James?"

This is a stimulating gambit in that it leaves it ambiguous to James and his classmates whether the answer was right or wrong as they start reworking the problem. There's a bit of suspense over a mystery they will have to figure out for themselves.

For a more vanilla clarity,

"Let's try that again, James. What's the first thing we have to do . . . ?"

| 16 **BREAK IT DOWN** |
| 18 **CFU** |
| 39 **DO IT AGAIN** |

"Not quite. What parts does *every* hypothesis include?"

"What is it that Yasmin may have overlooked?"

"Say it again, but shift the stress to syllable three."

Don't Normally Praise or Fuss over Right Answers

Praising relatively routine right answers often affects students perversely. If you make too much of a fuss, they infer that you're surprised they got it right. Praise exceptional answers and hard work.

Acknowledge Work of Correction

When a student answers correctly, move on with no big deal. When the student shows effort in making a correction, acknowledge it and move on:

| 44 **PRECISE PRAISE** |

"That's right, Avi. Good work on that."

Normalize

Following are a teacher's question, the correct answer, and a student's answer. Write a next response for the teacher that best serves the ideas behind *Normalize Error*. Incorporate other relevant techniques. If you see the response as a short sequence of further questions and likely student replies, write it out that way.

1. "Which way does the Missouri flow, Elias?" (*East to the Mississippi*)

   Elias: "It either flows to the Great Lakes or the Pacific Ocean."

Teacher: _____

_____

_____

_____

_____

_____

2. "How do we convert miles to kilometers, Eva?" (*We multiply miles times 1.6.*)

   Eva: "We use the Internet."

Teacher: _____

_____

_____

_____

_____

_____

_____

3. "What's the synonym we just used for *healthy,* Sophia?" (*The synonym was* hale.)

    Sophia: "Wealthy."

Teacher: _____

_____

_____

_____

_____

_____

4. "How would you translate *Cogito ergo sum,* Aris? (*Cogito,* I think; *ergo,* therefore; *sum,* I am.)

    Aris: "I think of ... so ... the *big* picture?"

Teacher: _____

_____

_____

_____

_____

_____

5. "If I left Los Angeles at 2:00 PM on a six-hour flight to DC, what time would it be when I landed? Wyatt." (*It would be 11:00* PM, *due to the three-hour time difference between east and west coasts.*)

    Wyatt: "It would be ... 11:00 PM No, wait ... five!"

Teacher: _____

_____

_____

_____

_____

_____

NORMALIZE ERROR

6. "Spell *rose,* the flower, Bahati."

   Bahati: "R-o ... wait, w—... z or e."

Teacher: _____

_____

_____

_____

_____

_____

7. "What party did Jefferson found, Earl?" (*The Republican Party or the Democratic-Republican Party—created in the early 1790s by Jefferson and James Madison*)

   Earl: "I'm not sure. I don't think most Republicans like him too much."

Teacher: _____

_____

_____

_____

_____

_____

8. "Square root of 64, Ernesto?" *(8)*

   Ernesto: "Ask me a smaller one."

Teacher: _____

_____

_____

_____

_____

_____

PRACTICE WITH A STUDY GROUP OR PARTNERS

Group Discussion

1. Share and compare your answers for the activity in "Normalize." Within your group, did one first response stand out? How so? Did someone's sequence stand out? How so?

2. Using examples from earlier activities or from your own classroom experience, discuss opportunities and challenges that arise when combining *Normalize Error* with other techniques like *No Opt Out*.

Role Play: *Check for Understanding* and *Normalize Error*

This exercise requires at least three participants and assumes you have already practiced *Check for Understanding*. Also freshen up on it as a group before you begin. Rotate *Teacher* and *Student* roles. Try rounds of each of the following patterns.

The *Facilitator* can prepare questions in advance, or the group can create a pool of questions (and answers) before the rounds begin.

Pattern 1
Practice this way of *Normalizing Error* so that it makes the *Students* feel normality in getting answers wrong and right. After several rounds, discuss how well the technique is working.

1. *Teacher* asks first *Student* a simple question (for example, "What's 3 plus 5?")
2. *Student* is unable to answer, but responds in a way that suggests genuine effort.
3. *Teacher* asks second *Student* to provide a correct answer.
4. Second *Student* answers directly and correctly.
5. *Teacher* returns to first *Student* for repetition of correct answer.
6. First *Student* answers correctly.
7. *Teacher* acknowledges correct answer.

Pattern 2
Again, practice so that this process makes the *Student* feel normality in erring and then getting it right. After each round, discuss how well it worked, including how much it likely improved the *Student*'s understanding.

1. *Teacher* asks a *Student* a simple question (for example, "Spell *conversion*")
2. *Student* answers with something that suggests both effort and some, but not complete, understanding.
3. *Teacher* responds to the *Student* with words that acknowledge the normality of error.
4. *Student* and *Teacher* continue until *Student* answers correctly.
5. *Teacher* acknowledges correct answer.

Pattern 3
Again, practice until the process feels normal. After each round, discuss how well it worked, including how much it likely improved the *Student*'s understanding.

1. *Teacher* asks a *Student* a question (for example, "Which city is closer to New York—Chicago or Los Angeles?")

2. *Student* answers with something that suggests both effort and some, but not complete, understanding.

3. *Teacher* poses the question to a second *Student,* including words that acknowledge the normality of error.

4. Second *Student* also answers with something that suggests both effort and some, but not complete, understanding.

5. Continuing to acknowledge the normality of error, *Teacher* calls on another *Student* or works with the two on whom she has already called.

> **1 NO OPT OUT**

6. The round continues until all *Students* who have participated answer correctly.

7. *Teacher* acknowledges or praises as appropriate.

Your takeaways:

_____

_____

_____

_____

TRY *NORMALIZE ERROR* IN THE CLASSROOM

1. If you have or can create a recording of yourself in the course of questioning, listen to it to notice and write down patterns you use that *Normalize Error.* For any of your statements that may have run contrary, script what you might otherwise have said.

2. If you can't arrange a recording, ask someone to observe you in class, and use their input to finish step 1. As a fallback, do step 1 using observations and notes you are able to take in an upcoming lesson.

3. As you plan an upcoming lesson, notice where you plan to question. Write out some of the questions along with erroneous answers you are likely to receive. Then write out your first response in keeping with *Normalize Error, No Opt Out,* and other closely related techniques.

4. After class, reflect on and write down evidence of moments when error caused some unnecessary ripple in a student or in the class at large. How might you prevent that ripple next time without draining your questions of valuable challenge?

TROUBLE-SHOOT

Steady On

It's tempting to try to reduce concern about errors by ignoring or trivializing them. It's also tempting to use them to bring some emotional drama into the class. Resist both temptations.

Other Challenges

Possible Challenge	Possible Solutions

BE CREATIVE

Naturally, your goal is for students to answer always to the best of their ability. Is there a special phrase or a physical sign or object you can use frequently to emphasize and positively frame some point that's likely to be tricky for students to master? (For example, in elementary grades, you might use a Wizard hand puppet through whom you can "teach" an especially challenging point in a math process or in reading or spelling.)

> 27 **VEGAS**
> 43 **POSITIVE FRAMING**

SUSTAIN YOUR PROGRESS

1. Using feedback from your study group or other peers, and reviewing your own lesson notes and observations, monitor your progress on *Normalize Error.*

Date	When Error Seemed Not to Be Normal	A Way to Improve

2. Revisit "Where Am I Now?" Are you ready to build out to some other new technique?

NORMALIZE ERROR

INDEX

A

Accountability: culture of, 11; *Explain Everything* on dynamics of, 433; peer-to-peer, 6

Achievement: *Emotional Constancy* to promote, 426–431; tying your language to, 427

Acknowledgment: differentiating praise from, 396; *Precise Praise* use of, 395, 396, 397, 402, 403, 406, 407; responding with praise, criticism, or, 397–399; search for situational, 403; for work of correction, 440

Active listening, 98

"Active Reading Job" objective, 78

Activities: *Begin with the End* reading lesson, 78; Bounce (game), 30–31; Brainstorm Game, 230; choosing those that work toward the goal, 76; "Cutting Edges," 94, 95; *Exit Tickets* assessment, 78; *Joy Factor*'s The faucet whistles and waters, 417, 424; library skill work, 117–118; "The Other Dr. J," 94–95; PEMDAS, 156–159; *Pepper*/Oral drill, 76; *Positive Framing*, 392–393; practice teaching a song, 423; proven success of using these, 7; *Ratio*'s centering more on the students, 155–156; *Shortest Path* on simplifying, 93; "Sorry!," 71; *Vegas* "Spice It Up," 254–255; *Wait Time*'s The Waiting Game, 240–241; within each technique, 4. *See also* Brainstorming; Role playing

Administrators, 6–7

Affect (managing as teacher), 354, 356

Ahn, Stephanie, *Ratio* (Grade 6), 151–152, 162

"Almost right" answers, 29–30, 33

Anger, 326, 376, 377, 411

Anonymity (plausible), 380, 382, 389, 390

Anonymous individual correction, 303–305

Answer formats: audible, 52, 54; complete sentence, 52, 53–54; grammatical, 52, 53; unit, 52, 54

Answers: "almost right," 29–30, 33; building evidence to support, 42–43; calling out, 310, 312, 340, 349, 389; *Cold Call* for calling on any student for, 195–210; countering "I don't know," 11–21; delaying a few seconds before taking student, 233–244; don't normally praise or fuss over right, 440; group choral response form of, 211–226; learning to "format" responses to questions, 52–64; narrowing or eliminating false choices, 138; precise, 23; providing example as, 135–136; rolling back, 138; "rounding up" student, 34; student judgment on other students', 190–194; three-legged stool, 439; unison, 211, 212, 214, 220, 293, 296, 297; verifying reliability of, 164–165. *See also* Complete sentence answers; Questions; Students

Apologizing: responding to student excuses and, 72; Sorry! activity on, 71; typical teacher, 66; *Without Apology* on, 65–72

Aspirations, 394

At Bats: homework tasks, 181–182; On the Mound Role Play, 182; repetition for learning new skills, 179–184; template for reinforcing/extending objectives, 75; video clips on champion teachers, 186

At Bats/combined techniques: *Begin with the End* used with, 75, 78; *Call and Response* used with, 180, 214–216; *Check for Understanding* used with, 169, 183; *Circulate* used with, 183; *Cold Call* used with, 180; *Do It Again* used with, 356; *Everybody Writes* used with, 246; *Exit Ticket* used with, 179, 183, 185; *Format Matters* used with, 183; *Joy Factor* used with, 418; *Pepper* used with, 180; *Ratio* used with, 183

Attention: *Slant* acronym for behaviors that boost, 284–287; small group discussion application of *Slant* on, 31; STAR and S-SLANT variations of *Slant* for, 286

Audible answer format, 52, 54, 56, 59

Audible greeting, 372

Audio-recording teaching: *Ratio* in the classroom, 160; of teacher behaviors and register, 345; *Tight Transitions*, 273–274; tips for, 4–5

Austin, Janelle: *Positive Framing* Part 1 transcript from class of, 386–388; *Positive Framing* Part 2 transcript from class of, 388–389

Austin, Will, 169–171

Authority: circulating through classroom to establish, 128; establishing teacher confidence and, 333–353. *See also* Controlling the classroom

B

Batch-processing, 150–151

Bathroom trips: *Draw the Map* on, 107; *100%* on, 302, 304; routines for, 258; *Seat Signals* on, 292, 293; *Strong Voice* on, 347

Begin with the End: breaking down learning objectives using, 73–81; framework for lesson planning provided by, 73; lesson planning progress, 74–77; lesson plans for teaching reading, 77–78

Begin with the End/combined techniques: *At Bats* used with, 75, 78; *Board=Paper* used with, 123; *Check for Understanding* used with, 76; *Cold Call* used with, 207–208; *Do It Again* used with, 268; *Do Now* used with, 75; *Double Plan* used with, 76, 101; *Everybody Writes* used with, 76, 246, 249; *Exit Ticket* used with, 73, 76, 78, 186–187; *4 MS* used with, 75, 83; *Joy Factor* used with, 417, 423; *No Opt Out* used with, 18, 19; *100%* used with, 317; *Pepper* used with, 75, 76; *Positive Framing* used with, 81; *Post It* used with, 89, 90; *Ratio* used with, 73; *Right Is Right* used with, 31; *Shortest Path* used with, 76, 92, 94; *Vegas* used with, 252; *Wait Time* used with, 241; *Without Apology* used with, 66, 71

Behaviors: misbehavior, 301–316, 326–327, 332, 374–379; modeling, 122–124, 234, 241, 258, 303, 410

Bellucci, Katie: *Do It Again* (Grade 5), 355; *Wait Time* (Grade 5), 234, 244

Binder Control: creating strong automatic routines, 259; helping students to get organized, 281–283

Binder Control/combined techniques: *Board=Paper* used with, 282; *Double Plan* used with, 282; *Draw the Map* used with, 282; *Entry Routine* used with, 282; *Everyone Writes* used with, 247; *No Opt Out* used with, 282; *On Your Mark* used with, 290; *Sweat the Details* used with, 364; *Tight Transitions* used with, 276, 282

Blackboard, 104

Blaming, 65, 69, 71

Board=Paper: modeling habit of taking classroom notes, 121–124; note taking basics and marking up the text, 122

Board=Paper/combined techniques: *Begin with the End* used with, 123; *Binder Control* used with, 282; *Check for Understanding* used with, 123; *Circulate* used with, 123; *Double Plan* used with, 101; *Explain Everything* used with, 123; *Name the Steps* used with, 119; *Ratio* used with, 160; *Stretch It* used with, 124

H

I

J

K

L

Seat Signals: creating strong automatic routines, 259; student signals to attend to necessary business, 292–294

Seat Signals/combined techniques: *No Warnings* used with, 376; *100%* used with, 302, 304, 305, 318

Seating arrangements: aisles and alleys around the, 107; considerations for, 104; pods versus rows, 105–106; rows, 106–107*fig*

Segel, Marisa, 272, 280

Self-improvement journey: charting and navigating your, 2–3; choosing which techniques to start with for, 2; identifying your goals, 3; improving both your strengths and weaknesses as part of, 1–2; journaling during your, 6; self-assessment role in, 1; "Where Am I Now?" charts as tools for, 1; working with a group or partner on your, 5. *See also* Teaching

Sequential consequences, 377–378

Sequential directions, 320

Shaking hands, 369

Shells, Stacey: *Do It Again* (Grade 7), 355; *Format Matters* (Grade 7), 53, 64; *Slant* (Grade 7), 285; *Take a Stand* (Grade 7), 191

Shepherd, Dinah: *Circulate* (Grade 8), 126; *Without Apology* (Grade 8), 66

Shift in tone and volume in-cues, 214, 215–216

Shortest Path: applied to your lesson plan, 95; *Begin with the End* used with, 76; breaking down activities for the, 93; finding direct route to student mastery, 92–96; to reach objectives, 94–95

Shortest Path/combined therapies: *Begin with the End* used with, 92, 94; *Check for Understanding* used with, 92; *Format Matters* used with, 94; *4 MS* used with, 94; *The Hook* used with, 112; *No Opt Out* used with, 94; *Right Is Right* used with, 94; *Stretch It* used with, 94; *Take a Stand* used with, 193

"Shorthand Corrections for Written Work" (*Format Matters*), 54–55, 62

Shout outs, 295

"Show me," 167

Simplifying lesson plans, 73–81

Situational envelopes role play, 349–351

Situational praise role play, 402–403

Skills: applying to new situations, 45; breaking down tasks for learning new, 114–120; bridging gap between knowledge and, 135; finding direct route to student mastery of, 92–96; integrating related, 443–444; library, 115–118; note taking, 99, 101, 121–124; repetition for learning new, 179–184. *See also* Objectives

Slant: acronym for student behaviors that boost attention, 284–287; creating strong automatic routines, 259; nonverbal signals to reinforce or correct, 285; small group discussion application of, 31; STAR and S-SLANT variations of, 286; video clips on champion teachers, 285

Slant/combined techniques: *Cold Call* used with, 205; *Do It Again* used with, 286; *Draw the Map* used with, 286; *Entry Routine* used with, 265; *Joy Factor* used with, 424; *No Warnings* used with, 285; *100%* used with, 284, 302, 317; *Positive Framing* used with, 286; *Ratio* used with, 160; *Right Is Right* used with, 31; *Tight Transitions* used with, 276

Slates (*Check for Understanding*), 167, 177

Small group discussion: *Format Matters* used during, 31; *No Opt Out* used during, 31; *100%* used during, 31; related techniques to use during, 31; *Right Is Right* use of, 31; *Slant* used during, 31; *Wait Time* video clip of, 240. *See also* Classroom discussion

Songs: *Call and Response* use of, 214; "Core Song" (Melcher), 254–255; "Indiana Fight Song" (*Vegas*), 254; *Joy Factor* use of, 418, 419, 420, 423; "Planets Song" (*Vegas*), 254; practice teaching a, 423. *See also* Chants

"Sorry!" activity, 71

Specialized in-cue, 214, 215–216

Specific directions, 320

Speed Role Play, 59–61

"Spice It Up" activity, 254–255

Square up/stand still, 334, 345, 353

Standardized tests, 71

STAR *Slant* variation, 286

Starting class, 289

Stickiness, 115–116

Stopwatch, 196, 272, 275, 276, 361

Storytelling, *Vegas*, 253

Strengths: identifying and considering your, 3; improving upon your weaknesses and, 1–2; *No Opt Out* self-assessment of, 11; *Right Is Right* self-assessment of, 22; *Stretch It* a self-assessment of, 37

Stretch It: comparing *Right Is Right* to, 38; rewarding "right" answers using, 37–51; vocabulary case study on, 45–47

Stretch It/combined techniques: *Board=Paper* used with, 124; *Break It Down* used with, 134; *Check for Understanding* used with, 164–165; *Cold Call* used with, 38; *Name the Steps* used with, 117; *No Opt Out* used with, 15, 38, 49; *Positive Framing* used with, 50; *Precise Praise* used with, 38, 396; *Props* used with, 50; *Ratio* used with, 148, 149; *Shortest Path* used with, 94; *Take a Stand* used with, 190; *Wait Time* used with, 244

Strong Voice: body language role plays, 346–349; default register of teachers, 343–345, 348–349; don't engage distractions, 337–343; use economical language, 334–337; establishing teacher authority and confidence, 333–353; situational envelopes role play, 349–351; steady and positive correction of routines, 259; synthesizing principles of, 345–346; using video and audio recordings, 345

Strong Voice/combined techniques: *Circulate* used with, 127, 132, 351; *Cold Call* used with, 208; *Do It Again* used with, 356, 361; *Explain Everything* used with, 351, 432, 434; *No Opt Out* used with, 12; *No Warnings* used with, 376, 377; *100%* used with, 302, 306, 317; *Positive Framing* used with, 381; *Vegas* used with, 253; *What to Do* used with, 327, 330, 338

Student behavior: distinguishing between possible causes of, 326–327, 332; interventions for, 301–316; *No Warnings* on, 374–379; *Slant* behavior, 285. *See also* Consequences

Student engagement: *Call and Response* group choral response to build, 211–226; *Double Plan* for sustaining, 97–102; *Everybody Writes* to prepare for classroom discussions, 245–250; *The Hook* for, 65, 72, 110–113; *Pepper* for building energy and, 227–232; *Ratio*'s group PEMDAS for, 159; suggestions for, 97–100; while circulating through classroom, 127; *Without Apology* for, 65–72

Student names: *Circulate* on using, 128; *Cold Call* on using, 201; *Joy Factor* on using, 418; *Name the Steps* on using, 115–116; nicknames, 418, 424; *Positive Framing* on using, 382; *Precise Praise* on using, 401

Students: "almost right" answers by, 29–30; bridging knowledge-skill gap of, 135; challenging, 383–384; circulating to leverage blind spots of, 128; countering "I don't know" responses by, 11–21; encouraging technical vocabulary use by, 27–28; finding direct route to skill mastery by, 92–96; greeting, 368–369, 372; learning the names of your, 201; note taking by, 99, 101, 121–124; posture of, 286, 303, 343, 344; responding to apologies made by, 72; rewarding "right" answers of, 37–51; setting standards of correctness for, 22–36; shifting cognitive effort to, 148–162. *See also* Answers; Challenging students; Classrooms

Suspense and surprise, 420

Sweat the Details: organizing your classroom, 363–365; types of orderly details and preparation, 363–364

Sweat the Details/combined techniques: *Binder Control* used with, 364; *Circulate* used with, 364; *Do It Again* used with, 364; *Format Matters* used with, 364; *Tight Transitions* used with, 364

T

Take a Stand: avoiding letting it become a cursory routine, 193; student judgment on answers by other students, 190–194; video clip of champion teacher, 191

HOW TO USE THE DVD

SYSTEM REQUIREMENTS

PC with Microsoft Windows 2003 or later
Mac with Apple OS version 10.1 or later

USING THE DVD WITH WINDOWS

To view the items located on the DVD, follow these steps:

1. Insert the DVD into your computer's DVD drive.
2. A window appears with the following options:

    Contents: Allows you to view the files included on the DVD.

    Links: Displays a page of associated websites for further information.

    Author: Displays a page with information about the author.
3. Click once to select a set of clips that you would like to view. Click again to open the sub-menu of individual clips; double-click to view the menu on full screen. To exit full screen, press escape.
4. Click once to select the clip you would like to view. Click once again to view the small version of the clip; double-click to view the clip on full screen. To exit full screen, press escape.
5. To end the clip, select "Root menu" or "Title menu" from the DVD drop down menu.
6. To return to the Title menu, select "Title menu" from the DVD drop down menu, or select "Home" from the upper right corner.

IN CASE OF TROUBLE

If you experience difficulty using the DVD, please follow these steps:

1. Make sure your hardware and systems configurations conform to the systems requirements noted under "System Requirements" above.
2. Review the installation procedure for your type of hardware and operating system. It is possible to reinstall the software if necessary.

To speak with someone in Product Technical Support, call 800-762-2974 or 317-572-3994 Monday through Friday from 8:30 a.m. to 5:00 p.m. EST. You can also contact Product Technical Support and get support information through our website at www.wiley.com/techsupport.

Before calling or writing, please have the following information available:

- Type of computer and operating system
- Any error messages displayed
- Complete description of the problem
- The DVD ID number from the DVD label

It is best if you are sitting at your computer when making the call.